Everyman, I will go with thee,
and be thy guide

William Wordsworth

SELECTED POEMS

Edited by
DAMIAN WALFORD DAVIES
Balliol College, Oxford

EVERYMAN
J. M. DENT · LONDON
CHARLES E. TUTTLE
VERMONT

This new edition first published in Everyman in 1994

© Introduction, chronology, selection and other critical apparatus
J. M. Dent 1994

J. M. Dent
Orion Publishing Group
Orion House
5 Upper St Martin's Lane, London WC2H 9EA
and
Charles E. Tuttle Co. Inc.
28 South Main Street,
Rutland, Vermont 05701, USA

Typeset at The Spartan Press Ltd,
Lymington, Hants
Printed in Great Britain by
The Guernsey Press Co. Ltd,
Guernsey, Channel Islands

British Library Cataloguing-in-Publication Data is available
upon request.

ISBN 0 460 87429 2

CONTENTS

NOTE ON THE AUTHOR AND EDITOR

WILLIAM WORDSWORTH was born at Cockermouth, Cumbria on 7 April 1770, the son of an attorney. He was educated at Hawkshead Grammar School and St John's College, Cambridge. In November 1791 he left England to spend a year in France, experiencing the French Revolution at first hand. During his stay he cultivated a formative friendship with Michel Beaupuy, an officer in the French Republican Army, and from a relationship with Annette Vallon he fathered a child, Caroline. After his return from the Continent he became a familiar figure in radical London circles. At Racedown, Dorset (from September 1795), and at Alfoxden, Somerset (from July 1797), he established an important literary partnership with Samuel Taylor Coleridge that culminated in the *annus mirabilis* of 1797–8 and in the publication of *Lyrical Ballads* (1798). Having visited Goslar, Germany, with his sister Dorothy, Wordsworth settled in late 1799 at Dove Cottage, Grasmere. January 1801 saw the publication of the second edition of *Lyrical Ballads*, and the following year Wordsworth married Mary Hutchinson. After the publication in 1807 of *Poems in Two Volumes*, Wordsworth still found himself battling against critical disparagement. Appointed Distributor of Stamps for Westmoreland in 1813, he settled at Rydal Mount, Ambleside, in May of the same year. *The Excursion* (1814) was followed by many editions of Wordsworth's poetry, and many honours – honorary doctorates, a Civil List Pension, the Poet Laureateship in 1843 – were conferred on him. He died on 23 April 1850 at Rydal Mount, after the appearance of a finally corrected six-volume *Poetical Works*. *The Prelude*, completed in thirteen books as early as 1805, was published posthumously in July 1850 by his wife and executors.

DAMIAN WALFORD DAVIES is the Andrew Bradley–J. C. Maxwell Junior Research Fellow Elect at Balliol College, Oxford. His previous publications include a translation of Friedrich Dürrenmatt's

Die Physiker and articles on medieval elegy and critical theory. He is currently preparing a study of the theme of solitude in Romantic poetry.

CHRONOLOGY OF WORDSWORTH'S LIFE

Year	Age	Life
1766	–	Marriage of parents
1770		Born 7 April at Cockermouth, Cumbria; Mary Hutchinson, future wife, born
1771	1	Birth of sister Dorothy
1778	8	Death of mother
1779	9	Enters Hawkshead Grammar School until 1787
1783	13	Death of father
1786	16	Claim to the Wordsworth inheritance lodged with Lord Lonsdale (settled 1802)
1787	17	Enters St John's College, Cambridge (until 1791)
1790	20	In France and Switzerland with Robert Jones (July–October)
1791	21	In London. Climbs Snowdon and leaves St John's with pass degree; returns to France and sees revolutionary Paris

CHRONOLOGY OF HIS TIMES

Year	Literary Context	Historical Events
1757	Blake born	
1769		Napoleon born
		Watt patents steam engine
1770		Beethoven born
1771	Scott born	
1772	Coleridge born	
	Morning Post begins	
1774	Southey born	
1775	Turner and Charles Lamb born	War of American Independence (ends 1783)
1776	Adam Smith, *Wealth of Nations*	US Declaration of Independence
	Gibbon, *Decline and Fall*	
1778	Hazlitt born	
	Death of Rousseau and Voltaire	
1781	Kant, *Critique of Pure Reason*	
	Rousseau, *Confessions*	
1783		Pitt's first Ministry
1784	Death of Samuel Johnson	
1785	De Quincey born	
1788	Byron born	
1789	Blake engraves *Songs of Innocence*	Fall of the Bastille, 14 July
	Bowles, *Sonnets*	
1790	Burke, *Reflections on the Revolution in France*	
1791	Paine, *Rights of Man*, Part I	
	Boswell, *Life of Johnson*	

Year	Age	Life
1792	22	Relationship with Annette Vallon; Caroline, daughter by Annette, born (Orleans, 15 December, after departure from France); friendship with Michel Beaupuy
1793	23	In London. Publishes *An Evening Walk* and *Descriptive Sketches*; writes the *Letter to the Bishop of Llandaff* and *Salisbury Plain*; visits Tintern Abbey on his way to North Wales
1794	24	In Lake District
1795	25	Left a legacy of £900 by Raisley Calvert. Meets Godwin in London; meets Coleridge. Moves to Racedown, Dorset (until July 1797)
1796	26	Crisis of disillusionment
1797	27	Wordsworths rent Alfoxden House so as to be near Coleridge; Wordsworth writes first version of *The Ruined Cottage* and completes writing *The Borderers*
1798	28	Wye Valley walking tour in July (Tintern Abbey revisited); publication in September of *Lyrical Ballads*; 16 September: Coleridge and the Wordsworths arrive in Germany; Wordsworth and Dorothy at Goslar from October to February; Wordsworth writes autobiographical verse that will eventually form basis of *The Prelude*
1799	29	Back in England (April). Settles with Dorothy at Dove Cottage, Grasmere, in December

Year	Literary Context	Historical Events
1792	Blake engraves *Marriage of Heaven and Hell*	France declares war on Austria and Prussia
	Shelley born	August: Louis XVI imprisoned
		September Massacres in Paris
1793	Godwin, *Political Justice*	21 January: Louis XVI executed
		February: France declares war on England
		September: Reign of Terror begins
		16 October: Marie Antoinette executed
1794	Blake, *Songs of Innocence and Experience*	Hardy, Horne Tooke, Thelwall and others arrested for High Treason
	Coleridge and Southey, *The Fall of Robespierre*	23 May: Suspension of Habeas Corpus
	Southey and Lovell, *Poems*	28 July: Execution of Robespierre
	Paine, *The Age of Reason* (1794–5)	
1795	Lewis, *The Monk*	Establishment of Directory
	Keats born	18 December: In England, the Two Bills become law
	Coleridge, *Conciones ad Populum*	
1796	Death of Burns	Napoleon's Italian campaign
	Coleridge, *Poems on Various Subjects*	
	Coleridge, *The Watchman*, Nos 1–10	
1797	Coleridge writes *Kubla Khan* and first version of *The Ancient Mariner*	
	With Lamb and Lloyd, Coleridge publishes *Poems*	
	Death of Burke	
1798	Coleridge, *Fears in Solitude*	Irish Rebellion (February–October)
		The French take Malta
		Nelson's victory in the battle of the Nile
1799	Schiller, *Death of Wallenstein*	November: Napoleon made First Consul
	Royal Institution founded	

Year	Age	Life
1800	30	*Home at Grasmere* begun; lines printed as 'Prospectus' to *The Recluse* and the preface and new poems for second edition of *Lyrical Ballads* written
1801	31	25 January: Second edition of *Lyrical Ballads*
1802	32	'Ode: Intimations of Immortality' begun; 'Resolution and Independence' composed (first version). With Dorothy visits Calais to see Annette and Caroline; 4 October: Wordsworth marries Mary Hutchinson. Third edition of *Lyrical Ballads*
1803	33	Tours Scotland; birth of first son, John
1804	34	Much work on *The Prelude*; 5-book structure enlarged after March; 'Ode to Duty' composed and 'Ode: Intimations of Immortality' completed
1805	35	Brother John drowned. Fourth edition of *Lyrical Ballads*. Completes *The Prelude* (13 Books)
1807	37	*Poems in Two Volumes* published
1808	38	Leaves Dove Cottage and moves to Allen bank
1809	39	*On the Convention of Cintra*; essays *Upon Epitaphs* written (1809–10)
1810	40	Quarrels with Coleridge; *Guide to the Lakes* published
1811	41	Moves to the Rectory, Grasmere
1812	42	Reconciliation with Coleridge. Deaths of his children Catherine and Thomas
1813	43	Settles at Rydal Mount. Appointed Distributor of Stamps

Year	Literary Context	Historical Events
1800	Death of Cowper Burns, *Works*, ed. Currie	Union of Great Britain and Ireland English capture Malta
1801	Southey, *Thalaba*	Addington's Ministry replaces Pitt's (until 1804)
1802	Coleridge, first version of 'Dejection: an Ode'	25 March: Peace of Amiens Napoleon Life Consul
1803	Coleridge, *Poems*	War with France resumed
1804	Blake completes *Milton* Death of Kant	Napoleon becomes Emperor Addington Ministry collapses 2nd Pitt Ministry (until 1806) Spain declares war on Britain
1805	Scott, *Lay of the Last Minstrel* Death of Schiller Hazlitt, *Principles of Human Action*	21 October: Battle of Trafalgar
1806		Death of Fox and Pitt
1807		Abolition of Slave Trade Peninsular War begins
1808	Goethe, *Faust*, Part I Scott, *Marmion* *The Examiner* begins	Convention of Cintra
1809	Coleridge first issues *The Friend* (27 vols) Byron, *English Bards and Scotch Reviewers* *Quarterly Review* founded	Perceval Ministry (until 1812)
1810	Blake working on *Jerusalem* and *Vala* (later *The Four Zoas*) Scott, *Lady of the Lake*	1st Reform Bill since 1797 George III's insanity officially acknowledged
1811	Shelley, *The Necessity of Atheism* Austen, *Sense and Sensibility*	Prince of Wales made Regent
1812	Byron, *Childe Harold*, I–II	Napoleon invades Russia Retreat from Moscow US declares war on Britain
1813	Byron, *The Giaour*, *The Bride of Abydos* Shelley, *Queen Mab* Austen, *Pride and Prejudice*	Leigh Hunt imprisoned for libelling Prince Regent (until 1815)

Year	Age	Life
1814	44	*The Excursion* published
1815	45	Publishes his collected *Poems*, with a preface, and *The White Doe of Rylstone*
1816	46	Revises *The Prelude* (1816–19)
1817	47	Meets Keats
1819	49	*The Waggoner* and *Peter Bell*
1820	50	Visits the Continent; publishes *Miscellaneous Poems* (4 vols); *The River Duddon: A Series of Sonnets, Voudracour and Julia, and Other Poems*
1822	52	*Ecclesiastical Sketches*; *A Description of the Scenery of the Lakes*; *Memorials of a Tour on the Continent, 1820*

Year	Literary Context	Historical Events
1814	Byron, *The Corsair* and *Lara*	Napoleon exiled to Elba
	Scott, *Waverley*	Congress of Vienna
	Austen, *Mansfield Park*	
	Cary's *Dante* completed	
1815	Scott, *Guy Mannering*	18 June: Battle of Waterloo
1816	Coleridge, *Christabel*	Death of Sheridan
	Shelley, *Alastor and other Poems*	The Lords reject a motion for the relief of Catholics
	Byron, *Childe Harold*, III	
	Austen, *Emma*	
	Peacock, *Headlong Hall*	
1817	Coleridge, *Biographia Literaria* and *Sibylline Leaves*	
	Keats, *Poems*	
	Death of Jane Austen	
	Blackwood's Magazine founded	
1818	Keats, *Endymion*, and attack in *Quarterly* on Keats	
	Hazlitt, *Lectures on the English Poets*	
	Peacock, *Nightmare Abbey*	
	Mary Shelley, *Frankenstein*	
	Austen, *Northanger Abbey* and *Persuasion*	
	Byron, *Childe Harold*, IV, and *Beppo*	
1819	Byron, *Don Juan,* I–II	Peterloo Massacre
1820	Keats, *Lamia, Isabella, The Eve of St Agnes, and other Poems*	Death of George III
	Lamb, *Essays of Elia*	Prince Regent becomes
	Shelley, *Prometheus Unbound*	George IV
1821	Death of Keats	
	De Quincey, *Confessions of an English Opium Eater*	
	Shelley, *Adonais*	
	Southey, *A Vision of Judgment*	
	Byron, *Don Juan,* III–V	
1822	Shelley, *Hellas*	
	Death of Shelley	
	Byron, *The Vision of Judgment*	
1823	Byron, *Don Juan,* VI–XIV	

Year	Age	Life
1824	54	*Poetical Works* (4 vols)
1827	57	*Poetical Works* (revised)
1829	59	Dorothy seriously ill
1831	61	Last meeting with Coleridge; tours Scotland
1832	62	Another Collected Edition
1835	65	*Yarrow Revisited and Other Poems*
		Dorothy's mental condition deteriorates
1837	67	Tours France and Italy
1838	68	D.C.L. (Durham). *The Sonnets*
1839	69	D.C.L. (Oxford); final revision of *The Prelude*
1842	72	*Poems, Chiefly of Early and Late Years*; pension from Civil List of £300 a year
1843	73	Appointed Poet Laureate on the death of Southey; dictates Fenwick notes
1845	75	Supervises single-volume Collection Edition
1849	79	Final edition of *Poetical Works* (6 vols)
1850	80	23 April: Death at Rydal Mount
		The Prelude published by wife and executors (July)
1855	–	Death of Dorothy
1859	–	Death of Mary

Year	Literary Context	Historical Events
1824	Byron, *Don Juan*, XV–XVI	
	Death of Byron	
	Hogg, *The Private Memoirs and Confessions of a Justified Sinner*	
1825	Hazlitt, *The Spirit of the Age*	
1827	Death of Blake	Death of Beethoven
	Tennyson, *Poems by Two Brothers*	
1829	Coleridge, *On the Constitution of the Church and State*	Catholic Relief Bill passed
1830	Tennyson, *Poems, Chiefly Lyrical*	Death of George IV
		William IV ascends throne
	Death of Hazlitt	
1831	J. S. Mill, 'The Spirit of the Age'	
1832	Death of Scott and Goethe	Reform Bill
1833	Carlyle, *Sartor Resartus*	
	Lamb, *Last Essays of Elia*	
	Newman et al., *Tracts for the Times*	
1834	Death of Coleridge	Poor Law Amendment Act
	Death of Lamb	Tolpuddle Martyrs
1837		William IV dies
		Victoria ascends throne
1839		Copyright Bill
1842	Tennyson, *Poems*	Chartist agitation
		The Mines Act
1847	Anne Brontë, *Agnes Grey*	
	Emily Brontë, *Wuthering Heights*	
	Charlotte Brontë, *Jane Eyre*	

Jason's

INTRODUCTION

I
A 'public road'?

The 72-year-old Wordsworth of Benjamin Haydon's 1842 portrait –
alone on the heights of Helvellyn, head bowed, arms crossed, seeing
nothing but himself and the universe – suggests an archetypal image
of the man and poet. The face of Keats in Haydon's *Christ's Entry
into Jerusalem* is that of a man involved in the passion of a dramatic
moment; below him, Wordsworth's head is bowed, his eyes closed
and his arms crossed again – the man as if self-absorbed. 'The power
of his mind preys on itself,' William Hazlitt remarked; 'it resists all
change of character, all variety of scenery, all the hustle, machinery,
and pantomime of the stage or of real life.' Hazlitt's reviews of
Wordsworth's *Excursion* in *The Examiner* evoke a man whose
sympathy is rooted in self, whose interest lies in those elemental
forms of feeling which immediately become part of his own person
and experience, or 'mingle . . . with the stream of general humanity'.
His interest in others is primarily an interest in self, in self-definition.
Shunning the hustle of an external world, Wordsworth's power is
that of a 'busy solitude' of the heart. Poised oxymoron-like between
the inner, contemplative life, and the outer world of the 'hustle . . . of
real life' suggested by 'busy', Hazlitt's phrase momentarily pulls the
poet in two directions before firmly, regretfully perhaps, establishing
in that inner world a totally self-sufficient emotional and intellectual
life.

'Fit audience let me find though few' Wordsworth sings in January
1800, two years into his Great Decade of creativity and as a start to
the main philosophical section of the projected but ultimately
unfinished *magnum opus*, *The Recluse*. Three years later, Coleridge
was to 'tremble' at the idea of Wordsworth 'living wholly among his
Devotees', and Keats in a letter of 1818 was to refer with character-
istic colour to Wordsworth's 'fireside Divan'. Both comments place
Wordsworth at the centre of a snug coterie. The poetry of 1798 to

1807 had been met with much scorn, and the support and faith of a small circle of admirers had certainly helped sustain a vision. But Coleridge's trembling in 1803 reveals doubts about the exact nature of Wordsworth's appeal and relevance. The redemptive *Recluse* which Grasmere should have fostered was just not being written, despite some very impressive trailers. Wordsworth was not enjoying the recognition and readership which were to be his by virtue of a different *kind* of poetry in the Victorian era – that of Christian comfort and moral instruction turned to social and educational use by a new generation. To see him as a poet at a sometimes disturbing distance from the world, as the poet of the 'egotistical sublime', of disillusioned retreats into non-political contemplation and of un-happy human relationships, is to perceive Wordsworth as many of his contemporaries did. But it is also as he himself wished to be seen in the complex texture of the poetry. Tension between the social and sociable on the one hand and on the other the simple desire for peace not at the heart of, but often at a remove from, the 'endless agitation' of society is what makes the poetry from *Salisbury Plain* to *The Excursion* so honest. The fantasy that is developed through 'These chairs, they have no words to utter' – that one could be oblivious to human suffering but conscious of the comforting presence of others – was to be acted out bizarrely in 1802: 'William heard me breathing and rustling now and then,' Dorothy records in her *Journal*,

> but we both lay still, and unseen by one another. He thought that it would be as sweet thus to lie so in the grave, and hear the *peaceful* sounds of the earth and just to know that our dear friends were near.

A compelling thought, but the balance between involvement and peaceful removal had to be a more realistic one. Settling down away from society could never be a simple matter of renouncing the world. Grasmere seemed to Wordsworth like 'the fixed centre of a troubled world'. What we find in *Home at Grasmere*, whether or not we believe the claims of the poem as we test them against the facts of life, is not a retreat but a meaningful move to a relevant 'centre' from which the redemptive philosophical poem could be written.

Despite Wordsworth's claim in *Home at Grasmere* that he and Dorothy are 'seceding from the common world' in order to anticipate the coming of the 'milder day' with millenarian hope, the poem is not a piece of writing that deals blithely with that secession. Wordsworth knew that he would be open to the charge of selfishness disguised 'under the soft titles of domestic attachment' in refusing, at Coleridge's prompting, to enter the world of political controversy. The parting in 1799 of Wordsworth and Coleridge – the latter, as the concluding lines of the 1799 *Prelude* state, to seek 'the haunts of men' in the great metropolis – was to lead to an existence at Grasmere that had to be justified. A later period of political upheaval was to move W. B. Yeats, as it had moved Andrew Marvell before Wordsworth, to confront the question of retreat versus involvement, and their influence on 'the mind of man'. In 'Meditations in Time of Civil War', Yeats considers whether a retreat from the world of action does away not only with our violent natures, but with our resources of power: 'O what if levelled lawns and gravelled ways / Where slippered Contemplation finds his ease / And Childhood a delight for every sense / But take our greatness with our violence?' In 'Easter, 1916', the Irish revolutionaries are seen in their blinkered devotion to their cause as a stone troubling 'the living stream'. Despite its pejorative associations, the stone is the very thing that gives life to that stream. Wordsworth, trying to work out a rationale in *Home at Grasmere* for that secession and seeking assurance that such a retreat will *not* diminish the strength of the mind, also uses the image of the living stream of involvement in public and political life:

> What if I floated down a pleasant stream
> And now am landed, and the motion gone,
> Shall I reprove myself? Ah no, the stream
> Is flowing and will never cease to flow,
> And I shall float upon that stream again.

'The motion gone': the impressive phrase brings to mind not only Yeats's thoughts on the lost greatness that a retreat from the world might bring and on the possible stagnation of a stream *not* troubled by the stone, but also the 'world not moving' of the Solitary of Wordsworth's *Excursion*. But the thoroughly Wordsworthian metaphor of the stream in *Home at Grasmere* is extended to insist that this retreat is not one of solipsism or disillusionment like that of the 'Lines left upon a Seat in a Yew-Tree' or that presented in *The Excursion*. Rather, it extends into a promise that the retreat from the world is temporary – a gathering of strength that is to precede joyful reintegration. Much of *Home at Grasmere* speaks of an imaginative understanding of what is valuable in human relationships. God himself, a sufferer and mourner, is seen in thoroughly human terms. 'I look for man,' declares Wordsworth, placing his faith in the strength of his affection for Dorothy, which will then radiate towards all mankind. But defending himself against the charge of acting out the role of the recluse was a constant battle. At many points, the impressiveness of the poem consists not so much in our belief that what the poet is claiming is true as in the superb rhetoric of *how* he says it. The poem often seems one of grand gestures only.

The 'Prospectus' to *The Recluse* announces a vision that promises not to shun the ugly side of human experience:

> ... if I oft
> Must turn elsewhere, and travel near the tribes
> And fellowships of men, and see ill sights
> Of passions ravenous from each other's rage,
> Must hear humanity in fields and groves
> Pipe solitary anguish, or must hang
> Brooding above the fierce confederate storm
> Of sorrow, barricadoed evermore
> Within the walls of cities – may these sounds
> Have their authentic comment, that even these
> Hearing, I be not heartless or forlorn.
> Come, thou prophetic spirit, soul of man,
> Thou human soul of the wide earth that hast
> Thy metropolitan temple in the hearts
> Of mighty poets ...

The human life of cities will have its 'authentic comment', but after the promise is made, the Miltonic language expands its frames of reference, and its afflatus seems to weaken that promise (already made suspect by the extravagance of its language – 'Pipe solitary anguish', 'hang / Brooding above the fierce confederate storm . . .'), despite the final gravitational pull towards the human heart. We remain to be convinced. 'Metropolitan', linked here with 'temple', carries religious connotations and is designed to evoke, for example, the supreme authority of a *metropolitan*, the title of the Church of England's archbishops and of those bishops of the Roman Catholic Church with jurisdiction over all others. After the reference to the human life of cities, however, what is carried across the intervening lines into the heart of 'mighty poets' by an important filament of connection is the great metropolis itself and its human life. In such poetry, the promise to attend to humanity is made literally from the heart. Books VII and VIII of *The Prelude* were to fulfil, and renege on, that promise.

Seeing the poetry as Haydon saw the man on Helvellyn – removed, self-contemplating – 'will never do'. 'I love a public road,' Wordsworth declares in *The Prelude*. His letter to John Wilson of 7 June 1802, anticipating the definition of a poet in the third edition of the *Lyrical Ballads*, defines the duty of the poet as traveller and fellow traveller:

> [A great Poet] ought, to a certain degree, to rectify men's feelings . . .
> He ought to travel before them occasionally as well as at their sides.

The poetry reveals both the close company Wordsworth keeps and the distance between the poet and his fellow travellers. For the man who concluded that 'we have all of us one human heart' and that the workaday world is 'the world of all of us', the place in which 'we find our happiness, or not at all', so much of his poetry was a struggle to define a poetic voice, a position from which he could identify for whom he wrote and for whom he would like to write. This involved a constant repositioning in relation to human lives and to the events that shaped them, a re-evaluation of what the poet feels as 'reality' and what as 'the idea, the abstraction'. His early contact with those on the fringes of society, his experience of the 'tragic super-tragic' of youth – the wilful fancy's heightening of the intensity of human suffering – helped define human-heartedness and what it really means to 'sympathise'. Personal relationships inevitably brought with them the pain of loss and, following the death of his children Catherine and Thomas in 1812, a sense of blankness. Re-entry into the world was to win the poet back to his kind, as it had done in 1806 in 'Elegiac Stanzas' after the death of his brother John. As Catherine Clarkson wrote to Henry Crabb Robinson:

> [Wordsworth and Mary] need the sight of *equals* who are not intimate friends – in whose company they must put some restraint upon themselves and in return they w^d be won from their sadness by hearing of other things – the goings on of life . . .

II
'An approach towards mortal business'
The Prelude

From the old Cumberland beggar, Wordsworth writes in 1797–8, 'lofty minds and meditative', those who have communicated delight and comfort to others, have received

> That first mild touch of sympathy and thought
> In which they found their kindred with a world
> Where want and sorrow were.

Two years later the narrator of 'Michael', echoing the grandiose 'Prospectus' to *The Recluse*, declares that the tale he is about to relate has led him 'to feel / For passions that were not [his] own, and think / (At random and imperfectly indeed) / On man, the heart of man, and human life'. The 1805 *Prelude* was to make the experience of social integration one of its main concerns as it charted the growth of the poet's mind, making the development of a social self part of a poetic, not a chronologically factual, vision. A concern with social and psychic integration had been part of the 1799 *Prelude*, in which 'gravitation' towards the world, towards 'mortal business', is seen in relation to the 'filial bond' between the child and the mother. Larger, more public relationships between man and society, between the individual and Nature, are securely based on this most important of early bonds –

> No outcast he, bewildered and depressed;
> Along his infant veins are interfused
> The gravitation and the filial bond
> Of Nature that connect him to the world.

– though the fifth and sixth stanzas of the 'Ode: Intimations of Immortality' testify to a very different position five years later on the question of man's relation to others and to the natural world. Changing personal and political circumstances effected a change in Wordsworth's poetic vision, especially with regard to something as complex as the integration of the individual into larger worlds. Tensions within individual passages of poetry, between lines separated by only a few minutes' writing time, much less the space of five years, show how complex Wordsworth's relation to the question of 'others' could be.

With 'an eddy's force', the beginning of Book III of the 1805 *Prelude* 'sucks' Wordsworth towards Cambridge. The passages that follow locate Wordsworth at the heart of the bustle of a new academic term, but the force of that eddy soon diminishes. There follows an extended description, not of joyfully relating to others in a new environment, but of turning the mind inwards 'upon itself' towards self-sufficiency:

> Oft did I leave
> My comrades, and the crowd, buildings and groves . . .
>
> . . . my mind
> Seemed busier in itself than heretofore –
> At least I more directly recognised
> My powers and habits. Let me dare to speak
> A higher language, say that now I felt
> The strength and consolation which were mine.
>
> But peace, it is enough
> To notice that I was ascending now
> To such community with highest truth.

'Ascending' towards a higher 'community' defies the gravitational pull of that eddy. But there is a reminder in that final line of the existence of a very different 'community': not so much a communion, a shared state of being, as the ordinary fellowship of Cambridge that he has left behind him in that crowd, those buildings and groves. Keats the 'camelion Poet', his personal identity 'annihilated' as he put it in a celebrated letter of 1818, could imagine 'innernesses' of feeling in billiard balls and sparrows; Wordsworth assigns a moral life during his Cambridge walks to 'the loose stones that cover the highway' – 'I saw them feel, / Or linked them to some feeling.' This animism leads not to his fellows, but back to the self, in lines which Wordsworth takes from his earlier poem *The Pedlar*, giving them the fully autobiographical 'I'. The tone is petulant:

> So was it with me in my solitude:
> So often among multitudes of men.
> Unknown, unthought of, yet I was most rich,
> I had a world about me – 'twas my own,
> I made it; for it only lived to me,
> And to the God who looked into my mind.

'Not of outward things / Done visibly for other minds . . . but of my own heart / Have I been speaking . . . and all my tale is of myself,' Wordsworth declares to Coleridge. The 31-year-old Wordsworth places his own self at the heart of his Cambridge experience. Sometimes a sociable temper does enter the poetry:

> . . . if a throng was near
> That way I leaned by nature, for my heart
> Was social and loved idleness and joy.

But it is rarely developed further. Such simple claims can hardly outweigh the extended analysis of the poet's solitary musings. Towards the end of Book III, however, a sense of integration begins to be charted, though by means of magisterial statements unsupported by illustration. Cambridge is now seen as a 'midway residence' between the life of the child and the 'substantial life' of society, and the terms used of the poet's pre-Cambridge remoteness are significant:

> Hitherto I had stood
> In my own mind remote from human life,
> At least from what we commonly so name,
> Even as a shepherd on a promontory,
> Who, lacking occupation, looks far forth
> Into the endless sea, and rather makes
> Than finds what he beholds.

Drawing on Thomson's *The Castle of Indolence* (1748), the picture of the uninitiated Wordsworth unfamiliar with 'mortal business' as a solitary observer on a promontory takes the reader back to an earlier passage in Book III, in which the poet informs Coleridge that he has 'traced [his] life / Up to an eminence' – to a peak of intellectual understanding, certainly, but also to a place removed from the 'populous plain' of Cambridge life. 'But this is human life: the war, the deeds, the disappointment . . . so stand / Upon a misty, jutting head of land – / Alone? . . . I'd rather stand upon this misty peak', declares Keats's persona in *Endymion*. Keats must be remembering his own sonnet on Chapman's Homer. Endymion rejects that sonnet's vision of earthly discovery, its sense of human fellowship high upon that peak in Darien. Endymion thinks he knows what human life is, and expresses his desire to distance himself from it. By his own admission, Wordsworth, also standing on an eminence, has yet to learn the meaning of 'substantial life'.

Book IV of *The Prelude* records the growth of a faculty of sympathy that is accompanied by an awareness of loss, of what time can do to others. Returning for the summer holidays from Cambridge, Wordsworth sees the two faces of time's effect on human life. Inevitable change ('Pale-faced babes . . . now rosy prattlers'), a falling away and a vanishing ('some sheltered seat in which / An old man had been used to sun himself / Now empty') are beginning to be proved upon the pulses. In Book IV, then, Wordsworth locates the dawn of human-heartedness around 1788. His position has obviously shifted since 'Tintern Abbey' (1798), where Nature is seen as having been 'all in all' as late as 1793, with the ability to hear the still, sad music of humanity being only a recent acquisition. In Book IV it is as if he wishes to push back the dawn of human-heartedness as far as possible to redeem, but also, chronologically, to confuse, the issue of his aloofness at Cambridge.

Book VI is where the public *Prelude* begins to assert itself. Wordsworth is on the public roads, and the rhetoric joyfully reaches outwards after dwelling painfully on a mind that had become a 'life unto itself' – not Wordsworth's own, but Coleridge's:

> But 'twas a time when Europe was rejoiced,
> France standing at the top of golden hours,
> And human nature seeming born again.
>
>   . . . we walked
> And found benevolence and blessedness
> Spread like a fragrance everywhere.

But again, there is a drawing back, a retreat into self. The admission at the end of Book VI that the poet is a 'stripling', 'scarcely of the household then / Of social life', is something in which Wordsworth, going on to explain why this is so, almost seems to delight:

>   I looked upon these things
> As from a distance – heard, and saw, and felt,
> Was touched but with no intimate concern –
> I seemed to move among them as a bird
> Moves through the air, or as a fish pursues
> Its business in its proper element.
> I needed not that joy, I did not need
> Such help . . .

'Proper' here carries its literal meaning, appropriately in this French context, of 'belonging to itself'. This focus on the individual self as distinct from the social self wards off the surrounding ferment of society. The petulant tone again brings into question whether such self-sufficiency was indeed 'proper' – 'right' – at this time. In this way *The Prelude* sets up a subtle dialectic that questions both the ostensible argument and our response to it.

*   *   *

> [I] pitched my vagrant tent,
> A casual dweller and at large, among
> The unfenced regions of society.
>
> *The Prelude*

More than a century and a half after Wordsworth had written these
lines, Larkin would describe a landscape removed from the 'termin-
ate and fishy-smelling / Pastoral of ships up streets' in terms of
'unfenced existence: / Facing the sun, untalkative, out of reach'.
Larkin might be remembering Wordsworth's phrase, but Words-
worth is depicting something very different from Larkin's sense of
space. The lines, from Book VII of *The Prelude*, tell of an entry into
the public life of London, a world at a remove from the enclosed
bowers of Cambridge. Living in London between January and May
1791, Wordsworth could not have remained isolated from 'mortal
business'. 'Substantial life' was something with which he became
increasingly familiar. Visits to the meeting house at the Old Jewry to
hear the Calvinist preacher Joseph Fawcett lecture, friendships with
Unitarian dissenters and with men who had thrown themselves into
parliamentary and pamphlet debates, and the experience of life in the
largest city in the world meant that Wordsworth was 'at large'.

The first extended description of London in Book VII presents a
place in which the city's inanimate objects are much more interesting
and lively than its people. The crowd is a 'weary throng', coming and
going with the impersonality of a march-past, the language not only
describing the two-way traffic, but suggesting a possible confronta-
tion that the crowd would be too weary to pursue. They flow on:

> Here, there, and everywhere, a weary throng,
> The comers and the goers face to face –
> Face after face.

The wares on sale are far more colourful than those who sell and buy
them, the shop façades more meaningful than the faces of the crowd,
and the allegoric shapes and physiognomies 'of real men' much more
alive and specific than the anonymous throng:

> – the string of dazzling wares,
> Shop after shop, with symbols, blazoned names . . .

> Here, fronts of houses, like a title-page
> With letters huge inscribed from top to toe;
> Stationed above the door like guardian saints,
> There, allegoric shapes, female or male,
> Or physiognomies of real men . . .
> Boyle, Shakespear, Newton . . .

When the desire to focus on real faces *is* present a few lines later, Wordsworth's tone suggests the rather cursory interest of a mind not wholly taken, or taken in, by London life, by the city's human inhabitants –

> Briefly we find (if tired of random sights,
> And haply to that search our thoughts should turn)
> Among the crowd, conspicuous less or more
> As we proceed, all specimens of men . . .
> And all the character of form and face.

'Briefly' suggests both the difficulty of glimpsing the busy citizens ('conspicuous less or more / As we proceed') and also a less-than-enthusiastic interest in them. The plural 'we' has a distancing effect, as does the parenthesis, while the word 'specimens' suggests the language of the naturalist – a title Hazlitt actually applied to Wordsworth. There is also a drawing back in the language of the 1850 revision, the double negative forcing into view that which its meaning dismisses: 'Enough; – the mighty concourse I surveyed / With no unthinking mind, well pleased to note / Among the crowd . . .' 'Well pleased to note': the language protests too much.

Early in Book VII, Wordsworth considers one of the observations that had baffled him as a child in a community where familiarity with others was the norm: 'how men lived / Even next-door neighbours, as we say, yet still / Strangers'. By the end of Book VII, Wordsworth is describing the sensation of confronting not only that which is unfamiliar, but that which is blankly unmeaning and alien:

> How often in the overflowing streets
> Have I gone forwards with the crowd, and said
> Unto myself, 'The face of every one
> That passes by me is a mystery'.

The lines feed directly into T. S. Eliot's *The Waste Land*: 'A crowd flowed over London Bridge – so many / I had not thought death had undone so many'. Wordsworth's London streets are a nightmare of impersonality. The verbalisation of those last two lines throws the poet's predicament into greater relief. But the act of enunciation is also one of self-comfort, placing what is outside the self in perspective, establishing meaning, asserting a measure of power, in a blank world. This 'blank confusion' and 'one identity' of London life are later seen as threatening specifically to 'higher minds'. The fear is that the poetic faculty risks being deadened – something which the quintessentially Wordsworthian piece of comfort that follows ('It is not wholly so to him who looks / In steadiness, who hath among least things / An under-sense of greatness') does little to dispel. The face of everyone who passes Wordsworth, *The Prelude* states, remains 'a mystery' communicating no meaning. Then the human faces and the 'ballast of familiar life' become spectral shapes. Not only is Wordsworth's mind being pushed away from these pictures of human impenetrability by a feeling of 'oppression'; his mind is retreating from the metropolis to the country, and, significantly, to the earlier verse of *An Evening Walk* recording the Lake District tradition of spectral horsemen:

> . . . the shapes before my eyes became
> A second-sight procession, such as glides
> Over still mountains, or appears in dreams.

The mind moves from human life in the city to the country and its dead, as well as to literature, looking for meaning in more personal resources. It is the London beggar who brings the poet back to the company of men. But again, much about this encounter suggests distancing. The beggar is 'propped against a wall' for support, but he seems far more active than the poet. It is as if he emerges from 'the moving pageant'; the poet does not see the beggar but is 'smitten with the view' of him, and the beggar's face is 'upright' – the very face seeming to stand up, ready to walk towards the motionless poet. The poet is one who is acted upon. The story on the label placed on the beggar's chest is of an individual human life, but Wordsworth spins it into philosophy – an 'emblem of the utmost that we know / Both of ourselves and of the universe'. The beggar, one of London's 'individual sights', is reduced to a label. He isn't even given the status of the hunger-bitten girl of Book IX who moved Beaupuy to comment, ' " 'Tis against *that* / Which we are fighting" ', much less the elaborate description of the child at the theatre in Book VII. 'I looked, as if admonished from another world': Wordsworth is remembering his leech-gatherer of 1802, and, as with that encounter, there is here a drive to transform ordinary experience into something otherworldly, to give status and meaning to 'common indications'. It might be the action of a mind that had been disturbed by the city's ability to deaden the imagination. An inevitable effect of that reaction, however, is the loss of human individuality, and, in the case of the blind beggar, a great silence on the subject of that individual's tragedy.

Whereas Wordsworth's French tour of 1790 had been, in Jonathan Wordsworth's phrase, 'protected from realities' by the speed of the visit and by the unusual events shaping France, the 1792 tour produced a 'poetry of experience' written over a decade later in Book IX of *The Prelude*. It is certainly, despite the enthusiastic statements seeking to register excited fellow-feeling ('My heart was all / Given to the people, and my love was theirs'), the poetry of a considered relationship with individuals who exerted an influence on the poet's mind – with men whose very physiognomies made Wordsworth see the effects of 'substantial life' on human beings at a momentous period in history.

Take the Royalist Soldier, for instance, observed at a moment of emotional crisis and in minute detail. The effect of the 'noisier world' on one human life, of larger social forces on the individual heart, is now seen and grasped:

> His temper was quite mastered by the times,
> And they had blighted him, and eat away
> The beauty of his person, doing wrong
> Alike to body and to mind . . .
>   . . . a face,
> By nature lovely in itself, expressed,
> As much as any that was ever seen,
> A ravage out of season . . .
>
>   At the hour,
> The most important of each day, in which
> The public news was read, the fever came,
> A punctual visitant, to shake this man,
> Disarmed his voice and fanned his yellow cheek
> Into a thousand colours. While he read,
> Or mused, his sword was haunted by his touch
> Continually, like an uneasy place
> In his own body.

There is real attention here to the man's personal crisis. Such contact with individuals like this fallen Royalist angel, this blighted Lucifer, and Beaupuy, is what made Wordsworth, back in England before his own emotional trial in 1796, into a social planner. His fervour as a man contemplating the management of nations, Book X informs us, was firmly grounded in his knowledge of 'what there is best in individual man . . . what there is strong and pure in household love / Benevolent in small societies / And great ones also . . .' His experience in France before his disillusionment and his loss of faith in a *public* role for himself ('A poet only to myself, to men / Useless') were later to create a desire to plan for *this* world:

> [Schemers] were called upon to exercise their skill
> Not in Utopia – subterraneous fields,
> Or some secreted island, heaven knows where –
> But in the very world which is the world
> Of all of us, the place in which, in the end,
> We find our happiness, or not at all.

That inclusive 'we' implies a greater weight of experience than does the casual 'we' of those London lines in Book VII. *The Prelude*'s ordering of experience infuses into its nuances, as well as into its general argument, the sense of a developing sympathy with others. But that sympathy remains a complex thing.

III

> It was the voice of one that sleeping mourned,
> A human voice!
>
> *Salisbury Plain*

Book IV of *The Prelude* located the dawn of human-heartedness around 1788. Manuscript evidence suggests that Wordsworth was working on the story of the soldier's widow in *An Evening Walk* around the same time. It is the earliest poetry of human suffering that survives, pointing forwards to the suffering figures in *Salisbury Plain* and *Adventures on Salisbury Plain* and to many of the concerns of *The Ruined Cottage*, *The Pedlar* and the *Lyrical Ballads*. So often, Wordsworth's poetry (and prose) of social protest is that of human suffering, but the poet's precise relationship with the suffering individuals he portrays needs further definition.

The self-parody of *The Prelude*, Book VIII's description of the young poet's craving for the tragic super-tragic, recalls an early portrayal of suffering in *An Evening Walk*:

> . . . behold,
> If such a sight were seen, would fancy bring
> Some vagrant thither, with her babes . . .
> . . . the stately flower,
> Drooping in sympathy and making so
> A melancholy crest above the head
> Of the lorn creature, while her little ones . . .
> Were sporting with the purple cups . . .

The preposterousness of the foxglove's sympathetic drooping is amplified by the indulgent 'lorn' and 'creature', the language of the period's sentimental poetry. The mature poet who had written the *Salisbury Plain* poems, *The Ruined Cottage* and the *Lyrical Ballads* is distancing himself from the kind of sentimental writing embodied in *An Evening Walk* not only through direct criticism ('Through wild obliquities could I pursue . . . / These cravings') but more subtly by incorporating the idiom of *An Evening Walk* into the mature verse of *The Prelude* and allowing it to remain there without comment. What the *Prelude* account of the tragic super-tragic implies is that human suffering, such as that of the female beggar in *An Evening Walk* (the direct antithesis in her crisis of a ready-to-hand female swan), was an appeal to contemporary sensibility. When the human sigh is heaved in *Descriptive Sketches*, the figures who emerge from the poetry are there for the same purpose and carry a symbolic, not an individual, significance:

> . . . thy poor babes that, hurrying from the door . . .
> Dead muttering lips, and hair of hungry white,
> Besiege the traveller whom they half affright.

What *Salisbury Plain* and *Adventures on Salisbury Plain* announce is a commitment not only to a poetry of social protest influenced by the radical strictures of William Godwin's *Enquiry Concerning Political Justice* of 1793 (in which vice and crime are seen as the products of an unjust social and political state) but also to a far more considered treatment of individual predicaments within an unjust society. The aim of the *Adventures*, Wordsworth informed Francis Wrangham in 1795, was 'partly to expose the vices of the penal law and the calamities of war as they affect individuals'. It is those last four words that are significant: the *concerns* of the poem are social and political – the stuff of Coleridge's lecture 'On the Present War' in *Conciones ad Populum* (1795); its *concern* is for the individual. At Racedown, the moralistic commentary of *Salisbury Plain* gave way in the *Adventures* to a dramatised presentation of the human tragedy of figures whose sense of alienation Wordsworth, in 1793, was sharing. The revised poem, moving further away from the descriptive and reflective mode of *An Evening Walk*, now develops through interlocking human stories as the suffering individuals narrate their own histories. Human individuality and its vulnerability in the face of an uncaring social system rather than a coolly presented symbolic significance form the basis of Wordsworth's humanist concern.

But both *Salisbury Plain* poems remained unpublished until *Guilt and Sorrow* appeared eight years before Wordsworth's death. A reaching out towards suffering individuals did not at the time gain an extended life, a wider sympathy. The prose *Letter to the Bishop of Llandaff* was just such a private outburst – a political polemic, never published by Wordsworth, emphasising the importance of under-standing human passions. The radical Wordsworth's view of monarchy, for instance, is of an office that requires 'more than human talents' from its incumbent who is isolated from ordinary life and prevented from developing a sense of general sympathy:

> It is from the passion thus directed that the men of whom I have just spoken are afflicted by the catastrophe of the fallen monarch. They are sorry that the prejudice and weakness of mankind have made it necessary to force an individual into an unnatural situation, which requires more than human talents and human virtues, and at the same time precludes him from feeling a particular share in the interests of mankind.

Fifteen years later, after excursions into politics in the narrow rooms of his sonnets 'on the subject of national liberty', Wordsworth was again to turn his hand to radical prose in his pamphlet *The Convention of Cintra*. There was a sense of 'reaching out' about the whole enterprise of *Cintra*: Wordsworth first intended to publish it in the *Courier* 'for the sake of immediate and wide circulation', and then as a sizeable pamphlet. In Coleridge's mind, too, *Cintra* had an extended life:

> . . . a considerable part [of the pamphlet] is almost a self-robbery from some great philosophical poem, of which it would form an appropriate part, & be fitl[ier] attuned to the high dogmatic Elo-quence, the oracular [tone] of impassioned Blank Verse.

He is thinking, of course, of *The Recluse* – the redemptive, millenarian scheme which Wordsworth still hadn't substantially tackled by 1809. The poet who was supposed to be writing *The Recluse* – a believer in universal benevolence, in human perfectibility, in a redemptive philosophy of progress and in the value of millen-arian hope – was writing his prose tract in Coleridge's mind *as if* for that great philosophical poem. As in the *Bishop of Llandaff* letter, what is urged in *Cintra* is a 'knowledge of human kind'. There is a desire to psychologise man's reaction and see the upheaval in Spain and Portugal in relation to the mind of man:

The true sorrow of humanity consists in this; – not that the mind of man fails, but that the course and demands of action and of life so rarely correspond with the dignity and intensity of human desires . . . Here then they, with whom I *hope*, take their stand. There is a spiritual community binding together the living and the dead . . . We would not be rejected from this community: and therefore do we hope.

Throughout *Cintra* Wordsworth had appealed to those who 'are not dead to the common feelings of . . . human nature', emphasising the importance of 'community'. Here, that notion is extended to include a sense of belonging to a society that transcends death and the ravages of 'things that perish'. It was an idea Wordsworth had already touched on in such poems as the *Lyrical Ballads*' 'We are seven' and 'To a Sexton', and one which he was to explore a year after *The Convention of Cintra* in his essays *Upon Epitaphs*, in which there is an attempt, informed by sympathy and understanding, to imagine what the lives of the now dead members of a rural community amounted to.

'Lines left upon a Seat in a Yew-Tree' is a poem in which Wordsworth seeks to define the kind of poet he wants to be. It is an intellectual and emotional manifesto. The Fenwick note identifies 'a gentleman of the neighbourhood' as the subject of the poem, but the lines have much of Wordsworth in them. Defining his present self against the intellectual individualism of Godwinism, Wordsworth chooses to register past disillusionment, and with it a new rejuvenating faith, in terms of the relation between man and mankind, the self and the world. A 'going forth' into the world is followed by a turning away and an arrogant reliance on the self-in-solitude:

> . . . he to the world
> Went forth, pure in his heart, against the taint
> Of dissolute tongues, 'gainst jealousy, and hate,
> And scorn, against all enemies prepared,
> All but neglect; and so, his spirit damped
> At once, with rash disdain he turned away,
> And with the food of pride sustained his soul
> In solitude.

'The man, whose eye / Is ever on himself' abuses his own dignity of mind. The poem ends in the silent hour of inward thought, but the thoughts are those of a mind that recognises that true knowledge – not that of an intellectual all in all – will lead to the love of others; not to solitude, but society. A decade later, reacting to another emotional crisis, Wordsworth was again to end a poem with a hopeful reaching out after evoking a picture of a mind content to preserve distance between itself and mankind. That mind, chastened by familiarity with the tragedy of life's 'frequent sights', is 'humanised' – meaning both 'brought down to earth', 'reconciled with realities' in the words of *The Prelude*, and, importantly, 'made humane'. Life's shocks lead the patient soul out into the world of the *Lyrical Ballads'* 'relationship and love':

> Farewell, farewell the heart that lives alone,
> Housed in a dream, at distance from the kind!
> Such happiness, wherever it be known,
> Is to be pitied, for 'tis surely blind.
>
> But welcome fortitude, and patient cheer,
> And frequent sights of what is to be borne!
> Such sights, or worse, as are before me here –
> Not without hope we suffer and we mourn.

Similarly, the passage in Book X of *The Prelude* referring to the effect on young radical minds of Godwin's *Political Justice* is an indictment of blind self-sufficiency:

> What delight! –
> How glorious! – in self-knowledge and self-rule
> To look through all the frailties of the world,
> And, with a resolute mastery shaking off
> The accidents of nature, time, and place,
> That make up the weak being of the past,
> Build social freedom on its only basis:
> The freedom of the individual mind,
> Which, to the blind restraint of general laws
> Superior, magisterially adopts
> One guide – the light of circumstances, flashed
> Upon an independent intellect.

Wordsworth claims to be 'speaking more in charity', but the tone of the passage is clearly mocking. The effusiveness of the opening, the self-satisfied emphasis on *self*-knowledge and *self*-rule and on the mind as an independent power, the implicit arrogance of the reference to the world's frailties and of Godwinism's disregard for the circumstances of nature, time and place, and the foregrounding of 'superior' with its literal meaning ('prouder') heightened, all combine to distance Wordsworth's present self from the undesirable aspects of Godwinian rationalism. Furthermore, those Victorian readers of the

1850 *Prelude*, who in 1842 had bought Wordsworth's *Poems, chiefly of Early and Late Years* (the volume containing the revised version of the post-Godwinian play *The Borderers*), would have been alerted to an indictment of Godwinism far more subtle and damning than the mocking tone of the above *Prelude* passage – namely, the status of its final two lines, taken from *The Borderers*, in which they are spoken by the villain Rivers. The prefatory note to *The Borderers* presents in Rivers another misanthrope who, like the subject of the 'Yew-Tree' lines, 'went forth', then with 'disdain . . . turned away'. But Rivers is more dangerous since his perverted sense of rationalism compels him to re-enter the world to see his crime of murder repeated by another. In this case, entering 'substantial life' from misanthropic retirement ends in death and alienation. It does not bring with it relationship and love.

After Wordsworth's moral crisis of 1796, rehabilitation, Book XII of *The Prelude* asserts, brought with it a desire to attend to man as a being bound to a community and to man in the true, not selfish, grandeur of the mind. Wordsworth speaks of a power that

> . . . lifts
> The being into magnanimity,
> Holds up before the mind, intoxicate
> With present objects and the busy dance
> Of things that pass away, a temperate shew
> Of objects that endure – and by this cause
> Disposes her, when over-fondly set
> On leaving her incumbrances behind,
> To seek in man, and in the frame of life
> Social and individual, what there is
> Desirable, affecting, good or fair,
> Of kindred permanence, the pervading grace
> That hath been, is, and shall be.

The being now sought is no 'idea' or 'abstraction of the kind' as he was at one stage in Book VIII, no 'composition of the thought, / Abstraction, shadow, image, but the man / Of whom we read, the man whom we behold / With our own eyes'. There is a levelling down here from what Wordsworth once referred to as 'general notions', to the representation of man in books (works of history, biography and literature) to a man actually met. The retrospect of *The Prelude* sees this time of emotional rehabilitation as a reawakening of faith in man, a process of empirical observation that involved a decision to look 'Among the natural abodes of men, / Fields with their rural works'. The poet who wished to be comforted by the leech-gatherer, the lover of public roads who felt the need to find a voice of human sympathy, sees himself as having been educated from childhood in the schools of the open lanes into a new way of seeing:

> When I began to inquire,
> To watch and question those I met, and held
> Familiar talk with them, the lonely roads
> Were schools to me in which I daily read
> With most delight the passions of mankind,
> There saw into the depth of human souls –
> Souls that appear to have no depth at all
> To vulgar eyes.

It is this kind of observation that leads in the 1805 *Prelude* to the great statements of the final books, to the faith that we begin and end our lives in the 'pervading love' of Book XIII, and to the development of a manifesto of the Imagination culminating in the great Ascent of Snowdon.

IV
'A stranger's privilege'
'Resolution and Independence' (Revised)

I return then to [the] question, please whom? or what? I answer, human nature . . . But where are we to find the best measure of this? I answer, [with]in; by stripping our own hearts naked, and by looking out of ourselves to [me]n who lead the simplest lives . . . And yet few ever consider books but with reference to their power of pleasing [persons of fortune] and men of a higher rank; few descend lower, among cottages and fields, and among children. A man must have done this habitually before his judgment upon 'The Idiot Boy' would be in any way decisive with me.

Here, in his letter of 7 June 1802 to John Wilson, Wordsworth effectively defines his ideal audience and points to the qualities essential to an appreciative reading of the *Lyrical Ballads*. The act of divesting the gentlemanly heart of 'false refinements, wayward and artificial desires, false criticisms' is not in itself enough; it must be followed by an act of moving outside that now naked heart towards the life of 'cottages and fields'. The description of this movement towards rural life is framed in a way that suggests that the act of self-purging prepares the mind for true literary taste and true grandeur which can then be carried back into the mind and heart after that excursion into a society where the 'best measure' of human nature may be found. Wordsworth proceeds to emphasise the importance of a familiarity with the lives and feelings of a section of the population that was frequently excluded from contemporary ruling-class views of who 'the people' were. 'Few descend lower': the verb is significant, pointing not only to a descent into rural valleys from solitary poetic promontories but to a descent through the social ranks. The *Lyrical Ballads*, both in the Preface and in the poems, expresses a strikingly confident faith in the extent to which man can reach out to man across social, intellectual and linguistic divides, but the volume also reveals a number of tensions in Wordsworth's vision of sympathetic contact with others – tensions that cannot easily be resolved by the confident assertions of the general democratic and egalitarian design of the work.

In the 1800 Preface, Wordsworth speaks of his decision to avoid 'poetic diction' as having cut him off from the 'common inheritance of Poets'. The rejection of poetic diction is absolutely necessary if poetry is to be written in 'the language of men'. But by cutting himself off from one community, Wordsworth establishes a new one through the radical theory of language propounded in the Preface. 'Arbitrary expression' is throughout the Preface a negative term that is seen to have socially divisive consequences – '[poets] think that they are conferring honour upon themselves and their art in proportion as they separate themselves from the sympathies of men, and indulge in arbitrary and capricious habits of expression.' The casual confidence with which Wordsworth is prepared to use such phrases as 'the real language of men' is remarkable. The view of language put forward by the Preface focuses on an easily defined, unproblematic language that forms the basis of every man's speech and which, when used as the basis of a poetry of feeling, enables readers to achieve a greater understanding of the workings of an idiot child's mind and, indeed, of the fluxes and refluxes of their own mental processes. There is no talk, as there would be in Coleridge's *Biographia Literaria*, of language as a medium whose characteristics distinguish and divide one class from another. Nor is there mention of the danger of an essential incongruity of style in poems where Wordsworth's own poetic register (it cannot be entirely suppressed) and that of the subject are in uneasy alliance. Wordsworth takes the existence of a 'shared' language very much for granted. What the Preface aims at by means of significant omissions and sometimes great silences is a sweeping democratic design. But the assertions of that manifesto mute the unusualness of some of the Preface's main claims.

'The Poet binds together by passion and knowledge the vast empire of human society, as it is spread over the whole earth': Wordsworth sees himself, in the grand 1802 additions to the Preface, as one who unites 'the Kind' across the centuries. 'What is a Poet? He is a man speaking to men'; 'Poets do not write for Poets alone, but for men': the extent to which others are involved in the enterprise of the *Lyrical Ballads* creates a compelling illusion which is not borne out consistently by the poetry itself. Indeed, Wordsworth is also careful to preserve a strong faith in his own powers and poetic creed. The otherness of the poet, his status as the creator distinct from the reader who is not 'so well acquainted with the various stages of meaning through which words have passed', and having a mind of his own, is unequivocally asserted:

> Such [feelings which to the reader appear ludicrous], were I convinced they were faulty at present, I would willingly take all reasonable pains to correct. But it is dangerous to make these alterations on the simple authority of a few individuals, or even of certain classes of men; for where the understanding of an Author is not convinced . . . this cannot be done without great injury to himself; for his own feelings are his stay and support and if he sets them aside in one instance, he may be induced to repeat this act till his mind loses all confidence in itself and becomes utterly debilitated.

With the sharing, then, there is a standing back. Towards the end of the Preface what emerges is the poet's desire to be read very much on his own terms.

The tone of sympathy running through the *Lyrical Ballads* was seen by the volume's more appreciative critics as one of its main claims to permanence. A review in the *British Critic* of February 1801, written most probably by Francis Wrangham, focuses on the ability of Wordsworth's poems to bridge class divides. The vision is of a poetry that unifies:

> It would be no mean, it would indeed be a very lofty praise, to assert of a writer, that he is able to pour into other bosoms powerful feelings of a particular class, or belonging to a particular order of men. To this praise, Mr Wordsworth lays a well-supported claim.

John Wilson's enthusiastic letter goes further. The *Lyrical Ballads* are seen as educating polite readers into sympathy and compassion, not only for our 'fellow-men', but for living things the world over. This fraternizing drive appears on a number of levels throughout the volume. Reading the poet Gottfried August Bürger in Germany, Wordsworth was searching for an *eradication* of self, objecting to the fact that Bürger does not lose himself in that which he creates. According to the 1802 Preface at least, this loss of self is part of an identification devoutly to be wished:

> It will be the wish of the Poet to bring his feelings near to those of the persons whose feelings he describes, nay, for short spaces of time, perhaps, to let himself slip into an entire delusion, and even confound and identify his own feelings with theirs.

The poet gains an extended life in that of his characters. But this process of identification is hardly unproblematic. The question of poetic voice, the existence in 'The Thorn' of two stylistic registers, of 'sinkings and re-elevations', and the title of the volume itself (suggesting both personal involvement and a measure of dramatic distancing), preserve a distance between poet and narrator, and consequently between the poet and the subject of the poem. 'There is . . . in Mr Wordsworth's mind', Hazlitt states, 'an evident repugnance to admit anything that tells for itself, without the interpretation of the poet . . . a systematic unwillingness to share the palm with his subject.' It is an astute comment justified by the way in which so many poems turn in their closing movements to focus attention and authority on the speaker. A portrait of others becomes personal interpretation as the individual mind takes over from a 'tale', as with 'Simon Lee':

> – I've heard of hearts unkind, kind deeds
> With coldness still returning;
> Alas! the gratitude of men
> Has oftener left me mourning.

A poem in which Simon himself achieves no stature whatever is pitched towards a sententious piece of wisdom belonging to the world of Wordsworth's polite speaker and to other scenes and encounters. In 'Hart-Leap Well' the shepherd, when called upon by the polite speaker to explain the significance of the 'doleful place', proceeds to relate a tale that has already been told by the speaker. The speaker is careful to emphasise that this is so: 'that same story told /

Which in my former rhyme I have rehearsed'. Authority now clearly begins to shift towards the speaker: 'Grey-headed shepherd, thou hast spoken well – / Small difference lies between thy creed and mine'. That is precisely why the shepherd has spoken *well*. The moral lecture of the ending, where the shepherd, by now probably baffled by the strangely philosophical visitor, is asked to remember the Blakean idea that 'everything that lives is holy', distances the polite speaker still further. The tensions apparent in such poems point to a problem of poetic voice, of intellectual and social compatibility, of which Wordsworth was aware. Such distance as exists in poems like 'Simon Lee' and 'Hart-Leap Well' is preserved by a poet whose faith is in a generous desire to reach out with love and sympathy but who realises that he cannot falsify the true nature of social relations or the suffering and isolation of many of his subjects.

Figures like the old man in 'Old Man Travelling', the Cumberland beggar, or the leech-gatherer of the 1807 volume, provide intimations of universal human nature, but they also stubbornly remain distinct individuals with whom Wordsworth's polite speakers have to deal. *Lyrical Ballads* is a volume of poetry that dramatises the difficulty of relating to others, the tensions felt not only by a man seeking to make contact with his fellow men, but by the poet-as-gentleman who is trying to relate to subjects from rustic life and from beyond the social pale in order to justify the great claims of the Preface. In its generality the *Lyrical Ballads*' vision of social sympathy – taking as subjects those pathetic figures familiar enough from contemporary magazine verse, lamenting the fact that men are imprisoned in workhouses, crying out against 'what man has made of man', and proposing for convicts radical education theories designed to restore deep levels of psychic health – is far less problematic than having to relate directly to the old man travelling or the leech-gatherer or having to come to terms with the guilt occasioned by an encounter such as that in the fourth of the 'Poems on the Naming of Places'. And the poetry registers and sometimes, embarrassed, evades these tensions. The sense of awkwardness in the last five lines of 'Old Man Travelling' is a dead end for a speaker aware of great distance between himself and the sailor's father. The prosaic ending and embarrassed after-vacancy are a way of indicating an awareness of a troubling poetic and social problem.

Dorothy's *Journal* entry for 3 October 1800 describes an encounter that was later to be given poetic life in 'Resolution and Independence':

When Wm and I returned from accompanying Jones we met an old
man almost double; he had on a coat thrown over his shoulders
above his waistcoat and coat . . . His face was interesting.

Transforming this real-life encounter in the company of Dorothy
with the leech-gatherer into the poetic encounter of 'Resolution and
Independence', Wordsworth is stage-managing a meeting in a poem
in which he seeks – indeed, needs – to analyse the nature of his
relationship with another human being. Dorothy and Wordsworth
met the leech-gatherer on a public road; the setting of the poem is an
isolated one. Most significantly, perhaps, Dorothy is excluded from
the poetic encounter. Wordsworth's poetic editing of actual experi-
ence focuses attention on the nature of the central meeting with the
old man and on the difficulty of communicating meaningfully in such
an unlooked-for encounter. The lonely figure is recognisably human
as the poet first catches sight of him. But immediately, the human
frame, bent double, is transformed:

> As a huge stone is sometimes seen to lie
> Couched on the bald top of an eminence . . .
>
> So that it seems a thing endued with sense:
> Like a sea-beast crawled forth . . .
>
> Such seemed this man . . .

The similes complicate any identification with the leech-gatherer as
an individual human being of a tough workaday (not primaeval)
world. Even the 1815 Preface speaks of him as being 'divested . . . of
the indications of life and motion'. The old man is 'in his extreme old
age', with 'a more than human weight' upon him and with a 'lofty
utterance . . . above the reach / Of ordinary men' to his speech. That
speech suddenly becomes a stream as the man who had earlier been
'as a cloud' is now seen as being like a figure in a dream. Everything
seems to be pushing the leech-gatherer away from what he actually is,
despite the fact that Wordsworth is careful always to employ similes,
not metaphors. Similes do not *utterly* transform things into other
things, but Wordsworth's repeated use of them does have the effect
of obscuring the human individual at the centre of the visionary
experience. Such is the strength of this movement away from the
leech-gatherer-as-man that on rereading the poem, the locution in
that initial description of the leech-gatherer – 'The oldest man he
seemed that ever wore grey hairs' – throws the weight of 'seemed' not
forwards to the relative clause as it would if the locution were

different ('He seemed the oldest man *that ever wore grey hairs*') but
back onto 'man': it is as if he only *seems* a man, even at this early stage
of the poem. The same effect is produced later in the poem:

> . . . the whole body of the man did seem
> Like one whom I had met with in a dream,
> Or *like a man* from some far region sent . . .

Momentarily, the leech-gatherer is something entirely different that
is being *compared* to a man. Before meeting the old man, Words-
worth has been thinking of fellow poets and of the waning of poetic
power and mental health. Viewed in relation to these fears, expanded
further in stanza XVIII ('And mighty poets in their misery dead'), the
movement in the poem away from the leech-gatherer as a human
individual becomes significant. The transforming drive of the dis-
tressed poetic mind is a way of exercising those poetic faculties –
imagination, in particular – which the speaker feels are threatened
with extinction. Imaginative vitality becomes a way of combating
vulnerability, but it does so to the exclusion of the leech-gatherer's
human status. Comparing him to sea-beasts, stones and clouds also
reveals uncertainty as to how to relate to the old man. The distressed
mind sets up a visionary mode of thought for itself in an attempt to
locate anything that might furnish it with a measure of comfort. A
geographical distance, too, is revealed by stanza XIII: 'And now such
freedom as I could I took, / And drawing to his side . . .' So far, the
speaker has been eyeing him, transforming him, from a distance.
Stanza XIII, then, augurs well, as it seems to mark a desire to make
contact with the old man not as a sea-beast or stone – the products of
the imagination or fancy – but as a man. But the human encounter
has its problems. There is awkwardness in the polite speaker's first
move:

> And drawing to his side, to him did say,
> 'This morning gives us promise of a glorious day.'

He can talk, in rather grand terms, too, only about the weather, and
when the old man begins to explain what his business is on the moor,
the transforming drive comes into play again, broken briefly by the
mundane details of stanza XVI, but reasserted in XVII. Seeing the old
man in terms of sea-beasts and stones might be viewed in terms of a
social dilemma, as a way of avoiding the awkwardness of having to
deal with him as a man. Stanza XVII, however, marks a change.
What the speaker gains at the end of that stanza is a specifically

human strength, not otherworldly or spiritual, but a strength for *this* world, there to help him cope with the 'cold, pain, and labour, and all fleshly ills' of the next stanza. What the final four stanzas express is a need for human comfort, a need to make contact with the life of another. As the mind's fears return in stanza XVIII with greater force, the question that had previously been asked in a rather different register as awkward banter is repeated, since the poet now really does need to know, '"How is it that you live, and what is it you do?"' The old man had heard and answered the first time – '"He with a smile did then his words repeat"' – but this is a different and more valuable experience for the speaker. The lonely moor and the shape of the old man are still 'troubling', but we are left with a picture of the leech-gatherer as one resolutely going about his business as a man.

A letter to Sara Hutchinson, dated 14 June 1802, sheds light on Wordsworth's relationship with his subject. Sara and her sister Mary had been displeased with certain aspects of Wordsworth's presentation of the leech-gatherer in an early version of the poem, which had referred to the old man's history, his wife and ten children. Wordsworth responds to their disapprobation, justifying the impressiveness of his poetic subject:

> I then describe him, whether ill or well is not for me to judge with perfect confidence, but this I can *confidently* affirm, that, though I believe that God has given me a strong imagination, I cannot conceive a figure more impressive than that of an old Man like this, the survivor of a Wife and ten children, travelling alone among the mountains and all lonely places, carrying with him his own fortitude, and the necessities which an unjust state of society has entailed upon him.

That 'though' after Wordsworth's bold underlining is significant. Yes, he has been blessed with a powerful imagination capable of transforming the ordinary into the supernatural and visionary, but what that 'though' announces is Wordsworth's reverence for the *ordinary*, untransformed by higher poetic faculties – his admiration for the man in the sheer dignity of survival. Though 'Resolution and Independence' is not resolved in any tidy way, there is at the end of the poem a coming to terms, as a poetic creed is worked out, with the true nature of the chosen poetic subject and with what that poetic creed is to focus on. The value of the transforming imaginative life of the mind is not dismissed; rather, it is securely rooted in the final stanzas in the tough existence of a man whose life the poet needs to understand.

DAMIAN WALFORD DAVIES

NOTE ON THE TEXT

The texts of *An Evening Walk* (1793), *Descriptive Sketches* (1793), *Lyrical Ballads* (1798 and 1800), *Poems in Two Volumes* (1807), *Poems* (1815), *Peter Bell* (1819), and the later poems have been edited from the first published editions. Seven poems – 'Argument for Suicide', the 'Baker's Cart' fragment, 'Are there no groans, no breeze or wind?', 'Away, away, it is the air', 'These chairs, they have no words to utter', 'I only looked for pain and grief', and 'St Paul's' – have been edited from manuscripts at the Wordsworth Library, Grasmere, and I am grateful to the Wordsworth Trust, Dove Cottage, Grasmere, for allowing me to print from them. I wish also to record my warm thanks to the following people for permission to print individual texts: Stephen Gill for the text of *Salisbury Plain* from *The Salisbury Plain Poems of William Wordsworth* (Ithaca, 1975), and Jonathan Wordsworth for the text of *The Ruined Cottage* from *The Ruined Cottage, The Brothers, and Michael* (Cambridge, 1985), the texts of *The Pedlar* and *The Prelude, 1799* from *The Pedlar, Tintern Abbey, and the Two-Part Prelude* (Cambridge, 1985), the text of 'Not useless do I deem' from *The Music of Humanity* (London, 1969), and the text of *Home at Grasmere* from *William Wordsworth: The Borders of Vision* (Oxford, 1982). For permission to use the text of *The Prelude*, 1805 and 1850 from *The Prelude: 1799, 1805, 1850*, eds Jonathan Wordsworth, M. H. Abrams, and Stephen Gill (New York and London, 1979), I would like to thank both Jonathan Wordsworth and Stephen Gill.

For *An Evening Walk* and *Descriptive Sketches*, original spelling, initial capitals and apostrophe 'd' have been retained. Punctuation is editorial. For the manuscript poems, the *Lyrical Ballads, Poems in Two Volumes, Poems, 1815, Peter Bell*, and the later poems, spelling has been modernised, initial capitals have been deleted (retained, however, for 'God', 'Nature', titles and personifications), ampersands have been replaced with 'and', and apostrophe 'd' replaced by 'ed'. Punctuation is editorial.

I wish to record my gratitude to Jonathan Wordsworth, Stephen Gill, and Robert Woof for their invaluable advice and assistance.

SELECTED POEMS

From *An Evening Walk*, 1793

Far from my dearest friend, 'tis mine to rove
Thro' bare grey dell, high wood, and pastoral cove;
His wizard course where hoary Derwent takes
Thro' craggs, and forest glooms, and opening lakes,
Staying his silent waves, to hear the roar   5
That stuns the tremulous cliffs of high Lodore:
Where silver rocks the savage prospect chear
Of giant yews that frown on Rydale's mere;
Where peace to Grasmere's lonely island leads,
To willowy hedgerows, and to emerald meads –   10
Leads to her bridge, rude church, and cottag'd grounds,
Her rocky sheepwalks, and her woodland bounds;
Where, bosom'd deep, the shy Winander peeps
Mid' clust'ring isles, and holly-sprinkl'd steeps;
Where twilight glens endear my Esthwaite's shore,   15
And memory of departed pleasures, more.

Fair scenes! with other eyes, than once, I gaze,
The ever-varying charm your round displays,
Than when, ere-while, I taught, 'a happy child',
The echoes of your rocks my carols wild: 20
Then did no ebb of chearfulness demand
Sad tides of joy from Melancholy's hand;
In youth's wild eye the livelong day was bright,
The sun at morning, and the stars of night
Alike, when first the vales the bittern fills,   25
Or the first woodcocks roam'd the moonlight hills.

Return, Delights! with whom my road begun,
When Life rear'd laughing up her morning sun;
When Transport kiss'd away my april tear,
'Rocking as in a dream the tedious year';   30
When link'd with thoughtless Mirth I cours'd the plain,
And hope itself was all I knew of pain.
For then, ev'n then, the little heart would beat
At times, while young Content forsook her seat,
And wild Impatience, panting upward, show'd   35
Where tipp'd with gold the mountain-summits glow'd.

Alas! the idle tale of man is found
Depicted in the dial's moral round;
With Hope Reflexion blends her social rays
To gild the total tablet of his days;   40
Yet still, the sport of some malignant Pow'r,
He knows but from its shade the present hour.

While, Memory at my side, I wander here,
Starts at the simplest sight th' unbidden tear,
A form discover'd at the well-known seat,   45
A spot, that angles at the riv'let's feet,
The ray the cot of morning trav'ling nigh,
And sail that glides the well-known alders by.

   But why, ungrateful, dwell on idle pain?
To shew her yet some joys to me remain,   50
Say, will my friend, with soft affection's ear,
The history of a poet's ev'ning hear?

                *   *   *

   How pleasant, as the yellowing sun declines,
And with long rays and shades the landscape shines,
To mark the birches' stems all golden light,
That lit the dark slant woods with silvery white!   100
The willows, weeping trees, that twinkling hoar,
Glanc'd oft upturn'd along the breezy shore,
Low bending o'er the colour'd water, fold
Their moveless boughs and leaves like threads of gold;
The skiffs with naked masts at anchor laid,   105
Before the boat-house peeping thro' the shade;
Th' unwearied glance of woodman's echo'd stroke,
And curling from the trees the cottage smoke.

   Their pannier'd train a groupe of potters goad,
Winding from side to side up the steep road;   110
The peasant from yon cliff of fearful edge
Shot, down the headlong pathway darts his sledge;
Bright beams the lonely mountain horse illume,
Feeding mid' purple heath, 'green rings', and broom,
While the sharp slope the slacken'd team confounds,   115
Downward the pond'rous timber-wain resounds.

Beside their sheltering cross of wall, the flock
Feeds on in light, nor thinks of winter's shock;
In foamy breaks the rill, with merry song,
Dash'd down the rough rock, lightly leaps along;   120
From lonesome chapel at the mountain's feet,
Three humble bells their rustic chime repeat;
Sounds from the water-side the hammer'd boat,
And blasted quarry thunders heard remote.

Ev'n here, amid the sweep of endless woods,   125
Blue pomp of lakes, high cliffs, and falling floods,
Not undelightful are the simplest charms
Found by the verdant door of mountain farms.

Sweetly ferocious round his native walks,
Gaz'd by his sister-wives, the monarch stalks;   130
Spur-clad his nervous feet, and firm his tread,
A crest of purple tops his warrior head.
Bright sparks his black and haggard eye-ball hurls
Afar; his tail he closes and unfurls,
Whose state, like pine-trees, waving to and fro,   135
Droops, and o'er canopies his regal brow.
On tiptoe rear'd he blows his clarion throat,
Threaten'd by faintly answering farms remote.

Bright'ning the cliffs between, where sombrous pine
And yew-trees o'er the silver rocks recline,   140
I love to mark the quarry's moving trains,
Dwarf pannier'd steeds, and men, and numerous wains:
How busy the enormous hive within,
While Echo dallies with the various din!
Some, hardly heard their chissel's clinking sound,   145
Toil, small as pigmies, in the gulph profound;
Some, dim between th' aëreal cliffs descry'd,
O'erwalk the viewless plank from side to side;
These, by the pale-blue rocks that ceaseless ring,
Glad from their airy baskets hang and sing.   150

Hung o'er a cloud, above the steep that rears
It's edge all flame, the broad'ning sun appears;

A long blue bar it's aegis orb divides,
And breaks the spreading of it's golden tides;
And now it touches on the purple steep   155
That flings his shadow on the pictur'd deep.
Cross the calm lake's blue shades the cliffs aspire,
With tow'rs and woods a 'prospect all on fire';
The coves and secret hollows thro' a ray
Of fainter gold a purple gleam betray;   160
The gilded turf arrays in richer green
Each speck of lawn the broken rocks between;
Deep yellow beams the scatter'd boles illume,
Far in the level forest's central gloom.
Waving his hat, the shepherd in the vale   165
Directs his winding dog the cliffs to scale,
That, barking busy 'mid the glittering rocks,
Hunts, where he points, the intercepted flocks;
Where oaks o'erhang the road the radiance shoots
On tawny earth, wild weeds, and twisted roots;   170
The Druid stones their lighted fane unfold,
And all the babbling brooks are liquid gold;
Sunk to a curve the day-star lessens still,
Gives one bright glance, and sinks behind the hill.
In these lone vales, if aught of faith may claim,   175
Thin silver hairs, and ancient hamlet fame;
When up the hills, as now, retreats the light,
Strange apparitions mock the village sight.

A desperate form appears that spurs his steed
Along the midway cliff with violent speed;   180
Unhurt pursues his lengthen'd flight, while all
Attend, at every stretch, his headlong fall.
Anon, in order mounts a gorgeous show
Of horsemen shadows winding to and fro;
And now the van is gilt with evening's beam,   185
The rear thro' iron brown betrays a sullen gleam;
Lost gradual o'er the heights in pomp they go
While silent stands th' admiring vale below,
Till but the lonely beacon all is fled,
That tips with eve's last gleam his spiry head.   190

*   *   *

Fair swan! by all a mother's joys caress'd,
Haply some wretch has ey'd, and call'd thee bless'd;
Who faint, and beat by summer's breathless ray,
Hath dragg'd her babes along this weary way,
While arrowy fire extorting feverish groans   245
Shot stinging through her stark o'erlabour'd bones.
With backward gaze, lock'd joints, and step of pain,
Her seat scarce left, she strives, alas! in vain
To teach their limbs along the burning road
A few short steps to totter with their load,   250
Shakes her numb arm that slumbers with its weight,
And eyes through tears the mountain's shadeless height,
And bids her soldier come her woes to share,
Asleep on Bunker's charnel hill afar.
For hope's deserted well why wistful look?   255
Chok'd is the pathway, and the pitcher broke.

    I see her now, deny'd to lay her head,
On cold blue nights, in hut or straw-built shed,
Turn to a silent smile their sleepy cry,
By pointing to a shooting star on high.   260
I hear, while in the forest depth he sees,
The Moon's fix'd gaze between the opening trees,
In broken sounds her elder grief demand,
And skyward lift, like one that prays, his hand,
If, in that country, where he dwells afar,   265
His father views that good, that kindly star;
– Ah me! all light is mute amid the gloom,
The interlunar cavern of the tomb.
When low-hung clouds each star of summer hide,
And fireless are the valleys far and wide,   270
Where the brook brawls along the painful road,
Dark with bat haunted ashes stretching broad,
The distant clock forgot, and chilling dew,
Pleas'd thro' the dusk their breaking smiles to view,
Oft has she taught them on her lap to play   275
Delighted, with the glow-worm's harmless ray
Toss'd light from hand to hand, while on the ground
Small circles of green radiance gleam around.

    Oh! when the bitter showers her path assail,
And roars between the hills the torrent gale,   280

No more her breath can thaw their fingers cold,
Their frozen arms her neck no more can fold;
Scarce heard, their chattering lips her shoulder chill,
And her cold back their colder bosoms thrill;
All blind she wilders o'er the lightless heath,   285
Led by Fear's cold wet hand, and dogg'd by Death;
Death, as she turns her neck the kiss to seek,
Breaks off the dreadful kiss with angry shriek.
Snatch'd from her shoulder with despairing moan,
She clasps them at that dim-seen roofless stone.   290
'Now ruthless Tempest launch thy deadliest dart!
Fall fires – but let us perish heart to heart.'
Weak roof a cow'ring form two babes to shield,
And faint the fire a dying heart can yield;
Press the sad kiss, fond mother! vainly fears   295
Thy flooded cheek to wet them with its tears;
Soon shall the Light'ning hold before thy head
His torch, and shew them slumbering in their bed,
No tears can chill them, and no bosom warms,
Thy breast their death-bed, coffin'd in thine arms.   300

                    *   *   *

   Now with religious awe the farewel light
Blends with the solemn colouring of the night;   330
Mid groves of clouds that crest the mountain's brow,
And round the West's proud lodge their shadows throw,
Like Una shining on her gloomy way,
The half seen form of Twilight roams astray.
Thence, from three paly loopholes mild and small,   335
Slow lights upon the lake's still bosom fall,
Beyond the mountain's giant reach that hides
In deep determin'd gloom his subject tides.
Mid the dark steeps repose the shadowy streams,
As touch'd with dawning moonlight's hoary gleams;   340
Long streaks of fairy light the wave illume
With bordering lines of intervening gloom;
Soft o'er the surface creep the lustres pale,
Tracking with silvering path the changeful gale.
'Tis restless magic all; at once the bright   345
Breaks on the shade, the shade upon the light;
Fair Spirits are abroad – in sportive chase

Brushing with lucid wands the water's face,
While music stealing round the glimmering deeps
Charms the tall circle of th' enchanted steeps.   350
As thro' th' astonish'd woods the notes ascend,
The mountain streams their rising song suspend;
Below Eve's listening Star, the sheep walk stills
It's drowsy tinklings on th' attentive hills;
The milkmaid stops her ballad, and her pail   355
Stays it's low murmur in th' unbreathing vale;
No night-duck clamours for his wilder'd mate,
Aw'd; while below the Genii hold their state.
The pomp is fled, and mute the wondrous strains,
No wrack of all the pageant scene remains;   360
So vanish those fair Shadows, human Joys,
But Death alone their vain regret destroys.
Unheeded Night has overcome the vales;
On the dark earth the baffl'd vision fails.
If peep between the clouds a star on high,   365
There turns for glad repose the weary eye;
The latest lingerer of the forest train,
The lone-black fir, forsakes the faded plain;
Last evening sight, the cottage smoke no more,
Lost in the deepen'd darkness, glimmers hoar;   370
High towering from the sullen dark-brown mere,
Like a black wall, the mountain steeps appear;
Thence red from different heights with restless gleam
Small cottage lights across the water stream.
Nought else of man or life remains behind   375
To call from other worlds the wilder'd mind,
Till pours the wakeful bird her solemn strains,
Heard by the night-calm of the watry plains.
– No purple prospects now the mind employ,
Glowing in golden sunset tints of joy,   380
But o'er the sooth'd accordant heart we feel
A sympathetic twilight slowly steal,
And ever, as we fondly muse, we find
The soft gloom deep'ning on the tranquil mind.
Stay! pensive, sadly-pleasing visions, stay!   385
Ah no! as fades the vale, they fade away.
Yet still the tender, vacant gloom remains,
Still the cold cheek its shuddering tear retains.

From *Descriptive Sketches*, 1793

How bless'd, delicious Scene! the eye that greets   120
Thy open beauties, or thy lone retreats;
Th' unwearied sweep of wood thy cliffs that scales,
The never-ending waters of thy vales;
The cots, those dim religious groves embow'r,
Or, under rocks that from the water tow'r   125
Insinuated, sprinkling all the shore,
Each with his household boat beside the door,
Whose flaccid sails in forms fantastic droop,
Bright'ning the gloom where thick the forests stoop;
– Thy torrents shooting from the clear-blue sky,   130
Thy towns, like swallows' nests that cleave on high,
That glimmer hoar in eve's last light, descry'd
Dim from the twilight water's shaggy side,
Whence lutes and voices down th' enchanted woods
Steal, and compose the oar-forgotten floods,   135
While Evening's solemn bird melodious weeps,
Heard, by star-spotted bays, beneath the steeps.
– Thy lake, mid smoking woods, that blue and grey
Gleams, streak'd or dappled, hid from morning's
      ray
Slow-travelling down the western hills, to fold   140
It's green-ting'd margin in a blaze of gold;
From thickly-glittering spires the matin-bell
Calling the woodman from his desert cell –
A summons to the sound of oars, that pass,
Spotting the steaming deeps, to early mass;   145
Slow swells the service o'er the water born,
While fill each pause the ringing woods of morn.
    Farewell! those forms that, in thy noon-tide
      shade,
Rest near their little plots of wheaten glade;
Those stedfast eyes, that beating breasts inspire   150
To throw the 'sultry ray' of young Desire;
Those lips, whose tides of fragrance come and go,
Accordant to the cheek's unquiet glow;
Those shadowy breasts in love's soft light array'd,
And rising, by the moon of passion sway'd.   155

Thy fragrant gales and lute-resounding streams
Breathe o'er the failing soul voluptuous dreams,
While Slavery, forcing the sunk mind to dwell
On joys that might disgrace the captive's cell,
Her shameless timbrel shakes along thy marge,   160
And winds between thine isles the vocal barge.
Yet arts are thine that rock th' unsleeping heart,
And smiles to Solitude and Want impart.
I lov'd, mid thy most desert woods astray,
With pensive step to measure my slow way,   165
By lonely, silent cottage-doors to roam —
The far-off peasant's day-deserted home.
Once did I pierce to where a cabin stood,
The red-breast peace had bury'd it in wood,
There, by the door a hoary-headed sire   170
Touch'd with his wither'd hand an aged lyre;
Beneath an old-grey oak as violets lie,
Stretch'd at his feet with stedfast, upward eye,
His children's children join'd the holy sound,
A hermit — with his family around.   175
Hence shall we seek where fair Locarno smiles
Embower'd in walnut slopes and citron isles,
Or charms that smile on Tusa's evening stream,
While mid dim towers and woods her waters gleam.
From the bright wave, in solemn gloom, retire   180
The dull-red steeps, and darkening still, aspire
To where afar rich orange lustres glow
Round undistinguish'd clouds, and rocks, and snow;
Or, led where Viamala's chasms confine
Th' indignant waters of the infant Rhine,   185
Bend o'er th' abyss? — the else impervious gloom
His burning eyes with fearful light illume.
The Grison gypsey here her tent has plac'd,
Sole human tenant of the piny waste;
Her tawny skin, dark eyes, and glossy locks,   190
Bend o'er the smoke that curls beneath the rocks.

The mind condemn'd, without reprieve, to go
O'er life's long deserts with it's charge of woe,
With sad congratulation joins the train,
Where beasts and men together o'er the plain   195

Move on – a mighty caravan of pain;
Hope, strength, and courage, social suffering brings,
Freshening the waste of sand with shades and springs.
– She solitary through the desert drear
Spontaneous wanders, hand in hand with Fear.   200
    A giant moan along the forest swells
Protracted, and the twilight storm foretells,
And, ruining from the cliffs, their deafening load
Tumbles; the wildering Thunder slips abroad.
On the high summits Darkness comes and goes,   205
Hiding their fiery clouds, their rocks, and snows;
The torrent, travers'd by the lustre broad,
Starts like a horse beside the flashing road;
In the roof'd bridge, at that despairing hour,
She seeks a shelter from the battering show'r.   210
Fierce comes the river down; the crashing wood
Gives way, and half it's pines torment the flood;
Fearful, beneath, the Water-spirits call,
And the bridge vibrates, tottering to its fall.
    Heavy, and dull, and cloudy is the night,   215
No star supplies the comfort of it's light;
Glimmer the dim-lit Alps, dilated, round,
And one sole light shifts in the vale profound
While, opposite, the waning moon hangs still
And red, above her melancholy hill.   220
By the deep quiet gloom appall'd, she sighs,
Stoops her sick head, and shuts her weary eyes.
Breaking th' ascending roar of desert floods,
And insect buzz, that stuns the sultry woods,
She hears, upon the mountain forest's brow,   225
The death-dog, howling loud and long, below;
On viewless fingers counts the valley-clock,
Followed by drowsy crow of midnight cock.
– Bursts from the troubl'd Larch's giant boughs
The pie, and chattering breaks the night's repose.   230
Low barks the fox; by Havoc rouz'd the bear
Quits, growling, the white bones that strew his lair.
The dry leaves stir as with the serpent's walk,
And far beneath, Banditti voices talk;
Behind her hill the Moon, all crimson, rides,   235
And his red eyes the slinking Water hides;

Then all is hush'd; the bushes rustle near,
And with strange tinglings sings her fainting ear.
Vex'd by the darkness, from the piny gulf
Ascending, nearer howls the famish'd wolf,   240
While thro' the stillness scatters wild dismay
Her babe's small cry, that leads him to his prey.
   Now, passing Urseren's open vale serene,
Her quiet streams, and hills of downy green,
Plunge with the Russ embrown'd by Terror's breath,   245
Where danger roofs the narrow walks of death,
By floods, that, thundering from their dizzy height,
Swell more gigantic on the stedfast sight;
Black drizzling craggs, that beaten by the din,
Vibrate, as if a voice complain'd within;   250
Bare steeps, where Desolation stalks, afraid,
Unstedfast, by a blasted yew upstay'd,
By cells whose image, trembling as he prays,
Awe-struck, the kneeling peasant scarce surveys;
Loose-hanging rocks the Day's bless'd eye that hide,   255
And crosses rear'd to Death on every side,
Which with cold kiss Devotion planted near,
And, bending, water'd with the human tear,
Soon fading 'silent' from her upward eye,
Unmov'd with each rude form of Danger nigh,   260
Fix'd on the anchor left by him who saves
Alike in whelming snows and roaring waves.

*   *   *

   'Tis storm; and hid in mist from hour to hour
All day the floods a deeper murmur pour,
And mournful sounds, as of a Spirit lost,
Pipe wild along the hollow-blustering coast,   335
'Till the Sun walking on his western field
Shakes from behind the clouds his flashing shield.
Triumphant on the bosom of the storm,
Glances the fire-clad eagle's wheeling form;
Eastward, in long perspective glittering, shine   340
The wood-crown'd cliffs that o'er the lake recline;
Wide o'er the Alps a hundred streams unfold,
At once to pillars turn'd that flame with gold;

Behind his sail the peasant strives to shun
The west that burns like one dilated sun,   345
Where in a mighty crucible expire
The mountains, glowing hot, like coals of fire.

          *   *   *

'Tis morn: with gold the verdant mountain glows,
More high, the snowy peaks with hues of rose.
Far stretch'd beneath the many-tinted hills
A mighty waste of mist the valley fills —   495
A solemn sea! whose vales and mountains round
Stand motionless, to awful silence bound.
A gulf of gloomy blue, that opens wide
And bottomless, divides the midway tide.
Like leaning masts of stranded ships appear   500
The pines that near the coast their summits rear;
Of cabins, woods, and lawns a pleasant shore
Bounds calm and clear the chaos still and hoar;
Loud thro' that midway gulf ascending, sound
Unnumber'd streams with hollow roar profound.   505
Mounts thro' the nearer mist the chaunt of birds,
And talking voices, and the low of herds,
The bark of dogs, the drowsy tinkling bell,
And wild-wood mountain lutes of saddest swell.
Think not, suspended from the cliff on high   510
He looks below with undelighted eye.
No vulgar joy is his, at even tide
Stretch'd on the scented mountain's purple side.
For as the pleasures of his simple day
Beyond his native valley hardly stray,   515
Nought round it's darling precincts can he find
But brings some past enjoyment to his mind,
While Hope that ceaseless leans on Pleasure's urn
Binds her wild wreathes, and whispers his return.
    Once Man entirely free, alone and wild,   520
Was bless'd as free — for he was Nature's child.
He, all superior but his God disdain'd,
Walk'd none restraining, and by none restrain'd,
Confess'd no law but what his reason taught,
Did all he wish'd, and wish'd but what he ought.   525

As Man in his primæval dower array'd
The image of his glorious sire display'd,
Ev'n so, by vestal Nature guarded, here
The traces of primæval Man appear.
The native dignity no forms debase,   530
The eye sublime, and surly lion-grace.
The slave of none, of beasts alone the lord,
He marches with his flute, his book, and sword,
Well taught by that to feel his rights, prepar'd
With this 'the blessings he enjoys to guard'.   535
  And as on glorious ground he draws his breath,
Where Freedom oft, with Victory and Death,
Hath seen in grim array amid their Storms
Mix'd with auxiliar Rocks, three hundred Forms,
While twice ten thousand corselets at the view   540
Dropp'd loud at once, Oppression shriek'd, and flew.
Oft as those sainted Rocks before him spread,
An unknown power connects him with the dead.
For images of other worlds are there —
Awful the light, and holy is the air.   545
Uncertain thro' his fierce uncultur'd soul
Like lighted tempests troubled transports roll;
To viewless realms his Spirit towers amain,
Beyond the senses and their little reign.

                *   *   *

  When downward to his winter hut he goes,
Dear and more dear the lessening circle grows,
That hut which from the hills his eyes employs   570
So oft, the central point of all his joys.
And as a swift by tender cares oppress'd
Peeps often ere she dart into her nest,
So to th' untrodden floor, where round him looks
His father helpless as the babe he rocks,   575
Oft he descends to nurse the brother pair,
Till storm and driving ice blockade him there;
There hears, protected by the woods behind,
Secure, the chiding of the baffled wind,
Hears Winter, calling all his Terrors round,   580
Rush down the living rocks with whirlwind sound.

Thro' Nature's vale his homely pleasures glide
Unstain'd by envy, discontent, and pride,
The bound of all his vanity to deck
With one bright bell a favourite heifer's neck;   585
Content upon some simple annual feast,
Remember'd half the year, and hop'd the rest,
If dairy produce, from his inner hoard,
Of thrice ten summers consecrate the board.
Alas! in every clime a flying ray   590
Is all we have to chear our wintry way:
Condemn'd, in mists and tempests ever rife,
To pant slow up the endless Alp of life.
'Here', cried a swain, whose venerable head
Bloom'd with the snow-drops of Man's narrow bed,   595
Last night, while by his dying fire, as clos'd
The day, in luxury my limbs repos'd,
'Here Penury oft from misery's mount will guide
Ev'n to the summer door his icy tide,
And here the avalanche of Death destroy   600
The little cottage of domestic Joy.
But, ah! th' unwilling mind may more than trace
The general sorrows of the human race:
The churlish gales, that unremitting blow
Cold from necessity's continual snow,   605
To us the gentle groups of bliss deny
That on the noon-day bank of leisure lie.
Yet more; the tyrant Genius, still at strife
With all the tender Charities of life,
When close and closer they begin to strain,   610
No fond hand left to staunch th' unclosing vein;
Tearing their bleeding ties leaves Age to groan
On his wet bed, abandon'd and alone.
For ever, fast as they of strength become
To pay the filial debt, for food to roam,   615
The father, forc'd by Powers that only deign
That solitary Man disturb their reign,
From his bare nest amid the storms of heaven
Drives, eagle-like, his sons as he was driven —
His last dread pleasure! watches to the plain,   620
And never, eagle-like, beholds again.'

                         *   *   *

At such an hour I heav'd the human sigh,
When roar'd the sullen Arve in anger by,
That not for thee, delicious vale! unfold
Thy reddening orchards, and thy fields of gold;   705
That thou, the slave of slaves, art doom'd to pine,
While no Italian arts their charms combine
To teach the skirt of thy dark cloud to shine;
For thy poor babes that, hurrying from the door,
With pale-blue hands, and eyes that fix'd implore,   710
Dead muttering lips, and hair of hungry white,
Besiege the traveller whom they half affright.
— Yes, were it mine, the cottage meal to share,
Forc'd from my native mountains bleak and bare,
O'er Anet's hopeless seas of marsh to stray,   715
Her shrill winds roaring round my lonely way;
To scent the sweets of Piedmont's breathing rose,
And orange gale that o'er Lugano blows;
In the wide range of many a weary round,
Still have my pilgrim feet unfailing found,   720
As despot courts their blaze of gems display,
Ev'n by the secret cottage far away
The lilly of domestic joy decay,
While Freedom's farthest hamlets blessings share,
Found still beneath her smile, and only there.   725
The casement shade more luscious woodbine binds,
And to the door a neater pathway winds;
At early morn the careful housewife, led
To cull her dinner from it's garden bed
Of weedless herbs, a healthier prospect sees,   730
While hum with busier joy her happy bees;
In brighter rows her table wealth aspires,
And laugh with merrier blaze her evening fires;
Her infant's cheeks with fresher roses glow,
And wilder graces sport around their brow;   735
By clearer taper lit a cleanlier board
Receives at supper hour her tempting hoard;
The chamber hearth with fresher boughs is spread,
And whiter is the hospitable bed.
— And thou! fair favoured region! which my soul   740
Shall love, 'till Life has broke her golden bowl,
Till Death's cold touch her cistern-wheel assail,

And vain regret and vain desire shall fail;
Tho' now, where erst the grey-clad peasant stray'd,
To break the quiet of the village shade   745
Gleam war's discordant habits thro' the trees,
And the red banner mock the sullen breeze;
Tho' now no more thy maids their voices suit
To the low-warbled breath of twilight lute,
And heard, the pausing village hum between,   750
No solemn songstress lull the fading green —
Scared by the fife, and rumbling drum's alarms,
And the short thunder, and the flash of arms,
While, as Night bids the startling uproar die,
Sole sound, the sourd renews his mournful cry.   755
Yet hast thou found that Freedom spreads her pow'r
Beyond the cottage hearth, the cottage door:
All nature smiles, and owns beneath her eyes
Her fields peculiar, and peculiar skies.
Yes, as I roam'd where Loiret's waters glide   760
Thro' rustling aspins heard from side to side,
When from october clouds a milder light
Fell, where the blue flood rippled into white,
Methought from every cot the watchful bird
Crowed with ear-piercing power 'till then unheard;   765
Each clacking mill, that broke the murmuring streams,
Rock'd the charm'd thought in more delightful dreams.
Chasing those long long dreams, the falling leaf
Awoke a fainter pang of moral grief;
The measured echo of the distant flail   770
Winded in sweeter cadence down the vale;
A more majestic tide the water roll'd,
And glowed the sun-gilt groves in richer gold.
— Tho' Liberty shall soon, indignant, raise
Red on his hills his beacon's comet blaze,   775
Bid from on high his lonely cannon found,
And on ten thousand hearths his shout rebound,
His larum-bell from village-tow'r to tow'r
Swing on th' astounded ear it's dull undying roar,
Yet, yet rejoice, tho' Pride's perverted ire   780
Rouze Hell's own aid, and wrap thy hills in fire.
Lo! from th' innocuous flames, a lovely birth!
With it's own Virtues springs another earth:

Nature, as in her prime, her virgin reign
Begins, and Love and Truth compose her train.   785
With pulseless hand, and fix'd unwearied gaze,
Unbreathing Justice her still beam surveys;
No more, along thy vales and viny groves,
Whole hamlets disappearing as he moves,
With cheeks o'erspread by smiles of baleful glow,   790
On his pale horse shall fell Consumption go.
   Oh give, great God, to Freedom's waves to ride
Sublime o'er Conquest, Avarice, and Pride,
To break, the vales where Death with Famine scow'rs,
And dark Oppression builds her thick-ribb'd tow'rs,   795
Where Machination her fell soul resigns,
Fled panting to the centre of her mines;
Where Persecution decks with ghastly smiles
Her bed, his mountains mad Ambition piles;
Where Discord stalks dilating, every hour,   800
And crouching fearful at the feet of Pow'r,
Like Lightnings eager for th' almighty word,
Look up for sign of havoc, Fire, and Sword;
– Give them, beneath their breast while Gladness springs,
To brood the nations o'er with Nile-like wings,   805
And grant that every sceptred child of clay,
Who cries, presumptuous, 'here their tides shall stay',
Swept in their anger from th' affrighted shore,
With all his creatures sink – to rise no more.
   To-night, my friend, within this humble cot   810
Be the dead load of mortal ills forgot,
Renewing, when the rosy summits glow
At morn, our various journey, sad and slow.

Salisbury Plain

1

Hard is the life when naked and unhouzed
And wasted by the long day's fruitless pains,
The hungry savage, 'mid deep forests, rouzed
By storms, lies down at night on unknown plains
And lifts his head in fear, while famished trains   5
Of boars along the crashing forests prowl,
And heard in darkness, as the rushing rains
Put out his watch-fire, bears contending growl
And round his fenceless bed gaunt wolves in armies howl.

2

Yet is he strong to suffer, and his mind   10
Encounters all his evils unsubdued;
For happier days since at the breast he pined
He never knew, and when by foes pursued
With life he scarce has reached the fortress rude,
While with the war-song's peal the valleys shake,   15
What in those wild assemblies has he viewed
But men who all of his hard lot partake,
Repose in the same fear, to the same toil awake?

3

The thoughts which bow the kindly spirits down
And break the springs of joy, their deadly weight   20
Derive from memory of pleasures flown
Which haunts us in some sad reverse of fate,
Or from reflection on the state
Of those who on the couch of Affluence rest
By laughing Fortune's sparkling cup elate,   25
While we of comfort reft, by pain depressed,
No other pillow know than Penury's iron breast.

4

Hence where Refinement's genial influence calls
The soft affections from their wintry sleep
And the sweet tear of Love and Friendship falls   30
The willing heart in tender joy to steep,
When men in various vessels roam the deep
Of social life, and turns of chance prevail
Various and sad, how many thousands weep
Beset with foes more fierce than e'er assail   35
The savage without home in winter's keenest gale.

5

The troubled west was red with stormy fire,
O'er Sarum's plain the traveller with a sigh
Measured each painful step, the distant spire
That fixed at every turn his backward eye   40
Was lost, tho' still he turned, in the blank sky.
By thirst and hunger pressed he gazed around
And scarce could any trace of man descry,
Save wastes of corn that stretched without a bound,
But where the sower dwelt was nowhere to be found.   45

6

No shade was there, no meads of pleasant green,
No brook to wet his lips or soothe his ear,
Huge piles of corn-stack here and there were seen
But thence no smoke upwreathed his sight to cheer;
And see the homeward shepherd dim appear   50
Far off – He stops his feeble voice to strain;
No sound replies but winds that whistling near
Sweep the thin grass and passing, wildly plain;
Or desert lark that pours on high a wasted strain.

7

Long had each slope he mounted seemed to hide   55
Some cottage whither his tired feet might turn,
But now, all hope resigned, in tears he eyed
The crows in blackening eddies homeward borne,
Then sought, in vain, a shepherd's lowly thorn
Or hovel from the storm to shield his head.   60
On as he passed more wild and more forlorn
And vacant the huge plain around him spread;
Ah me! the wet cold ground must be his only bed.

8

Hurtle the rattling clouds together piled
By fiercer gales, and soon the storm must break.   65
He stood the only creature in the wild
On whom the elements their rage could wreak,
Save that the bustard of those limits bleak,
Shy tenant, seeing there a mortal wight
At that dread hour, outsent a mournful shriek   70
And half upon the ground, with strange affright,
Forced hard against the wind a thick unwieldy flight.

9

The Sun unheeded sunk, while on a mound
He stands beholding with astonished gaze,
Frequent upon the deep entrenched ground,   75
Strange marks of mighty arms of former days,
Then looking up at distance he surveys
What seems an antique castle spreading wide.
Hoary and naked are its walls and raise
Their brow sublime; while to those walls he hied   80
A voice as from a tomb in hollow accents cried:

10

'Oh from that mountain-pile avert thy face
Whate'er betide at this tremendous hour.
To hell's most cursed sprites the baleful place
Belongs, upreared by their magic power.   85
Though mixed with flame rush down the crazing shower
And o'er thy naked bed the thunder roll
Fly ere the fiends their prey unwares devour
Or grinning, on thy endless tortures scowl
Till very madness seem a mercy to thy soul.   90

11

'For oft at dead of night, when dreadful fire
Reveals that powerful circle's reddening stones,
'Mid priests and spectres grim and idols dire,
Far heard the great flame utters human moans,
Then all is hushed: again the desert groans,   95
A dismal light its farthest bounds illumes,
While warrior spectres of gigantic bones,
Forth-issuing from a thousand rifted tombs,
Wheel on their fiery steeds amid the infernal glooms.'

12

The voice was from beneath but face or form   100
He saw not, mocked as by a hideous dream.
Three hours he wildered through the watery storm
No moon to open the black clouds and stream
From narrow gulph profound one friendly beam;
No watch-dog howled from shepherd's homely shed.   105
Once did the lightning's pale abortive beam
Disclose a naked guide-post's double head,
Sole object where he stood had day its radiance spread.

13

'Twas dark and waste as ocean's shipless flood
Roaring with storms beneath night's starless gloom.   110
[   ]

Where the wet gypsey in her straw-built home
Warmed her wet limbs by fire of fern and broom.
No transient meteor burst upon his sight
Nor taper glimmered dim from sick man's room.   115
Along the moor no line of mournful light
From lamp of lonely toll-gate streamed athwart the night.

14

At length, deep hid in clouds, the moon arose
And spread a sickly glare. With flight unwilled,
Worn out and wasted, wishing the repose   120
Of death, he came where, antient vows fulfilled,
Kind pious hands did to the Virgin build
A lonely Spital, the belated swain
From the night-terrors of that waste to shield.
But there no human being could remain   125
And now the walls are named the dead house of the plain.

15

Till then as if his terror dogged his road
He fled, and often backward cast his face;
And when the ambiguous gloom that ruin shewed
How glad he was at length to find a place   130
That bore of human hands the chearing trace:
Here shall he rest till Morn her eye unclose.
Ah me! that last of hopes is fled apace;
For, entering in, his hair in horror rose
To hear a voice that seemed to mourn in sorrow's throes.   135

16

It was the voice of one that sleeping mourned,
A human voice! and soon his terrors fled;
At dusk a female wanderer hither turned
And found a comfortless half-sheltered bed.
The moon a wan dead light around her shed;   140
He waked her and at once her spirits fail
Thrill'd by the poignant dart of sudden dread,
For of that ruin she had heard a tale
That might with a child's fears the stoutest heart assail.

17

Had heard of one who forced from storms to shroud 145
Felt the loose walls of this decayed retreat
Rock to his horse's neighings shrill and loud,
While the ground rang by ceaseless pawing beat,
Till on a stone that sparkled to his feet
Struck and still struck again the troubled horse. 150
The man half raised that stone by pain and sweat,
Half raised; for well his arm might lose its force
Disclosing the grim head of a new murdered corse.

18

Such tales of the lone Spital she had learned,
And when that shape with eyes in sleep half-drowned 155
By the moon's sullen lamp she scarce discerned,
Cold stony horror all her senses bound.
But he to her low words of chearing sound
Addressed. With joy she heard such greeting kind
And much they conversed of that desert ground, 160
Which seemed to those of other worlds consigned
Whose voices still they heard as paused the hollow wind.

19

The Woman told that through a hollow deep
As on she journeyed, far from spring or bower,
An old man beckoning from the naked steep 165
Came tottering sidelong down to ask the hour;
There never clock was heard from steeple tower.
From the wide corn the plundering crows to scare
He held a rusty gun. In sun and shower,
Old as he was, alone he lingered there, 170
His hungry meal too scant for dog that meal to share.

20

Much of the wonders of that boundless heath
He spoke, and of a swain who far astray
Reached unawares a height and saw beneath
Gigantic beings ranged in dread array. 175

Such beings thwarting oft the traveller's way
With shield and stone-ax stride across the wold,
Or, throned on that dread circle's summit gray
Of mountains hung in air, their state unfold,
And like a thousand Gods mysterious council hold.   180

21

And oft a night-fire mounting to the clouds
Reveals the desert and with dismal red
Clothes the black bodies of encircling crowds.
It is the sacrificial altar fed
With living men. How deep it groans – the dead   185
Thrilled in their yawning tombs their helms uprear;
The sword that slept beneath the warriour's head
Thunders in fiery air: red arms appear
Uplifted thro' the gloom and shake the rattling spear.

22

Not thus where clear moons spread their pleasing light.   190
– Long bearded forms with wands uplifted shew
To vast assemblies, while each breath of night
Is hushed, the living fires that bright and slow
Rounding th'aetherial field in order go.
Then as they trace with awe their various files   195
All figured on the mystic plain below,
Still prelude of sweet sounds the moon beguiles
And charmed for many a league the hoary desert smiles.

23

While thus they talk the churlish storms relent;
And round those broken walls the dying wind   200
In feeble murmurs told his rage was spent.
With sober sympathy and tranquil mind
Gently the Woman gan her wounds unbind.
Might Beauty charm the canker worm of pain
The rose on her sweet cheek had ne'er declined: 205
Moved she not once the prime of Keswick's plain
While Hope and Love and Joy composed her smiling train?

24

Like swans, twin swans, that when on the sweet brink
Of Derwent's stream the south winds hardly blow,
'Mid Derwent's water-lillies swell and sink   210
In union, rose her sister breasts of snow,
(Fair emblem of two lovers' hearts that know
No separate impulse) or like infants played,
Like infants strangers yet to pain and woe.
Unwearied Hope to tend their motions made   215
Long Vigils, and Delight her cheek between them laid.

25

And are ye spread ye glittering dews of youth
For this, – that Frost may gall the tender flower
In Joy's fair breast with more untimely tooth?
Unhappy man! thy sole delightful hour   220
Flies first; it is thy miserable dower
Only to taste of joy that thou may'st pine
A loss, which rolling suns shall ne'er restore.
New suns roll on and scatter as they shine
No second spring, but pain, till death release thee, thine.   225

26

'By Derwent's side my father's cottage stood,'
The mourner thus her artless story told.
'A little flock and what the finny flood
Supplied, to him were more than mines of gold.
Light was my sleep; my days in transport rolled: 230
With thoughtless joy I stretched along the shore
My parent's nets, or watched, when from the fold
High o'er the cliffs I led his fleecy store,
A dizzy depth below! his boat and twinkling oar.

27

'Can I forget my seat beneath the thorn,   235
My garden stored with peas and mint and thyme,
And rose and lilly for the sabbath morn;

The church-inviting bell's delightful chime,
The merriment and song at shearing time,
My hen's rich nest with long grass overgrown,   240
The cowslip gathering at the morning prime,
The hazel copse with teeming clusters brown,
[   ]

28

'Can I forget the casement where I fed
The red-breast when the fields were whitened o'er,   245
My snowy kerchiefs on the hawthorn spread,
My humming wheel and glittering table store,
The well-known knocking at the evening door,
The hunted slipper and the blinded game,
The dance that loudly beat the merry floor,   250
The ballad chaunted round the brightening flame
While down the ravaged hills the storm unheeded came?

29

'The suns of eighteen summers danced along
Joyous as in the pleasant morn of May.
At last by cruel chance and wilful wrong   255
My father's substance fell into decay.
Oppression trampled on his tresses grey:
His little range of water was denied;
Even to the bed where his old body lay
His all was seized; and weeping side by side   260
Turned out on the cold winds, alone we wandered wide.

30

'Can I forget that miserable hour
When from the last hill-top my sire surveyed,
Peering above the trees, the steeple-tower
That on his marriage-day sweet music made?   265
There at my birth my mother's bones were laid
And there, till then, he hoped his own might rest.

Bidding me trust in God he stood and prayed:
I could not pray, by human grief oppressed,
Viewing our glimmering cot through tears that never ceased.   270

31

'There was a youth whose tender voice and eye
Might add fresh happiness to happiest days.
At uprise of the sun when he was by
The birds prolonged with joy their choicest lays,
The soft pipe warbled out a wilder maze,   275
The silent moon of evening, hung above,
Showered through the waving lime-trees mellower rays;
Warm was the breath of night: his voice of love
Charmed the rude winds to sleep by river, field, or grove.

32

'His father bid him to a distant town   280
To ply remote from groves the artist's trade.
What tears of bitter grief till then unknown,
What tender vows our last sad kiss delayed!
To him our steps we turned, by hope upstayed.
Oh with what bliss upon his neck I wept;   285
And her whom he had loved in joy, he said,
He well could love in grief: his faith he kept,
And sheltered from the winds once more my father slept.

33

'Four years each day with daily bread was blessed,
By constant toil and constant prayer supplied.   290
Three lovely infants lay within my breast
And often viewing their sweet smiles I sighed
And knew not why. My happy father died
Just as the children's meal began to fail.
For War the nations to the field defied.   295
The loom stood still; unwatched, the idle gale
Wooed in deserted shrouds the unregarding sail.

34

'How changed at once! for Labor's chearful hum
Silence and Fear, and Misery's weeping train.
But soon with proud parade the noisy drum   300
Beat round to sweep the streets of want and pain.
My husband's arms now only served to strain
Me and his children hungering in his view.
He could not beg: my prayers and tears were vain;
To join those miserable men he flew.   305
We reached the western world a poor devoted crew.

35

'Oh dreadful price of being! to resign
All that is dear in being; better far
In Want's most lonely cave till death to pine
Unseen, unheard, unwatched by any star.   310
Better before proud Fortune's sumptuous car
Obvious our dying bodies to obtrude,
Than dog-like wading at the heels of War
Protract a cursed existence with the brood
That lap, their very nourishment, their brother's blood.   315

36

'The pains and plagues that on our heads came down,
Disease and Famine, Agony and Fear,
In wood or wilderness, in camp or town,
It would thy brain unsettle even to hear.
All perished, all in one remorseless year,   320
Husband and children one by one, by sword
And scourge of fiery fever: every tear
Dried up, despairing, desolate, on board
A British ship I waked as from a trance restored.'

37

Here paused she of all present thought forlorn,   325
Living once more those hours that sealed her doom.
Meanwhile he looked and saw the smiling morn
All unconcerned with their unrest resume
Her progress through the brightening eastern gloom.
Oh when shall such fair hours their gleams bestow   330
To bid the grave its opening clouds illume?
Fled each fierce blast and hellish fiend, and lo!
Day fresh from ocean wave uprears his lovely brow.

38

'Oh come,' he said, 'come after weary night
So ruinous far other scene to view.'   335
So forth she came and eastward look'd. The sight
O'er her moist eyes meek dawn of gladness threw
That tinged with faint red smile her faded hue.
Not lovelier did the morning star appear
Parting the lucid mist and bathed in dew,   340
The whilst her comrade to her pensive chear
Tempered sweet words of hope and the lark warbled near.

39

They looked and saw a lengthening road and wain
Descending a bare slope not far remote.
The downs all glistered dropt with freshening rain;   345
The carman whistled loud with chearful note;
The cock scarce heard at distance sounds his throat;
But town or farm or hamlet none they viewed,
Only were told there stood a lonely cot
Full two miles distant. Then, while they pursued   350
Their journey, her sad tale the mourner thus renewed.

40

'Peaceful as this immeasurable plain
By these extended beams of dawn impressed,
In the calm sunshine slept the glittering main.

The very ocean has its hour of rest   355
Ungranted to the human mourner's breast.
Remote from man and storms of mortal care,
With wings which did the world of waves invest,
The Spirit of God diffused through balmy air
Quiet that might have healed, if aught could heal, Despair.   360

41

'Ah! how unlike each smell, each sight and sound
That late the stupor of my spirit broke.
Of noysome hospitals the groan profound,
The mine's dire earthquake, the bomb's thunder stroke;
Heart sickening Famine's grim despairing look;   365
The midnight flames in thundering deluge spread;
The stormed town's expiring shriek that woke
Far round the griesly phantoms of the dead,
And pale with ghastly light the victor's human head.

42

'Some mighty gulf of separation passed   370
I seemed transported to another world:
A dream resigned with pain when from the mast
The impatient mariner the sail unfurled,
And whistling called the wind that hardly curled
The silent seas. The pleasant thoughts of home   375
With tears his weather-beaten cheek impearled:
For me, farthest from earthly port to roam
Was best; my only wish to shun where man might come.

43

'And oft, robbed of my perfect mind, I thought
At last my feet a resting-place had found.   380
"Here will I weep in peace," so Fancy wrought,
"Roaming the illimitable waters round,
Here gaze, of every friend but Death disowned,
All day, my ready tomb the ocean flood."
To break my dream the vessel reached its bound   385
And homeless near a thousand homes I stood,
And near a thousand tables pined and wanted food.

44

'Three years a wanderer round my native coast
My eyes have watched yon sun declining tend
Down to the land where hope to me was lost;   390
And now across this waste my steps I bend:
Oh! tell me whither, for no earthly friend
Have I, no house in prospect but the tomb.'
She ceased. The city's distant spires ascend
Like flames which far and wide the west illume,   395
Scattering from out the sky the rear of night's thin gloom.

45

Along the fiery east the Sun, a show
More gorgeous still! pursued his proud career.
But human sufferings and that tale of woe
Had dimmed the traveller's eye with Pity's tear,   400
And in the youthful mourner's doom severe
He half forgot the terrors of the night,
Striving with counsel sweet her soul to chear,
Her soul for ever widowed of delight.
He too had withered young in sorrow's deadly blight.   405

46

But now from a hill summit down they look
Where through a narrow valley's pleasant scene
A wreath of vapour tracked a winding brook
Babbling through groves and lawns and meads of green.
A smoking cottage peeped the trees between,   410
The woods resound the linnet's amorous lays,
And melancholy lowings intervene
Of scattered herds that in the meadows graze,
While through the furrowed grass the merry milkmaid strays.

47

Adieu ye friendless hope-forsaken pair!   415
Yet friendless ere ye take your several road,
Enter that lowly cot and ye shall share
Comforts by prouder mansions unbestowed.

For you yon milkmaid bears her brimming load,
For you the board is piled with homely bread,   420
And think that life is like this desart broad,
Where all the happiest find is but a shed
And a green spot 'mid wastes interminably spread.

48

Though from huge wickers paled with circling fire
No longer horrid shrieks and dying cries   425
To ears of Dæmon-Gods in peals aspire,
To Dæmon-Gods a human sacrifice;
Though Treachery her sword no longer dyes
In the cold blood of Truce, still, reason's ray,
What does it more than while the tempests rise,   430
With starless glooms and sounds of loud dismay,
Reveal with still-born glimpse the terrors of our way?

49

For proof, if man thou lovest, turn thy eye
On realms which least the cup of Misery taste.
For want how many men and children die?   435
How many at Oppression's portal placed
Receive the scanty dole she cannot waste,
And bless, as she has taught, her hand benign?
How many by inhuman toil debased,
Abject, obscure, and brute to earth incline   440
Unrespited, forlorn of every spark divine?

50

Nor only is the walk of private life
Unblessed by Justice and the kindly train
Of Peace and Truth, while Injury and Strife,
Outrage and deadly Hate usurp their reign;   445
From the pale line to either frozen main
The nations, though at home in bonds they drink
The dregs of wretchedness, for empire strain,
And crushed by their own fetters helpless sink,
Move their galled limbs in fear and eye each silent link.   450

51

Lo! where the Sun exulting in his might
In haste the fiery top of Andes scales
And flings deep silent floods of purple light
Down to the sea through long Peruvian vales,
At once a thousand streams and gentle gales   455
Start from their slumber breathing scent and song.
But now no joy of man or woman hails
That star as once, ere with him came the throng
Of Furies and grim Death by Avarice lashed along.

52

Oh that a slave who on his naked knees   460
Weeps tears of fear at Superstition's nod,
Should rise a monster Tyrant and o'er seas
And mountains stretch so far his cruel rod
To bruise meek nature in her lone abode.
Is it for this the planet of the pole   465
Sends through the storms its stedfast light abroad?
Through storms we ride with Misery to her goal:
Nor star nor needle know the tempests of the soul.

53

How changed that paradise, those happy bounds
Where once through his own groves the Hindoo strayed;   470
No more the voice of jocund toil resounds
Along the crowded banyan's high arcade.

[*Lines 473–504 are missing.*]

57

How weak the solace such fond thoughts afford,   505
When with untimely stroke the virtuous bleed.
Say, rulers of the nations, from the sword
Can ought but murder, pain, and tears proceed?
Oh! what can war but endless war still breed?

Or whence but from the labours of the sage   510
Can poor benighted mortals gain the meed
Of happiness and virtue, how assuage
But by his gentle words their self-consuming rage?

58

Insensate they who think, at Wisdom's porch
That Exile, Terror, Bonds, and Force may stand: 515
That Truth with human blood can feed her torch,
And Justice balance with her gory hand
Scales whose dire weights of human heads demand
A Nero's arm. Must Law with iron scourge
Still torture crimes that grew a monstrous band   520
Formed by his care, and still his victim urge,
With voice that breathes despair, to death's tremendous verge?

[*Lines 523–539 are missing.*]

Who fierce on kingly crowns hurled his own lightning blaze.   540

61

Heroes of Truth pursue your march, uptear
Th'Oppressor's dungeon from its deepest base;
High o'er the towers of Pride undaunted rear
Resistless in your might the herculean mace
Of Reason; let foul Error's monster race   545
Dragged from their dens start at the light with pain
And die; pursue your toils, till not a trace
Be left on earth of Superstition's reign,
Save that eternal pile which frowns on Sarum's plain.

Argument for Suicide

Send this man to the mine, this to the battle;
Famish an aged beggar at your gates,
And let him die by inches – but for worlds
Lift not your hand against him. Live, live on,
As if this earth owned neither steel nor arsenic,   5
A rope, a river, or a standing pool.
Live, if you dread the pains of hell, or think
Your corpse would quarrel with a stake; alas,
Has misery then no friend? If you would die
By license, call the dropsy and the stone,   10
And let them end you. Strange it is,
And most fantastic are the magic circles
Drawn round the thing called life: till we have learned
To prize it less, we ne'er shall learn to prize
The things worth living for.   15

The Baker's Cart [fragment]

I have seen the baker's horse,
As he had been accustomed at your door,
Stop with the loaded wain, when o'er his head
Smack went the whip, and you were left as if
You were not born to live, or there had been   5
No bread in all the land. Five little ones –
They at the rumbling of the distant wheels
Had all come forth, and ere the grove of birch
Concealed the wain, into their wretched hut
They all returned. While in the road I stood   10
Pursuing with involuntary look
The wain now seen no longer, to my side
[   ] came, a pitcher in her hand
Filled from the spring. She saw what way my eyes
Were turned, and in a low and fearful voice   15
She said, 'That waggon does not care for us.'
The words were simple, but her look and voice
Made up their meaning, and bespoke a mind
Which being long neglected, and denied

The common food of hope, was now become   20
Sick and extravagant – by strong access
Of momentary pangs driv'n to that state
In which all past experience melts away
And the rebellious heart to its own will
Fashions the laws of nature.   25

'Are there no groans, no breeze or wind?'

Are there no groans, no breeze or wind?
Does misery leave no track behind?
Why is the earth without a shape, and why
Thus silent is the sky?
Is every glimmering of the sky,   5
Is every loophole in the world an eye?
Has every star a tongue?

'Away, away, it is the air'

Away, away, it is the air
That stirs among the withered leaves;
Away, away, it is not there –
Go hunt among the harvest sheaves.
There is a bed in shape as plain   5
As form of hare or lion's lair:
It is the bed where we have lain
In anguish and despair.

Away, and take the eagle's eyes,
The tiger's smell,   10
Ears that can hear the agonies
And murmurings of hell.
And when you there have stood
By that same bed of pain –
The groans are gone, the tears remain –   15
Then tell me if the thing be clear:
The difference betwixt a tear
Of water and of blood.

The Ruined Cottage

'Twas Summer and the sun was mounted high;
Along the south the uplands feebly glared
Through a pale steam, and all the northern downs,
In clearer air ascending, shewed far off
Their surfaces with shadows dappled o'er   5
Of deep embattled clouds. Far as the sight
Could reach those many shadows lay in spots
Determined and unmoved, with steady beams
Of clear and pleasant sunshine interposed –
Pleasant to him who on the soft cool moss   10
Extends his careless limbs beside the root
Of some huge oak whose aged branches make
A twilight of their own, a dewy shade
Where the wren warbles while the dreaming man,
Half-conscious of that soothing melody,   15
With side-long eye looks out upon the scene,
By those impending branches made more soft,
More soft and distant.

            Other lot was mine.
Across a bare wide common I had toiled
With languid feet which by the slipp'ry ground   20
Were baffled still; and when I stretched myself
On the brown earth my limbs from very heat
Could find no rest, nor my weak arm disperse
The insect host which gathered round my face
And joined their murmurs to the tedious noise   25
Of seeds of bursting gorse that crackled round.
I rose and turned towards a group of trees
Which midway in that level stood alone;
And thither come at length, beneath a shade
Of clustering elms that sprang from the same root   30
I found a ruined house, four naked walls
That stared upon each other. I looked round,
And near the door I saw an aged man

Alone and stretched upon the cottage bench;
An iron-pointed staff lay at his side.   35
With instantanious joy I recognized
That pride of Nature and of lowly life,
The venerable Armytage, a friend
As dear to me as is the setting sun.
                  Two days before   40
We had been fellow-travellers. I knew
That he was in this neighbourhood, and now
Delighted found him here in the cool shade.
He lay, his pack of rustic merchandize
Pillowing his head. I guess he had no thought   45
Of his way-wandering life. His eyes were shut,
The shadows of the breezy elms above
Dappled his face. With thirsty heat oppressed
At length I hailed him, glad to see his hat
Bedewed with water-drops, as if the brim   50
Had newly scooped a running stream. He rose
And pointing to a sun-flower, bade me climb
The [   ] wall where that same gaudy flower
Looked out upon the road.

                It was a plot
Of garden-ground now wild, its matted weeds   55
Marked with the steps of those whom as they passed,
The gooseberry-trees that shot in long lank slips,
Or currants hanging from their leafless stems
In scanty strings, had tempted to o'erleap
The broken wall. Within that cheerless spot,   60
Where two tall hedgerows of thick alder boughs
Joined in a damp cold nook, I found a well
Half covered up with willow-flowers and grass.
I slaked my thirst and to the shady bench
Returned, and while I stood unbonneted   65
To catch the motion of the cooler air
The old man said, 'I see around me here
Things which you cannot see. We die, my friend,
Nor we alone, but that which each man loved
And prized in his peculiar nook of earth   70
Dies with him, or is changed, and very soon
Even of the good is no memorial left.

The poets, in their elegies and songs
Lamenting the departed, call the groves,
They call upon the hills and streams to mourn,   75
And senseless rocks — nor idly, for they speak
In these their invocations with a voice
Obedient to the strong creative power
Of human passion. Sympathies there are
More tranquil, yet perhaps of kindred birth,   80
That steal upon the meditative mind
And grow with thought. Beside yon spring I stood,
And eyed its waters till we seemed to feel
One sadness, they and I. For them a bond
Of brotherhood is broken: time has been   85
When every day the touch of human hand
Disturbed their stillness, and they ministered
To human comfort. When I stooped to drink
A spider's web hung to the water's edge,
And on the wet and slimy foot-stone lay   90
The useless fragment of a wooden bowl.
It moved my very heart.

                    The day has been
When I could never pass this road but she
Who lived within these walls, when I appeared,
A daughter's welcome gave me, and I loved her   95
As my own child. Oh sir, the good die first,
And they whose hearts are dry as summer dust
Burn to the socket. Many a passenger
Has blessed poor Margaret for her gentle looks
When she upheld the cool refreshment drawn   100
From that forsaken spring, and no one came
But he was welcome, no one went away
But that it seemed she loved him. She is dead,
The worm is on her cheek, and this poor hut,
Stripped of its outward garb of household flowers,   105
Of rose and sweetbriar, offers to the wind
A cold bare wall whose earthy top is tricked
With weeds and the rank speargrass. She is dead,
And nettles rot and adders sun themselves
Where we have sate together while she nursed   110
Her infant at her breast. The unshod colt,

The wandring heifer and the potter's ass,
Find shelter now within the chimney-wall
Where I have seen her evening hearth-stone blaze
And through the window spread upon the road   115
Its chearful light. You will forgive me, sir,
But often on this cottage do I muse
As on a picture, till my wiser mind
Sinks, yielding to the foolishness of grief.

She had a husband, an industrious man,   120
Sober and steady. I have heard her say
That he was up and busy at his loom
In summer ere the mower's scythe had swept
The dewy grass, and in the early spring
Ere the last star had vanished. They who passed   125
At evening, from behind the garden-fence
Might hear his busy spade, which he would ply
After his daily work till the daylight
Was gone, and every leaf and flower were lost
In the dark hedges. So they passed their days   130
In peace and comfort, and two pretty babes
Were their best hope next to the God in heaven.

You may remember, now some ten years gone,
Two blighting seasons when the fields were left
With half a harvest. It pleased heaven to add   135
A worse affliction in the plague of war;
A happy land was stricken to the heart —
'Twas a sad time of sorrow and distress.
A wanderer among the cottages,
I with my pack of winter raiment saw   140
The hardships of that season. Many rich
Sunk down as in a dream among the poor,
And of the poor did many cease to be,
And their place knew them not. Meanwhile, abridged
Of daily comforts, gladly reconciled   145
To numerous self-denials, Margaret
Went struggling on through those calamitous years
With chearful hope. But ere the second autumn
A fever seized her husband. In disease
He lingered long, and when his strength returned   150

He found the little he had stored to meet
The hour of accident, or crippling age,
Was all consumed. As I have said, 'twas now
A time of trouble: shoals of artizans
Were from their daily labour turned away   155
To hang for bread on parish charity,
They and their wives and children – happier far
Could they have lived as do the little birds
That peck along the hedges, or the kite
That makes her dwelling in the mountain rocks.   160
Ill fared it now with Robert, he who dwelt
In this poor cottage. At his door he stood
And whistled many a snatch of merry tunes
That had no mirth in them, or with his knife
Carved uncouth figures on the heads of sticks;   165
Then idly sought about through every nook
Of house or garden any casual task
Of use or ornament, and with a strange
Amusing but uneasy novelty
He blended where he might the various tasks   170
Of summer, autumn, winter, and of spring.
But this endured not, his good-humour soon
Became a weight in which no pleasure was,
And poverty brought on a petted mood
And a sore temper. Day by day he drooped,   175
And he would leave his home, and to the town
Without an errand would he turn his steps,
Or wander here and there among the fields.
One while he would speak lightly of his babes
And with a cruel tongue; at other times   180
He played with them wild freaks of merriment,
And 'twas a piteous thing to see the looks
Of the poor innocent children. "Every smile",
Said Margaret to me here beneath these trees,
"Made my heart bleed." '   185

                    At this the old man paused,
And looking up to those enormous elms
He said, ' 'Tis now the hour of deepest noon.
At this still season of repose and peace,
This hour when all things which are not at rest

Are chearful, while this multitude of flies 190
Fills all the air with happy melody,
Why should a tear be in an old man's eye?
Why should we thus with an untoward mind,
And in the weakness of humanity,
From natural wisdom turn our hearts away, 195
To natural comfort shut our eyes and ears,
And, feeding on disquiet, thus disturb
The calm of Nature with our restless thoughts?'

SECOND PART

He spake with somewhat of a solemn tone,
But when he ended there was in his face 200
Such easy chearfulness, a look so mild,
That for a little time it stole away
All recollection, and that simple tale
Passed from my mind like a forgotten sound.
A while on trivial things we held discourse, 205
To me soon tasteless. In my own despite
I thought of that poor woman as of one
Whom I had known and loved. He had rehearsed
Her homely tale with such familiar power,
With such an active countenance, an eye 210
So busy, that the things of which he spake
Seemed present, and, attention now relaxed,
There was a heartfelt chillness in my veins.
I rose, and turning from that breezy shade
Went out into the open air, and stood 215
To drink the comfort of the warmer sun.
Long time I had not stayed ere, looking round
Upon that tranquil ruin, I returned
And begged of the old man that for my sake
He would resume his story. 220
                              He replied,
'It were a wantonness, and would demand
Severe reproof, if we were men whose hearts
Could hold vain dalliance with the misery
Even of the dead, contented thence to draw
A momentary pleasure, never marked 225
By reason, barren of all future good.

But we have known that there is often found
In mournful thoughts, and always might be found,
A power to virtue friendly; were't not so
I am a dreamer among men, indeed   230
An idle dreamer. 'Tis a common tale
By moving accidents uncharactered,
A tale of silent suffering, hardly clothed
In bodily form, and to the grosser sense
But ill adapted — scarcely palpable   235
To him who does not think. But at your bidding
I will proceed.

        While thus it fared with them
To whom this cottage till that hapless year
Had been a blessed home, it was my chance
To travel in a country far remote;   240
And glad I was when, halting by yon gate
That leads from the green lane, again I saw
These lofty elm-trees. Long I did not rest —
With many pleasant thoughts I cheered my way
O'er the flat common. At the door arrived,   245
I knocked, and when I entered, with the hope
Of usual greeting, Margaret looked at me
A little while, then turned her head away
Speechless, and sitting down upon a chair
Wept bitterly. I wist not what to do,   250
Or how to speak to her. Poor wretch, at last
She rose from off her seat, and then, oh sir,
I cannot tell how she pronounced my name.
With fervent love, and with a face of grief
Unutterably helpless, and a look   255
That seemed to cling upon me, she enquired
If I had seen her husband. As she spake
A strange surprize and fear came to my heart,
Nor had I power to answer ere she told
That he had disappeared — just two months gone.   260
He left his house: two wretched days had passed,
And on the third by the first break of light,
Within her casement full in view she saw
A purse of gold. "I trembled at the sight,"
Said Margaret, "for I knew it was his hand   265

That placed it there. And on that very day
By one, a stranger, from my husband sent,
The tidings came that he had joined a troop
Of soldiers going to a distant land.
He left me thus. Poor man, he had not heart   270
To take a farewell of me, and he feared
That I should follow with my babes, and sink
Beneath the misery of a soldier's life."

This tale did Margaret tell with many tears,
And when she ended I had little power   275
To give her comfort, and was glad to take
Such words of hope from her own mouth as served
To cheer us both. But long we had not talked
Ere we built up a pile of better thoughts,
And with a brighter eye she looked around,   280
As if she had been shedding tears of joy.
We parted. It was then the early spring;
I left her busy with her garden tools,
And well remember, o'er that fence she looked,
And, while I paced along the foot-way path,   285
Called out and sent a blessing after me,
With tender chearfulness, and with a voice
That seemed the very sound of happy thoughts.

I roved o'er many a hill and many a dale
With this my weary load, in heat and cold,   290
Through many a wood and many an open ground,
In sunshine or in shade, in wet or fair,
Now blithe, now drooping, as it might befal;
My best companions now the driving winds
And now the "trotting brooks" and whispering trees,   295
And now the music of my own sad steps,
With many a short-lived thought that passed between
And disappeared.

       I came this way again
Towards the wane of summer, when the wheat
Was yellow, and the soft and bladed grass   300
Sprang up afresh and o'er the hay-field spread
Its tender green. When I had reached the door

I found that she was absent. In the shade,
Where we now sit, I waited her return.
Her cottage in its outward look appeared   305
As chearful as before, in any shew
Of neatness little changed – but that I thought
The honeysuckle crowded round the door
And from the wall hung down in heavier tufts,
And knots of worthless stonecrop started out   310
Along the window's edge, and grew like weeds
Against the lower panes. I turned aside
And strolled into her garden. It was changed.
The unprofitable bindweed spread his bells
From side to side, and with unwieldy wreaths   315
Had dragged the rose from its sustaining wall
And bent it down to earth. The border tufts,
Daisy, and thrift, and lowly camomile,
And thyme, had straggled out into the paths
Which they were used to deck.   320

                              Ere this an hour
Was wasted. Back I turned my restless steps,
And as I walked before the door it chanced
A stranger passed, and guessing whom I sought,
He said that she was used to ramble far.
The sun was sinking in the west, and now   325
I sate with sad impatience. From within
Her solitary infant cried aloud.
The spot though fair seemed very desolate –
The longer I remained more desolate –
And looking round I saw the corner-stones,   330
Till then unmarked, on either side the door
With dull red stains discoloured, and stuck o'er
With tufts and hairs of wool, as if the sheep
That feed upon the commons thither came
Familiarly, and found a couching-place   335
Even at her threshold.

                              The house-clock struck eight:
I turned and saw her distant a few steps.
Her face was pale and thin, her figure too
Was changed. As she unlocked the door she said,

"It grieves me you have waited here so long, 340
But in good truth I've wandered much of late,
And sometimes – to my shame I speak – have need
Of my best prayers to bring me back again."
While on the board she spread our evening meal,
She told me she had lost her elder child, 345
That he for months had been a serving-boy,
Apprenticed by the parish. "I perceive
You look at me, and you have cause. Today
I have been travelling far, and many days
About the fields I wander, knowing this 350
Only, that what I seek I cannot find.
And so I waste my time: for I am changed,
And to myself," said she, "have done much wrong,
And to this helpless infant. I have slept
Weeping, and weeping I have waked. My tears 355
Have flowed as if my body were not such
As others are, and I could never die.
But I am now in mind and in my heart
More easy, and I hope," said she, "that heaven
Will give me patience to endure the things 360
Which I behold at home."

                                    It would have grieved
Your very soul to see her. Sir, I feel
The story linger in my heart. I fear
'Tis long and tedious, but my spirit clings
To that poor woman. So familiarly 365
Do I perceive her manner and her look
And presence, and so deeply do I feel
Her goodness, that not seldom in my walks
A momentary trance comes over me,
And to myself I seem to muse on one 370
By sorrow laid asleep or borne away,
A human being destined to awake
To human life, or something very near
To human life, when he shall come again
For whom she suffered. Sir, it would have grieved 375
Your very soul to see her: evermore
Her eyelids drooped, her eyes were downward cast,
And when she at her table gave me food

She did not look at me. Her voice was low,
Her body was subdued. In every act   380
Pertaining to her house-affairs appeared
The careless stillness which a thinking mind
Gives to an idle matter. Still she sighed,
But yet no motion of the breast was seen,
No heaving of the heart. While by the fire   385
We sate together, sighs came on my ear –
I knew not how, and hardly whence, they came.
I took my staff, and when I kissed her babe
The tears stood in her eyes. I left her then
With the best hope and comfort I could give: 390
She thanked me for my will, but for my hope
It seemed she did not thank me.
                                      I returned
And took my rounds along this road again
Ere on its sunny bank the primrose flower
Had chronicled the earliest day of spring.   395
I found her sad and drooping. She had learned
No tidings of her husband. If he lived,
She knew not that he lived: if he were dead,
She knew not he was dead. She seemed the same
In person or appearance, but her house   400
Bespoke a sleepy hand of negligence.
The floor was neither dry nor neat, the hearth
Was comfortless,
The windows too were dim, and her few books,
Which one upon the other heretofore   405
Had been piled up against the corner-panes
In seemly order, now with straggling leaves
Lay scattered here and there, open or shut,
As they had chanced to fall. Her infant babe
Had from its mother caught the trick of grief,   410
And sighed among its playthings. Once again
I turned towards the garden-gate, and saw
More plainly still that poverty and grief
Were now come nearer to her. The earth was hard,
With weeds defaced and knots of withered grass;   415
No ridges there appeared of clear black mould,
No winter greenness. Of her herbs and flowers
It seemed the better part were gnawed away

Or trampled on the earth. A chain of straw,
Which had been twisted round the tender stem   420
Of a young appletree, lay at its root;
The bark was nibbled round by truant sheep.
Margaret stood near, her infant in her arms,
And, seeing that my eye was on the tree,
She said, "I fear it will be dead and gone   425
Ere Robert come again."

                              Towards the house
Together we returned, and she inquired
If I had any hope. But for her babe,
And for her little friendless boy, she said,
She had no wish to live – that she must die   430
Of sorrow. Yet I saw the idle loom
Still in its place. His sunday garments hung
Upon the self-same nail, his very staff
Stood undisturbed behind the door. And when
I passed this way beaten by autumn winds,   435
She told me that her little babe was dead,
And she was left alone. That very time,
I yet remember, through the miry lane
She walked with me a mile, when the bare trees
Trickled with foggy damps, and in such sort   440
That any heart had ached to hear her, begged
That wheresoe'er I went I still would ask
For him whom she had lost. We parted then,
Our final parting; for from that time forth
Did many seasons pass ere I returned   445
Into this tract again.

                              Five tedious years
She lingered in unquiet widowhood,
A wife and widow. Needs must it have been
A sore heart-wasting. I have heard, my friend,
That in that broken arbour she would sit   450
The idle length of half a sabbath day –
There, where you see the toadstool's lazy head –
And when a dog passed by she still would quit
The shade and look abroad. On this old Bench
For hours she sate, and evermore her eye   455

Was busy in the distance, shaping things
Which made her heart beat quick. Seest thou that path? —
The green-sward now has broken its grey line —
There to and fro she paced through many a day
Of the warm summer, from a belt of flax   460
That girt her waist, spinning the long-drawn thread
With backward steps. Yet ever as there passed
A man whose garments shewed the soldier's red,
Or crippled mendicant in sailor's garb,
The little child who sate to turn the wheel   465
Ceased from his toil, and she, with faltering voice,
Expecting still to learn her husband's fate,
Made many a fond inquiry; and when they
Whose presence gave no comfort, were gone by,
Her heart was still more sad. And by yon gate,   470
Which bars the traveller's road, she often stood,
And when a stranger horseman came, the latch
Would lift, and in his face look wistfully,
Most happy if from aught discovered there
Of tender feeling she might dare repeat   475
The same sad question.
              Meanwhile her poor hut
Sunk to decay; for he was gone, whose hand
At the first nippings of October frost
Closed up each chink, and with fresh bands of straw
Chequered the green-grown thatch. And so she lived   480
Through the long winter, reckless and alone,
Till this reft house, by frost, and thaw, and rain,
Was sapped; and when she slept, the nightly damps
Did chill her breast, and in the stormy day
Her tattered clothes were ruffled by the wind   485
Even at the side of her own fire. Yet still
She loved this wretched spot, nor would for worlds
Have parted hence; and still that length of road,
And this rude bench, one torturing hope endeared,
Fast rooted at her heart. And here, my friend,   490
In sickness she remained; and here she died,
Last human tenant of these ruined walls.'

The old man ceased; he saw that I was moved.
From that low bench rising instinctively,

I turned aside in weakness, nor had power   495
To thank him for the tale which he had told.
I stood, and leaning o'er the garden gate
Reviewed that woman's sufferings; and it seemed
To comfort me while with a brother's love
I blessed her in the impotence of grief.   500
At length towards the cottage I returned
Fondly, and traced with milder interest
That secret spirit of humanity
Which, mid the calm oblivious tendencies
Of Nature, mid her plants, her weeds and flowers,   505
And silent overgrowings, still survived.
The old man seeing this resumed, and said,
'My friend, enough to sorrow have you given,
The purposes of wisdom ask no more:
Be wise and chearful, and no longer read   510
The forms of things with an unworthy eye.
She sleeps in the calm earth, and peace is here.
I well remember that those very plumes,
Those weeds, and the high speargrass on that wall,
By mist and silent raindrops silvered o'er,   515
As once I passed, did to my mind convey
So still an image of tranquility,
So calm and still, and looked so beautiful
Amid the uneasy thoughts which filled my mind,
That what we feel of sorrow and despair   520
From ruin and from change, and all the grief
The passing shews of being leave behind,
Appeared an idle dream that could not live
Where meditation was. I turned away,
And walked along my road in happiness.'   525

He ceased. By this the sun declining shot
A slant and mellow radiance, which began
To fall upon us where beneath the trees
We sate on that low bench. And now we felt,
Admonished thus, the sweet hour coming on: 530
A linnet warbled from those lofty elms,
A thrush sang loud, and other melodies
At distance heard peopled the milder air.
The old man rose and hoisted up his load;

Together casting then a farewell look 535
Upon those silent walls, we left the shade,
And ere the stars were visible attained
A rustic inn, our evening resting-place.

The Pedlar

Him had I seen the day before, alone
And in the middle of the public way
Standing to rest himself. His eyes were turned
Towards the setting sun, while, with that staff
Behind him fixed, he propped a long white pack   5
Which crossed his shoulders, wares for maids who live
In lonely villages or straggling huts.
I knew him – he was born of lowly race
On Cumbrian hills, and I have seen the tear
Stand in his luminous eye when he described   10
The house in which his early youth was passed,
And found I was no stranger to the spot.
I loved to hear him talk of former days
And tell how when a child, ere yet of age
To be a shepherd, he had learned to read   15
His bible in a school that stood alone,
Sole building on a mountain's dreary edge,
Far from the sight of city spire, or sound
Of minster clock. From that bleak tenement
He many an evening to his distant home   20
In solitude returning saw the hills
Grow larger in the darkness, all alone
Beheld the stars come out above his head,
And travelled through the wood, no comrade near,
To whom he might confess the things he saw.   25

So the foundations of his mind were laid.
In such communion, not from terror free,
While yet a child and long before his time,
He had perceived the presence and the power
Of greatness, and deep feelings had impressed   30
Great objects on his mind with portraiture
And colour so distinct that on his mind
They lay like substances, and almost seemed
To haunt the bodily sense. He had received
A precious gift, for as he grew in years   35
With these impressions would he still compare

All his ideal stores, his shapes and forms,
And, being still unsatisfied with aught
Of dimmer character, he thence attained
An *active* power to fasten images   40
Upon his brain, and on their pictured lines
Intensely brooded, even till they acquired
The liveliness of dreams. Nor did he fail,
While yet a child, with a child's eagerness
Incessantly to turn his ear and eye   45
On all things which the rolling seasons brought
To feed such appetite. Nor this alone
Appeased his yearning – in the after day
Of boyhood, many an hour in caves forlorn
And in the hollow depths of naked crags   50
He sate, and even in their fixed lineaments,
Or from the power of a peculiar eye,
Or by creative feeling overborne,
Or by predominance of thought oppressed,
Even in their fixed and steady lineaments   55
He traced an ebbing and a flowing mind,
Expression ever varying.
                         Thus informed,
He had small need of books; for many a tale
Traditionary round the mountains hung,
And many a legend peopling the dark woods   60
Nourished imagination in her growth,
And gave the mind that apprehensive power
By which she is made quick to recognize
The moral properties and scope of things.
But greedily he read and read again   65
Whate'er the rustic vicar's shelf supplied:
The life and death of martyrs who sustained
Intolerable pangs, and here and there
A straggling volume, torn and incomplete,
Which left half-told the preternatural tale,   70
Romance of giants, chronicle of fiends,
Profuse in garniture of wooden cuts
Strange and uncouth, dire faces, figures dire,
Sharp-kneed, sharp-elbowed, and lean-ankled too,
With long and ghostly shanks, forms which once seen   75
Could never be forgotten – things though low,

Though low and humble, not to be despised
By such as have observed the curious links
With which the perishable hours of life
Are bound together, and the world of thought   80
Exists and is sustained. Within his heart
Love was not yet, nor the pure joy of love,
By sound diffused, or by the breathing air,
Or by the silent looks of happy things,
Or flowing from the universal face   85
Of earth and sky. But he had felt the power
Of Nature, and already was prepared
By his intense conceptions to receive
Deeply the lesson deep of love, which he
Whom Nature, by whatever means, has taught   90
To feel intensely, cannot but receive.

Ere his ninth year he had been sent abroad
To tend his father's sheep; such was his task
Henceforward till the later day of youth.
Oh then what soul was his, when on the tops   95
Of the high mountains he beheld the sun
Rise up and bathe the world in light. He looked,
The ocean and the earth beneath him lay
In gladness and deep joy. The clouds were touched,
And in their silent faces he did read   100
Unutterable love. Sound needed none,
Nor any voice of joy: his spirit drank
The spectacle. Sensation, soul, and form,
All melted into him; they swallowed up
His animal being. In them did he live,   105
And by them did he live – they were his life.
In such access of mind, in such high hour
Of visitation from the living God,
He did not feel the God, he felt his works.
Thought was not; in enjoyment it expired.   110
Such hour by prayer or praise was unprofaned;
He neither prayed, nor offered thanks or praise;
His mind was a thanksgiving to the power
That made him. It was blessedness and love.

A shepherd on the lonely mountain-tops,   115
Such intercourse was his, and in this sort
Was his existence oftentimes possessed.
Oh *then* how beautiful, how bright, appeared
The written promise. He had early learned
To reverence the volume which displays   120
The mystery, the life which cannot die,
But in the mountains did he FEEL his faith,
There did he see the writing. All things there
Breathed immortality, revolving life,
And greatness still revolving, infinite.   125
There littleness was not, the least of things
Seemed infinite, and there his spirit shaped
Her prospects – nor did he *believe*; he saw.
What wonder if his being thus became
Sublime and comprehensive? Low desires,   130
Low thoughts, had there no place; yet was his heart
Lowly, for he was meek in gratitude
Oft as he called to mind those exstacies,
And whence they flowed; and from them he acquired
Wisdom which works through patience – thence he learned   135
In many a calmer hour of sober thought
To look on Nature with an humble heart,
Self-questioned where it did not understand,
And with a superstitious eye of love.

Thus passed the time, yet to the neighbouring town   140
He often went with what small overplus
His earnings might supply, and brought away
The book which most had tempted his desires
While at the stall he read. Among the hills
He gazed upon that mighty orb of song,   145
The divine Milton. Lore of different kind,
The annual savings of a toilsome life,
The schoolmaster supplied – books that explain
The purer elements of truth involved
In lines and numbers, and by charm severe,   150
Especially perceived where Nature droops
And feeling is suppressed, preserve the mind
Busy in solitude and poverty.
And thus employed he many a time o'erlooked

The listless hours when in the hollow vale,   155
Hollow and green, he lay on the green turf
In lonesome idleness. What could he do?
Nature was at his heart, and he perceived,
Though yet he knew not how, a wasting power
In all things which from her sweet influence   160
Might tend to wean him. Therefore with her hues,
Her forms, and with the spirit of her forms,
He clothed the nakedness of austere truth.
While yet he lingered in the elements
Of science, and among her simplest laws,   165
His triangles they were the stars of heaven,
The silent stars; his altitudes the crag
Which is the eagle's birth-place, or some peak
Familiar with forgotten years which shews
Inscribed, as with the silence of the thought,   170
Upon its bleak and visionary sides
The history of many a winter storm,
Or obscure records of the path of fire.
Yet with these lonesome sciences he still
Continued to amuse the heavier hours   175
Of solitude. Yet not the less he found
In cold elation, and the lifelessness
Of truth by oversubtlety dislodged
From grandeur and from love, an idle toy,
The dullest of all toys. He saw in truth   180
A holy spirit and a breathing soul;
He reverenced her and trembled at her look,
When with a moral beauty in her face
She led him through the worlds.

But now, before his twentieth year was passed,   185
Accumulated feelings pressed his heart
With an encreasing weight; he was o'erpowered
By Nature, and his spirit was on fire
With restless thoughts. His eye became disturbed,
And many a time he wished the winds might rage   190
When they were silent. Far more fondly now
Than in his earlier season did he love
Tempestuous nights, the uproar and the sounds
That live in darkness. From his intellect,

And from the stillness of abstracted thought, 195
He sought repose in vain. I have heard him say
That at this time he scanned the laws of light
Amid the roar of torrents, where they send
From hollow clefts up to the clearer air
A cloud of mist, which in the shining sun 200
Varies its rainbow hues. But vainly thus,
And vainly by all other means he strove
To mitigate the fever of his heart.

From Nature and her overflowing soul
He had received so much that all his thoughts 205
Were steeped in feeling. He was only then
Contented when with bliss ineffable
He felt the sentiment of being spread
O'er all that moves, and all that seemeth still,
O'er all which, lost beyond the reach of thought 210
And human knowledge, to the human eye
Invisible, yet liveth to the heart;
O'er all that leaps, and runs, and shouts, and sings,
Or beats the gladsome air; o'er all that glides
Beneath the wave, yea, in the wave itself, 215
And mighty depth of waters. Wonder not
If such his transports were; for in all things
He saw one life, and felt that it was joy.
One song they sang, and it was audible –
Most audible then when the fleshly ear, 220
O'ercome by grosser prelude of that strain,
Forgot its functions, and slept undisturbed.

These things he had sustained in solitude
Even till his bodily strength began to yield
Beneath their weight. The mind within him burnt, 225
And he resolved to quit his native hills.
The father strove to make his son perceive
As clearly as the old man did himself
With what advantage he might teach a school
In the adjoining village. But the youth, 230
Who of this service made a short essay,
Found that the wanderings of his thought were then
A misery to him, that he must resign

A task he was unable to perform.
He asked his father's blessing, and assumed   235
This lowly occupation. The old man
Blessed him and prayed for him, yet with a heart
Forboding evil.
                    From his native hills
He wandered far. Much did he see of men,
Their manners, their enjoyments and pursuits,   240
Their passions and their feelings, chiefly those
Essential and eternal in the heart,
Which mid the simpler forms of rural life
Exist more simple in their elements,
And speak a plainer language. Many a year   245
Of lonesome meditation and impelled
By curious thought he was content to toil
In this poor calling, which he now pursued
From habit and necessity. He walked
Among the impure haunts of vulgar men   250
Unstained; the talisman of constant thought
And kind sensations in a gentle heart
Preserved him. Every shew of vice to him
Was a remembrancer of what he knew,
Or a fresh seed of wisdom, or produced   255
That tender interest which the virtuous feel
Among the wicked, which when truly felt
May bring the bad man nearer to the good,
But, innocent of evil, cannot sink
The good man to the bad.   260
                    Among the woods
A lone enthusiast, and among the hills,
Itinerant in this labour he had passed
The better portion of his time, and there
From day to day had his affections breathed
The wholesome air of Nature; there he kept   265
In solitude and solitary thought,
So pleasant were those comprehensive views,
His mind in a just equipoise of love.
Serene it was, unclouded by the cares
Of ordinary life – unvexed, unwarped   270
By partial bondage. In his steady course
No piteous revolutions had he felt,

No wild varieties of joy or grief.
Unoccupied by sorrow of its own,
His heart lay open; and, by Nature tuned   275
And constant disposition of his thoughts
To sympathy with man, he was alive
To all that was enjoyed where'er he went,
And all that was endured; and, in himself
Happy, and quiet in his chearfulness,   280
He had no painful pressure from within
Which made him turn aside from wretchedness
With coward fears. He could afford to suffer
With those whom he saw suffer. Hence it was
That in our best experience he was rich,   285
And in the wisdom of our daily life.
For hence, minutely, in his various rounds
He had observed the progress and decay
Of many minds, of minds and bodies too –
The history of many families,   290
And how they prospered, how they were o'erthrown
By passion or mischance, or such misrule
Among the unthinking masters of the earth
As makes the nations groan. He was a man,
One whom you could not pass without remark –   295
If you had met him on a rainy day
You would have stopped to look at him. Robust,
Active, and nervous, was his gait; his limbs
And his whole figure breathed intelligence.
His body, tall and shapely, shewed in front   300
A faint line of the hollowness of age,
Or rather what appeared the curvature
Of toil; his head looked up steady and fixed.
Age had compressed the rose upon his cheek
Into a narrower circle of deep red,   305
But had not tamed his eye, which, under brows
Of hoary grey, had meanings which it brought
From years of youth, which, like a being made
Of many beings, he had wondrous skill
To blend with meanings of the years to come,   310
Human, or such as lie beyond the grave.
Long had I loved him. Oh, it was most sweet
To hear him teach in unambitious style

Reasoning and thought, by painting as he did
The manners and the passions. Many a time   315
He made a holiday and left his pack
Behind, and we two wandered through the hills
A pair of random travellers. His eye
Flashing poetic fire he would repeat
The songs of Burns, or many a ditty wild   320
Which he had fitted to the moorland harp –
His own sweet verse – and as we trudged along,
Together did we make the hollow grove
Ring with our transports.
                  Though he was untaught,
In the dead lore of schools undisciplined,   325
Why should he grieve? He was a chosen son.
He yet retained an ear which deeply felt
The voice of Nature in the obscure wind,
The sounding mountain, and the running stream.
From deep analogies by thought supplied,   330
Or consciousnesses not to be subdued,
To every natural form, rock, fruit, and flower,
Even the loose stones that cover the highway,
He gave a moral life; he saw them feel,
Or linked them to some feeling. In all shapes   335
He found a secret and mysterious soul,
A fragrance and a spirit of strange meaning.
Though poor in outward shew, he was most rich:
He had a world about him – 'twas his own,
He made it – for it only lived to him,   340
And to the God who looked into his mind.
Such sympathies would often bear him far
In outward gesture, and in visible look,
Beyond the common seeming of mankind.
Some called it madness; such it might have been,   345
But that he had an eye which evermore
Looked deep into the shades of difference
As they lie hid in all exterior forms,
Near or remote, minute or vast – an eye
Which from a stone, a tree, a withered leaf,   350
To the broad ocean and the azure heavens
Spangled with kindred multitudes of stars,
Could find no surface where its power might sleep –

Which spake perpetual logic to his soul,
And by an unrelenting agency   355
Did bind his feelings even as in a chain.

'Not useless do I deem'

Not useless do I deem
These quiet sympathies with things that hold
An inarticulate language, for the man
Once taught to love such objects as excite
No morbid passions, no disquietude,   5
No vengeance and no hatred, needs must feel
The joy of that pure principle of love
So deeply that, unsatisfied with aught
Less pure and exquisite, he cannot chuse
But seek for objects of a kindred love   10
In fellow-natures, and a kindred joy.
Accordingly he by degrees perceives
His feelings of aversion softened down,
A holy tenderness pervade his frame,
His sanity of reason not impaired,   15
Say rather all his thoughts now flowing clear
– From a clear fountain flowing – he looks round,
He seeks for good and finds the good he seeks;
Till execration and contempt are things
He only knows by name, and if he hears   20
From other mouth the language which they speak
He is compassionate, and has no thought,
No feeling, which can overcome his love.
      And further by contemplating these forms
In the relations which they bear to man   25
We shall discover what a power is theirs
To stimulate our minds, and multiply
The spiritual presences of absent things.
Then weariness will cease – We shall acquire
The [   ] habit by which sense is made   30
Subservient still to moral purposes,
A vital essence and a saving power;
Nor shall we meet an object but may read
Some sweet and tender lesson to our minds
Of human suffering or of human joy.   35

All things shall speak of man, and we shall read
Our duties in all forms; and general laws
And local accidents shall tend alike
To quicken and to rouze, and give the will
And power which by a [   ] chain of good   40
Shall link us to our kind. No naked hearts,
No naked minds, shall then be left to mourn
The burthen of existence. Science then
Shall be a precious visitant; and then,
And only then, be worthy of her name.   45
For then her heart shall kindle her dull eye
– Dull and inanimate – no more shall hang
Chained to its object in brute slavery;
But better taught and mindful of its use
Legitimate, and its peculiar power   50
While with a patient interest it shall watch
The processes of things, and serve the cause
Of order and distinctness; not for this
Shall it forget that its most noble end,
Its most illustrious province, must be found   55
In ministering to the excursive power
Of Intellect and thought. So build we up
The being that we are. For was it meant
That we should pore, and dwindle as we pore
Forever dimly pore on things minute,   60
On solitary objects, still beheld
In disconnection, dead and spiritless;
And still dividing, and dividing still,
Break down all grandeur, still unsatisfied
With our unnatural toil while littleness   65
May yet become more little, waging thus
An impious warfare with the very life
Of our souls? Or was it ever meant
That this majestic imagery, the clouds,
The ocean, and the firmament of heaven   70
Should be a barren picture on the mind?
Never for ends of vanity and pain
And sickly wretchedness were we endued
Amid this world of feeling and of life
With apprehension, reason, will and thought,   75
Affections, organs, passions. Let us rise

From this oblivious sleep, these fretful dreams
Of feverish nothingness. Thus disciplined
All things shall live in us, and we shall live
In all things that surround us. This I deem   80
Our tendency, and thus shall every day
Enlarge our sphere of pleasure and of pain.
For thus the senses and the intellect
Shall each to each supply a mutual aid,
Invigorate and sharpen and refine   85
Each other with a power that knows no bound,
And forms and feelings acting thus, and thus
Reacting, they shall each acquire
A living spirit and a character
Till then unfelt, and each be multiplied,   90
With a variety that knows no end.
Thus deeply drinking in the soul of things
We shall be wise perforce, and we shall move
From strict necessity along the path
Of order and of good. Whate'er we see,   95
Whate'er we feel, by agency direct
Or indirect, shall tend to feed and nurse
Our faculties and raise to loftier height
Our intellectual soul. The old man ceased.
The words he uttered shall not pass away;   100
They had sunk into me, but not as sounds
To be expressed by visible characters,
For while he spake my spirit had obeyed
The presence of his eye, my ear had drunk
The meanings of his voice. He had discoursed   105
Like one who in the slow and silent works,
The manifold conclusions of his thought,
Had brooded till Imagination's power
Condensed them to a passion whence she drew
Herself new energies, resistless force.   110

From

LYRICAL BALLADS
1798/1800

Lines

LEFT UPON A SEAT IN A YEW-TREE WHICH STANDS NEAR
THE LAKE OF ESTHWAITE, ON A DESOLATE PART OF THE
SHORE, YET COMMANDING A BEAUTIFUL PROSPECT

    — Nay, traveller! rest. This lonely yew-tree stands
Far from all human dwelling; what if here
No sparkling rivulet spread the verdant herb?
What if these barren boughs the bee not loves?
Yet, if the wind breathe soft, the curling waves   5
That break against the shore shall lull thy mind
By one soft impulse saved from vacancy.

          Who he was
That piled these stones, and with the mossy sod
First covered o'er, and taught this aged tree,   10
Now wild, to bend its arms in circling shade,
I well remember. He was one who owned
No common soul. In youth, by genius nursed,
And big with lofty views, he to the world
Went forth, pure in his heart, against the taint   15
Of dissolute tongues, 'gainst jealousy, and hate,
And scorn, against all enemies prepared,
All but neglect; and so, his spirit damped
At once, with rash disdain he turned away,
And with the food of pride sustained his soul   20
In solitude. — Stranger! these gloomy boughs
Had charms for him, and here he loved to sit,
His only visitants a straggling sheep,
The stone-chat, or the glancing sand-piper;
And on these barren rocks, with juniper,   25
And heath, and thistle, thinly sprinkled o'er,
Fixing his downward eye, he many an hour
A morbid pleasure nourished, tracing here
An emblem of his own unfruitful life,
And lifting up his head, he then would gaze   30
On the more distant scene: how lovely 'tis
Thou seest, and he would gaze till it became

Far lovelier, and his heart could not sustain
The beauty still more beauteous. Nor, that time,
Would he forget those beings, to whose minds,   35
Warm from the labours of benevolence,
The world, and man himself, appeared a scene
Of kindred loveliness; then he would sigh
With mournful joy, to think that others felt
What he must never feel; and so, lost man!   40
On visionary views would fancy feed,
Till his eye streamed with tears. In this deep vale
He died, this seat his only monument.

If thou be one whose heart the holy forms
Of young imagination have kept pure,   45
Stranger! henceforth be warned; and know that pride,
Howe'er disguised in its own majesty,
Is littleness; that he, who feels contempt
For any living thing, hath faculties
Which he has never used; that thought with him   50
Is in its infancy. The man whose eye
Is ever on himself doth look on one,
The least of nature's works, one who might move
The wise man to that scorn which wisdom holds
Unlawful, ever. O, be wiser thou!   55
Instructed that true knowledge leads to love,
True dignity abides with him alone
Who, in the silent hour of inward thought,
Can still suspect, and still revere himself,
In lowliness of heart.   60

Goody Blake and Harry Gill

A TRUE STORY

Oh! what's the matter? what's the matter?
What is't that ails young Harry Gill?
That evermore his teeth they chatter,
Chatter, chatter, chatter still.
Of waistcoats Harry has no lack,   5
Good duffle grey, and flannel fine;

He has a blanket on his back,
And coats enough to smother nine.

In March, December, and in July,
'Tis all the same with Harry Gill;   10
The neighbours tell, and tell you truly,
His teeth they chatter, chatter still.
At night, at morning, and at noon,
'Tis all the same with Harry Gill;
Beneath the sun, beneath the moon,   15
His teeth they chatter, chatter still.

Young Harry was a lusty drover,
And who so stout of limb as he?
His cheeks were red as ruddy clover,
His voice was like the voice of three.   20
Auld Goody Blake was old and poor,
Ill fed she was, and thinly clad;
And any man who passed her door
Might see how poor a hut she had.

All day she spun in her poor dwelling,   25
And then her three hours' work at night!
Alas! 'twas hardly worth the telling,
It would not pay for candle-light.
– This woman dwelt in Dorsetshire,
Her hut was on a cold hill-side,   30
And in that country coals are dear,
For they come far by wind and tide.

By the same fire to boil their pottage,
Two poor old dames, as I have known,
Will often live in one small cottage,   35
But she, poor woman, dwelt alone.
'Twas well enough when summer came,
The long, warm, lightsome summer-day,
Then at her door the *canty* dame
Would sit, as any linnet gay.   40

But when the ice our streams did fetter,
Oh! then how her old bones would shake!
You would have said, if you had met her,
'Twas a hard time for Goody Blake.
Her evenings then were dull and dead: 45
Sad case it was, as you may think,
For very cold to go to bed,
And then for cold not sleep a wink.

Oh joy for her! when e'er in winter
The winds at night had made a rout,   50
And scattered many a lusty splinter,
And many a rotten bough about.
Yet never had she, well or sick,
As every man who knew her says,
A pile before-hand, wood or stick,   55
Enough to warm her for three days.

Now, when the frost was past enduring,
And made her poor old bones to ache,
Could any thing be more alluring,
Than an old hedge to Goody Blake?   60
And now and then, it must be said,
When her old bones were cold and chill,
She left her fire, or left her bed,
To seek the hedge of Harry Gill.

Now Harry he had long suspected   65
This trespass of old Goody Blake,
And vowed that she should be detected,
And he on her would vengeance take.
And oft from his warm fire he'd go,
And to the fields his road would take,   70
And there, at night, in frost and snow,
He watched to seize old Goody Blake.

And once, behind a rick of barley,
Thus looking out did Harry stand;
The moon was full and shining clearly,   75
And crisp with frost the stubble-land.

— He hears a noise — he's all awake —
Again? — on tip-toe down the hill
He softly creeps — 'Tis Goody Blake,
She's at the hedge of Harry Gill.   80

Right glad was he when he beheld her:
Stick after stick did Goody pull,
He stood behind a bush of elder,
Till she had filled her apron full.
When with her load she turned about,   85
The bye-road back again to take,
He started forward with a shout,
And sprang upon poor Goody Blake.

And fiercely by the arm he took her,
And by the arm he held her fast,   90
And fiercely by the arm he shook her,
And cried, 'I've caught you then at last!'
Then Goody, who had nothing said,
Her bundle from her lap let fall,
And kneeling on the sticks, she prayed   95
To God that is the judge of all.

She prayed, her withered hand uprearing,
While Harry held her by the arm —
'God! who art never out of hearing,
O may he never more be warm!'   100
The cold, cold moon above her head,
Thus on her knees did Goody pray;
Young Harry heard what she had said,
And icy-cold he turned away.

He went complaining all the morrow   105
That he was cold and very chill:
His face was gloom, his heart was sorrow,
Alas that day for Harry Gill!
That day he wore a riding-coat,
But not a whit the warmer he: 110
Another was on Thursday brought,
And ere the Sabbath he had three.

'Twas all in vain, a useless matter,
And blankets were about him pinned;
Yet still his jaws and teeth they clatter,   115
Like a loose casement in the wind.
And Harry's flesh it fell away,
And all who see him say 'tis plain,
That live as long as live he may,
He never will be warm again.   120

No word to any man he utters,
A-bed or up, to young or old;
But ever to himself he mutters,
'Poor Harry Gill is very cold'.
A-bed or up, by night or day,   125
His teeth they chatter, chatter still.
Now think, ye farmers all, I pray,
Of Goody Blake and Harry Gill.

Lines

WRITTEN AT A SMALL DISTANCE FROM MY HOUSE,
AND SENT BY MY LITTLE BOY TO THE
PERSON TO WHOM THEY ARE
ADDRESSED

It is the first mild day of March:
Each minute sweeter than before;
The red-breast sings from the tall larch
That stands beside our door.

There is a blessing in the air,   5
Which seems a sense of joy to yield
To the bare trees, and mountains bare,
And grass in the green field.

My Sister! ('tis a wish of mine)
Now that our morning meal is done,   10
Make haste, your morning task resign;
Come forth and feel the sun.

Edward will come with you, and pray,
Put on with speed your woodland dress,
And bring no book, for this one day   15
We'll give to idleness.

No joyless forms shall regulate
Our living calendar:
We from to-day, my friend, will date
The opening of the year.   20

Love, now an universal birth,
From heart to heart is stealing –
From earth to man, from man to earth –
It is the hour of feeling.

One moment now may give us more   25
Than fifty years of reason;
Our minds shall drink at every pore
The spirit of the season.

Some silent laws our hearts may make,
Which they shall long obey;   30
We for the year to come may take
Our temper from to-day.

And from the blessed power that rolls
About, below, above,
We'll frame the measure of our souls –   35
They shall be tuned to love.

Then come, my sister! come, I pray,
With speed put on your woodland dress,
And bring no book, for this one day
We'll give to idleness.   40

Simon Lee

In the sweet shire of Cardigan,
Not far from pleasant Ivor-hall,
An old man dwells, a little man,
I've heard he once was tall.
Of years he has upon his back,   5
No doubt, a burthen weighty;
He says he is three score and ten,
But others say he's eighty.

A long blue livery-coat has he,
That's fair behind, and fair before;   10
Yet, meet him where you will, you see
At once that he is poor.
Full five and twenty years he lived
A running huntsman merry;
And, though he has but one eye left,   15
His cheek is like a cherry.

No man like him the horn could sound,
And no man was so full of glee;
To say the least, four counties round
Had heard of Simon Lee.   20
His master's dead, and no one now
Dwells in the hall of Ivor;
Men, dogs, and horses, all are dead;
He is the sole survivor.

His hunting feats have him bereft   25
Of his right eye, as you may see,
And then, what limbs those feats have left
To poor old Simon Lee!
He has no son, he has no child,
His wife, an aged woman,   30
Lives with him near the waterfall,
Upon the village common.

And he is lean and he is sick,
His little body's half awry;
His ankles they are swol'n and thick,   35
His legs are thin and dry.
When he was young he little knew
Of husbandry or tillage,
And now he's forced to work, though weak —
The weakest in the village.   40

He all the country could outrun,
Could leave both man and horse behind;
And often, ere the race was done,
He reeled and was stone-blind.
And still there's something in the world   45
At which his heart rejoices,
For when the chiming hounds are out,
He dearly loves their voices!

Old Ruth works out of doors with him,
And does what Simon cannot do;   50
For she, not over-stout of limb,
Is stouter of the two.
And though you with your utmost skill
From labour could not wean them,
Alas! 'tis very little, all   55
Which they can do between them.

Beside their moss-grown hut of clay,
Not twenty paces from the door,
A scrap of land they have, but they
Are poorest of the poor.   60
This scrap of land he from the heath
Enclosed when he was stronger,
But what avails the land to them,
Which they can till no longer?

Few months of life has he in store,   65
As he to you will tell,
For still, the more he works, the more
His poor old ankles swell.

My gentle reader, I perceive
How patiently you've waited,   70
And I'm afraid that you expect
Some tale will be related.

O reader! had you in your mind
Such stores as silent thought can bring,
O gentle reader! you would find   75
A tale in every thing.
What more I have to say is short,
I hope you'll kindly take it;
It is no tale; but should you think,
Perhaps a tale you'll make it.   80

One summer-day I chanced to see
This old man doing all he could
About the root of an old tree –
A stump of rotten wood.
The mattock tottered in his hand;   85
So vain was his endeavour
That at the root of the old tree
He might have worked for ever.

'You're overtasked, good Simon Lee,
Give me your tool' to him I said;   90
And at the word right gladly he
Received my proffered aid.
I struck, and with a single blow
The tangled root I severed,
At which the poor old man so long   95
And vainly had endeavoured.

The tears into his eyes were brought,
And thanks and praises seemed to run
So fast out of his heart, I thought
They never would have done.   100
– I've heard of hearts unkind, kind deeds
With coldness still returning;
Alas! the gratitude of men
Has oftener left me mourning.

Anecdote for Fathers

SHOWING HOW THE ART OF LYING MAY BE TAUGHT

I have a boy of five years old –
His face is fair and fresh to see;
His limbs are cast in beauty's mould,
And dearly he loves me.

One morn we strolled on our dry walk,   5
Our quiet house all full in view,
And held such intermitted talk
As we are wont to do.

My thoughts on former pleasures ran;
I thought of Kilve's delightful shore,   10
My pleasant home, when spring began,
A long, long year before.

A day it was when I could bear
To think, and think, and think again;
With so much happiness to spare,   15
I could not feel a pain.

My boy was by my side, so slim
And graceful in his rustic dress!
And oftentimes I talked to him
In very idleness.   20

The young lambs ran a pretty race;
The morning sun shone bright and warm;
'Kilve,' said I, 'was a pleasant place,
And so is Liswyn farm.

My little boy, which like you more,'   25
I said and took him by the arm,
'Our home by Kilve's delightful shore,
Or here at Liswyn farm?

And tell me, had you rather be,'
I said and held him by the arm,   30
'At Kilve's smooth shore by the green sea,
Or here at Liswyn farm?'

In careless mood he looked at me,
While still I held him by the arm,
And said, 'At Kilve I'd rather be   35
Than here at Liswyn farm.'

'Now, little Edward, say why so;
My little Edward, tell me why';
'I cannot tell, I do not know.'
'Why this is strange,' said I.   40

'For here are woods and green-hills warm;
There surely must some reason be
Why you would change sweet Liswyn farm
For Kilve by the green sea.'

At this, my boy, so fair and slim,   45
Hung down his head, nor made reply;
And five times did I say to him,
'Why? Edward, tell me, why?'

His head he raised – there was in sight,
It caught his eye, he saw it plain –   50
Upon the house-top, glittering bright,
A broad and gilded vane.

Then did the boy his tongue unlock,
And thus to me he made reply:
'At Kilve there was no weather-cock,   55
And that's the reason why.'

Oh dearest, dearest boy! my heart
For better lore would seldom yearn,
Could I but teach the hundredth part
Of what from thee I learn.   60

We are seven

A simple child, dear brother Jim,
That lightly draws its breath,
And feels its life in every limb,
What should it know of death?

I met a little cottage girl,   5
She was eight years old, she said;
Her hair was thick with many a curl
That clustered round her head.

She had a rustic, woodland air,
And she was wildly clad;   10
Her eyes were fair, and very fair –
Her beauty made me glad.

'Sisters and brothers, little maid,
How many may you be?'
'How many? seven in all,' she said,   15
And wondering looked at me.

'And where are they? I pray you, tell.'
She answered, 'Seven are we,
And two of us at Conway dwell,
And two are gone to sea.   20

Two of us in the church-yard lie,
My sister and my brother,
And in the church-yard cottage, I
Dwell near them with my mother.'

'You say that two at Conway dwell,   25
And two are gone to sea,
Yet you are seven; I pray you tell,
Sweet maid, how this may be.'

Then did the little maid reply,
'Seven boys and girls are we;   30
Two of us in the church-yard lie,
Beneath the church-yard tree.'

'You run about, my little maid,
Your limbs they are alive;
If two are in the church-yard laid,   35
Then ye are only five.'

'Their graves are green, they may be seen,'
The little maid replied;
'Twelve steps or more from my mother's door,
And they are side by side.   40

My stockings there I often knit,
My 'kerchief there I hem;
And there upon the ground I sit —
I sit and sing to them.

And often after sunset, sir,   45
When it is light and fair,
I take my little porringer,
And eat my supper there.

The first that died was little Jane;
In bed she moaning lay,   50
Till God released her of her pain,
And then she went away.

So in the church-yard she was laid,
And all the summer dry,
Together round her grave we played,   55
My brother John and I.

And when the ground was white with snow,
And I could run and slide,
My brother John was forced to go,
And he lies by her side.'   60

'How many are you then,' said I,
'If they two are in heaven?'
The little maiden did reply,
'O master! we are seven.'

'But they are dead; those two are dead! 65
Their spirits are in heaven!'
'Twas throwing words away, for still
The little maid would have her will,
And said, 'Nay, we are seven!'

Lines

WRITTEN IN EARLY SPRING

I heard a thousand blended notes,
While in a grove I sat reclined,
In that sweet mood when pleasant thoughts
Bring sad thoughts to the mind.

To her fair works did nature link 5
The human soul that through me ran;
And much it grieved my heart to think
What man has made of man.

Through primrose-tufts, in that sweet bower,
The periwinkle trailed its wreathes; 10
And 'tis my faith that every flower
Enjoys the air it breathes.

The birds around me hopped and played:
Their thoughts I cannot measure,
But the least motion which they made, 15
It seemed a thrill of pleasure.

The budding twigs spread out their fan
To catch the breezy air;
And I must think, do all I can,
That there was pleasure there. 20

If I these thoughts may not prevent,
If such be of my creed the plan,
Have I not reason to lament
What man has made of man?

The Thorn

1

There is a thorn; it looks so old,
In truth you'd find it hard to say
How it could ever have been young,
It looks so old and grey.
Not higher than a two-years' child,   5
It stands erect, this aged thorn;
No leaves it has, no thorny points;
It is a mass of knotted joints –
A wretched thing forlorn.
It stands erect, and like a stone   10
With lichens it is overgrown.

2

Like rock or stone, it is o'ergrown
With lichens to the very top,
And hung with heavy tufts of moss,
A melancholy crop;   15
Up from the earth these mosses creep,
And this poor thorn they clasp it round
So close, you'd say that they were bent
With plain and manifest intent
To drag it to the ground;   20
And all had joined in one endeavour
To bury this poor thorn for ever.

3

High on a mountain's highest ridge,
Where oft the stormy winter gale
Cuts like a scythe, while through the clouds   25
It sweeps from vale to vale,
Not five yards from the mountain-path
This thorn you on your left espy;

And to the left, three yards beyond,
You see a little muddy pond   30
Of water, never dry;
I've measured it from side to side:
'Tis three feet long, and two feet wide.

4

And close beside this aged thorn,
There is a fresh and lovely sight —   35
A beauteous heap, a hill of moss,
Just half a foot in height.
All lovely colours there you see,
All colours that were ever seen,
And mossy network too is there,   40
As if by hand of lady fair
The work had woven been,
And cups, the darlings of the eye,
So deep is their vermilion dye.

5

Ah me! what lovely tints are there!   45
Of olive-green and scarlet bright,
In spikes, in branches, and in stars,
Green, red, and pearly white.
This heap of earth o'ergrown with moss
Which close beside the thorn you see,   50
So fresh in all its beauteous dyes,
Is like an infant's grave in size,
As like as like can be:
But never, never any where
An infant's grave was half so fair.   55

6

Now would you see this aged thorn,
This pond and beauteous hill of moss,
You must take care and choose your time
The mountain when to cross.

For oft there sits, between the heap   60
That's like an infant's grave in size,
And that same pond of which I spoke,
A woman in a scarlet cloak,
And to herself she cries,
'Oh misery! oh misery!   65
Oh woe is me! oh misery!'

7

At all times of the day and night
This wretched woman thither goes,
And she is known to every star,
And every wind that blows;   70
And there beside the thorn she sits
When the blue day-light's in the skies,
And when the whirlwind's on the hill,
Or frosty air is keen and still,
And to herself she cries,   75
'Oh misery! oh misery!
Oh woe is me! oh misery!'

8

'Now wherefore thus, by day and night,
In rain, in tempest, and in snow,
Thus to the dreary mountain-top   80
Does this poor woman go?
And why sits she beside the thorn
When the blue day-light's in the sky,
Or when the whirlwind's on the hill,
Or frosty air is keen and still,   85
And wherefore does she cry? –
Oh wherefore? wherefore? tell me why
Does she repeat that doleful cry?'

9

I cannot tell; I wish I could,
For the true reason no one knows;   90
But if you'd gladly view the spot,
The spot to which she goes:

The heap that's like an infant's grave,
The pond and thorn, so old and grey;
Pass by her door — 'tis seldom shut — 95
And if you see her in her hut,
Then to the spot away! —
I never heard of such as dare
Approach the spot when she is there.

10

'But wherefore to the mountain-top 100
Can this unhappy woman go,
Whatever star is in the skies,
Whatever wind may blow?'
Nay rack your brain — 'tis all in vain,
I'll tell you every thing I know; 105
But to the thorn, and to the pond
Which is a little step beyond,
I wish that you would go:
Perhaps when you are at the place
You something of her tale may trace. 110

11

I'll give you the best help I can:
Before you up the mountain go,
Up to the dreary mountain-top,
I'll tell you all I know.
'Tis now some two and twenty years, 115
Since she (her name is Martha Ray)
Gave with a maiden's true good will
Her company to Stephen Hill;
And she was blithe and gay,
And she was happy, happy still 120
Whene'er she thought of Stephen Hill.

12

And they had fixed the wedding-day,
The morning that must wed them both;

But Stephen to another maid
Had sworn another oath,   125
And with this other maid to church
Unthinking Stephen went –
Poor Martha! on that woeful day
A cruel, cruel fire, they say,
Into her bones was sent: 130
It dried her body like a cinder,
And almost turned her brain to tinder.

13

They say, full six months after this,
While yet the summer-leaves were green,
She to the mountain-top would go,   135
And there was often seen.
'Tis said, a child was in her womb,
As now to any eye was plain;
She was with child, and she was mad,
Yet often she was sober sad   140
From her exceeding pain.
Oh me! ten thousand times I'd rather
That he had died, that cruel father!

14

Sad case for such a brain to hold
Communion with a stirring child!   145
Sad case, as you may think, for one
Who had a brain so wild!
Last Christmas when we talked of this,
Old Farmer Simpson did maintain,
That in her womb the infant wrought   150
About its mother's heart, and brought
Her senses back again;
And when at last her time drew near,
Her looks were calm, her senses clear.

15

No more I know, I wish I did,   155
And I would tell it all to you,
For what became of this poor child
There's none that ever knew;
And if a child was born or no,
There's no one that could ever tell,   160
And if 'twas born alive or dead,
There's no one knows, as I have said,
But some remember well,
That Martha Ray about this time
Would up the mountain often climb.   165

16

And all that winter, when at night
The wind blew from the mountain-peak,
'Twas worth your while, though in the dark,
The church-yard path to seek:
For many a time and oft were heard   170
Cries coming from the mountain-head,
Some plainly living voices were,
And others, I've heard many swear,
Were voices of the dead;
I cannot think, whate'er they say,   175
They had to do with Martha Ray.

17

But that she goes to this old thorn,
The thorn which I've described to you,
And there sits in a scarlet cloak,
I will be sworn is true.   180
For one day with my telescope,
To view the ocean wide and bright,
When to this country first I came,
Ere I had heard of Martha's name,
I climbed the mountain's height;   185
A storm came on, and I could see
No object higher than my knee.

18

'Twas mist and rain, and storm and rain,
No screen, no fence could I discover,
And then the wind! in faith, it was   190
A wind full ten times over.
I looked around, I thought I saw
A jutting crag, and off I ran,
Head-foremost, through the driving rain,
The shelter of the crag to gain,   195
And, as I am a man,
Instead of jutting crag, I found
A woman seated on the ground.

19

I did not speak – I saw her face,
Her face it was enough for me;   200
I turned about and heard her cry,
'O misery! O misery!'
And there she sits, until the moon
Through half the clear blue sky will go,
And when the little breezes make   205
The waters of the pond to shake,
As all the country know,
She shudders and you hear her cry,
'Oh misery! oh misery!'

20

'But what's the thorn? and what's the pond?   210
And what's the hill of moss to her?
And what's the creeping breeze that comes
The little pond to stir?'
I cannot tell; but some will say
She hanged her baby on the tree,   215
Some say she drowned it in the pond,
Which is a little step beyond,
But all and each agree,
The little babe was buried there,
Beneath that hill of moss so fair.   220

21

I've heard the scarlet moss is red
With drops of that poor infant's blood;
But kill a new-born infant thus!
I do not think she could.
Some say, if to the pond you go,   225
And fix on it a steady view,
The shadow of a babe you trace –
A baby and a baby's face –
And that it looks at you;
Whene'er you look on it, 'tis plain   230
The baby looks at you again.

22

And some had sworn an oath that she
Should be to public justice brought,
And for the little infant's bones
With spades they would have sought.   235
But then the beauteous hill of moss
Before their eyes began to stir,
And for full fifty yards around,
The grass it shook upon the ground;
But all do still aver   240
The little babe is buried there,
Beneath that hill of moss so fair.

23

I cannot tell how this may be,
But plain it is, the thorn is bound
With heavy tufts of moss that strive   245
To drag it to the ground.
And this I know, full many a time,
When she was on the mountain high,
By day, and in the silent night,
When all the stars shone clear and bright,   250
That I have heard her cry,
'Oh misery! oh misery!
O woe is me! oh misery!'

The Idiot Boy

'Tis eight o'clock – a clear March night;
The moon is up – the sky is blue;
The owlet in the moonlight air,
He shouts from nobody knows where;
He lengthens out his lonely shout,   5
Halloo! halloo! a long halloo!

– Why bustle thus about your door,
What means this bustle, Betty Foy?
Why are you in this mighty fret?
And why on horseback have you set   10
Him whom you love, your idiot boy?

Beneath the moon that shines so bright,
Till she is tired, let Betty Foy
With girt and stirrup fiddle-faddle;
But wherefore set upon a saddle   15
Him whom she loves, her idiot boy?

There's scarce a soul that's out of bed;
Good Betty! put him down again;
His lips with joy they burr at you,
But, Betty! what has he to do   20
With stirrup, saddle, or with rein?

The world will say 'tis very idle –
Bethink you of the time of night;
There's not a mother, no not one,
But when she hears what you have done,   25
Oh! Betty, she'll be in a fright.

But Betty's bent on her intent,
For her good neighbour, Susan Gale,
Old Susan, she who dwells alone,
Is sick, and makes a piteous moan,   30
As if her very life would fail.

There's not a house within a mile,
No hand to help them in distress:
Old Susan lies a-bed in pain,
And sorely puzzled are the twain,   35
For what she ails they cannot guess.

And Betty's husband's at the wood,
Where by the week he doth abide,
A woodman in the distant vale;
There's none to help poor Susan Gale,   40
What must be done? what will betide?

And Betty from the lane has fetched
Her pony, that is mild and good,
Whether he be in joy or pain,
Feeding at will along the lane,   45
Or bringing faggots from the wood.

And he is all in travelling trim,
And by the moonlight, Betty Foy
Has up upon the saddle set –
The like was never heard of yet –   50
Him whom she loves, her idiot boy.

And he must post without delay
Across the bridge that's in the dale,
And by the church, and o'er the down,
To bring a doctor from the town,   55
Or she will die, old Susan Gale.

There is no need of boot or spur,
There is no need of whip or wand,
For Johnny has his holly-bough,
And with a hurly-burly now   60
He shakes the green bough in his hand.

And Betty o'er and o'er has told
The boy who is her best delight,
Both what to follow, what to shun,
What do, and what to leave undone,   65
How turn to left, and how to right.

And Betty's most especial charge,
Was, 'Johnny! Johnny! mind that you
Come home again, nor stop at all,
Come home again, whate'er befall,   70
My Johnny do, I pray you do.'

To this did Johnny answer make,
Both with his head and with his hand,
And proudly shook the bridle too,
And then! his words were not a few,   75
Which Betty well could understand.

And now that Johnny is just going,
Though Betty's in a mighty flurry,
She gently pats the pony's side
On which her idiot boy must ride,   80
And seems no longer in a hurry.

But when the pony moved his legs,
Oh! then for the poor idiot boy!
For joy he cannot hold the bridle,
For joy his head and heels are idle –   85
He's idle all for very joy.

And while the pony moves his legs,
In Johnny's left-hand you may see
The green bough's motionless and dead;
The moon that shines above his head   90
Is not more still and mute than he.

His heart it was so full of glee
That till full fifty yards were gone
He quite forgot his holly whip
And all his skill in horsemanship,   95
Oh! happy, happy, happy John.

And Betty's standing at the door,
And Betty's face with joy o'erflows,
Proud of herself, and proud of him,
She sees him in his travelling trim;   100
How quietly her Johnny goes!

The silence of her idiot boy,
What hopes it sends to Betty's heart!
He's at the guide-post — he turns right,
She watches till he's out of sight,   105
And Betty will not then depart.

Burr, burr — now Johnny's lips they burr,
As loud as any mill, or near it,
Meek as a lamb the pony moves,
And Johnny makes the noise he loves,   110
And Betty listens, glad to hear it.

Away she hies to Susan Gale;
And Johnny's in a merry tune,
The owlets hoot, the owlets curr,
And Johnny's lips they burr, burr, burr,   115
And on he goes beneath the moon.

His steed and he right well agree,
For of this pony there's a rumour,
That should he lose his eyes and ears,
And should he live a thousand years,   120
He never will be out of humour.

But then he is a horse that thinks!
And when he thinks, his pace is slack;
Now, though he knows poor Johnny well,
Yet for his life he cannot tell   125
What he has got upon his back.

So through the moonlight lanes they go,
And far into the moonlight dale,
And by the church, and o'er the down,
To bring a doctor from the town   130
To comfort poor old Susan Gale.

And Betty, now at Susan's side,
Is in the middle of her story —
What comfort Johnny soon will bring,
With many a most diverting thing   135
Of Johnny's wit and Johnny's glory.

And Betty's still at Susan's side:
By this time she's not quite so flurried;
Demure with porringer and plate
She sits, as if in Susan's fate   140
Her life and soul were buried.

But Betty, poor good woman! she,
You plainly in her face may read it,
Could lend out of that moment's store
Five years of happiness or more,   145
To any that might need it.

But yet I guess that now and then
With Betty all was not so well,
And to the road she turns her ears,
And thence full many a sound she hears,   150
Which she to Susan will not tell.

Poor Susan moans, poor Susan groans;
'As sure as there's a moon in heaven,'
Cries Betty, 'he'll be back again;
They'll both be here, 'tis almost ten,   155
They'll both be here before eleven.'

Poor Susan moans, poor Susan groans,
The clock gives warning for eleven;
'Tis on the stroke – 'If Johnny's near,'
Quoth Betty, 'he will soon be here,   160
As sure as there's a moon in heaven.'

The clock is on the stroke of twelve,
And Johnny is not yet in sight;
The moon's in heaven, as Betty sees,
But Betty is not quite at ease,   165
And Susan has a dreadful night.

And Betty, half an hour ago,
On Johnny vile reflections cast:
'A little idle sauntering thing!'
With other names, an endless string,   170
But now that time is gone and past.

And Betty's drooping at the heart,
That happy time all past and gone,
'How can it be he is so late?
The doctor he has made him wait –   175
Susan! they'll both be here anon.'

And Susan's growing worse and worse,
And Betty's in a sad quandary;
And then there's nobody to say
If she must go or she must stay: 180
She's in a sad quandary.

The clock is on the stroke of one,
But neither doctor nor his guide
Appear along the moonlight road;
There's neither horse nor man abroad,   185
And Betty's still at Susan's side.

And Susan she begins to fear
Of sad mischances not a few,
That Johnny may perhaps be drowned,
Or lost perhaps, and never found,   190
Which they must both for ever rue.

She prefaced half a hint of this
With, 'God forbid it should be true!'
At the first word that Susan said,
Cried Betty, rising from the bed,   195
'Susan, I'd gladly stay with you.

I must be gone, I must away,
Consider, Johnny's but half-wise;
Susan, we must take care of him,
If he is hurt in life or limb.'   200
'Oh God forbid!' poor Susan cries.

'What can I do?' says Betty, going,
'What can I do to ease your pain?
Good Susan tell me, and I'll stay;
I fear you're in a dreadful way,   205
But I shall soon be back again.'

'Good Betty go, good Betty go,
There's nothing that can ease my pain.'
Then off she hies, but with a prayer
That God poor Susan's life would spare,   210
Till she comes back again.

So through the moonlight lane she goes,
And far into the moonlight dale;
And how she ran, and how she walked,
And all that to herself she talked   215
Would surely be a tedious tale.

In high and low, above, below,
In great and small, in round and square,
In tree and tower was Johnny seen,
In bush and brake, in black and green,   220
'Twas Johnny, Johnny, every where.

She's past the bridge that's in the dale,
And now the thought torments her sore –
Johnny perhaps his horse forsook,
To hunt the moon that's in the brook,   225
And never will be heard of more.

And now she's high upon the down,
Alone amid a prospect wide;
There's neither Johnny nor his horse
Among the fern or in the gorse;   230
There's neither doctor nor his guide.

'Oh saints! what is become of him?
Perhaps he's climbed into an oak,
Where he will stay till he is dead;
Or sadly he has been misled,   235
And joined the wandering gipsy-folk.

Or him that wicked pony's carried
To the dark cave, the goblins' hall,
Or in the castle he's pursuing,
Among the ghosts, his own undoing,   240
Or playing with the waterfall.'

At poor old Susan then she railed,
While to the town she posts away:
'If Susan had not been so ill,
Alas! I should have had him still,   245
My Johnny, till my dying day.'

Poor Betty! in this sad distemper,
The doctor's self would hardly spare;
Unworthy things she talked and wild,
Even he, of cattle the most mild,   250
The pony had his share.

And now she's got into the town,
And to the doctor's door she hies;
'Tis silence all on every side –
The town so long, the town so wide,   255
Is silent as the skies.

And now she's at the doctor's door,
She lifts the knocker, rap, rap, rap;
The doctor at the casement shows
His glimmering eyes that peep and doze,   260
And one hand rubs his old night-cap.

'Oh Doctor! Doctor! where's my Johnny?'
'I'm here – what is't you want with me?'
'Oh sir! you know I'm Betty Foy,
And I have lost my poor dear boy,   265
You know him – him you often see;

He's not so wise as some folks be.'
'The devil take his wisdom!' said
The doctor, looking somewhat grim;
'What, woman! should I know of him?'   270
And, grumbling, he went back to bed.

'O woe is me! O woe is me!
Here will I die, here will I die;
I thought to find my Johnny here,
But he is neither far nor near,   275
Oh! what a wretched mother I!'

She stops, she stands, she looks about,
Which way to turn she cannot tell;
Poor Betty! it would ease her pain
If she had heart to knock again;   280
The clock strikes three – a dismal knell!

Then up along the town she hies –
No wonder if her senses fail;
This piteous news so much it shocked her,
She quite forgot to send the doctor   285
To comfort poor old Susan Gale.

And now she's high upon the down,
And she can see a mile of road;
'Oh cruel! I'm almost three-score;
Such night as this was ne'er before,   290
There's not a single soul abroad.'

She listens, but she cannot hear
The foot of horse, the voice of man;
The streams with softest sound are flowing,
The grass you almost hear it growing –   295
You hear it now if e'er you can.

The owlets through the long blue night
Are shouting to each other still:
Fond lovers, yet not quite hob nob,
They lengthen out the tremulous sob   300
That echoes far from hill to hill.

Poor Betty now has lost all hope,
Her thoughts are bent on deadly sin;
A green-grown pond she just has passed,
And from the brink she hurries fast,   305
Lest she should drown herself therein.

And now she sits her down and weeps;
Such tears she never shed before;
'Oh dear, dear pony! my sweet joy!
Oh carry back my idiot boy!   310
And we will ne'er o'erload thee more.'

A thought is come into her head:
'The pony he is mild and good,
And we have always used him well;
Perhaps he's gone along the dell,   315
And carried Johnny to the wood.'

Then up she springs as if on wings;
She thinks no more of deadly sin;
If Betty fifty ponds should see,
The last of all her thoughts would be   320
To drown herself therein.

Oh reader! now that I might tell
What Johnny and his horse are doing!
What they've been doing all this time,
Oh could I put it into rhyme,   325
A most delightful tale pursuing!

Perhaps, and no unlikely thought!
He with his pony now doth roam
The cliffs and peaks so high that are,
To lay his hands upon a star,   330
And in his pocket bring it home.

Perhaps he's turned himself about,
His face unto his horse's tail,
And still and mute, in wonder lost,
All like a silent horseman-ghost,   335
He travels on along the vale.

And now, perhaps, he's hunting sheep,
A fierce and dreadful hunter he!
Yon valley, that's so trim and green,
In five months' time, should he be seen,   340
A desert wilderness will be.

Perhaps, with head and heels on fire,
And like the very soul of evil,
He's galloping away, away,
And so he'll gallop on for aye,   345
The bane of all that dread the devil.

I to the muses have been bound,
These fourteen years, by strong indentures;
Oh gentle Muses! let me tell
But half of what to him befell,   350
For sure he met with strange adventures.

Oh gentle Muses! is this kind?
Why will ye thus my suit repel?
Why of your further aid bereave me?
And can ye thus unfriended leave me?   355
Ye Muses! whom I love so well.

Who's yon, that near the waterfall,
Which thunders down with headlong force,
Beneath the moon, yet shining fair,
As careless as if nothing were,   360
Sits upright on a feeding horse?

Unto his horse, that's feeding free,
He seems, I think, the rein to give;
Of moon or stars he takes no heed –
Of such we in romances read –   365
'Tis Johnny! Johnny! as I live.

And that's the very pony too.
Where is she, where is Betty Foy?
She hardly can sustain her fears;
The roaring water-fall she hears,   370
And cannot find her idiot boy.

Your pony's worth his weight in gold,
Then calm your terrors, Betty Foy!
She's coming from among the trees,
And now, all full in view, she sees   375
Him whom she loves, her idiot boy.

And Betty sees the pony too:
Why stand you thus, Good Betty Foy?
It is no goblin, 'tis no ghost,
'Tis he whom you so long have lost –   380
He whom you love, your idiot boy.

She looks again – her arms are up –
She screams – she cannot move for joy;
She darts as with a torrent's force,
She almost has o'erturned the horse,   385
And fast she holds her idiot boy.

And Johnny burrs and laughs aloud,
Whether in cunning or in joy
I cannot tell; but while he laughs,
Betty a drunken pleasure quaffs   390
To hear again her idiot boy.

And now she's at the pony's tail,
And now she's at the pony's head,
On that side now, and now on this,
And almost stifled with her bliss,   395
A few sad tears does Betty shed.

She kisses o'er and o'er again
Him whom she loves, her idiot boy;
She's happy here, she's happy there,
She is uneasy every where;   400
Her limbs are all alive with joy.

She pats the pony, where or when
She knows not, happy Betty Foy!
The little pony glad may be,
But he is milder far than she: 405
You hardly can perceive his joy.

'Oh! Johnny, never mind the doctor;
You've done your best, and that is all.'
She took the reins, when this was said,
And gently turned the pony's head   410
From the loud water-fall.

By this the stars were almost gone,
The moon was setting on the hill,
So pale you scarcely looked at her;
The little birds began to stir,   415
Though yet their tongues were still.

The pony, Betty, and her boy,
Wind slowly through the woody dale;
And who is she, be-times abroad,
That hobbles up the steep rough road?   420
Who is it, but old Susan Gale?

Long Susan lay deep lost in thought,
And many dreadful fears beset her,
Both for her messenger and nurse;
And as her mind grew worse and worse,   425
Her body it grew better.

She turned, she tossed herself in bed,
On all sides doubts and terrors met her;
Point after point did she discuss;
And while her mind was fighting thus,   430
Her body still grew better.

'Alas! what is become of them?
These fears can never be endured,
I'll to the woods.' The word scarce said,
Did Susan rise up from her bed,   435
As if by magic cured.

Away she posts up hill and down,
And to the wood at length is come;
She spies her friends, she shouts a greeting:
Oh me! it is a merry meeting,   440
As ever was in Christendom.

The owls have hardly sung their last,
While our four travellers homeward wend;
The owls have hooted all night long,
And with the owls began my song,   445
And with the owls must end.

For while they all were travelling home,
Cried Betty, 'Tell us Johnny, do,
Where all this long night you have been,
What you have heard, what you have seen,   450
And Johnny, mind you tell us true.'

Now Johnny all night long had heard
The owls in tuneful concert strive;
No doubt too he the moon had seen,
For in the moonlight he had been   455
From eight o'clock till five.

And thus to Betty's question, he
Made answer, like a traveller bold,
(His very words I give to you)
'The cocks did crow to-whoo, to-whoo,   460
And the sun did shine so cold.'
– Thus answered Johnny in his glory,
And that was all his travel's story.

Lines

WRITTEN NEAR RICHMOND, UPON THE THAMES,
AT EVENING

How rich the wave, in front, impressed
With evening-twilight's summer hues,
While, facing thus the crimson west,
The boat her silent path pursues!
And see how dark the backward stream!   5
A little moment past, so smiling!
And still, perhaps, with faithless gleam,
Some other loiterer beguiling.

Such views the youthful bard allure,
But, heedless of the following gloom,   10
He deems their colours shall endure
Till peace go with him to the tomb.
– And let him nurse his fond deceit,
And what if he must die in sorrow!
Who would not cherish dreams so sweet,   15
Though grief and pain may come to-morrow?

Glide gently, thus for ever glide,
O Thames! that other bards may see
As lovely visions by thy side
As now, fair river! come to me.   20
Oh glide, fair stream! for ever so;
Thy quiet soul on all bestowing,
'Till all our minds for ever flow
As thy deep waters now are flowing.

Vain thought! yet be as now thou art,   25
That in thy waters may be seen
The image of a poet's heart,
How bright, how solemn, how serene!
Such heart did once the poet bless,
Who, pouring here a *later* ditty,   30
Could find no refuge from distress,
But in the milder grief of pity.

Remembrance! as we glide along,
For him suspend the dashing oar,
And pray that never child of song   35
May know his freezing sorrows more.
How calm! how still! the only sound,
The dripping of the oar suspended!
– The evening darkness gathers round
By virtue's holiest powers attended.   40

Expostulation and Reply

'Why William, on that old grey stone,
Thus for the length of half a day,
Why William, sit you thus alone,
And dream your time away?

Where are your books? that light bequeathed   5
To beings else forlorn and blind!
Up! Up! and drink the spirit breathed
From dead men to their kind.

You look round on your mother earth
As if she for no purpose bore you –   10
As if you were her first-born birth,
And none had lived before you!'

One morning thus, by Esthwaite lake,
When life was sweet, I knew not why,
To me my good friend Matthew spake,   15
And thus I made reply.

'The eye it cannot choose but see,
We cannot bid the ear be still;
Our bodies feel, where'er they be,
Against, or with our will.   20

Nor less I deem that there are powers,
Which of themselves our minds impress,
That we can feed this mind of ours
In a wise passiveness.

Think you, mid all this mighty sum   25
Of things for ever speaking,
That nothing of itself will come,
But we must still be seeking?

Then ask not wherefore, here, alone,
Conversing as I may,   30
I sit upon this old grey stone,
And dream my time away.'

The Tables Turned

AN EVENING SCENE
ON THE SAME SUBJECT

Up! up! my friend, and clear your looks,
Why all this toil and trouble?
Up! up! my friend, and quit your books,
Or surely you'll grow double.

The sun above the mountain's head 5
A freshening lustre mellow
Through all the long green fields has spread –
His first sweet evening yellow.

Books! 'tis a dull and endless strife,
Come, hear the woodland linnet – 10
How sweet his music; on my life
There's more of wisdom in it.

And hark! how blithe the throstle sings!
And he is no mean preacher;
Come forth into the light of things, 15
Let Nature be your teacher.

She has a world of ready wealth,
Our minds and hearts to bless –
Spontaneous wisdom breathed by health,
Truth breathed by cheerfulness. 20

One impulse from a vernal wood
May teach you more of man,
Of moral evil and of good,
Than all the sages can.

Sweet is the lore which nature brings; 25
Our meddling intellect
Misshapes the beauteous forms of things:
We murder to dissect.

Enough of science and of art;
Close up these barren leaves; 30
Come forth, and bring with you a heart
That watches and receives.

Old Man Travelling

       The little hedge-row birds
That peck along the road regard him not.
He travels on, and in his face, his step,
His gait, is one expression; every limb,
His look and bending figure, all bespeak   5
A man who does not move with pain, but moves
With thought. He is insensibly subdued
To settled quiet: he is one by whom
All effort seems forgotten – one to whom
Long patience has such mild composure given   10
That patience now doth seem a thing of which
He hath no need. He is by nature led
To peace so perfect, that the young behold
With envy, what the old man hardly feels.
– I asked him whither he was bound, and what   15
The object of his journey; he replied
'Sir! I am going many miles to take
A last leave of my son, a mariner,
Who from a sea-fight has been brought to Falmouth,
And there is dying in an hospital.'   20

The Complaint
of a forsaken Indian Woman

When a Northern Indian, from sickness, is unable to continue
his journey with his companions, he is left behind, covered over
with deer-skins, and is supplied with water, food, and fuel if the
situation of the place will afford it. He is informed of the track
which his companions intend to pursue, and if he is unable to
follow or overtake them, he perishes alone in the desert, unless
he should have the good fortune to fall in with some other tribes
of Indians. It is unnecessary to add that the females are equally,
or still more, exposed to the same fate. See that very interesting
work, Hearne's Journey from Hudson's Bay to the Northern
Ocean. When the Northern Lights, as the same writer informs
us, vary their position in the air, they make a rustling and a
crackling noise. This circumstance is alluded to in the first stanza
of the following poem.

Before I see another day,
Oh let my body die away!
In sleep I heard the northern gleams;
The stars they were among my dreams;
In sleep did I behold the skies —   5
I saw the crackling flashes drive,
And yet they are upon my eyes,
And yet I am alive.
Before I see another day,
Oh let my body die away!   10

My fire is dead: it knew no pain,
Yet is it dead, and I remain.
All stiff with ice the ashes lie,
And they are dead, and I will die.
When I was well, I wished to live   15
For clothes, for warmth, for food, and fire;
But they to me no joy can give,
No pleasure now, and no desire.
Then here contented will I lie;
Alone I cannot fear to die.   20

Alas! you might have dragged me on
Another day, a single one!
Too soon despair o'er me prevailed;
Too soon my heartless spirit failed;
When you were gone my limbs were stronger,   25
And oh! how grievously I rue,
That afterwards, a little longer,
My friends, I did not follow you!
For strong and without pain I lay,
My friends, when you were gone away.   30

My child! they gave thee to another,
A woman who was not thy mother.
When from my arms my babe they took,
On me how strangely did he look!
Through his whole body something ran –   35
A most strange something did I see –
As if he strove to be a man,
That he might pull the sledge for me.
And then he stretched his arms, how wild!
Oh mercy! like a little child.   40

My little joy! my little pride!
In two days more I must have died.
Then do not weep and grieve for me;
I feel I must have died with thee.
Oh wind that o'er my head art flying   45
The way my friends their course did bend,
I should not feel the pain of dying
Could I with thee a message send.
Too soon, my friends, you went away,
For I had many things to say.   50

I'll follow you across the snow,
You travel heavily and slow:
In spite of all my weary pain,
I'll look upon your tents again.
My fire is dead, and snowy white   55
The water which beside it stood;
The wolf has come to me to-night,
And he has stolen away my food.

For ever left alone am I,
Then wherefore should I fear to die?   60

My journey will be shortly run;
I shall not see another sun;
I cannot lift my limbs to know
If they have any life or no.
My poor forsaken child! If I   65
For once could have thee close to me,
With happy heart I then would die,
And my last thoughts would happy be.
I feel my body die away:
I shall not see another day.   70

The Convict

The glory of evening was spread through the west;
   On the slope of a mountain I stood,
While the joy that precedes the calm season of rest
   Rang loud through the meadow and wood.

'And must we then part from a dwelling so fair?'   5
   In the pain of my spirit I said,
And with a deep sadness I turned, to repair
   To the cell where the convict is laid.

The thick-ribbed walls that o'ershadow the gate
   Resound, and the dungeons unfold;   10
I pause, and at length, through the glimmering grate,
   That outcast of pity behold.

His black matted head on his shoulder is bent,
   And deep is the sigh of his breath,
And with stedfast dejection his eyes are intent   15
   On the fetters that link him to death.

'Tis sorrow enough on that visage to gaze,
   That body dismissed from his care;
Yet my fancy has pierced to his heart, and portrays
   More terrible images there.   20

His bones are consumed, and his life-blood is dried,
    With wishes the past to undo;
And his crime, through the pains that o'erwhelm him,
        descried,
    Still blackens and grows on his view.

When from the dark synod, or blood-reeking field,   25
    To his chamber the monarch is led,
All soothers of sense their soft virtue shall yield,
    And quietness pillow his head.

But if grief, self-consumed, in oblivion would doze,
    And conscience her tortures appease,   30
'Mid tumult and uproar this man must repose —
    In the comfortless vault of disease.

When his fetters at night have so pressed on his limbs
    That the weight can no longer be borne,
If, while a half-slumber his memory bedims,   35
    The wretch on his pallet should turn,

While the jail-mastiff howls at the dull clanking chain,
    From the roots of his hair there shall start
A thousand sharp punctures of cold-sweating pain,
    And terror shall leap at his heart.   40

But now he half-raises his deep-sunken eye,
    And the motion unsettles a tear;
The silence of sorrow it seems to supply,
    And asks of me why I am here.

'Poor victim! no idle intruder has stood   45
    With o'erweening complacence our state to compare,
But one, whose first wish is the wish to be good,
    Is come as a brother thy sorrows to share.

At thy name though compassion her nature resign,
    Though in virtue's proud mouth thy report be a stain,   50
My care, if the arm of the mighty were mine,
    Would plant thee where yet thou might'st blossom again.'

Lines
written a few miles above Tintern Abbey

ON REVISITING THE BANKS OF THE WYE
DURING A TOUR
July 13, 1798

Five years have passed; five summers, with the length
Of five long winters! and again I hear
These waters, rolling from their mountain-springs
With a sweet inland murmur. Once again
Do I behold these steep and lofty cliffs,   5
Which on a wild secluded scene impress
Thoughts of more deep seclusion, and connect
The landscape with the quiet of the sky.
The day is come when I again repose
Here, under this dark sycamore, and view   10
These plots of cottage-ground, these orchard-tufts,
Which, at this season, with their unripe fruits,
Among the woods and copses lose themselves,
Nor, with their green and simple hue, disturb
The wild green landscape. Once again I see   15
These hedge-rows, hardly hedge-rows, little lines
Of sportive wood run wild; these pastoral farms
Green to the very door, and wreaths of smoke
Sent up, in silence, from among the trees,
With some uncertain notice, as might seem,   20
Of vagrant dwellers in the houseless woods,
Or of some hermit's cave, where by his fire
The hermit sits alone.

                    Though absent long,
These forms of beauty have not been to me
As is a landscape to a blind man's eye;   25
But oft, in lonely rooms, and mid the din
Of towns and cities, I have owed to them,
In hours of weariness, sensations sweet,
Felt in the blood, and felt along the heart,
And passing even into my purer mind   30
With tranquil restoration; feelings too

Of unremembered pleasure – such, perhaps,
As may have had no trivial influence
On that best portion of a good man's life:
His little, nameless, unremembered acts   35
Of kindness and of love. Nor less, I trust,
To them I may have owed another gift,
Of aspect more sublime – that blessed mood
In which the burthen of the mystery,
In which the heavy and the weary weight   40
Of all this unintelligible world
Is lightened; that serene and blessed mood
In which the affections gently lead us on,
Until, the breath of this corporeal frame,
And even the motion of our human blood   45
Almost suspended, we are laid asleep
In body, and become a living soul,
While with an eye made quiet by the power
Of harmony, and the deep power of joy,
We see into the life of things.   50

　　　　　If this
Be but a vain belief, yet oh! how oft
In darkness, and amid the many shapes
Of joyless day-light, when the fretful stir
Unprofitable, and the fever of the world
Have hung upon the beatings of my heart,   55
How oft, in spirit, have I turned to thee
O sylvan Wye! Thou wanderer through the woods,
How often has my spirit turned to thee!

And now, with gleams of half-extinguished thought,
With many recognitions dim and faint,   60
And somewhat of a sad perplexity,
The picture of the mind revives again
While here I stand, not only with the sense
Of present pleasure, but with pleasing thoughts
That in this moment there is life and food   65
For future years. And so I dare to hope
Though changed, no doubt, from what I was when first
I came among these hills; when like a roe
I bounded o'er the mountains, by the sides

Of the deep rivers and the lonely streams,   70
Wherever nature led; more like a man
Flying from something that he dreads, than one
Who sought the thing he loved. For nature then
(The coarser pleasures of my boyish days
And their glad animal movements all gone by)   75
To me was all in all. I cannot paint
What then I was. The sounding cataract
Haunted me like a passion; the tall rock,
The mountain, and the deep and gloomy wood,
Their colours and their forms, were then to me   80
An appetite – a feeling and a love
That had no need of a remoter charm,
By thought supplied, or any interest
Unborrowed from the eye. That time is past,
And all its aching joys are now no more,   85
And all its dizzy raptures. Not for this
Faint I, nor mourn nor murmur: other gifts
Have followed – for such loss, I would believe,
Abundant recompense. For I have learned
To look on nature, not as in the hour   90
Of thoughtless youth, but hearing oftentimes
The still, sad music of humanity,
Not harsh nor grating, though of ample power
To chasten and subdue. And I have felt
A presence that disturbs me with the joy   95
Of elevated thoughts: a sense sublime
Of something far more deeply interfused,
Whose dwelling is the light of setting suns,
And the round ocean, and the living air,
And the blue sky, and in the mind of man –   100
A motion and a spirit that impels
All thinking things, all objects of all thought,
And rolls through all things. Therefore am I still
A lover of the meadows and the woods,
And mountains, and of all that we behold   105
From this green earth; of all the mighty world
Of eye and ear, both what they half-create,
And what perceive; well pleased to recognise
In Nature and the language of the sense
The anchor of my purest thoughts, the nurse,   110

The guide, the guardian of my heart, and soul
Of all my moral being.

              Nor, perchance,
If I were not thus taught, should I the more
Suffer my genial spirits to decay:
For thou art with me, here, upon the banks   115
Of this fair river; thou, my dearest friend,
My dear, dear friend, and in thy voice I catch
The language of my former heart, and read
My former pleasures in the shooting lights
Of thy wild eyes. Oh! yet a little while   120
May I behold in thee what I was once,
My dear, dear sister! And this prayer I make,
Knowing that Nature never did betray
The heart that loved her; 'tis her privilege,
Through all the years of this our life, to lead   125
From joy to joy: for she can so inform
The mind that is within us, so impress
With quietness and beauty, and so feed
With lofty thoughts, that neither evil tongues,
Rash judgements, nor the sneers of selfish men,   130
Nor greetings where no kindness is, nor all
The dreary intercourse of daily life
Shall e'er prevail against us, or disturb
Our cheerful faith that all which we behold
Is full of blessings. Therefore let the moon   135
Shine on thee in thy solitary walk,
And let the misty mountain winds be free
To blow against thee; and in after years,
When these wild ecstasies shall be matured
Into a sober pleasure, when thy mind   140
Shall be a mansion for all lovely forms,
Thy memory be as a dwelling-place
For all sweet sounds and harmonies, oh! then,
If solitude, or fear, or pain, or grief,
Should be thy portion, with what healing thoughts   145
Of tender joy wilt thou remember me,
And these my exhortations! Nor, perchance,
If I should be where I no more can hear
Thy voice, nor catch from thy wild eyes these gleams

Of past existence, wilt thou then forget   150
That on the banks of this delightful stream
We stood together, and that I, so long
A worshipper of Nature, hither came
Unwearied in that service – rather say
With warmer love, oh! with far deeper zeal   155
Of holier love. Nor wilt thou then forget,
That after many wanderings, many years
Of absence, these steep woods and lofty cliffs,
And this green pastoral landscape, were to me
More dear, both for themselves, and for thy sake.   160

From

LYRICAL BALLADS,

1800

Hart-Leap Well

Hart-Leap Well is a small spring of water, about five miles from Richmond in Yorkshire, and near the side of the road which leads from Richmond to Askrigg. Its name is derived from a remarkable chase, the memory of which is preserved by the monuments spoken of in the second part of the following poem, which monuments do now exist as I have there described them.

The knight had ridden down from Wensley moor
With the slow motion of a summer's cloud;
He turned aside towards a vassal's door,
And, 'Bring another horse!' he cried aloud.

'Another horse!' – That shout the vassal heard,   5
And saddled his best steed, a comely grey;
Sir Walter mounted him; he was the third
Which he had mounted on that glorious day.

Joy sparkled in the prancing courser's eyes;
The horse and horseman are a happy pair;   10
But though Sir Walter like a falcon flies,
There is a doleful silence in the air.

A rout this morning left Sir Walter's hall,
That as they galloped made the echoes roar;
But horse and man are vanished, one and all;   15
Such race, I think, was never seen before.

Sir Walter, restless as a veering wind,
Calls to the few tired dogs that yet remain:
Brach, Swift and Music, noblest of their kind,
Follow, and up the weary mountain strain.   20

The knight hallooed, he chid and cheered them on
With suppliant gestures and upbraidings stern;
But breath and eye-sight fail, and, one by one,
The dogs are stretched among the mountain fern.

Where is the throng, the tumult of the chase?   25
The bugles that so joyfully were blown?
– This race it looks not like an earthly race;
Sir Walter and the hart are left alone.

The poor hart toils along the mountain side;
I will not stop to tell how far he fled,   30
Nor will I mention by what death he died;
But now the knight beholds him lying dead.

Dismounting then, he leaned against a thorn;
He had no follower, dog, nor man, nor boy;
He neither smacked his whip, nor blew his horn,   35
But gazed upon the spoil with silent joy.

Close to the thorn on which Sir Walter leaned
Stood his dumb partner in this glorious act –
Weak as a lamb the hour that it is yeaned,
And foaming like a mountain cataract.   40

Upon his side the hart was lying stretched:
His nose half-touched a spring beneath a hill,
And with the last deep groan his breath had fetched,
The waters of the spring were trembling still.

And now, too happy for repose or rest   45
(Was never man in such a joyful case),
Sir Walter walked all round, north, south, and west,
And gazed and gazed upon that darling place.

And turning up the hill – it was at least
Nine roods of sheer ascent – Sir Walter found   50
Three several marks which with his hoofs the beast
Had left imprinted on the verdant ground.

Sir Walter wiped his face, and cried, 'Till now
Such sight was never seen by living eyes:
Three leaps have borne him from this lofty brow,   55
Down to the very fountain where he lies.

I'll build a pleasure-house upon this spot,
And a small arbour, made for rural joy;
'Twill be the traveller's shed, the pilgrim's cot,
A place of love for damsels that are coy. 60

A cunning artist will I have to frame
A basin for that fountain in the dell;
And they, who do make mention of the same,
From this day forth, shall call it Hart-leap Well.

And, gallant brute! to make thy praises known, 65
Another monument shall here be raised:
Three several pillars, each a rough-hewn stone,
And planted where thy hoofs the turf have grazed.

And in the summer-time when days are long,
I will come hither with my paramour, 70
And with the dancers and the minstrel's song
We will make merry in that pleasant bower.

Till the foundations of the mountains fail
My mansion with its arbour shall endure –
The joy of them who till the fields of Swale, 75
And them who dwell among the woods of Ure.'

Then home he went, and left the hart, stone-dead,
With breathless nostrils stretched above the spring.
And soon the knight performed what he had said,
The fame whereof through many a land did ring. 80

Ere thrice the moon into her port had steered,
A cup of stone received the living well;
Three pillars of rude stone Sir Walter reared,
And built a house of pleasure in the dell.

And near the fountain, flowers of stature tall 85
With trailing plants and trees were intertwined,
Which soon composed a little sylvan hall,
A leafy shelter from the sun and wind.

And thither, when the summer days were long,
Sir Walter journeyed with his paramour; 90
And with the dancers and the minstrel's song
Made merriment within that pleasant bower.

The knight, Sir Walter, died in course of time,
And his bones lie in his paternal vale;
But there is matter for a second rhyme, 95
And I to this would add another tale.

PART SECOND

The moving accident is not my trade,
To freeze the blood I have no ready arts;
'Tis my delight, alone in summer shade,
To pipe a simple song to thinking hearts. 100

As I from Hawes to Richmond did repair,
It chanced that I saw standing in a dell
Three aspins at three corners of a square,
And one, not four yards distant, near a well.

What this imported I could ill divine, 105
And, pulling now the rein my horse to stop,
I saw three pillars standing in a line,
The last stone pillar on a dark hill-top.

The trees were grey, with neither arms nor head;
Half-wasted the square mound of tawny green, 110
So that you just might say, as then I said,
'Here in old time the hand of man has been.'

I looked upon the hills both far and near;
More doleful place did never eye survey;
It seemed as if the spring-time came not here, 115
And Nature here were willing to decay.

I stood in various thoughts and fancies lost
When one who was in shepherd's garb attired
Came up the hollow. Him did I accost,
And what this place might be I then inquired. 120

The shepherd stopped, and that same story told
Which in my former rhyme I have rehearsed.
'A jolly place,' said he, 'in times of old,
But something ails it now; the spot is cursed.

You see these lifeless stumps of aspin wood? –   125
Some say that they are beeches, others elms;
These were the bower, and here a mansion stood –
The finest palace of a hundred realms.

The arbour does its own condition tell;
You see the stones, the fountain, and the stream;   130
But as to the great lodge, you might as well
Hunt half a day for a forgotten dream.

There's neither dog nor heifer, horse nor sheep,
Will wet his lips within that cup of stone;
And, oftentimes, when all are fast asleep,   135
This water doth send forth a dolorous groan.

Some say that here a murder has been done,
And blood cries out for blood; but, for my part,
I've guessed, when I've been sitting in the sun,
That it was all for that unhappy hart.   140

What thoughts must through the creature's brain have
          passed!
From the stone on the summit of the steep
Are but three bounds, and look, sir, at this last!
O master! it has been a cruel leap.

For thirteen hours he ran a desperate race,   145
And in my simple mind we cannot tell
What cause the hart might have to love this place,
And come and make his death-bed near the well.

Here on the grass perhaps asleep he sank,
Lulled by this fountain in the summer-tide;   150
This water was perhaps the first he drank
When he had wandered from his mother's side.

In April here beneath the scented thorn
He heard the birds their morning carols sing;
And he, perhaps, for aught we know, was born   155
Not half a furlong from that self-same spring.

But now here's neither grass nor pleasant shade;
The sun on drearier hollow never shone;
So will it be, as I have often said,
Till trees, and stones, and fountain all are gone.'   160

'Grey-headed shepherd, thou hast spoken well –
Small difference lies between thy creed and mine;
This beast not unobserved by Nature fell;
His death was mourned by sympathy divine.

The being, that is in the clouds and air,   165
That is in the green leaves among the groves,
Maintains a deep and reverential care
For them, the quiet creatures whom he loves.

The pleasure-house is dust; behind, before,
This is no common waste, no common gloom;   170
But Nature, in due course of time, once more
Shall here put on her beauty and her bloom.

She leaves these objects to a slow decay
That what we are, and have been, may be known;
But, at the coming of the milder day,   175
These monuments shall all be overgrown.

One lesson, shepherd, let us two divide,
Taught both by what she shows, and what conceals:
Never to blend our pleasure or our pride
With sorrow of the meanest thing that feels.'   180

'There was a boy'

There was a boy: ye knew him well, ye cliffs
And islands of Winander! Many a time,
At evening, when the stars had just begun
To move along the edges of the hills,

Rising or setting, would he stand alone 5
Beneath the trees, or by the glimmering lake,
And there, with fingers interwoven, both hands
Pressed closely palm to palm and to his mouth
Uplifted, he, as through an instrument,
Blew mimic hootings to the silent owls 10
That they might answer him. And they would shout
Across the wat'ry vale and shout again,
Responsive to his call, with quivering peals,
And long halloos, and screams, and echoes loud
Redoubled and redoubled: a wild scene 15
Of mirth and jocund din. And, when it chanced
That pauses of deep silence mocked his skill,
Then, sometimes, in that silence, while he hung
Listening, a gentle shock of mild surprise
Has carried far into his heart the voice 20
Of mountain torrents, or the visible scene
Would enter unawares into his mind
With all its solemn imagery: its rocks,
Its woods, and that uncertain heaven, received
Into the bosom of the steady lake. 25

    Fair are the woods, and beauteous is the spot,
The vale where he was born; the church-yard hangs
Upon a slope above the village school,
And there along that bank when I have passed
At evening, I believe that near his grave 30
A full half-hour together I have stood,
Mute – for he died when he was ten years old.

'Strange fits of passion'

Strange fits of passion I have known,
And I will dare to tell,
But in the lover's ear alone,
What once to me befell.

When she I loved was strong and gay 5
And like a rose in June,
I to her cottage bent my way
Beneath the evening moon.

Upon the moon I fixed my eye,
All over the wide lea;   10
My horse trudged on, and we drew nigh
Those paths so dear to me.

And now we reached the orchard plot,
And, as we climbed the hill,
Towards the roof of Lucy's cot   15
The moon descended still.

In one of those sweet dreams I slept,
Kind Nature's gentlest boon!
And, all the while, my eyes I kept
On the descending moon.   20

My horse moved on: hoof after hoof
He raised and never stopped;
When down behind the cottage roof
At once the planet dropped.

What fond and wayward thoughts will slide   25
Into a lover's head —
'O mercy!' to myself I cried,
'If Lucy should be dead!'

Song

She dwelt among th' untrodden ways
    Beside the springs of Dove:
A maid whom there were none to praise
    And very few to love.

A violet by a mossy stone   5
    Half-hidden from the eye!
— Fair as a star when only one
    Is shining in the sky!

She lived unknown, and few could know
    When Lucy ceased to be;   10
But she is in her grave, and oh!
    The difference to me.

'A slumber did my spirit seal'

A slumber did my spirit seal,
   I had no human fears;
She seemed a thing that could not feel
   The touch of earthly years.

No motion has she now, no force;   5
   She neither hears nor sees,
Rolled round in earth's diurnal course
   With rocks and stones and trees!

'Three years she grew in sun and shower'

Three years she grew in sun and shower,
Then Nature said, 'A lovelier flower
On earth was never sown;
This child I to myself will take,
She shall be mine, and I will make   5
A Lady of my own.

Myself will to my darling be
Both law and impulse, and with me
The girl in rock and plain,
In earth and heaven, in glade and bower,   10
Shall feel an overseeing power
To kindle or restrain.

She shall be sportive as the fawn
That wild with glee across the lawn
Or up the mountain springs;   15
And hers shall be the breathing balm,
And hers the silence and the calm
Of mute insensate things.

The floating clouds their state shall lend
To her, for her the willow bend,   20
Nor shall she fail to see
Even in the motions of the storm

Grace that shall mould the maiden's form
By silent sympathy.

The stars of midnight shall be dear   25
To her, and she shall lean her ear
In many a secret place
Where rivulets dance their wayward round,
And beauty born of murmuring sound
Shall pass into her face.   30

And vital feelings of delight
Shall rear her form to stately height,
Her virgin bosom swell;
Such thoughts to Lucy I will give
While she and I together live   35
Here in this happy dell.'

Thus Nature spake. The work was done.
How soon my Lucy's race was run!
She died and left to me
This heath, this calm and quiet scene,   40
The memory of what has been,
And never more will be.

Lucy Gray

Oft I had heard of Lucy Gray,
And when I crossed the wild,
I chanced to see at break of day
The solitary child.

No mate, no comrade Lucy knew;   5
She dwelt on a wild moor –
The sweetest thing that ever grew
Beside a human door!

You yet may spy the fawn at play,
The hare upon the green;   10
But the sweet face of Lucy Gray
Will never more be seen.

'To-night will be a stormy night,
You to the town must go,
And take a lantern, child, to light   15
Your mother thro' the snow.'

'That, Father! will I gladly do;
'Tis scarcely afternoon –
The minster-clock has just struck two,
And yonder is the moon.'   20

At this the father raised his hook
And snapped a faggot-band;
He plied his work, and Lucy took
The lantern in her hand.

Not blither is the mountain roe: 25
With many a wanton stroke
Her feet disperse the powd'ry snow
That rises up like smoke.

The storm came on before its time;
She wandered up and down,   30
And many a hill did Lucy climb,
But never reached the town.

The wretched parents all that night
Went shouting far and wide,
But there was neither sound nor sight   35
To serve them for a guide.

At day-break on a hill they stood
That overlooked the moor,
And thence they saw the bridge of wood
A furlong from their door.   40

And now they homeward turned, and cried
'In Heaven we all shall meet!'
When in the snow the mother spied
The print of Lucy's feet.

Then downward from the steep hill's edge   45
They tracked the footmarks small,
And through the broken hawthorn-hedge,
And by the long stone-wall;

And then an open field they crossed –
The marks were still the same;   50
They tracked them on, nor ever lost,
And to the bridge they came.

They followed from the snowy bank
The footmarks, one by one,
Into the middle of the plank,   55
And further there were none.

Yet some maintain that to this day
She is a living child:
That you may see sweet Lucy Gray
Upon the lonesome wild.   60

O'er rough and smooth she trips along,
And never looks behind;
And sings a solitary song
That whistles in the wind.

''Tis said that some have died for love'

'Tis said that some have died for love,
And here and there a church-yard grave is found
In the cold North's unhallowed ground,
Because the wretched man himself had slain,
His love was such a grievous pain.   5
And there is one whom I five years have known;
He dwells alone
Upon Helvellyn's side.
He loved; the pretty Barbara died,
And thus he makes his moan;   10
Three years had Barbara in her grave been laid
When thus his moan he made:

'Oh! move thou cottage from behind that oak
Or let the aged tree uprooted lie,
That in some other way yon smoke   15
May mount into the sky!
The clouds pass on; they from the heavens depart:
I look – the sky is empty space;
I know not what I trace;
But when I cease to look, my hand is on my heart.   20

O! what a weight is in these shades! Ye leaves,
When will that dying murmur be suppressed?
Your sound my heart of peace bereaves –
It robs my heart of rest.
Thou thrush, that singest loud and loud and free,   25
Into yon row of willows flit,
Upon that alder sit,
Or sing another song, or choose another tree.

Roll back, sweet rill! back to thy mountain bounds,
And there for ever be thy waters chained!   30
For thou dost haunt the air with sounds
That cannot be sustained;
If still beneath that pine-tree's ragged bough
Headlong yon waterfall must come,
Oh let it then be dumb! –   35
Be any thing, sweet rill, but that which thou art now.

Thou eglantine whose arch so proudly towers,
(Even like a rainbow spanning half the vale)
Thou one fair shrub, oh! shed thy flowers,
And stir not in the gale.   40
For thus to see thee nodding in the air,
To see thy arch thus stretch and bend,
Thus rise and thus descend,
Disturbs me, till the sight is more than I can bear.'

The man who makes this feverish complaint   45
Is one of giant stature, who could dance
Equipped from head to foot in iron mail.

Ah gentle Love! if ever thought was thine
To store up kindred hours for me, thy face
Turn from me, gentle Love, nor let me walk   50
Within the sound of Emma's voice, or know
Such happiness as I have known to-day.

Poor Susan

At the corner of Wood-Street, when daylight appears,
There's a thrush that sings loud, it has sung for three years;
Poor Susan has passed by the spot and has heard
In the silence of morning the song of the bird.

'Tis a note of enchantment; what ails her? She sees   5
A mountain ascending, a vision of trees;
Bright volumes of vapour through Lothbury glide,
And a river flows on through the vale of Cheapside.

Green pastures she views in the midst of the dale,
Down which she so often has tripped with her pail;   10
And a single small cottage, a nest like a dove's,
The only one dwelling on earth that she loves.

She looks, and her heart is in heaven; but they fade,
The mist and the river, the hill and the shade;
The stream will not flow, and the hill will not rise,   15
And the colours have all passed away from her eyes.

Poor outcast! return – to receive thee once more
The house of thy father will open its door,
And thou once again, in thy plain russet gown,
May'st hear the thrush sing from a tree of its own.   20

To a Sexton

Let thy wheel-barrow alone.
Wherefore, Sexton, piling still
In thy bone-house bone on bone?
'Tis already like a hill
In a field of battle made,   5
Where three thousand skulls are laid.
– These died in peace each with the other,
Father, sister, friend, and brother.

Mark the spot to which I point!
From this platform eight feet square   10
Take not even a finger-joint:
Andrew's whole fire-side is there.
Here, alone, before thine eyes,
Simon's sickly daughter lies –
From weakness, now, and pain defended,   15
Whom he twenty winters tended.

Look but at the gardener's pride,
How he glories, when he sees
Roses, lilies, side by side,
Violets in families.   20
By the heart of man, his tears,
By his hopes and by his fears,
Thou, old grey-beard! art the warden
Of a far superior garden.

Thus then, each to other dear,   25
Let them all in quiet lie,
Andrew there and Susan here,
Neighbours in mortality.
And should I live through sun and rain
Seven widowed years without my Jane,   30
O Sexton, do not then remove her:
Let one grave hold the loved and lover!

'A whirl-blast from behind the hill'

A whirl-blast from behind the hill
Rushed o'er the wood with startling sound;
Then all at once the air was still,
And showers of hail-stones pattered round.
Where leafless oaks towered high above,   5
I sat within an undergrove
Of tallest hollies, tall and green –
A fairer bower was never seen.
From year to year the spacious floor
With withered leaves is covered o'er: 10
You could not lay a hair between,
And all the year the bower is green.
But see! where'er the hailstones drop
The withered leaves all skip and hop:
There's not a breeze – no breath of air –   15
Yet here, and there, and every where
Along the floor, beneath the shade
By those embowering hollies made,
The leaves in myriads jump and spring,
As if with pipes and music rare   20
Some Robin Good-fellow were there,
And all those leaves that jump and spring
Were each a joyous, living thing.

Oh! grant me, heaven, a heart at ease,
That I may never cease to find,   25
Even in appearances like these,
Enough to nourish and to stir my mind!

Song

FOR THE WANDERING JEW

Though the torrents from their fountains
Roar down many a craggy steep,
Yet they find among the mountains
Resting-places calm and deep.

Though almost with eagle pinion   5
O'er the rocks the chamois roam,
Yet he has some small dominion
Which no doubt he calls his home.

If on windy days the raven
Gambol like a dancing skiff,   10
Not the less he loves his haven
On the bosom of the cliff.

Though the sea-horse in the ocean
Own no dear domestic cave,
Yet he slumbers without motion   15
On the calm and silent wave.

Day and night my toils redouble!
Never nearer to the goal;
Night and day I feel the trouble
Of the Wanderer in my soul.   20

Lines
written on a Tablet in a School

*In the School of —— is a tablet on which are inscribed, in gilt
letters, the names of the several persons who have been school-
masters there since the foundation of the school, with the time at
which they entered upon and quitted their office. Opposite one of
those names the author wrote the following lines.*

If Nature, for a favourite child
In thee hath tempered so her clay,
That every hour thy heart runs wild
Yet never once doth go astray,

Read o'er these lines, and then review   5
This tablet, that thus humbly rears
In such diversity of hue
Its history of two hundred years.

– When through this little wreck of fame,
Cypher and syllable, thine eye   10
Has travelled down to Matthew's name,
Pause with no common sympathy.

And if a sleeping tear should wake,
Then be it neither checked nor stayed;
For Matthew a request I make   15
Which for himself he had not made.

Poor Matthew, all his frolics o'er,
Is silent as a standing pool,
Far from the chimney's merry roar,
And murmur of the village school.   20

The sighs which Matthew heaved were sighs
Of one tired out with fun and madness;
The tears which came to Matthew's eyes
Were tears of light, the oil of gladness.

Yet sometimes when the secret cup   25
Of still and serious thought went round,
It seemed as if he drank it up,
He felt with spirit so profound.

– Thou soul of God's best earthly mould,
Thou happy soul! and can it be   30
That these two words of glittering gold
Are all that must remain of thee?

The Two April Mornings

We walked along while bright and red
Uprose the morning sun,
And Matthew stopped; he looked, and said,
'The will of God be done!'

A village schoolmaster was he,   5
With hair of glittering grey –
As blithe a man as you could see
On a spring holiday.

And on that morning, through the grass,
And by the steaming rills, 10
We travelled merrily to pass
A day among the hills.

'Our work,' said I, 'was well begun;
Then, from thy breast what thought,
Beneath so beautiful a sun, 15
So sad a sigh has brought?'

A second time did Matthew stop,
And fixing still his eye
Upon the eastern mountain-top
To me he made reply. 20

'Yon cloud with that long purple cleft
Brings fresh into my mind
A day like this which I have left
Full thirty years behind.

And on that slope of springing corn 25
The self-same crimson hue
Fell from the sky that April morn,
The same which now I view!

With rod and line my silent sport
I plied by Derwent's wave, 30
And, coming to the church, stopped short
Beside my daughter's grave.

Nine summers had she scarcely seen —
The pride of all the vale;
And then she sang! — she would have been 35
A very nightingale.

Six feet in earth my Emma lay,
And yet I loved her more,
For so it seemed, than till that day
I e'er had loved before. 40

And, turning from her grave, I met
Beside the church-yard yew
A blooming girl, whose hair was wet
With points of morning dew.

A basket on her head she bare,   45
Her brow was smooth and white;
To see a child so very fair,
It was a pure delight!

No fountain from its rocky cave
E'er tripped with foot so free;   50
She seemed as happy as a wave
That dances on the sea.

There came from me a sigh of pain
Which I could ill confine;
I looked at her and looked again,   55
And did not wish her mine.'

Matthew is in his grave, yet now
Methinks I see him stand,
As at that moment, with his bough
Of wilding in his hand.   60

The Fountain

A CONVERSATION

We talked with open heart, and tongue
Affectionate and true –
A pair of friends, though I was young,
And Matthew seventy-two.

We lay beneath a spreading oak   5
Beside a mossy seat,
And from the turf a fountain broke,
And gurgled at our feet.

'Now, Matthew, let us try to match
This water's pleasant tune   10
With some old border-song or catch
That suits a summer's noon,

Or of the church-clock and the chimes
Sing here beneath the shade —
That half-mad thing of witty rhymes   15
Which you last April made!'

In silence Matthew lay, and eyed
The spring beneath the tree;
And thus the dear old man replied,
The grey-haired man of glee: 20

'Down to the vale this water steers —
How merrily it goes!
'Twill murmur on a thousand years,
And flow as now it flows.

And here, on this delightful day,   25
I cannot choose but think
How oft, a vigorous man, I lay
Beside this fountain's brink.

My eyes are dim with childish tears,
My heart is idly stirred,   30
For the same sound is in my ears
Which in those days I heard.

Thus fares it still in our decay,
And yet the wiser mind
Mourns less for what age takes away   35
Than what it leaves behind.

The blackbird in the summer trees,
The lark upon the hill,
Let loose their carols when they please,
Are quiet when they will.   40

With Nature never do *they* wage
A foolish strife; they see
A happy youth, and their old age
Is beautiful and free;

But we are pressed by heavy laws,   45
And often, glad no more,
We wear a face of joy, because
We have been glad of yore.

If there is one who need bemoan
His kindred laid in earth,   50
The household hearts that were his own,
It is the man of mirth.

My days, my friend, are almost gone,
My life has been approved,
And many love me, but by none   55
Am I enough beloved.'

'Now both himself and me he wrongs,
The man who thus complains!
I live and sing my idle songs
Upon these happy plains,   60

And, Matthew, for thy children dead
I'll be a son to thee!'
At this he grasped his hands, and said,
'Alas! that cannot be.'

We rose up from the fountain-side,   65
And down the smooth descent
Of the green sheep-track did we glide,
And through the wood we went,

And, ere we came to Leonard's Rock,
He sang those witty rhymes   70
About the crazy old church-clock
And the bewildered chimes.

Nutting

It seems a day
(I speak of one from many singled out),
One of those heavenly days which cannot die,
When forth I sallied from our cottage-door,
And with a wallet o'er my shoulder slung, 5
A nutting crook in hand, I turned my steps
Towards the distant woods, a figure quaint,
Tricked out in proud disguise of beggar's weeds
Put on for the occasion, by advice
And exhortation of my frugal Dame. 10
Motley accoutrement! of power to smile
At thorns, and brakes, and brambles, and, in truth,
More ragged than need was. Among the woods,
And o'er the pathless rocks, I forced my way
Until, at length, I came to one dear nook 15
Unvisited, where not a broken bough
Drooped with its withered leaves (ungracious sign
Of devastation), but the hazels rose
Tall and erect, with milk-white clusters hung –
A virgin scene! A little while I stood, 20
Breathing with such suppression of the heart
As joy delights in, and with wise restraint
Voluptuous, fearless of a rival, eyed
The banquet, or beneath the trees I sat
Among the flowers, and with the flowers I played: 25
A temper known to those, who, after long
And weary expectation, have been blessed
With sudden happiness beyond all hope.
– Perhaps it was a bower beneath whose leaves
The violets of five seasons re-appear 30
And fade, unseen by any human eye,
Where fairy water-breaks do murmur on
For ever, and I saw the sparkling foam,
And with my cheek on one of those green stones
That, fleeced with moss, beneath the shady trees, 35
Lay round me scattered like a flock of sheep,
I heard the murmur and the murmuring sound,

In that sweet mood when pleasure loves to pay
Tribute to ease, and, of its joy secure,
The heart luxuriates with indifferent things,   40
Wasting its kindliness on stocks and stones,
And on the vacant air. Then up I rose,
And dragged to earth both branch and bough, with crash
And merciless ravage, and the shady nook
Of hazels, and the green and mossy bower   45
Deformed and sullied, patiently gave up
Their quiet being; and unless I now
Confound my present feelings with the past,
Even then, when from the bower I turned away,
Exulting, rich beyond the wealth of kings,   50
I felt a sense of pain when I beheld
The silent trees and the intruding sky.

Then, dearest maiden! move along these shades
In gentleness of heart; with gentle hand
Touch – for there is a spirit in the woods.   55

The Old Cumberland Beggar

A DESCRIPTION

The class of beggars to which the old man here described
belongs, will probably soon be extinct. It consisted of poor, and,
mostly, old and infirm persons, who confined themselves to a
stated round in their neighbourhood, and had certain fixed days
on which, at different houses, they regularly received charity –
sometimes in money, but mostly in provisions.

I saw an aged beggar in my walk,
And he was seated by the highway side
On a low structure of rude masonry
Built at the foot of a huge hill, that they
Who lead their horses down the steep rough road   5
May thence remount at ease. The aged man
Had placed his staff across the broad smooth stone
That overlays the pile, and from a bag
All white with flour, the dole of village dames,

He drew his scraps and fragments, one by one, 10
And scanned them with a fixed and serious look
Of idle computation. In the sun,
Upon the second step of that small pile,
Surrounded by those wild unpeopled hills
He sat, and ate his food in solitude; 15
And ever, scattered from his palsied hand
That still attempting to prevent the waste
Was baffled still, the crumbs in little showers
Fell on the ground, and the small mountain birds,
Not venturing yet to peck their destined meal, 20
Approached within the length of half his staff.

Him from my childhood have I known, and then
He was so old, he seems not older now;
He travels on, a solitary man,
So helpless in appearance, that for him 25
The sauntering horseman-traveller does not throw
With careless hand his alms upon the ground,
But stops, that he may safely lodge the coin
Within the old man's hat; nor quits him so,
But still when he has given his horse the rein 30
Towards the aged beggar turns a look,
Sidelong and half-reverted. She who tends
The toll-gate, when in summer at her door
She turns her wheel, if on the road she sees
The aged beggar coming, quits her work, 35
And lifts the latch for him that he may pass.
The post-boy when his rattling wheels o'ertake
The aged beggar in the woody lane,
Shouts to him from behind, and if perchance
The old man does not change his course, the boy 40
Turns with less noisy wheels to the road-side,
And passes gently by, without a curse
Upon his lips, or anger at his heart.
He travels on, a solitary man,
His age has no companion. On the ground 45
His eyes are turned, and as he moves along,
They move along the ground; and evermore,
Instead of common and habitual sight
Of fields with rural works, of hill and dale,

And the blue sky, one little span of earth   50
Is all his prospect. Thus, from day to day,
Bowbent, his eyes for ever on the ground,
He plies his weary journey, seeing still,
And never knowing that he sees, some straw,
Some scattered leaf, or marks which, in one track,   55
The nails of cart or chariot wheel have left
Impressed on the white road, in the same line,
At distance still the same. Poor traveller!
His staff trails with him; scarcely do his feet
Disturb the summer dust. He is so still   60
In look and motion that the cottage curs,
Ere he have passed the door, will turn away,
Weary of barking at him. Boys and girls,
The vacant and the busy, maids and youths,
And urchins newly breeched all pass him by;   65
Him even the slow-paced waggon leaves behind.

But deem not this man useless. — Statesmen! ye
Who are so restless in your wisdom, ye
Who have a broom still ready in your hands
To rid the world of nuisances; ye proud,   70
Heart-swol'n, while in your pride ye contemplate
Your talents, power, and wisdom, deem him not
A burthen of the earth. 'Tis Nature's law
That none, the meanest of created things,
Of forms created the most vile and brute,   75
The dullest or most noxious, should exist
Divorced from good, a spirit and pulse of good,
A life and soul to every mode of being
Inseparably linked. While thus he creeps
From door to door, the villagers in him   80
Behold a record which together binds
Past deeds and offices of charity
Else unremembered, and so keeps alive
The kindly mood in hearts which lapse of years,
And that half-wisdom half-experience gives   85
Make slow to feel, and by sure steps resign
To selfishness and cold oblivious cares.
Among the farms and solitary huts,
Hamlets, and thinly-scattered villages,

Where'er the aged beggar takes his rounds,   90
The mild necessity of use compels
To acts of love, and habit does the work
Of reason, yet prepares that after joy
Which reason cherishes. And thus the soul,
By that sweet taste of pleasure unpursued,   95
Doth find itself insensibly disposed
To virtue and true goodness. Some there are,
By their good works exalted, lofty minds
And meditative, authors of delight
And happiness, which to the end of time   100
Will live, and spread, and kindle; minds like these,
In childhood, from this solitary being,
This helpless wanderer, have perchance received
(A thing more precious far than all that books
Or the solicitudes of love can do!)   105
That first mild touch of sympathy and thought
In which they found their kindred with a world
Where want and sorrow were. The easy man
Who sits at his own door, and like the pear
Which overhangs his head from the green wall,   110
Feeds in the sunshine; the robust and young,
The prosperous and unthinking, they who live
Sheltered, and flourish in a little grove
Of their own kindred, all behold in him
A silent monitor, which on their minds   115
Must needs impress a transitory thought
Of self-congratulation, to the heart
Of each recalling his peculiar boons,
His charters and exemptions; and perchance,
Though he to no one give the fortitude   120
And circumspection needful to preserve
His present blessings, and to husband up
The respite of the season, he, at least —
And 'tis no vulgar service — makes them felt.

Yet further. Many, I believe, there are   125
Who live a life of virtuous decency:
Men who can hear the Decalogue and feel
No self-reproach, who of the moral law
Established in the land where they abide

Are strict observers, and not negligent,   130
Meanwhile, in any tenderness of heart
Or act of love to those with whom they dwell,
Their kindred, and the children of their blood.
Praise be to such, and to their slumbers peace!
– But of the poor man ask, the abject poor,   135
Go and demand of him, if there be here,
In this cold abstinence from evil deeds,
And these inevitable charities,
Wherewith to satisfy the human soul.
No – man is dear to man: the poorest poor   140
Long for some moments in a weary life
When they can know and feel that they have been
Themselves the fathers and the dealers out
Of some small blessings, have been kind to such
As needed kindness, for this single cause,   145
That we have all of us one human heart.
Such pleasure is to one kind being known –
My neighbour – when with punctual care, each week,
Duly as Friday comes, though pressed herself
By her own wants, she from her chest of meal   150
Takes one unsparing handful for the scrip
Of this old mendicant, and from her door
Returning with exhilarated heart,
Sits by her fire and builds her hope in heaven.

Then let him pass, a blessing on his head!   155
And while, in that vast solitude to which
The tide of things has led him, he appears
To breathe and live but for himself alone,
Unblamed, uninjured, let him bear about
The good which the benignant law of heaven   160
Has hung around him, and, while life is his,
Still let him prompt the unlettered villagers
To tender offices and pensive thoughts.
Then let him pass, a blessing on his head!
And, long as he can wander, let him breathe   165
The freshness of the valleys, let his blood
Struggle with frosty air and winter snows,
And let the chartered wind that sweeps the heath
Beat his grey locks against his withered face.

Reverence the hope whose vital anxiousness 170
Gives the last human interest to his heart.
May never house, misnamed of industry,
Make him a captive; for that pent-up din,
Those life-consuming sounds that clog the air,
Be his the natural silence of old age. 175
Let him be free of mountain solitudes,
And have around him, whether heard or not,
The pleasant melody of woodland birds.
Few are his pleasures; if his eyes, which now
Have been so long familiar with the earth, 180
No more behold the horizontal sun
Rising or setting, let the light at least
Find a free entrance to their languid orbs.
And let him, where and when he will, sit down
Beneath the trees, or by the grassy bank 185
Of high-way side, and with the little birds
Share his chance-gathered meal, and finally,
As in the eye of Nature he has lived,
So in the eye of Nature let him die.

A Poet's Epitaph

Art thou a Statesman, in the van
Of public business trained and bred?
— First learn to love one living man;
Then may'st thou think upon the dead.

A Lawyer art thou? — draw not nigh; 5
Go, carry to some other place
The hardness of thy coward eye,
The falsehood of thy sallow face.

Art thou a man of purple cheer?
A rosy man, right plump to see? 10
Approach; yet Doctor, not too near:
This grave no cushion is for thee.

Art thou a man of gallant pride,
A Soldier, and no man of chaff?
Welcome! – but lay thy sword aside,   15
And lean upon a peasant's staff.

Physician art thou? One, all eyes,
Philosopher! a fingering slave,
One that would peep and botanise
Upon his mother's grave?   20

Wrapped closely in thy sensual fleece,
O turn aside, and take, I pray,
That he below may rest in peace,
Thy pin-point of a soul away!

A Moralist perchance appears,   25
Led, heaven knows how! to this poor sod,
And he has neither eyes nor ears –
Himself his world, and his own God;

One to whose smooth-rubbed soul can cling
Nor form nor feeling great nor small,
A reasoning, self-sufficing thing,   30
An intellectual All in All!

Shut close the door! press down the latch;
Sleep in thy intellectual crust;
Nor lose ten tickings of thy watch   35
Near this unprofitable dust.

But who is he with modest looks,
And clad in homely russet brown?
He murmurs near the running brooks
A music sweeter than their own.   40

He is retired as noontide dew,
Or fountain in a noonday grove;
And you must love him, ere to you
He will seem worthy of your love.

The outward shows of sky and earth,   45
Of hill and valley he has viewed,
And impulses of deeper birth
Have come to him in solitude.

In common things that round us lie
Some random truths he can impart –   50
The harvest of a quiet eye
That broods and sleeps on his own heart.

But he is weak, both man and boy –
Hath been an idler in the land:
Contented if he might enjoy   55
The things which others understand.

Come hither in thy hour of strength;
Come, weak as is a breaking wave!
Here stretch thy body at full length,
Or build thy house upon this grave.   60

From *Poems on the Naming of Places*

IV

A narrow girdle of rough stones and crags,
A rude and natural causeway, interposed
Between the water and a winding slope
Of copse and thicket, leaves the eastern shore
Of Grasmere safe in its own privacy.   5
And there, myself and two beloved friends,
One calm September morning, ere the mist
Had altogether yielded to the sun,
Sauntered on this retired and difficult way.
– Ill suits the road with one in haste, but we   10
Played with our time; and, as we strolled along,
It was our occupation to observe
Such objects as the waves had tossed ashore –
Feather, or leaf, or weed, or withered bough –
Each on the other heaped along the line   15
Of the dry wreck. And in our vacant mood,

Not seldom did we stop to watch some tuft
Of dandelion seed or thistle's beard,
Which, seeming lifeless half, and half impelled
By some internal feeling, skimmed along   20
Close to the surface of the lake that lay
Asleep in a dead calm, ran closely on
Along the dead calm lake, now here, now there,
In all its sportive wanderings all the while
Making report of an invisible breeze   25
That was its wings, its chariot, and its horse,
Its very playmate, and its moving soul.
– And often, trifling with a privilege
Alike indulged to all, we paused, one now,
And now the other, to point out, perchance   30
To pluck, some flower or water-weed, too fair
Either to be divided from the place
On which it grew, or to be left alone
To its own beauty. Many such there are,
Fair ferns and flowers, and chiefly that tall plant   35
So stately, of the Queen Osmunda named –
Plant lovelier in its own retired abode
On Grasmere's beach, than Naid by the side
Of Grecian brook, or Lady of the Mere
Sole-sitting by the shores of old romance.   40
– So fared we that sweet morning. From the fields
Meanwhile, a noise was heard – the busy mirth
Of reapers, men and women, boys and girls.
Delighted much to listen to those sounds,
And in the fashion which I have described,   45
Feeding unthinking fancies, we advanced
Along the indented shore; when suddenly,
Through a thin veil of glittering haze, we saw
Before us on a point of jutting land
The tall and upright figure of a man   50
Attired in peasant's garb, who stood alone
Angling beside the margin of the lake.
That way we turned our steps; nor was it long,
Ere making ready comments on the sight
Which then we saw, with one and the same voice   55
We all cried out, that he must be indeed
An idle man who thus could lose a day

Of the mid harvest, when the labourer's hire
Is ample, and some little might be stored
Wherewith to cheer him in the winter time.   60
Thus talking of that peasant we approached
Close to the spot where with his rod and line
He stood alone; whereat he turned his head
To greet us, and we saw a man worn down
By sickness – gaunt and lean, with sunken cheeks   65
And wasted limbs, his legs so long and lean
That for my single self I looked at them,
Forgetful of the body they sustained.
Too weak to labour in the harvest field,
The man was using his best skill to gain   70
A pittance from the dead unfeeling lake
That knew not of his wants. I will not say
What thoughts immediately were ours, nor how
The happy idleness of that sweet morn,
With all its lovely images, was changed   75
To serious musing and to self-reproach.
Nor did we fail to see within ourselves
What need there is to be reserved in speech,
And temper all our thoughts with charity.
– Therefore, unwilling to forget that day,   80
My friend, myself, and she who then received
The same admonishment, have called the place
By a memorial name, uncouth indeed
As e'er by mariner was giv'n to bay
Or foreland on a new-discovered coast,   85
And POINT RASH-JUDGEMENT is the name it bears.

Michael

If from the public way you turn your steps
Up the tumultuous brook of Greenhead Gill,
You will suppose that with an upright path
Your feet must struggle; in such bold ascent
The pastoral mountains front you, face to face.　　　　5
But courage! for beside that boisterous brook
The mountains have all opened out themselves,
And made a hidden valley of their own.
No habitation there is seen, but such
As journey thither find themselves alone　　　　10
With a few sheep, with rocks and stones, and kites
That overhead are sailing in the sky.

It is in truth an utter solitude,
Nor should I have made mention of this dell
But for one object which you might pass by –　　　　15
Might see and notice not. Beside the brook
There is a straggling heap of unhewn stones,
And to that place a story appertains,
Which, though it be ungarnished with events,
It is unfit, I deem, for the fireside　　　　20
Or for the summer shade. It was the first,
The earliest of those tales that spake to me
Of shepherds, dwellers in the valleys – men
Whom I already loved, not verily
For their own sakes, but for the fields and hills　　　　25
Where was their occupation and abode.
And hence this tale, while I was yet a boy,
Careless of books, yet having felt the power
Of Nature, by the gentle agency
Of natural objects led me on to feel　　　　30
For passions that were not my own, and think
At random and imperfectly indeed
On man, the heart of man, and human life.
Therefore, although it be a history
Homely and rude, I will relate the same　　　　35

For the delight of a few natural hearts,
And with yet fonder feeling for the sake
Of youthful poets who among these hills
Will be my second self when I am gone.

Upon the forest-side in Grasmere vale   40
There dwelt a shepherd – Michael was his name:
An old man, stout of heart and strong of limb.
His bodily frame had been from youth to age
Of an unusual strength; his mind was keen,
Intense, and frugal, apt for all affairs,   45
And in his shepherd's calling he was prompt
And watchful more than ordinary men.
Hence he had learned the meaning of all winds,
Of blasts of every tone, and often-times
When others heeded not, he heard the south   50
Make subterraneous music, like the noise
Of bagpipers on distant Highland hills.
The shepherd, at such warning, of his flock
Bethought him, and he to himself would say,
'The winds are now devising work for me!'   55
And truly at all times the storm that drives
The traveller to a shelter summoned him
Up to the mountains: he had been alone
Amid the heart of many thousand mists
That came to him and left him on the heights.   60
So lived he till his eightieth year was passed.

And grossly that man errs who should suppose
That the green valleys, and the streams and rocks,
Were things indifferent to the shepherd's thoughts.
Fields, where with cheerful spirits he had breathed   65
The common air, the hills which he so oft
Had climbed with vigorous steps, which had impressed
So many incidents upon his mind
Of hardship, skill or courage, joy or fear,
Which like a book preserved the memory   70
Of the dumb animals whom he had saved,
Had fed or sheltered, linking to such acts,
So grateful in themselves, the certainty
Of honourable gains – these fields, these hills,

Which were his living being even more   75
Than his own blood (what could they less?) had
        laid
Strong hold on his affections, were to him
A pleasurable feeling of blind love,
The pleasure which there is in life itself.

He had not passed his days in singleness.   80
He had a wife, a comely matron – old,
Though younger than himself full twenty years.
She was a woman of a stirring life,
Whose heart was in her house. Two wheels she had
Of antique form – this, large for spinning wool,   85
That, small for flax – and if one wheel had rest
It was because the other was at work.
The pair had but one inmate in their house,
An only child, who had been born to them
When Michael telling o'er his years began   90
To deem that he was old – in shepherd's phrase,
With one foot in the grave. This only son,
With two brave sheep dogs tried in many a storm
(The one of an inestimable worth),
Made all their household. I may truly say   95
That they were as a proverb in the vale
For endless industry. When day was gone,
And from their occupations out of doors
The son and father were come home, even then
Their labour did not cease, unless when all   100
Turned to their cleanly supper-board, and there
Each with a mess of pottage and skimmed milk
Sat round their basket piled with oaten cakes
And their plain home-made cheese. Yet when their
        meal
Was ended, Luke (for so the son was named)   105
And his old father both betook themselves
To such convenient work as might employ
Their hands by the fireside – perhaps to card
Wool for the housewife's spindle, or repair
Some injury done to sickle, flail, or scythe,   110
Or other implement of house or field.

Down from the ceiling by the chimney's edge
(Which in our ancient uncouth country style
Did with a huge projection overbrow
Large space beneath) as duly as the light 115
Of day grew dim, the housewife hung a lamp,
An aged utensil which had performed
Service beyond all others of its kind.
Early at evening did it burn, and late,
Surviving comrade of uncounted hours 120
Which going by from year to year had found
And left the couple neither gay perhaps
Nor cheerful, yet with objects and with hopes
Living a life of eager industry.
And now, when Luke was in his eighteenth year, 125
There by the light of this old lamp they sat,
Father and son, while late into the night
The housewife plied her own peculiar work,
Making the cottage through the silent hours
Murmur as with the sound of summer flies. 130
Not with a waste of words, but for the sake
Of pleasure which I know that I shall give
To many living now, I of this lamp
Speak thus minutely, for there are no few
Whose memories will bear witness to my tale. 135
The light was famous in its neighbourhood,
And was a public symbol of the life
The thrifty pair had lived. For, as it chanced,
Their cottage on a plot of rising ground
Stood single, with large prospect north and south, 140
High into Easedale, up to Dunmal-Raise,
And westward to the village near the lake.
And from this constant light so regular
And so far-seen, the house itself by all
Who dwelt within the limits of the vale, 145
Both old and young, was named 'The Evening Star'.

Thus living on through such a length of years
The shepherd, if he loved himself, must needs
Have loved his help-mate; but to Michael's heart
This son of his old age was yet more dear – 150
Effect which might perhaps have been produced

By that instinctive tenderness, the same
Blind spirit which is in the blood of all,
Or that a child, more than all other gifts,
Brings hope with it, and forward-looking thoughts,   155
And stirrings of inquietude, when they
By tendency of Nature needs must fail.
From such, and other causes, to the thoughts
Of the old man his only son was now
The dearest object that he knew on earth.   160
Exceeding was the love he bare to him,
His heart and his heart's joy! For oftentimes
Old Michael, while he was a babe in arms,
Had done him female service, not alone
For dalliance and delight, as is the use   165
Of fathers, but with patient mind enforced
To acts of tenderness, and he had rocked
His cradle with a woman's gentle hand.

And in a later time, ere yet the boy
Had put on boy's attire, did Michael love   170
(Albeit of a stern unbending mind)
To have the young one in his sight when he
Had work by his own door, or when he sat
With sheep before him on his shepherd's stool
Beneath that large old oak, which near their door   175
Stood, and from its enormous breadth of shade
Chosen for the shearer's covert from the sun,
Thence in our rustic dialect was called
The Clipping Tree – a name which yet it bears.
There, while they two were sitting in the shade   180
With others round them, earnest all and blithe,
Would Michael exercise his heart with looks
Of fond correction and reproof, bestowed
Upon the child if he disturbed the sheep
By catching at their legs, or with his shouts   185
Scared them while they lay still beneath the shears.
And when by Heaven's good grace the boy grew up
A healthy lad, and carried in his cheek
Two steady roses that were five years old,
Then Michael from a winter coppice cut   190
With his own hand a sapling, which he hooped

With iron, making it throughout in all
Due requisites a perfect shepherd's staff,
And gave it to the boy; wherewith equipped,
He as a watchman oftentimes was placed   195
At gate or gap, to stem or turn the flock,
And to his office prematurely called,
There stood the urchin, as you will divine,
Something between a hindrance and a help,
And for this cause not always, I believe,   200
Receiving from his father hire of praise,
Though nought was left undone which staff, or voice,
Or looks, or threatening gestures, could perform.
But soon as Luke, full ten years old, could stand
Against the mountain blasts, and to the heights,   205
Not fearing toil, nor length of weary ways,
He with his father daily went, and they
Were as companions. Why should I relate
That objects which the shepherd loved before
Were dearer now? – that from the boy there came   210
Feelings and emanations, things which were
Light to the sun and music to the wind,
And that the old man's heart seemed born again?
Thus in his father's sight the boy grew up,
And now when he had reached his eighteenth year,   215
He was his comfort and his daily hope.

While this good household thus were living on
From day to day, to Michael's ear there came
Distressful tidings. Long before the time
Of which I speak, the shepherd had been bound   220
In surety for his brother's son – a man
Of an industrious life and ample means –
But unforeseen misfortunes suddenly
Had pressed upon him, and old Michael now
Was summoned to discharge the forfeiture –   225
A grievous penalty, but little less
Than half his substance. This unlooked-for claim,
At the first hearing, for a moment took
More hope out of his life than he supposed
That any old man ever could have lost.   230

As soon as he had gathered so much strength
That he could look his trouble in the face,
It seemed that his sole refuge was to sell
A portion of his patrimonial fields.
Such was his first resolve; he thought again,   235
And his heart failed him. 'Isabel,' said he,
Two evenings after he had heard the news,
'I have been toiling more than seventy years,
And in the open sunshine of God's love
Have we all lived, yet if these fields of ours   240
Should pass into a stranger's hand, I think
That I could not lie quiet in my grave.
Our lot is a hard lot; the sun itself
Has scarcely been more diligent than I,
And I have lived to be a fool at last   245
To my own family. An evil man
That was, and made an evil choice, if he
Were false to us, and if he were not false,
There are ten thousand to whom loss like this
Had been no sorrow. I forgive him – but   250
'Twere better to be dumb than to talk thus.
When I began, my purpose was to speak
Of remedies, and of a cheerful hope.
Our Luke shall leave us, Isabel; the land
Shall not go from us, and it shall be free –   255
He shall possess it, free as is the wind
That passes over it. We have, thou knowest,
Another kinsman; he will be our friend
In this distress. He is a prosperous man,
Thriving in trade, and Luke to him shall go   260
And with his kinsman's help and his own thrift
He quickly will repair this loss, and then
May come again to us. If here he stay,
What can be done? Where every one is poor,
What can be gained?'   265
                        At this the old man paused
And Isabel sat silent, for her mind
Was busy, looking back into past times.
There's Richard Bateman, thought she to herself;
He was a parish-boy; at the church door
They made a gathering for him – shillings, pence,   270

And halfpennies – wherewith the neighbours bought
A basket, which they filled with pedlar's wares,
And with this basket on his arm the lad
Went up to London, found a master there,
Who out of many chose the trusty boy   275
To go and overlook his merchandise
Beyond the seas, where he grew wondrous rich
And left estates and monies to the poor,
And at his birthplace built a chapel, floored
With marble which he sent from foreign lands.   280
These thoughts, and many others of like sort,
Passed quickly through the mind of Isabel,
And her face brightened. The old man was glad,
And thus resumed: 'Well, Isabel, this scheme
These two days has been meat and drink to me;   285
Far more than we have lost is left us yet.
We have enough – I wish indeed that I
Were younger, but this hope is a good hope.
Make ready Luke's best garments; of the best
Buy for him more, and let us send him forth   290
Tomorrow, or the next day, or tonight –
If he could go, the boy should go tonight.'

Here Michael ceased, and to the fields went forth
With a light heart. The housewife for five days
Was restless morn and night, and all day long   295
Wrought on with her best fingers to prepare
Things needful for the journey of her son.
But Isabel was glad when Sunday came
To stop her in her work, for when she lay
By Michael's side, she for the last two nights   300
Heard him, how he was troubled in his sleep,
And when they rose at morning she could see
That all his hopes were gone. That day at noon
She said to Luke, while they two by themselves
Were sitting at the door: 'Thou must not go;   305
We have no other child but thee to lose,
None to remember – do not go away,
For if thou leave thy father he will die.'
The lad made answer with a jocund voice,
And Isabel, when she had told her fears,

Recovered heart. That evening her best fare
Did she bring forth, and all together sat
Like happy people round a Christmas fire.

Next morning Isabel resumed her work,
And all the ensuing week the house appeared   315
As cheerful as a grove in spring. At length
The expected letter from their kinsman came,
With kind assurances that he would do
His utmost for the welfare of the boy,
To which requests were added that forthwith   320
He might be sent to him. Ten times or more
The letter was read over; Isabel
Went forth to show it to the neighbours round;
Nor was there at that time on English land
A prouder heart than Luke's. When Isabel   325
Had to her house returned the old man said,
'He shall depart to-morrow.' To this word
The housewife answered, talking much of things
Which, if at such short notice he should go,
Would surely be forgotten. But at length   330
She gave consent, and Michael was at ease.

Near the tumultuous brook of Greenhead Gill
In that deep valley, Michael had designed
To build a sheepfold, and before he heard
The tidings of his melancholy loss   335
For this same purpose he had gathered up
A heap of stones, which close to the brook-side
Lay thrown together, ready for the work.
With Luke that evening thitherward he walked,
And soon as they had reached the place he stopped,   340
And thus the old man spake to him: 'My son,
To-morrow thou wilt leave me. With full heart
I look upon thee, for thou art the same
That wert a promise to me ere thy birth,
And all thy life hast been my daily joy.   345
I will relate to thee some little part
Of our two histories; 'twill do thee good
When thou art from me, even if I should speak

Of things thou canst not know of. After thou
First cam'st into the world, as it befalls
To newborn infants, thou didst sleep away   350
Two days, and blessings from thy father's tongue
Then fell upon thee. Day by day passed on,
And still I loved thee with increasing love.
Never to living ear came sweeter sounds   355
Than when I heard thee by our own fire-side
First uttering without words a natural tune –
When thou, a feeding babe, didst in thy joy
Sing at thy mother's breast. Month followed month,
And in the open fields my life was passed,   360
And in the mountains, else I think that thou
Hadst been brought up upon thy father's knees.
But we were playmates, Luke; among these hills,
As well thou knowest, in us the old and young
Have played together – nor with me didst thou   365
Lack any pleasure which a boy can know.'

Luke had a manly heart; but at these words
He sobbed aloud. The old man grasped his hand
And said, 'Nay do not take it so – I see
That these are things of which I need not speak.   370
Even to the utmost I have been to thee
A kind and a good father, and herein
I but repay a gift which I myself
Received at others' hands, for though now old
Beyond the common life of man I still   375
Remember them who loved me in my youth.
Both of them sleep together – here they lived
As all their forefathers had done, and when
At length their time was come, they were not loth
To give their bodies to the family mold.   380
I wished that thou should'st live the life they lived,
But 'tis a long time to look back, my son,
And see so little gain from sixty years.
These fields were burthened when they came to me;
Till I was forty years of age, not more   385
Than half of my inheritance was mine.
I toiled and toiled; God blessed me in my work,
And till these three weeks past the land was free –

It looks as if it never could endure
Another master. Heaven forgive me, Luke,   390
If I judge ill for thee, but it seems good
That thou should'st go.'
                    At this the old man paused,
Then pointing to the stones near which they stood,
Thus after a short silence he resumed:
'This was a work for us, and now, my son,   395
It is a work for me. But, lay one stone –
Here, lay it for me, Luke, with thine own hands –
I for the purpose brought thee to this place.
Nay, boy, be of good hope – we both may live
To see a better day. At eighty-four   400
I still am strong and stout; do thou thy part,
I will do mine. I will begin again
With many tasks that were resigned to thee;
Up to the heights, and in among the storms
Will I without thee go again, and do   405
All works which I was wont to do alone
Before I knew thy face. Heaven bless thee, boy!
Thy heart these two weeks has been beating fast
With many hopes. It should be so – yes, yes,
I knew that thou could'st never have a wish   410
To leave me, Luke – thou hast been bound to me
Only by links of love. When thou art gone
What will be left to us? – but I forget
My purposes. Lay now the corner-stone
As I requested, and hereafter, Luke,   415
When thou art gone away, should evil men
Be thy companions, let this sheepfold be
Thy anchor and thy shield. Amid all fear,
And all temptation, let it be to thee
An emblem of the life thy fathers lived,   420
Who, being innocent, did for that cause
Bestir them in good deeds. Now, fare thee well.
When thou return'st, thou in this place wilt see
A work which is not here. A covenant
'Twill be between us – but whatever fate   425
Befall thee, I shall love thee to the last,
And bear thy memory with me to the grave.'

The shepherd ended here, and Luke stooped down,
And as his father had requested, laid
The first stone of the sheepfold. At the sight   430
The old man's grief broke from him; to his heart
He pressed his son, he kissed him and wept,
And to the house together they returned.
Next morning, as had been resolved, the boy
Began his journey, and when he had reached   435
The public way he put on a bold face,
And all the neighbours as he passed their doors
Came forth with wishes and with farewell prayers
That followed him till he was out of sight.

A good report did from their kinsman come   440
Of Luke and his well-doing, and the boy
Wrote loving letters, full of wondrous news,
Which, as the housewife phrased it, were throughout
The prettiest letters that were ever seen.
Both parents read them with rejoicing hearts.   445
So many months passed on, and once again
The shepherd went about his daily work
With confident and cheerful thoughts; and now,
Sometimes when he could find a leisure hour,
He to that valley took his way, and there   450
Wrought at the sheepfold. Meantime Luke began
To slacken in his duty, and at length
He in the dissolute city gave himself
To evil courses; ignominy and shame
Fell on him, so that he was driven at last   455
To seek a hiding-place beyond the seas.

There is a comfort in the strength of love;
'Twill make a thing endurable which else
Would break the heart: old Michael found it so.
I have conversed with more than one who well   460
Remember the old man, and what he was
Years after he had heard this heavy news.
His bodily frame had been from youth to age
Of an unusual strength. Among the rocks
He went, and still looked up upon the sun,   465
And listened to the wind, and, as before,

Performed all kinds of labour for his sheep
And for the land, his small inheritance.
And to that hollow dell from time to time
Did he repair, to build the fold of which   470
His flock had need. 'Tis not forgotten yet
The pity which was then in every heart
For the old man, and 'tis believed by all
That many and many a day he thither went,
And never lifted up a single stone.   475

There by the sheepfold sometimes was he seen
Sitting alone, with that his faithful dog –
Then old – beside him, lying at his feet.
The length of full seven years from time to time
He at the building of this sheepfold wrought,   480
And left the work unfinished when he died.
Three years, or little more, did Isabel
Survive her husband; at her death the estate
Was sold, and went into a stranger's hand.
The cottage which was named 'The Evening Star'   485
Is gone; the ploughshare has been through the ground
On which it stood. Great changes have been wrought
In all the neighbourhood, yet the oak is left
That grew beside their door, and the remains
Of the unfinished sheepfold may be seen   490
Beside the boisterous brook of Greenhead Gill.

Home at Grasmere

and the 'Prospectus' to *The Recluse*

Once on the brow of yonder hill I stopped,
While I was yet a schoolboy (of what age
I cannot well remember, but the hour
I well remember though the year be gone),
And with a sudden influx overcome   5
At sight of this seclusion, I forgot
My haste – for hasty had my footsteps been,
As boyish my pursuits – and sighing said,
'What happy fortune were it here to live!
And if I thought of dying, if a thought   10
Of mortal separation could come in
With paradise before me, here to die.'
I was no prophet, nor had even a hope,
Scarcely a wish, but one bright pleasing thought,
A fancy in the heart of what might be   15
The lot of others, never could be mine.

    The place from which I looked was soft and green,
Not giddy yet aërial, with a depth
Of vale below, a height of hills above.
Long did I halt; I could have made it even   20
My business and my errand so to halt.
For rest of body 'twas a perfect place,
All that luxurious nature could desire,
But tempting to the spirit; who could look
And not feel motions there? I thought of clouds   25
That sail on winds; of breezes that delight
To play on water, or in endless chase
Pursue each other through the liquid depths
Of grass or corn, over and through and through
In billow after billow evermore;   30
Of sunbeams, shadows, butterflies and birds,
Angels, and wingèd creatures that are lords
Without restraint of all which they behold.
I sate, and, stirred in spirit as I looked,
I seemed to feel such liberty was mine,   35

Such power and joy – but only for this end,
To flit from field to rock, from rock to field,
From shore to island, and from isle to shore,
From open place to covert, from a bed
Of meadow-flowers into a tuft of wood,   40
From high to low, from low to high, yet still
Within the bounds of this huge concave; here
Should be my home, this valley be my world.

     From that time forward was the place to me
As beautiful in thought as it had been   45
When present to my bodily eyes: a haunt
Of my affections, oftentimes in joy
A brighter joy, in sorrow (but of that
I have known little), in such gloom, at least,
Such damp of the gay mind as stood to me   50
In place of sorrow, 'twas a gleam of light –
And now 'tis mine for life! Dear vale,
One of thy lowly dwellings is my home.

     Yes, the realities of life – so cold,
So cowardly, so ready to betray,   55
So stinted in the measure of their grace,
As we report them, doing them much wrong –
Have been to me more bountiful than hope,
Less timid than desire. Oh bold indeed
They have been, bold and bounteous unto me,   60
Who have myself been bold, not wanting trust,
Nor resolution, nor at last the hope
Which is of wisdom, for I feel it is.

     And did it cost so much, and did it ask
Such length of discipline, and could it seem   65
An act of courage, and the thing itself
A conquest? Shame that this was ever so,
Not to the boy or youth, but shame to thee,
Sage man, thou sun in its meridian strength,
Thou flower in its full blow, thou king and crown   70
Of human nature – shame to thee, sage man.
Thy prudence, thy experience, thy desires,
Thy apprehensions, blush thou for them all!

But I am safe – yes, one at least is safe –
What once was deemed so difficult is now   75
Smooth, easy, without obstacle; what once
Did to my blindness seem a sacrifice,
The same is now a choice of the whole heart.
If e'er the acceptance of such dower was deemed
A condescension or a weak indulgence   80
To a sick fancy, it is now an act
Of reason that exultingly aspires.
This solitude is mine; the distant thought
Is fetched out of the heaven in which it was.
The unappropriated bliss hath found   85
An owner, and that owner I am he! –
The lord of this enjoyment is on earth
And in my breast. What wonder if I speak
With fervour, am exalted with the thought
Of my possessions, of my genuine wealth   90
Inward and outward – what I keep, have gained,
Shall gain, must gain – if sound be my belief,
From past and present rightly understood,
That in my day of childhood I was less
The mind of Nature, less, take all in all,   95
Whatever may be lost, than I am now?
For proof behold this valley – and behold
Yon cottage, where with me my Emma dwells.

    Aye, think on that, my heart, and cease to stir;
Pause upon that, and let the breathing frame   100
No longer breathe, but all be satisfied.
Oh, if such silence be not thanks to God
For what hath been bestowed, then where, where then,
Shall gratitude find rest? Mine eyes did ne'er
Rest on a lovely object, nor my mind   105
Take pleasure in the midst of happy thoughts,
But either she whom now I have, who now
Divides with me this loved abode, was there
Or not far off. Where'er my footsteps turned,
Her voice was like a hidden bird that sang;   110
The thought of her was like a flash of light
Or an unseen companionship, a breath
Or fragrance independent of the wind

In all my goings, in the new and old
Of all my meditations – and in this   115
Favorite of all, in this the most of all.
What being, therefore, since the birth of man
Had ever more abundant cause to speak
Thanks, and if music and the power of song
Make him more thankful, then to call on these   120
To aid him, and with these resound his joy?
The boon is absolute: surpassing grace
To me hath been voutchsafed. Among the bowers
Of blissful Eden this was neither given,
Nor could be given – possession of the good   125
Which had been sighed for, antient thought fulfilled,
And dear imaginations realized
Up to their highest measure, yea, and more.

        Embrace me then, ye hills, and close me in;
Now in the clear and open day I feel   130
Your guardianship, I take it to my heart –
'Tis like the solemn shelter of the night.
But I would call thee beautiful, for mild
And soft and gay and beautiful thou art,
Dear valley, having in thy face a smile,   135
Though peaceful, full of gladness. Thou art pleased,
Pleased with thy crags and woody steeps, thy lake,
Its one green island and its winding shores,
The multitude of little rocky hills,
Thy church and cottages of mountain stone –   140
Clustered like stars, some few, but single most,
And lurking dimly in their shy retreats,
Or glancing at each other chearful looks,
Like separated stars with clouds between.
What want we? Have we not perpetual streams,   145
Warm woods and sunny hills, and fresh green fields,
And mountains not less green, and flocks and herds,
And thickets full of songsters, and the voice
Of lordly birds – an unexpected sound
Heard now and then from morn to latest eve   150
Admonishing the man who walks below
Of solitude and silence in the sky?

These have we, and a thousand nooks of earth
Have also these; but nowhere else is found –
Nowhere (or is it fancy?) can be found –   155
The one sensation that is here; 'tis here,
Here as it found its way into my heart
In childhood, here as it abides by day,
By night, here only; or in chosen minds
That take it with them hence, where'er they go.   160
'Tis (but I cannot name it), 'tis the sense
Of majesty and beauty and repose,
A blended holiness of earth and sky,
Something that makes this individual spot,
This small abiding-place of many men,   165
A termination and a last retreat,
A centre, come from whereso'er you will,
A whole without dependence or defect,
Made for itself and happy in itself,
Perfect contentment, unity entire.   170

   Long is it since we met to part no more,
Since I and Emma heard each other's call
And were companions once again, like birds
Which by the intruding fowler had been scared,
Two of a scattered brood that could not bear   175
To live in loneliness; 'tis long since we,
Remembering much and hoping more, found means
To walk abreast, though in a narrow path,
With undivided steps. Our home was sweet –
Could it be less? If we were forced to change,   180
Our home again was sweet; but still – for youth,
Strong as it seems and bold, is inly weak
And diffident – the destiny of life
Remained unfixed, and therefore we were still

[*Seven lines missing*]

We will be free, and, as we mean to live
In culture of divinity and truth,
Will chuse the noblest temple that we know.
Not in mistrust or ignorance of the mind,   195
And of the power she has within herself
To enoble all things, made we this resolve;

Far less from any momentary fit
Of inconsiderate fancy, light and vain;
But that we deemed it wise to take the help   200
Which lay within our reach; and here, we knew,
Help could be found of no mean sort – the spirit
Of singleness and unity and peace.
In this majestic, self-sufficing world,
This all in all of Nature, it will suit,   205
We said, no other [   ] on earth so well,
Simplicity of purpose, love intense,
Ambition not aspiring to the prize
Of outward things, but for the prize within –
Highest ambition. In the daily walks   210
Of business 'twill be harmony and grace
For the perpetual pleasure of the sense,
And for the soul – I do not say too much,
Though much be said – an image for the soul,
A habit of eternity and God.   215

    Nor have we been deceived; thus far the effect
Falls not below the loftiest of our hopes.
Bleak season was it, turbulent and bleak,
When hitherward we journeyed, and on foot,
Through bursts of sunshine and through flying snows,   220
Paced the long vales. How long they were, and yet
How fast that length of way was left behind –
Wensley's long vale and Sedbergh's naked heights.
The frosty wind, as if to make amends
For its keen breath, was aiding to our course   225
And drove us onward like two ships at sea.
Stern was the face of Nature; we rejoiced
In that stern countenance, for our souls had there
A feeling of their strength. The naked trees,
The icy brooks, as on we passed, appeared   230
To question us. 'Whence come ye? To what end?'
They seemed to say. 'What would ye?' said the shower,
'Wild wanderers, whither through my dark domain?'
The sunbeam said, 'Be happy.' They were moved –
All things were moved – they round us as we went,   235
We in the midst of them. And when the trance
Came to us as we stood by Hart-leap Well,

The intimation of the milder day
Which is to come, the fairer world than this,
And raised us up, dejected as we were   240
Among the records of that doleful place
By sorrow for the hunted beast who there
Had yielded up his breath – the awful trance,
The vision of humanity and of God
The mourner, God the sufferer, when the heart   245
Of his poor creatures suffers wrongfully –
Both in the sadness and the joy we found
A promise and an earnest that we twain,
A pair seceding from the common world,
Might in that hallowed spot to which our steps   250
Were tending, in that individual nook,
Might even thus early for ourselves secure,
And in the midst of these unhappy times,
A portion of the blessedness which love
And knowledge will, we trust, hereafter give   255
To all the vales of earth and all mankind.

    Thrice hath the winter moon been filled with light
Since that dear day when Grasmere, our dear vale,
Received us. Bright and solemn was the sky
That faced us with a passionate welcoming   260
And led us to our threshold, to a home
Within a home, what was to be, and soon,
Our love within a love. Then darkness came,
Composing darkness, with its quiet load
Of full contentment, in a little shed,   265
Disturbed, uneasy in itself, as seemed,
And wondering at its new inhabitants.
It loves us now – this vale so beautiful
Begins to love us. By a sullen storm,
Two months unwearied of severest storm,   270
It put the temper of our minds to proof,
And found us faithful through the gloom, and heard
The poet mutter his prelusive songs
With chearful heart, an unknown voice of joy
Among the silence of the woods and hills,   275
Silent to any gladsomeness of sound
With all their shepherds. But the gates of Spring

Are opened; churlish Winter hath given leave
That she should entertain for this one day –
Perhaps for many genial days to come –   280
His guests and make them happy. They are pleased,
But most of all, the birds that haunt the flood,
With the mild summons, inmates though they be
Of Winter's household. They are jubilant
This day, who drooped, or seemed to droop, so long;   285
They shew their pleasure, and shall I do less?
Happier of happy though I be, like them
I cannot take possession of the sky,
Mount with a thoughtless impulse, and wheel there,
One of a mighty multitude whose way   290
And motion is a harmony and dance
Magnificent. Behold them, how they shape
Orb after orb their course still round and round
Above the area of the lake, their own
Adopted region, girding it about   295
In wanton repetition, yet therewith –
With that large circle evermore renewed –
Hundreds of curves and circlets, high and low,
Backwards and forwards, progress intricate,
As if one spirit was in all and swayed   300
Their indefatigable flight. 'Tis done!
Ten times or more I fancied it had ceased,
And lo, the vanished company again
Ascending – list, again I hear their wings –
Faint, faint at first, and then an eager sound,   305
Passed in a moment, and as faint again.
They tempt the sun to sport among their plumes;
They tempt the water and the gleaming ice
To shew them a fair image. 'Tis themselves,
Their own fair forms upon the glimmering plain,   310
Painted more soft and fair as they descend
Almost to touch, then up again aloft,
Up with a sally and a flash of speed
As if they scorned both resting-place and rest.
Spring – for this day belongs to thee – rejoice!   315
Not upon me alone hath been bestowed –
Me, blessed with many onward-looking thoughts –
The sunshine and mild air. Oh, surely these

Are grateful: not the happy quires of love,
Thine own peculiar family, sweet Spring,   320
That sport among green leaves, so blithe a train.

    But two are missing—two, a lonely pair
Of milk-white swans. Ah, why are they not here?
These above all, ah, why are they not here
To share in this day's pleasure? From afar   325
They came, like Emma and myself, to live
Together here in peace and solitude,
Chusing this valley, they who had the choice
Of the whole world. We saw them day by day,
Through those two months of unrelenting storm,   330
Conspicuous in the centre of the lake,
Their safe retreat. We knew them well—I guess
That the whole valley knew them—but to us
They were more dear than may be well believed,
Not only for their beauty and their still   335
And placid way of life and faithful love
Inseparable, not for these alone,
But that their state so much resembled ours,
They also having chosen this abode —
They strangers, and we strangers—they a pair,   340
And we a solitary pair like them.
They should not have departed! Many days
I've looked for them in vain, nor on the wing
Have seen them, nor in that small open space
Of blue unfrozen water, where they lodged   345
And lived so long in quiet, side by side.
Companions, brethren, consecrated friends,
Shall we behold them yet another year
Surviving, they for us and we for them,
And neither pair be broken? Nay, perchance   350
It is too late already for such hope;
The shepherd may have seized the deadly tube
And parted them, incited by a prize
Which, for the sake of those he loves at home,
And for the lamb upon the mountain-tops,   355
He should have spared. Or haply both are gone —
One death—and that were mercy—given to both.

I cannot look upon this favoured vale
But that I seem, by harbouring this thought,
To wrong it, such unworthy recompense   360
Imagining, of confidence so pure.
Ah, if I wished to follow where the sight
Of all that is before my eyes, the voice
Which is as a presiding spirit here,
Would lead me, I should say unto myself,   365
'They who are dwellers in this holy place
Must needs themselves be hallowed.' They require
No benediction from the stranger's lips,
For they are blessed already. None would give
The greeting 'Peace be with you' unto them,   370
For peace they have – it cannot but be theirs –
And mercy and forbearance. Nay, not these,
There is no call for these – that office love
Performs, and charity beyond the bounds
Of charity – an overflowing love,   375
Not for the creature only, but for all
Which is around them; love for every thing
Which in this happy valley we behold.

          Thus do we soothe ourselves, and when the thought
Is passed, we blame it not for having come.   380
What if I floated down a pleasant stream
And now am landed, and the motion gone,
Shall I reprove myself? Ah no, the stream
Is flowing and will never cease to flow,
And I shall float upon that stream again.   385
By such forgetfulness the soul becomes
Words cannot say how beautiful. Then hail,
Hail to the visible presence! Hail to thee,
Delightful valley, habitation fair,
And to whatever else of outward form   390
Can give us inward help, can purify
And elevate and harmonize and soothe,
And steal away and for a while deceive
And lap in pleasing rest, and bear us on
Without desire in full complacency,   395
Contemplating perfection absolute
And entertained as in a placid sleep.

But not betrayed by tenderness of mind
That feared, or wholly overlooked, the truth
Did we come hither, with romantic hope   400
To find in midst of so much loveliness
Love, perfect love, of so much majesty
A like majestic frame of mind in those
Who here abide – the persons like the place.
Nor from such hope, or aught of such belief,   405
Hath issued any portion of the joy
Which I have felt this day. An awful voice,
'Tis true, I in my walks have often heard,
Sent from the mountains or the sheltered fields,
Shout after shout, reiterated whoop   410
In manner of a bird that takes delight
In answering to itself, or like a hound
Single at chace among the lonely woods –
A human voice (how awful in the gloom
Of coming night, when sky is dark, and earth   415
Not dark, nor yet enlightened, but by snow
Made visible) amid the noise of winds
And bleatings manifold of sheep that know
Their summons and are gathering round for food –
That voice, the same, the very same, that breath   420
Which was an utterance awful as the wind,
Or any sound the mountains ever heard!
That shepherd's voice, it may have reached mine ear
Debased and under prophanation, made
An organ for the sounds articulate   425
Of ribaldry and blasphemy and wrath,
Where drunkenness hath kindled senseless frays.
I came not dreaming of unruffled life,
Untainted manners; born among the hills,
Bred also there, I wanted not a scale   430
To regulate my hopes; pleased with the good,
I shrink not from the evil in disgust,
Or with immoderate pain. I look for man,
The common creature of the brotherhood,
But little differing from the man elsewhere   435
For selfishness and envy and revenge
(Ill neighbourhood! – folly that this should be),
Flattery and double-dealing, strife and wrong.

Yet is it something gained – it is in truth
A mighty gain – that labour here preserves   440
His rosy face, a servant only here
Of the fireside or of the open field,
A freeman, therefore sound and unenslaved;
That extreme penury is here unknown,
And cold and hunger's abject wretchedness,   445
Mortal to body and the heaven-born mind;
That they who want, are not too great a weight
For those who can relieve. Here may the heart
Breathe in the air of fellow-suffering
Dreadless, as in a kind of fresher breeze   450
Of her own native element – the hand
Be ready and unwearied, without plea,
From tasks too frequent and beyond its powers,
For languor or indifference or despair.
And as these lofty barriers break the force   455
Of winds (this deep vale as it doth in part
Conceal us from the storm) so here there is
A power and a protection for the mind –
Dispensed indeed to other solitudes
Favoured by noble privilege like this,   460
Where kindred independence of estate
Is prevalent, where he who tills the field,
He, happy man, is master of the field
And treads the mountain which his father trod.
Hence, and from other local circumstance,   465
In this enclosure many of the old
Substantial virtues have a firmer tone
Than in the base and ordinary world.

Yon cottage, would that it could tell a part
Of its own story; thousands might give ear –   470
Might hear it, and blush deep. There few years past
In this his native valley dwelt a man,
The master of a little plot of ground,
A man of mild deportment and discourse,
A scholar also (as the phrase is here),   475
For he drew much delight from those few books
That lay within his reach, and for this cause
Was by his fellow-dalesmen honoured more.

A shepherd and a tiller of the ground,
Studious withal, and healthy in his frame   480
Of body, and of just and placid mind,
He with his consort and his children saw
Days that were seldom touched by petty strife,
Years safe from large misfortune – long maintained
That course which men the wisest and most pure   485
Might look on with entire complacency.
Yet in himself and near him were there faults
At work to undermine his happiness
By little and by little. Active, prompt,
And lively was the housewife – in the vale   490
None more industrious – but her industry
Was of that kind, 'tis said, which tended more
To splendid neatness, to a shewy, trim,
And overlaboured purity of house,
Than to substantial thrift. He, on his part,   495
Generous and easy-minded, was not free
From carelessness, and thus in course of time
These joint infirmities, combined perchance
With other cause less obvious, brought decay
Of worldly substance and distress of mind,   500
Which to a thoughtful man was hard to shun,
And which he could not cure. A blooming girl
Served them, an inmate of the house. Alas!
Poor now in tranquil pleasure, he gave way
To thoughts of troubled pleasure; he became   505
A lawless suitor of the maid, and she
Yielded unworthily. Unhappy man –
That which he had been weak enough to do
Was misery in remembrance; he was stung,
Stung by his inward thoughts, and by the smiles   510
Of wife and children stung to agony.
His temper urged him not to seek relief
Amid the noise of revellers, nor from draught
Of lonely stupefaction; he himself –
A rational and suffering man – himself   515
Was his own world, without a resting-place.
Wretched at home, he had no peace abroad,
Ranged through the mountains, slept upon the earth,
Asked comfort of the open air, and found

No quiet in the darkness of the night,   520
No pleasure in the beauty of the day.
His flock he slighted; his paternal fields
Were as a clog to him, whose spirit wished
To fly, but whither? And yon gracious church,
That has a look so full of peace and hope   525
And love – benignant mother of the vale,
How fair amid her brood of cottages! –
She was to him a sickness and reproach.
I speak, conjecturing from the little known
The much that to the last remained unknown,   530
But this is sure: he died of his own grief –
He could not bear the weight of his own shame.

    That ridge, which elbowing from the mountain-side
Carries into the plain its rocks and woods,
Conceals a cottage where a father dwells   535
In widowhood, whose life's co-partner died
Long since, and left him solitary prop
Of many helpless children. I begin
With words which might be prelude to a tale
Of sorrow and dejection, but I feel –   540
Though in the midst of sadness, as might seem –
No sadness, when I think of what mine eyes
Have seen in that delightful family.
Bright garland make they for their father's brows,
Those six fair daughters, budding yet – not one,   545
Not one of all the band, a full-blown flower!
Go to the dwelling: there thou shalt have proof
That He who takes away, yet takes not half
Of what He seems to take, or gives it back
Not to our prayer, but far beyond our prayer;   550
He gives it, the boon-produce of a soil
Which Hope hath never watered. Thou shalt see
A house, which at small distance will appear
In no distinction to have passed beyond
Its fellows – will appear, like them, to have grown   555
Out of the native rock – but nearer view
Will shew it not so grave in outward mien
And soberly arrayed as for the most
Are these rude mountain-dwellings (Nature's care,
Mere friendless Nature's), but a studious work   560

Of many fancies and of many hands,
A plaything and a pride; for such the air
And aspect which the little spot maintains
In spite of lonely winter's nakedness.
They have their jasmine resting on the porch,   565
Their rose-trees, strong in health, that will be soon
Roof-high; and here and there the garden-wall
Is topped with single stones, a shewy file
Curious for shape or hue – some round, like balls,
Worn smooth and round by fretting of the brook   570
From which they have been gathered, others bright
And sparry, the rough scatterings of the hills.
These ornaments the cottage chiefly owes
To one, a hardy girl, who mounts the rocks
(Such is her choice; she fears not the bleak wind),   575
Companion of her father – does for him
Where'er he wanders in his pastoral course
The service of a boy, and with delight
More keen, and prouder daring. Yet hath she
Within the garden, like the rest, a bed   580
For her own flowers or favorite herbs, a space
Holden by sacred charter; and I guess
She also helped to frame that tiny plot
Of garden-ground which one day 'twas my chance
To find among the woody rocks that rise   585
Above the house, a slip of smoother earth
Planted with gooseberry-bushes – and in one,
Right in the centre of the prickly shrub,
A mimic bird's-nest, fashioned by the hand,
Was stuck, a staring thing of twisted hay,   590
And one quaint fir-tree towered above the whole.
But in the darkness of the night, then most
This dwelling charms me; covered by the gloom
Then, heedless of good manners, I stop short
And (who could help it?) feed by stealth my sight   595
With prospect of the company within,
Laid open through the blazing window. There
I see the eldest daughter at her wheel,
Spinning amain, as if to overtake
She knows not what, or teaching in her turn   600
Some little novice of the sisterhood
That skill or this, or other household work

Which from her father's honored hands, herself,
While she was yet a little one, had learned.
Mild man – he is not gay; but they are gay,   605
And the whole house is filled with gaiety.

    From yonder grey stone that stands alone
Close to the foaming stream, look up and see,
Not less than half way up the mountain-side,
A dusky spot, a little grove of firs –   610
And seems still smaller than it is. The dame
Who dwells below, she told me that this grove,
Just six weeks younger than her eldest boy,
Was planted by her husband and herself
For a convenient shelter, which in storm   615
Their sheep might draw to. 'And they know it well,'
Said she, 'for thither do we bear them food
In time of heavy snow.' She then began
In fond obedience to her private thoughts
To speak of her dead husband. Is there not   620
An art, a music, and a stream of words
That shall be life, the acknowledged voice of life –
Shall speak of what is done among the fields,
Done truly there, or felt, of solid good
And real evil, yet be sweet withal,   625
More grateful, more harmonious than the breath,
The idle breath of sweetest pipe attuned
To pastoral fancies? Is there such a stream,
Pure and unsullied, flowing from the heart
With motions of true dignity and grace –   630
Or must we seek these things where man is not?
Methinks I could repeat in tuneful verse,
Delicious as the gentlest breeze that sounds
Through that aërial fir-grove, could preserve
Some portion of its human history   635
As gathered from that matron's lips, and tell
Of tears that have been shed at sight of it,
And moving dialogues between this pair,
Who in the prime of wedlock with joint hands
Did plant this grove, now flourishing while they   640
No longer flourish – he entirely gone,
She withering in her loneliness. Be this

A task above my skill; the silent mind
Has its own treasures, and I think of these,
Love what I see, and honour humankind.   645

   No, we are not alone; we do not stand,
My Emma, here misplaced and desolate,
Loving what no one cares for but ourselves.
We shall not scatter through the plains and rocks
Of this fair vale and o'er its spatious heights   650
Unprofitable kindliness, bestowed
On objects unaccustomed to the gifts
Of feeling, that were cheerless and forlorn
But few weeks past, and would be so again
If we were not. We do not tend a lamp   655
Whose lustre we alone participate,
Which is dependent upon us alone,
Mortal though bright, a dying, dying flame.
Look where we will, some human heart has been
Before us with its offering; not a tree   660
Sprinkles these little pastures, but the same
Hath furnished matter for a thought, perchance
To some one is as a familiar friend.
Joy spreads and sorrow spreads; and this whole
    vale,
Home of untutored shepherds as it is,   665
Swarms with sensation, as with gleams of sunshine,
Shadows or breezes, scents or sounds. Nor deem
These feelings – though subservient more than ours
To every day's demand for daily bread,
And borrowing more their spirit and their shape   670
From self-respecting interests – deem them not
Unworthy therefore and unhallowed. No,
They lift the animal being, do themselves
By Nature's kind and ever present aid
Refine the selfishness from which they spring,   675
Redeem by love the individual sense
Of anxiousness with which they are combined.
Many are pure, the best of them are pure;
The best, and these, remember, most abound,
Are fit associates of the worthiest joy,   680
Joy of the highest and the purest minds.

They blend with it congenially; meanwhile,
Calmly they breathe their own undying life,
Lowly and unassuming as it is,
Through this, their mountain sanctuary (long,   685
Oh long may it remain inviolate!),
Diffusing health and sober chearfulness,
And giving to the moments as they pass
Their little boons of animating thought,
That sweeten labour, make it seem and feel   690
To be no arbitrary weight imposed,
But a glad function natural to man.

   Fair proof of this, newcomer though I be,
Already have I seen; the inward frame,
Though slowly opening, opens every day.   695
Nor am I less delighted with the show
As it unfolds itself, now here, now there,
Than is the passing traveller, when his way
Lies through some region then first trod by him
(Say this fair valley's self), when low-hung mists   700
Break up and are beginning to recede.
How pleased he is to hear the murmuring streams,
The many voices, from he knows not where,
To have about him, which way e'er he goes,
Something on every side concealed from view,   705
In every quarter some thing visible,
Half seen or wholly, lost and found again —
Alternate progress and impediment,
And yet a growing prospect in the main.

   Such pleasure now is mine, and what if I —   710
Herein less happy than the traveller —
Am sometimes forced to cast a painful look
Upon unwelcome things, which unawares
Reveal themselves? Not therefore is my mind
Depressed, nor do I fear what is to come;   715
But confident, enriched at every glance,
The more I see the more is my delight.
Truth justifies herself; and as she dwells
With Hope, who would not follow where she leads?

Nor let me overlook those other loves   720
Where no fear is, those humbler sympathies
That have to me endeared the quietness
Of this sublime retirement. I begin
Already to inscribe upon my heart
A liking for the small grey horse that bears   725
The paralytic man; I know the ass
On which the cripple, in the quarry maimed,
Rides to and fro: I know them and their ways.
The famous sheep-dog, first in all the vale,
Though yet to me a stranger, will not be   730
A stranger long; nor will the blind man's guide,
Meek and neglected thing, of no renown.
Whoever lived a winter in one place,
Beneath the shelter of one cottage-roof,
And has not had his red-breast or his wren?   735
I have them both; and I shall have my thrush
In spring-time, and a hundred warblers more;
And if the banished eagle pair return,
Helvellyn's eagles, to their antient hold,
Then shall I see, shall claim with those two birds   740
Acquaintance, as they soar amid the heavens.
The owl that gives the name to Owlet-crag
Have I heard shouting, and he soon will be
A chosen one of my regards. See there,
The heifer in yon little croft belongs   745
To one who holds it dear; with duteous care
She reared it, and in speaking of her charge
I heard her scatter once a word or two,
A term domestic, yea, and motherly,
She being herself a mother. Happy beast,   750
If the caresses of a human voice
Can make it so, and care of human hands.

    And ye, as happy under Nature's care,
Strangers to me and all men, or at least
Strangers to all particular amity,   755
All intercourse of knowledge or of love
That parts the individual from the kind;
Whether in large communities ye dwell
From year to year, not shunning man's abode,

A settled residence, or be from far,   760
Wild creatures, and of many homes, that come
The gift of winds, and whom the winds again
Take from us at your pleasure – yet shall ye
Not want for this, your own subordinate place,
According to your claim, an underplace   765
In my affections. Witness the delight
With which erewhile I saw that multitude
Wheel through the sky and see them now at rest,
Yet not at rest, upon the glassy lake.
They cannot rest – they gambol like young whelps,   770
Active as lambs and overcome with joy;
They try all frolic motions, flutter, plunge,
And beat the passive water with their wings.
Too distant are they for plain view, but lo!
Those little fountains, sparkling in the sun,   775
Which tell what they are doing, which rise up,
First one and then another silver spout,
As one or other takes the fit of glee –
Fountains and spouts, yet rather in the guise
Of plaything fire-works, which on festal nights   780
Hiss, hiss about the feet of wanton boys.
How vast the compass of this theatre,
Yet nothing to be seen but lovely pomp
And silent majesty. The birch-tree woods
Are hung with thousand thousand diamond drops   785
Of melted hoar-frost, every tiny knot
In the bare twigs, each little budding-place
Cased with its several bead; what myriads there
Upon one tree, while all the distant grove
That rises to the summit of the steep   790
Is like a mountain built of silver light!
See yonder the same pageant, and again
Behold the universal imagery
At what a depth, deep in the lake below.
Admonished of the days of love to come,   795
The raven croaks and fills the sunny air
With a strange sound of genial harmony;
And in and all about that playful band,
Incapable although they be of rest,
And in their fashion very rioters,   800

There is a stillness, and they seem to make
Calm revelry in that their calm abode.
I leave them to their pleasure, and I pass,
Pass with a thought the life of the whole year
That is to come – the throngs of mountain flowers   805
And lillies that will dance upon the lake.

   Then boldly say that solitude is not
Where these things are: he truly is alone,
He of the multitude, whose eyes are doomed
To hold a vacant commerce day by day   810
With that which he can neither know nor love –
Dead things, to him thrice dead – or worse than this,
With swarms of life, and worse than all, of men,
His fellow men, that are to him no more
Than to the forest hermit are the leaves   815
That hang aloft in myriads – nay, far less,
Far less for aught that comforts or defends
Or lulls or chears. Society is here:
The true community, the noblest frame
Of many into one incorporate;   820
That must be looked for here; paternal sway,
One household under God for high and low,
One family and one mansion; to themselves
Appropriate, and divided from the world
As if it were a cave, a multitude   825
Human and brute, possessors undisturbed
Of this recess, their legislative hall,
Their temple, and their glorious dwelling-place.

   Dismissing therefore all Arcadian dreams,
All golden fancies of the golden age,   830
The bright array of shadowy thoughts from times
That were before all time, or are to be
When time is not, the pageantry that stirs
And will be stirring when our eyes are fixed
On lovely objects and we wish to part   835
With all remembrance of a jarring world –
Give entrance to the sober truth; avow
That Nature to this favourite spot of ours
Yields no exemption, but her awful rights

Enforces to the utmost, and exacts   840
Her tribute of inevitable pain,
And that the sting is added, man himself
For ever busy to afflict himself.
Yet temper this with one sufficient hope –
What need of more? – that we shall neither droop   845
Nor pine for want of pleasure in the life
Which is about us, nor through dearth of aught
That keeps in health the insatiable mind;
That we shall have for knowledge and for love
Abundance; and that, feeling as we do,   850
How goodly, how exceeding fair, how pure
From all reproach is this aetherial frame
And this deep vale, its earthly counterpart,
By which and under which we are enclosed
To breathe in peace; we shall moreover find   855
(If sound, and what we ought to be ourselves,
If rightly we observe and justly weigh)
The inmates not unworthy of their home,
The dwellers of the dwelling. And if this
Were not, we have enough within ourselves,   860
Enough to fill the present day with joy
And overspread the future years with hope –
Our beautiful and quiet home, enriched
Already with a stranger whom we love
Deeply, a stranger of our father's house,   865
A never-resting pilgrim of the sea,
Who finds at last an hour to his content
Beneath our roof; and others whom we love
Will seek us also, sisters of our hearts,
And one, like them, a brother of our hearts,   870
Philosopher and poet, in whose sight
These mountains will rejoice with open joy.
Such is our wealth: O vale of peace, we are
And must be, with God's will, a happy band!

    But 'tis not to enjoy, for this alone   875
That we exist; no, something must be done.
I must not walk in unreproved delight
These narrow bounds and think of nothing more,
No duty that looks further and no care.

Each being has his office, lowly some   880
And common, yet all worthy if fulfilled
With zeal, acknowledgement that with the gift
Keeps pace a harvest answering to the seed.
Of ill-advised ambition and of pride
I would stand clear, yet unto me I feel   885
That an internal brightness is vouchsafed
That must not die, that must not pass away.
Why does this inward lustre fondly seek
And gladly blend with outward fellowship?
Why shine they round me thus, whom thus I love?   890
Why do they teach me, whom I thus revere?
Strange question, yet it answers not itself.
That humble roof, embowered among the trees,
That calm fireside – it is not even in them,
Blessed as they are, to furnish a reply   895
That satisfies and ends in perfect rest.
Possessions have I, wholly, solely mine,
Something within, which yet is shared by none –
Not even the nearest to me and most dear –
Something which power and effort may impart.   900
I would impart it; I would spread it wide,
Immortal in the world which is to come.
I would not wholly perish even in this,
Lie down and be forgotten in the dust,
I and the modest partners of my days   905
Making a silent company in death.
It must not be, if I, divinely taught
Am privileged to speak as I have felt
Of what in man is human or divine.

    While yet an innocent, a little one, a heart   910
That doubtless wanted not its tender moods,
I breathed (for this I better recollect)
Among wild appetites and blind desires,
Motions of savage instinct, my delight
And exaltation. No thing at that time   915
So welcome, no temptation half so dear
As that which [urged] me to a daring feat.
Deep pools, tall trees, black chasms, and dizzy crags –

I loved to look at them, to stand and read
Their looks forbidding, read and disobey,   920
Sometimes in act, and evermore in thought.
With impulses which only were by these
Surpassed in strength, I heard of danger met
Or sought with courage, enterprize forlorn,
By one, sole keeper of his own intent,   925
Or by a resolute few, who for the sake
Of glory fronted multitudes in arms.
Yea, to this day I swell with like desire;
I cannot at this moment read a tale
Of two brave vessels matched in deadly fight   930
And fighting to the death, but I am pleased
More than a wise man ought to be; I wish,
I burn, I struggle, and in soul am there.
But me hath Nature tamed and bade me seek
For other agitations or be calm,   935
Hath dealt with me as with a turbulent stream –
Some nurseling of the mountains which she leads
Through quiet meadows after it has learned
Its strength and had its triumph and its joy,
Its desperate course of tumult and of glee.   940
That which in stealth by Nature was performed
Hath reason sanctioned. Her deliberate voice
Hath said, 'Be mild and love all gentle things;
Thy glory and thy happiness be there.
Yet fear (though thou confide in me) no want   945
Of aspirations which have been – of foes
To wrestle with and victory to complete,
Bounds to be leapt and darkness to explore.
That which enflamed thy infant heart – the love,
The longing, the contempt, the undaunted quest –   950
These shall survive, though changed their office, these
Shall live; it is not in their power to die.'
Then farewell to the warrior's deeds, farewell
All hope, which once and long was mine, to fill
The heroic trumpet with the muse's breath!   955
Yet in this peaceful vale we will not spend
Unheard-of days, though loving peaceful thoughts;
A voice shall speak, and what will be the theme?

On man, on Nature, and on human life,
Thinking in solitude, from time to time   960
I feel sweet passions traversing my soul
Like music; unto these, where'er I may,
I would give utterance in numerous verse.
Of truth, of grandeur, beauty, love, and hope –
Hope for this earth and hope beyond the grave –   965
Of virtue and of intellectual power,
Of blessed consolations in distress,
Of joy in widest commonalty spread,
Of the individual mind that keeps its own
Inviolate retirement, and consists   970
With being limitless, the one great life,
I sing; fit audience let me find, though few!

'Fit audience find, though few' – thus prayed the bard,
Holiest of men. Urania, I shall need
Thy guidance, or a greater muse, if such   975
Descend to earth or dwell in highest heaven;
For I must tread on shadowy ground, must sink
Deep, and aloft ascending, breathe in worlds
To which the heaven of heavens is but a veil.
All strength, all terror, single or in bands,   980
That ever was put forth in personal forms –
Jehovah, with his thunder, and the quire
Of shouting angels and the empyreal thrones –
I pass them unalarmed. The darkest pit
Of the profoundest hell, chaos, night,   985
Nor aught of blinder vacancy scooped out
By help of dreams, can breed such fear and awe
As fall upon us often when we look
Into our minds, into the mind of man,
My haunt, and the main region of my song.   990
Beauty, whose living home is the green earth,
Surpassing the most fair ideal forms
The craft of delicate spirits hath composed
From earth's materials, waits upon my steps,
Pitches her tents before me where I move,   995
An hourly neighbour. Paradise and groves
Elysian, fortunate islands, fields like those of old
In the deep ocean – wherefore should they be

A history, or but a dream, when minds
Once wedded to this outward frame of things   1000
In love, find these the growth of common day?
I, long before the blessèd hour arrives,
Would sing in solitude the spousal verse
Of this great consummation, would proclaim –
Speaking of nothing more than what we are –   1005
How exquisitely the individual mind
(And the progressive powers perhaps no less
Of the whole species) to the external world
Is fitted; and how exquisitely too –
Theme this but little heard of among men –   1010
The external world is fitted to the mind;
And the creation (by no lower name
Can it be called) which they with blended might
Accomplish: this is my great argument.

    Such pleasant haunts foregoing, if I oft   1015
Must turn elsewhere, and travel near the tribes
And fellowships of men, and see ill sights
Of passions ravenous from each other's rage,
Must hear humanity in fields and groves
Pipe solitary anguish, or must hang   1020
Brooding above the fierce confederate storm
Of sorrow, barricadoed evermore
Within the walls of cities – may these sounds
Have their authentic comment, that even these
Hearing, I be not heartless or forlorn.   1025
Come, thou prophetic spirit, soul of man,
Thou human soul of the wide earth that hast
Thy metropolitan temple in the hearts
Of mighty poets; unto me vouchsafe
Thy guidance, teach me to discern, and part   1030
Inherent things from casual, what is fixed
From fleeting, that my verse may live, and be
Even as a light hung up in heaven to chear
Mankind in times to come. And if with this
I blend more lowly matter, with the thing   1035
Contemplated describe the mind and man
Contemplating, and who and what he was,
The transitory being that beheld

This vision, when and where and how he lived,
With all his little realties of life –   1040
Be not this labour useless. If such theme
With highest things may [   ], then great God,
Thou who art breath and being, way and guide,
And power and understanding, may my life
Express the image of a better time;   1045
More wise desires and simpler manners nurse
My heart in genuine freedom; all pure thoughts
Be with me, and uphold me to the end!

The Forsaken

The peace which others seek, they find;
The heaviest storms not longest last;
Heaven grants even to the guiltiest mind
An amnesty for what is past.
When will my sentence be reversed?   5
I only pray to know the worst,
And wish as if my heart would burst.

O weary struggle! silent years
Tell seemingly no doubtful tale,
And yet they leave it short, and fears   10
And hopes are strong and will prevail.
My calmest faith escapes not pain,
And feeling that the hope is vain,
I think that he will come again.

'These chairs, they have no words to utter'

These chairs, they have no words to utter;
No fire is in the grate to stir or flutter;
The ceiling and floor are mute as a stone.
My chamber is hushed and still,
        And I am alone,
        Happy and alone.   5

Oh! who would be afraid of life?
  The passion, the sorrow, and the strife,
    When he may lie
      Sheltered so easily? —   10
May lie in peace on his bed,
Happy as they who are dead.

HALF AN HOUR AFTERWARDS

I have thoughts that are fed by the sun:
  The things which I see
    Are welcome to me —   15
    Welcome every one.
    I do not wish to lie
      Dead, dead,
Dead without any company;
  Here alone on my bed,   20
With thoughts that are fed by the sun,
And hopes that are welcome everyone,
    Happy am I.

O life, there is about thee
A deep delicious peace;   25
I would not be without thee —
    Stay, oh stay!
Yet be thou ever as now,
Sweetness and breath with the quiet of death;
    Peace, peace, peace.   30

'I only looked for pain and grief'

I only looked for pain and grief
And trembled as I drew more near;
But God's unbounded love is here,
And I have found relief.
The precious spot is all my own,   5
Save only that this plant unknown —
A little one and lowly sweet,
Not surely now without heaven's grace,
First seen, and seen, too, in this place —
Is flowering at my feet.   10

The shepherd boy hath disappeared;
The buzzard, too, hath soared away;
And undisturbed I now may pay
My debt to what I feared.
Sad register! but this is sure: 15
Peace built on suffering will endure.
But such the peace that will be ours,
Though many suns, alas! must shine
Ere tears shall cease from me and mine
To fall in bitter show'rs.   20

The sheep-boy whistled loud, and lo!
Thereafter, having felt the shock,
The buzzard mounted from the rock
Deliberate and slow:
Lord of the air, he took his flight;   25
Oh could he on that woeful night
Have lent his wing, my brother dear!
For one poor moment's space to thee,
And all who struggle with the sea
When safety is so near.   30

Thus in the weakness of my heart
I said (but let that pang be still),
When rising from the rock at will,
I saw the bird depart.
And let me calmly bless the power   35
That meets me in this unknown flower —
Affecting type of him I mourn!
With calmness suffer and believe,
And grieve, and know that I must grieve,
Not cheerless, though forlorn.   40

Here did we stop, and here looked round
While each into himself descends
For that last thought of parting friends
That is not to be found.
Our Grasmere vale was out of sight,   45
Our home and his, his heart's delight,
His quiet heart's delicious home.
But time before him melts away,

And he hath feeling of a day
Of blessedness to come.   50

Here did we part, and halted here
With one he loved, I saw him bound
Downwards along the rocky ground
As if with eager cheer.
A lovely sight as on he went,   55
For he was bold and innocent,
Had lived a life of self-command.
Heaven, did it seem to me and her,
Had laid on such a mariner
A consecrating hand.   60

And therefore also do we weep,
To find that such a faith was dust –
With sorrow, but for higher trust,
How miserably deep!
All vanished, in a single word,   65
A breath, a sound, and scarcely heard.
Sea, ship, drowned, shipwreck – so it came;
The meek, the brave, the good was gone –
He who had been our living John
Was nothing but a name.   70

That was indeed a parting! oh,
Glad am I, glad that it is past,
For there were some on whom it cast
Unutterable woe.
But they as well as I have gains,   75
The worthiest and the best; to pains
Like these, there comes a mild release –
Even here I feel it, even this plant
So peaceful is ministrant
Of comfort and of peace.   80

He would have loved thy modest grace,
Meek flower! To him I would have said,
'It grows upon its native bed
Beside our parting-place;
Close to the ground like dew it lies   85

With multitude of purple eyes
Spangling a cushion green like moss;
But we will see it, joyful tide!
Some day to see it in its pride
The mountain we will cross.'   90

Well, well, if ever verse of mine
Have power to make his merits known,
Then let a monumental stone
Stand here – a sacred shrine –
And to the few who come this way,   95
Traveller or shepherd, let it say,
Long as these mighty rocks endure:
Oh do not thou too fondly brood,
Although deserving of all good,
On any earthly hope, however pure!   100

THE PRELUDE
1799

The Prelude, 1799

Was it for this
That one, the fairest of all rivers, loved
To blend his murmurs with my nurse's song,
And from his alder shades and rocky falls,
And from his fords and shallows, sent a voice   5
That flowed along my dreams? For this didst thou,
O Derwent, travelling over the green plains
Near my 'sweet birthplace', didst thou, beauteous stream,
Make ceaseless music through the night and day,
Which with its steady cadence tempering   10
Our human waywardness, composed my thoughts
To more than infant softness, giving me
Among the fretful dwellings of mankind
A knowledge, a dim earnest, of the calm
Which Nature breathes among the fields and groves?   15
Beloved Derwent, fairest of all streams,
Was it for this that I, a four years' child,
A naked boy, among thy silent pools
Made one long bathing of a summer's day,
Basked in the sun, or plunged into thy streams,   20
Alternate, all a summer's day, or coursed
Over the sandy fields, and dashed the flowers
Of yellow grunsel; or, when crag and hill,
The woods, and distant Skiddaw's lofty height,
Were bronzed with a deep radiance, stood alone   25
A naked savage in the thunder-shower?
    And afterwards ('twas in a later day,
Though early), when upon the mountain slope
The frost and breath of frosty wind had snapped
The last autumnal crocus, 'twas my joy   30
To wander half the night among the cliffs
And the smooth hollows where the woodcocks ran
Along the moonlight turf. In thought and wish
That time, my shoulder all with springes hung,
I was a fell destroyer. Gentle powers,   35
Who give us happiness and call it peace,

When scudding on from snare to snare I plied
My anxious visitation, hurrying on,
Still hurrying, hurrying onward, how my heart
Panted! – among the scattered yew-trees and the crags   40
That looked upon me, how my bosom beat
With expectation! Sometimes strong desire
Resistless overpowered me, and the bird
Which was the captive of another's toils
Became my prey; and when the deed was done   45
I heard among the solitary hills
Low breathings coming after me, and sounds
Of undistinguishable motion, steps
Almost as silent as the turf they trod.
    Nor less in springtime, when on southern banks   50
The shining sun had from his knot of leaves
Decoyed the primrose flower, and when the vales
And woods were warm, was I a rover then
In the high places, on the lonesome peaks,
Among the mountains and the winds. Though mean   55
And though inglorious were my views, the end
Was not ignoble. Oh, when I have hung
Above the raven's nest, by knots of grass
Or half-inch fissures in the slippery rock
But ill sustained, and almost, as it seemed,   60
Suspended by the blast which blew amain,
Shouldering the naked crag, oh, at that time,
While on the perilous ridge I hung alone,
With what strange utterance did the loud dry wind
Blow through my ears; the sky seemed not a sky   65
Of earth, and with what motion moved the clouds!
    The mind of man is fashioned and built up
Even as a strain of music. I believe
That there are spirits which, when they would form
A favored being, from his very dawn   70
Of infancy do open out the clouds
As at the touch of lightning, seeking him
With gentle visitation – quiet powers,
Retired, and seldom recognized, yet kind,
And to the very meanest not unknown –   75
With me, though rarely, in my boyish days
They communed. Others too there are, who use,

Yet haply aiming at the self-same end,
Severer interventions, ministry
More palpable – and of their school was I.   80
   They guided me: one evening led by them
I went alone into a shepherd's boat,
A skiff, that to a willow-tree was tied
Within a rocky cave, its usual home.
The moon was up, the lake was shining clear   85
Among the hoary mountains; from the shore
I pushed, and struck the oars, and struck again
In cadence, and my little boat moved on
Just like a man who walks with stately step
Though bent on speed. It was an act of stealth   90
And troubled pleasure. Not without the voice
Of mountain echoes did my boat move on,
Leaving behind her still on either side
Small circles glittering idly in the moon,
Until they melted all into one track   95
Of sparkling light. A rocky steep uprose
Above the cavern of the willow-tree,
And now, as suited one who proudly rowed
With his best skill, I fixed a steady view
Upon the top of that same craggy ridge,   100
The bound of the horizon – for behind
Was nothing but the stars and the grey sky.
She was an elfin pinnace; twenty times
I dipped my oars into the silent lake,
And as I rose upon the stroke my boat   105
Went heaving through the water like a swan –
When from behind that rocky steep, till then
The bound of the horizon, a huge cliff,
As if with voluntary power instinct,
Upreared its head. I struck, and struck again,   110
And, growing still in stature, the huge cliff
Rose up between me and the stars, and still,
With measured motion, like a living thing
Strode after me. With trembling hands I turned,
And through the silent water stole my way   115
Back to the cavern of the willow-tree.
There in her mooring-place I left my bark,

And through the meadows homeward went with grave
And serious thoughts; and after I had seen
That spectacle, for many days my brain   120
Worked with a dim and undetermined sense
Of unknown modes of being. In my thoughts
There was a darkness—call it solitude,
Or blank desertion—no familiar shapes
Of hourly objects, images of trees,   125
Of sea or sky, no colours of green fields,
But huge and mighty forms that do not live
Like living men moved slowly through my mind
By day, and were the trouble of my dreams.
  Ah, not in vain ye beings of the hills,   130
And ye that walk the woods and open heaths
By moon or star-light, thus, from my first dawn
Of childhood, did ye love to intertwine
The passions that build up our human soul
Not with the mean and vulgar works of man,   135
But with high objects, with eternal things,
With life and Nature, purifying thus
The elements of feeling and of thought,
And sanctifying by such discipline
Both pain and fear, until we recognise   140
A grandeur in the beatings of the heart.
Nor was this fellowship vouchsafed to me
With stinted kindness. In November days,
When vapours rolling down the valleys made
A lonely scene more lonesome, among woods   145
At noon, and mid the calm of summer nights
When by the margin of the trembling lake
Beneath the gloomy hills I homeward went
In solitude, such intercourse was mine.
  And in the frosty season, when the sun   150
Was set, and visible for many a mile
The cottage windows through the twilight blazed,
I heeded not the summons. Clear and loud
The village clock tolled six; I wheeled about
Proud and exulting, like an untired horse   155
That cares not for its home. All shod with steel
We hissed along the polished ice in games
Confederate, imitative of the chace

And woodland pleasures, the resounding horn,
The pack loud bellowing, and the hunted hare. 160
So through the darkness and the cold we flew,
And not a voice was idle. With the din,
Meanwhile, the precipices rang aloud;
The leafless trees and every icy crag
Tinkled like iron; while the distant hills 165
Into the tumult sent an alien sound
Of melancholy, not unnoticed; while the stars,
Eastward, were sparkling clear, and in the west
The orange sky of evening died away.
   Not seldom from the uproar I retired 170
Into a silent bay, or sportively
Glanced sideway, leaving the tumultuous throng,
To cut across the shadow of a star
That gleamed upon the ice. And oftentimes
When we had given our bodies to the wind, 175
And all the shadowy banks on either side
Came sweeping through the darkness, spinning still
The rapid line of motion, then at once
Have I, reclining back upon my heels,
Stopped short – yet still the solitary cliffs 180
Wheeled by me, even as if the earth had rolled
With visible motion her diurnal round.
Behind me did they stretch in solemn train,
Feebler and feebler, and I stood and watched
Till all was tranquil as a summer sea. 185
   Ye powers of earth, ye genii of the springs,
And ye that have your voices in the clouds,
And ye that are familiars of the lakes
And of the standing pools, I may not think
A vulgar hope was yours when ye employed 190
Such ministry – when ye through many a year
Thus by the agency of boyish sports,
On caves and trees, upon the woods and hills,
Impressed upon all forms the characters
Of danger or desire, and thus did make 195
The surface of the universal earth
With meanings of delight, of hope and fear,
Work like a sea.

                           Not uselessly employed,
I might pursue this theme through every change
Of exercise and sport to which the year   200
Did summon us in its delightful round.
We were a noisy crew; the sun in heaven
Beheld not vales more beautiful than ours,
Nor saw a race in happiness and joy
More worthy of the fields where they were sown.   205
I would record with no reluctant voice
Our home amusements by the warm peat fire
At evening, when with pencil and with slate,
In square divisions parcelled out, and all
With crosses and with cyphers scribbled o'er,   210
We schemed and puzzled, head opposed to head,
In strife too humble to be named in verse;
Or round the naked table, snow-white deal,
Cherry, or maple, sate in close array,
And to the combat – lu or whist – led on   215
A thick-ribbed army, not as in the world
Discarded and ungratefully thrown by
Even for the very service they had wrought,
But husbanded through many a long campaign.
Oh, with what echoes on the board they fell –   220
Ironic diamonds, hearts of sable hue,
Queens gleaming through their splendour's last decay,
Knaves wrapt in one assimilating gloom,
And kings indignant at the shame incurred
By royal visages. Meanwhile abroad   225
The heavy rain was falling, or the frost
Raged bitterly with keen and silent tooth,
And, interrupting the impassioned game,
Oft from the neighbouring lake the splitting ice,
While it sank down towards the water, sent   230
Among the meadows and the hills its long
And frequent yellings, imitative some
Of wolves that howl along the Bothnic main.
    Nor with less willing heart would I rehearse
The woods of autumn, and their hidden bowers   235
With milk-white clusters hung; the rod and line –
True symbol of the foolishness of hope –
Which with its strong enchantment led me on

By rocks and pools, where never summer star
Impressed its shadow, to forlorn cascades 240
Among the windings of the mountain-brooks;
The kite in sultry calms from some high hill
Sent up, ascending thence till it was lost
Among the fleecy clouds – in gusty days
Launched from the lower grounds, and suddenly 245
Dashed headlong and rejected by the storm.
All these, and more, with rival claims demand
Grateful acknowledgement. It were a song
Venial, and such as – if I rightly judge –
I might protract unblamed, but I perceive 250
That much is overlooked, and we should ill
Attain our object if, from delicate fears
Of breaking in upon the unity
Of this my argument, I should omit
To speak of such effects as cannot here 255
Be regularly classed, yet tend no less
To the same point, the growth of mental power
And love of Nature's works.
                              Ere I had seen
Eight summers – and 'twas in the very week
When I was first transplanted to thy vale, 260
Beloved Hawkshead; when thy paths, thy shores
And brooks, were like a dream of novelty
To my half-infant mind – I chanced to cross
One of those open fields which, shaped like ears,
Make green peninsulas on Esthwaite's lake. 265
Twilight was coming on, yet through the gloom
I saw distinctly on the opposite shore,
Beneath a tree and close by the lake side,
A heap of garments, as if left by one
Who there was bathing. Half an hour I watched 270
And no one owned them; meanwhile the calm lake
Grew dark with all the shadows on its breast,
And now and then a leaping fish disturbed
The breathless stillness. The succeeding day
There came a company, and in their boat 275
Sounded with iron hooks and with long poles.
At length the dead man, mid that beauteous scene
Of trees and hills and water, bolt upright

Rose with his ghastly face. I might advert
To numerous accidents in flood or field,   280
Quarry or moor, or mid the winter snows,
Distresses and disasters, tragic facts
Of rural history that impressed my mind
With images to which in following years
Far other feelings were attached – with forms   285
That yet exist with independent life,
And, like their archetypes, know no decay.
   There are in our existence spots of time
Which with distinct preeminence retain
A fructifying virtue, whence, depressed   290
By trivial occupations and the round
Of ordinary intercourse, our minds –
Especially the imaginative power –
Are nourished and invisibly repaired.
Such moments chiefly seem to have their date   295
In our first childhood. I remember well
('Tis of an early season that I speak,
The twilight of rememberable life),
While I was yet an urchin, one who scarce
Could hold a bridle, with ambitious hopes   300
I mounted, and we rode towards the hills.
We were a pair of horsemen: honest James
Was with me, my encourager and guide.
We had not travelled long ere some mischance
Disjoined me from my comrade, and, through fear   305
Dismounting, down the rough and stony moor
I led my horse, and stumbling on, at length
Came to a bottom where in former times
A man, the murderer of his wife, was hung
In irons. Mouldered was the gibbet-mast;   310
The bones were gone, the iron and the wood;
Only a long green ridge of turf remained
Whose shape was like a grave. I left the spot,
And reascending the bare slope I saw
A naked pool that lay beneath the hills,   315
The beacon on the summit, and more near
A girl who bore a pitcher on her head
And seemed with difficult steps to force her way
Against the blowing wind. It was in truth

An ordinary sight, but I should need   320
Colours and words that are unknown to man
To paint the visionary dreariness
Which, while I looked all round for my lost guide,
Did at that time invest the naked pool,
The beacon on the lonely eminence,   325
The woman and her garments vexed and tossed
By the strong wind.
           Nor less I recollect —
Long after, though my childhood had not ceased —
Another scene which left a kindred power
Implanted in my mind. One Christmas time,   330
The day before the holidays began,
Feverish, and tired, and restless, I went forth
Into the fields, impatient for the sight
Of those three horses which should bear us home,
My brothers and myself. There was a crag,   335
An eminence, which from the meeting-point
Of two highways ascending overlooked
At least a long half-mile of those two roads,
By each of which the expected steeds might come —
The choice uncertain. Thither I repaired   340
Up to the highest summit. 'Twas a day
Stormy, and rough, and wild, and on the grass
I sate half sheltered by a naked wall.
Upon my right hand was a single sheep,
A whistling hawthorn on my left, and there,   345
Those two companions at my side, I watched
With eyes intensely straining, as the mist
Gave intermitting prospects of the wood
And plain beneath. Ere I to school returned
That dreary time, ere I had been ten days   350
A dweller in my father's house, he died,
And I and my two brothers, orphans then,
Followed his body to the grave. The event,
With all the sorrow which it brought, appeared
A chastisement; and when I called to mind   355
That day so lately passed, when from the crag
I looked in such anxiety of hope,
With trite reflections of morality,

Yet with the deepest passion, I bowed low
To God who thus corrected my desires.   360
And afterwards the wind and sleety rain,
And all the business of the elements,
The single sheep, and the one blasted tree,
And the bleak music of that old stone wall,
The noise of wood and water, and the mist   365
Which on the line of each of those two roads
Advanced in such indisputable shapes –
All these were spectacles and sounds to which
I often would repair, and thence would drink
As at a fountain. And I do not doubt   370
That in this later time, when storm and rain
Beat on my roof at midnight, or by day
When I am in the woods, unknown to me
The workings of my spirit thence are brought.
   Nor, sedulous as I have been to trace   370
How Nature by collateral interest,
And by extrinsic passion, peopled first
My mind with forms or beautiful or grand
And made me love them, may I well forget
How other pleasures have been mine, and joys   380
Of subtler origin – how I have felt
Not seldom, even in that tempestuous time,
Those hallowed and pure motions of the sense
Which seem in their simplicity to own
An intellectual charm, that calm delight   385
Which, if I err not, surely must belong
To those first-born affinities that fit
Our new existence to existing things,
And, in our dawn of being, constitute
The bond of union betwixt life and joy.   390
   Yes, I remember when the changeful earth
And twice five seasons on my mind had stamped
The faces of the moving year, even then,
A child, I held unconscious intercourse
With the eternal beauty, drinking in   395
A pure organic pleasure from the lines
Of curling mist, or from the level plain
Of waters coloured by the steady clouds.

The sands of Westmoreland, the creeks and bays
Of Cumbria's rocky limits, they can tell   400
How when the sea threw off his evening shade
And to the shepherd's hut beneath the crags
Did send sweet notice of the rising moon,
How I have stood, to images like these
A stranger, linking with the spectacle   405
No body of associated forms,
And bringing with me no peculiar sense
Of quietness or peace – yet I have stood
Even while my eye has moved o'er three long leagues
Of shining water, gathering, as it seemed,   410
Through the wide surface of that field of light
New pleasure, like a bee among the flowers.
    Thus often in those fits of vulgar joy
Which through all seasons on a child's pursuits
Are prompt attendants, mid that giddy bliss   415
Which like a tempest works along the blood
And is forgotten, even then I felt
Gleams like the flashing of a shield. The earth
And common face of Nature spake to me
Rememberable things – sometimes, 'tis true,   420
By quaint associations, yet not vain
Nor profitless, if haply they impressed
Collateral objects and appearances,
Albeit lifeless then, and doomed to sleep
Until maturer seasons called them forth   425
To impregnate and to elevate the mind.
And if the vulgar joy by its own weight
Wearied itself out of the memory,
The scenes which were a witness of that joy
Remained, in their substantial lineaments   430
Depicted on the brain, and to the eye
Were visible, a daily sight. And thus
By the impressive agency of fear,
By pleasure and repeated happiness –
So frequently repeated – and by force   435
Of obscure feelings representative
Of joys that were forgotten, these same scenes,
So beauteous and majestic in themselves,

Though yet the day was distant, did at length
Become habitually dear, and all   440
Their hues and forms were by invisible links
Allied to the affections.
              I began
My story early, feeling, as I fear,
The weakness of a human love for days
Disowned by memory – ere the birth of spring   445
Planting my snowdrops among winter snows.
Nor will it seem to thee, my friend, so prompt
In sympathy, that I have lengthened out
With fond and feeble tongue a tedious tale.
Meanwhile my hope has been that I might fetch   450
Reproaches from my former years, whose power
May spur me on, in manhood now mature,
To honourable toil. Yet should it be
That this is but an impotent desire –
That I by such inquiry am not taught   455
To understand myself, nor thou to know
With better knowledge how the heart was framed
Of him thou lovest – need I dread from thee
Harsh judgements if I am so loth to quit
Those recollected hours that have the charm   460
Of visionary things, and lovely forms
And sweet sensations, that throw back our life
And make our infancy a visible scene
On which the sun is shining?

SECOND PART

Thus far, my friend, have we retraced the way
Through which I travelled when I first began
To love the woods and fields. The passion yet
Was in its birth, sustained, as might befal,
By nourishment that came unsought – for still   5
From week to week, from month to month, we lived
A round of tumult. Duly were our games
Prolonged in summer till the daylight failed:
No chair remained before the doors, the bench
And threshold steps were empty, fast asleep   10
The labourer and the old man who had sate

A later lingerer, yet the revelry
Continued and the loud uproar. At last,
When all the ground was dark and the huge clouds
Were edged with twinkling stars, to bed we went   15
With weary joints and with a beating mind.
Ah, is there one who ever has been young
And needs a monitory voice to tame
The pride of virtue and of intellect?
And is there one, the wisest and the best   20
Of all mankind, who does not sometimes wish
For things which cannot be, who would not give,
If so he might, to duty and to truth
The eagerness of infantine desire?
A tranquillizing spirit presses now   25
On my corporeal frame, so wide appears
The vacancy between me and those days,
Which yet have such self-presence in my heart
That sometimes when I think of them I seem
Two consciousnesses – conscious of myself,   30
And of some other being.
                A grey stone
Of native rock, left midway in the square
Of our small market-village, was the home
And centre of these joys; and when, returned
After long absence thither I repaired,   35
I found that it was split and gone to build
A smart assembly-room that perked and flared
With wash and rough-cast, elbowing the ground
Which had been ours. But let the fiddle scream,
And be ye happy! Yet I know, my friends,   40
That more than one of you will think with me
Of those soft starry nights, and that old dame
From whom the stone was named, who there had sate
And watched her table with its huckster's wares,
Assiduous, for the length of sixty years.   45
    We ran a boisterous race, the year span round
With giddy motion; but the time approached
That brought with it a regular desire
For calmer pleasures – when the beauteous scenes
Of Nature were collaterally attached   50
To every scheme of holiday delight,

And every boyish sport, less grateful else
And languidly pursued. When summer came
It was the pastime of our afternoons
To beat along the plain of Windermere   55
With rival oars; and the selected bourn
Was now an island musical with birds
That sang for ever, now a sister isle
Beneath the oak's umbrageous covert, sown
With lilies-of-the-valley like a field,   60
And now a third small island where remained
An old stone table and one mouldered cave –
A hermit's history. In such a race,
So ended, disappointment could be none,
Uneasiness, or pain, or jealousy;   65
We rested in the shade, all pleased alike,
Conquered or conqueror. Thus our selfishness
Was mellowed down, and thus the pride of strength
And the vainglory of superior skill
Were interfused with objects which subdued   70
And tempered them, and gradually produced
A quiet independence of the heart.
And to my friend who knows me I may add,
Unapprehensive of reproof, that hence
Ensued a diffidence and modesty,   75
And I was taught to feel – perhaps too much –
The self-sufficing power of solitude.
    No delicate viands sapped our bodily strength:
More than we wished we knew the blessing then
Of vigorous hunger, for our daily meals   80
Were frugal, Sabine fare – and then, exclude
A little weekly stipend, and we lived
Through three divisions of the quartered year
In pennyless poverty. But now, to school
Returned from the half-yearly holidays,   85
We came with purses more profusely filled,
Allowance which abundantly sufficed
To gratify the palate with repasts
More costly than the dame of whom I spake,
That ancient woman, and her board, supplied.   90
Hence inroads into distant vales, and long
Excursions far away among the hills,

Hence rustic dinners on the cool green ground —
Or in the woods, or by a river-side
Or fountain — festive banquets, that provoked   95
The languid action of a natural scene
By pleasure of corporeal appetite.
  Nor is my aim neglected if I tell
How twice in the long length of those half-years
We from our funds perhaps with bolder hand   100
Drew largely, anxious for one day at least
To feel the motion of the galloping steed;
And with the good old inkeeper, in truth
I needs must say, that sometimes we have used
Sly subterfuge, for the intended bound   105
Of the day's journey was too distant far
For any cautious man: a structure famed
Beyond its neighbourhood, the antique walls
Of a large abbey, with its fractured arch,
Belfry, and images, and living trees —   110
A holy scene. Along the smooth green turf
Our horses grazed. In more than inland peace,
Left by the winds that overpass the vale,
In that sequestered ruin trees and towers —
Both silent and both motionless alike —   115
Hear all day long the murmuring sea that beats
Incessantly upon a craggy shore.
  Our steeds remounted, and the summons given,
With whip and spur we by the chantry flew
In uncouth race, and left the cross-legged knight   120
And the stone abbot, and that single wren
Which one day sang so sweetly in the nave
Of the old church that, though from recent showers
The earth was comfortless, and, touched by faint
Internal breezes, from the roofless walls   125
The shuddering ivy dripped large drops, yet still
So sweetly mid the gloom the invisible bird
Sang to itself that there I could have made
My dwelling-place, and lived for ever there,
To hear such music. Through the walls we flew   130
And down the valley, and, a circuit made
In wantonness of heart, through rough and smooth
We scampered homeward. O, ye rocks and streams,

And that still spirit of the evening air,
Even in this joyous time I sometimes felt   135
Your presence, when, with slackened step, we breathed
Along the sides of the steep hills, or when,
Lightened by gleams of moonlight from the sea,
We beat with thundering hoofs the level sand.
    There was a row of ancient trees, since fallen,   140
That on the margin of a jutting land
Stood near the lake of Coniston, and made,
With its long boughs above the water stretched,
A gloom through which a boat might sail along
As in a cloister. An old hall was near,   145
Grotesque and beautiful, its gavel-end
And huge round chimneys to the top o'ergrown
With fields of ivy. Thither we repaired –
'Twas even a custom with us – to the shore,
And to that cool piazza. They who dwelt   150
In the neglected mansion-house supplied
Fresh butter, tea-kettle and earthernware,
And chafing-dish with smoking coals; and so
Beneath the trees we sate in our small boat,
And in the covert eat our delicate meal   155
Upon the calm smooth lake. It was a joy
Worthy the heart of one who is full grown
To rest beneath those horizontal boughs
And mark the radiance of the setting sun,
Himself unseen, reposing on the top   160
Of the high eastern hills. And there I said,
That beauteous sight before me, there I said
(Then first beginning in my thoughts to mark
That sense of dim similitude which links
Our moral feelings with external forms)   165
That in whatever region I should close
My mortal life I would remember you,
Fair scenes – that dying I would think on you,
My soul would send a longing look to you,
Even as that setting sun, while all the vale   170
Could nowhere catch one faint memorial gleam,
Yet with the last remains of his last light
Still lingered, and a farewell lustre threw
On the dear mountain-tops where first he rose.

'Twas then my fourteenth summer, and these words   175
Were uttered in a casual access
Of sentiment, a momentary trance
That far outran the habit of my mind.
   Upon the eastern shore of Windermere
Above the crescent of a pleasant bay   180
There was an inn, no homely-featured shed,
Brother of the surrounding cottages,
But 'twas a splendid place, the door beset
With chaises, grooms, and liveries, and within
Decanters, glasses and the blood-red wine.   185
In ancient times, or ere the hall was built
On the large island, had the dwelling been
More worthy of a poet's love, a hut
Proud of its one bright fire and sycamore shade;
But though the rhymes were gone which once inscribed   190
The threshold, and large golden characters
On the blue-frosted signboard had usurped
The place of the old lion, in contempt
And mockery of the rustic painter's hand,
Yet to this hour the spot to me is dear   195
With all its foolish pomp. The garden lay
Upon a slope surmounted by the plain
Of a small bowling-green; beneath us stood
A grove, with gleams of water through the trees
And over the tree-tops – nor did we want   200
Refreshment, strawberries and mellow cream –
And there through half an afternoon we played
On the smooth platform, and the shouts we sent
Made all the mountains ring. But ere the fall
Of night, when in our pinnace we returned   205
Over the dusky lake, and to the beach
Of some small island steered our course, with one,
The minstrel of our troop, and left him there,
And rowed off gently, while he blew his flute
Alone upon the rock, oh, then the calm   210
And dead still water lay upon my mind
Even with a weight of pleasure, and the sky,
Never before so beautiful, sank down
Into my heart and held me like a dream.
   Thus day by day my sympathies increased,   215

And thus the common range of visible things
Grew dear to me. Already I began
To love the sun – a boy I loved the sun
Not as I since have loved him (as a pledge
And surety of my earthly life, a light   220
Which while I view I feel I am alive),
But for this cause, that I had seen him lay
His beauty on the morning hills, had seen
The western mountain touch his setting orb
In many a thoughtless hour, when from excess   225
Of happiness my blood appeared to flow
With its own pleasure, and I breathed with joy.
And from like feelings, humble though intense,
To patriotic and domestic love
Analogous, the moon to me was dear: 230
For I would dream away my purposes
Standing to look upon her, while she hung
Midway between the hills as if she knew
No other region but belonged to thee,
Yea appertained by a peculiar right   235
To thee and thy grey huts, my native vale.
      Those incidental charms which first attached
My heart to rural objects, day by day
Grew weaker, and I hasten on to tell
How Nature, intervenient till this time   240
And secondary, now at length was sought
For her own sake. But who shall parcel out
His intellect by geometric rules
Split like a province into round and square?
Who knows the individual hour in which   245
His habits were first sown even as a seed?
Who that shall point as with a wand, and say
'This portion of the river of my mind
Came from yon fountain'? Thou, my friend, art one
More deeply read in thy own thoughts, no slave   250
Of that false secondary power by which
In weakness we create distinctions, then
Believe our puny boundaries are things
Which we perceive, and not which we have made.
To thee, unblinded by these outward shews,   255
The unity of all has been revealed;

And thou wilt doubt with me, less aptly skilled
Than many are to class the cabinet
Of their sensations, and in voluble phrase
Run through the history and birth of each   260
As of a single independent thing.
Hard task to analyse a soul, in which
Not only general habits and desires,
But each most obvious and particular thought –
Not in a mystical and idle sense,   265
But in the words of reason deeply weighed –
Hath no beginning.
        Blessed the infant babe –
For with my best conjectures I would trace
The progress of our being – blest the babe
Nursed in his mother's arms, the babe who sleeps   270
Upon his mother's breast, who, when his soul
Claims manifest kindred with an earthly soul,
Doth gather passion from his mother's eye.
Such feelings pass into his torpid life
Like an awakening breeze, and hence his mind,   275
Even in the first trial of its powers,
Is prompt and watchful, eager to combine
In one appearance all the elements
And parts of the same object, else detached
And loth to coalesce. Thus day by day,   280
Subjected to the discipline of love,
His organs and recipient faculties
Are quickened, are more vigorous; his mind spreads,
Tenacious of the forms which it receives.
In one beloved presence – nay and more,   285
In that most apprehensive habitude
And those sensations which have been derived
From this beloved presence – there exists
A virtue which irradiates and exalts
All objects through all intercourse of sense.   290
No outcast he, bewildered and depressed;
Along his infant veins are interfused
The gravitation and the filial bond
Of Nature that connect him with the world.
Emphatically such a being lives,   295
An inmate of this *active* universe.

From Nature largely he receives, nor so
Is satisfied, but largely gives again;
For feeling has to him imparted strength,
And – powerful in all sentiments of grief,   300
Of exultation, fear and joy – his mind,
Even as an agent of the one great mind,
Creates, creator and receiver both,
Working but in alliance with the works
Which it beholds. Such, verily, is the first   305
Poetic spirit of our human life –
By uniform control of after years
In most abated and suppressed, in some
Through every change of growth or of decay
Preeminent till death.   310
      From early days,
Beginning not long after that first time
In which, a babe, by intercourse of touch
I held mute dialogues with my mother's heart,
I have endeavoured to display the means
Whereby this infant sensibility,   315
Great birthright of our being, was in me
Augmented and sustained. Yet is a path
More difficult before me, and I fear
That in its broken windings we shall need
The chamois' sinews and the eagle's wing.   320
For now a trouble came into my mind
From obscure causes. I was left alone
Seeking this visible world, nor knowing why.
The props of my affections were removed,
And yet the building stood, as if sustained   325
By its own spirit. All that I beheld
Was dear to me, and from this cause it came
That now to Nature's finer influxes
My mind lay open – to that more exact
And intimate communion which our hearts   330
Maintain with the minuter properties
Of objects which already are beloved,
And of those only.
      Many are the joys
Of youth, but oh, what happiness to live
When every hour brings palpable access   335

Of knowledge, when all knowledge is delight,
And sorrow is not there. The seasons came,
And every season brought a countless store
Of modes and temporary qualities
Which but for this most watchful power of love   340
Had been neglected, left a register
Of permanent relations else unknown.
Hence life, and change, and beauty, solitude
More active even than 'best society',
Society made sweet as solitude   345
By silent inobtrusive sympathies,
And gentle agitations of the mind
From manifold distinctions – difference
Perceived in things where to the common eye
No difference is – and hence, from the same source,   350
Sublimer joy. For I would walk alone
In storm and tempest, or in starlight nights
Beneath the quiet heavens, and at that time
Would feel whate'er there is of power in sound
To breathe an elevated mood, by form   355
Or image unprofaned; and I would stand
Beneath some rock, listening to sounds that are
The ghostly language of the ancient earth,
Or make their dim abode in distant winds.
Thence did I drink the visionary power.   360
I deem not profitless these fleeting moods
Of shadowy exaltation; not for this,
That they are kindred to our purer mind
And intellectual life, but that the soul –
Remembering how she felt, but what she felt   365
Remembering not – retains an obscure sense
Of possible sublimity, to which
With growing faculties she doth aspire,
With faculties still growing, feeling still
That whatsoever point they gain they still   370
Have something to pursue.
                          And not alone
In grandeur and in tumult, but no less
In tranquil scenes, that universal power
And fitness in the latent qualities
And essences of things, by which the mind   375

  Is moved with feelings of delight, to me
Came strengthened with a superadded soul,
A virtue not its own. My morning walks
Were early: oft before the hours of school
I travelled round our little lake, five miles   380
Of pleasant wandering – happy time, more dear
For this, that one was by my side, a friend
Then passionately loved. With heart how full
Will he peruse these lines, this page – perhaps
A blank to other men – for many years   385
Have since flowed in between us, and, our minds
Both silent to each other, at this time
We live as if those hours had never been.
Nor seldom did I lift our cottage latch
Far earlier, and before the vernal thrush   390
Was audible, among the hills I sate
Alone upon some jutting eminence
At the first hour of morning, when the vale
Lay quiet in an utter solitude.
How shall I trace the history, where seek   395
The origin of what I then have felt?
Oft in those moments such a holy calm
Did overpread my soul that I forgot
The agency of sight, and what I saw
Appeared like something in myself, a dream,   400
A prospect in my mind.
                                'Twere long to tell
What spring and autumn, what the winter snows,
And what the summer shade, what day and night,
The evening and the morning, what my dreams
And what my waking thoughts, supplied to nurse   405
That spirit of religious love in which
I walked with Nature. But let this at least
Be not forgotten, that I still retained
My first creative sensibility,
That by the regular action of the world   410
My soul was unsubdued. A plastic power
Abode with me, a forming hand, at times
Rebellious, acting in a devious mood,
A local spirit of its own, at war
With general tendency, but for the most   415

Subservient strictly to the external things
With which it communed. An auxiliar light
Came from my mind, which on the setting sun
Bestowed new splendour; the melodious birds,
The gentle breezes, fountains that ran on   420
Murmuring so sweetly in themselves, obeyed
A like dominion, and the midnight storm
Grew darker in the presence of my eye.
Hence my obeisance, my devotion hence,
And *hence* my transport.
                   Nor should this, perchance,   425
Pass unrecorded, that I still had loved
The exercise and produce of a toil
Than analytic industry to me
More pleasing, and whose character I deem
Is more poetic, as resembling more   430
Creative agency – I mean to speak
Of that interminable building reared
By observation of affinities
In objects where no brotherhood exists
To common minds. My seventeenth year was come,   435
And, whether from this habit rooted now
So deeply in my mind, or from excess
Of the great social principle of life
Coercing all things into sympathy,
To unorganic natures I transferred   440
My own enjoyments, or, the power of truth
Coming in revelation, I conversed
With things that really are, I at this time
Saw blessings spread around me like a sea.
Thus did my days pass on, and now at length   445
From Nature and her overflowing soul
I had received so much that all my thoughts
Were steeped in feeling. I was only then
Contented when with bliss ineffable
I felt the sentiment of being spread   450
O'er all that moves, and all that seemeth still,
O'er all that, lost beyond the reach of thought
And human knowledge, to the human eye
Invisible, yet liveth to the heart,
O'er all that leaps, and runs, and shouts, and sings,   455

Or beats the gladsome air, o'er all that glides
Beneath the wave, yea, in the wave itself
And mighty depth of waters. Wonder not
If such my transports were, for in all things
I saw one life, and felt that it was joy;   460
One song they sang and it was audible –
Most audible then when the fleshly ear,
O'ercome by grosser prelude of that strain,
Forgot its functions and slept undisturbed.
　　If this be error, and another faith   465
Find easier access to the pious mind,
Yet were I grossly destitute of all
Those human sentiments which make this earth
So dear if I should fail with grateful voice
To speak of you, ye mountains, and ye lakes   470
And sounding cataracts, ye mists and winds
That dwell among the hills where I was born.
If in my youth I have been pure in heart,
If, mingling with the world, I am content
With my own modest pleasures, and have lived   475
With God and Nature communing, removed
From little enmities and low desires,
The gift is yours; if in these times of fear,
This melancholy waste of hopes o'erthrown,
If, mid indifference and apathy   480
And wicked exultation, when good men
On every side fall off we know not how
To selfishness, disguised in gentle names
Of peace and quiet and domestic love –
Yet mingled, not unwillingly, with sneers   485
On visionary minds – if, in this time
Of dereliction and dismay, I yet
Despair not of our nature, but retain
A more than Roman confidence, a faith
That fails not, in all sorrow my support,   490
The blessing of my life, the gift is yours
Ye mountains, thine O Nature. Thou hast fed
My lofty speculations, and in thee
For this uneasy heart of ours I find
A never-failing principle of joy   495
And purest passion.

                    Thou, my friend, wast reared
In the great city, mid far other scenes,
But we by different roads at length have gained
The self-same bourne. And from this cause to thee
I speak unapprehensive of contempt,   500
The insinuated scoff of coward tongues,
And all that silent language which so oft
In conversation betwixt man and man
Blots from the human countenance all trace
Of beauty and of love. For thou hast sought   505
The truth in solitude, and thou art one
The most intense of Nature's worshippers,
In many things my brother, chiefly here
In this my deep devotion. Fare thee well:
Health and the quiet of a healthful mind   510
Attend thee, seeking oft the haunts of men –
But yet more often living with thyself,
And for thyself – so haply shall thy days
Be many, and a blessing to mankind.

From

THE PRELUDE
1805 and 1850

From *The Prelude*, 1850

The Evangelist St John my patron was:
Three Gothic courts are his, and in the first
Was my abiding-place, a nook obscure;
Right underneath, the College kitchens made
A humming sound, less tuneable than bees,   50
But hardly less industrious; with shrill notes
Of sharp command and scolding intermixed.
Near me hung Trinity's loquacious clock,
Who never let the quarters, night or day,
Slip by him unproclaimed, and told the hours   55
Twice over with a male and female voice.
Her pealing organ was my neighbour too;
And from my pillow, looking forth by light
Of moon or favouring stars, I could behold
The antechapel where the statue stood   60
Of Newton with his prism and silent face,
The marble index of a mind for ever
Voyaging through strange seas of Thought, alone.

* * *

From *The Prelude*, 1805

Of college labours, of the lecturer's room   60
All studded round, as thick as chairs could stand,
With loyal students faithful to their books,
Half-and-half idlers, hardy recusants,
And honest dunces; of important days,
Examinations, when the man was weighed   65
As in the balance; of excessive hopes,
Tremblings withal and commendable fears,

Small jealousies and triumphs good or bad –
I make short mention. Things they were which then
I did not love, nor do I love them now: 70
Such glory was but little sought by me,
And little won. But it is right to say
That even so early, from the first crude days
Of settling-time in this my new abode,
Not seldom I had melancholy thoughts   75
From personal and family regards,
Wishing to hope without a hope – some fears
About my future worldly maintenance,
And, more than all, a strangeness in my mind,
A feeling that I was not for that hour   80
Nor for that place. But wherefore be cast down,
Why should I grieve? – I was a chosen son.
For hither I had come with holy powers
And faculties, whether to work or feel:
To apprehend all passions and all moods   85
Which time, and place, and season do impress
Upon the visible universe, and work
Like changes there by force of my own mind.
I was a freeman, in the purest sense
Was free, and to majestic ends was strong –   90
I do not speak of learning, moral truth,
Or understanding – 'twas enough for me
To know that I was otherwise endowed.
When the first glitter of the show was passed,
And the first dazzle of the taper-light,   95
As if with a rebound my mind returned
Into its former self. Oft did I leave
My comrades, and the crowd, buildings and groves,
And walked along the fields, the level fields,
With heaven's blue concave reared above my head.   100
And now it was that through such change entire,
And this first absence from those shapes sublime
Wherewith I had been conversant, my mind
Seemed busier in itself than heretofore –
At least I more directly recognised   105
My powers and habits. Let me dare to speak
A higher language, say that now I felt
The strength and consolation which were mine.

As if awakened, summoned, rouzed, constrained,
I looked for universal things, perused   110
The common countenance of earth and heaven,
And, turning the mind in upon itself,
Pored, watched, expected, listened, spread my thoughts,
And spread them with a wider creeping, felt
Incumbences more awful, visitings   115
Of the upholder, of the tranquil soul,
Which underneath all passion lives secure
A steadfast life. But peace, it is enough
To notice that I was ascending now
To such community with highest truth.   120

                    *   *   *

   And here, O friend, have I retraced my life
Up to an eminence, and told a tale
Of matters which not falsely I may call   170
The glory of my youth. Of genius, power,
Creation, and divinity itself,
I have been speaking, for my theme has been
What passed within me. Not of outward things
Done visibly for other minds — words, signs,   175
Symbols or actions — but of my own heart
Have I been speaking, and my youthful mind.
O heavens, how awful is the might of souls,
And what they do within themselves while yet
The yoke of earth is new to them, the world   180
Nothing but a wild field where they were sown.
This is in truth heroic argument,
And genuine prowess — which I wished to touch,
With hand however weak — but in the main
It lies far hidden from the reach of words.   185
Points have we all of us within our souls
Where all stand single; this I feel, and make
Breathings for incommunicable powers.
Yet each man is a memory to himself,
And, therefore, now that I must quit this theme,   190
I am not heartless; for there's not a man
That lives who hath not had his god-like hours,
And knows not what majestic sway we have
As natural beings in the strength of Nature.

Enough, for now into a populous plain   195
We must descend. A traveller I am,
And all my tale is of myself – even so –
So be it, if the pure in heart delight
To follow me, and thou, O honored friend,
Who in my thoughts art ever at my side,   200
Uphold as heretofore my fainting steps.
It hath been told already how my sight
Was dazzled by the novel show, and how
Erelong I did into myself return.
So did it seem, and so in truth it was –   205
Yet this was but short-lived. Thereafter came
Observance less devout: I had made a change
In climate, and my nature's outward coat
Changed also, slowly and insensibly.
To the deep quiet and majestic thoughts   210
Of loneliness succeeded empty noise
And superficial pastimes, now and then
Forced labour, and more frequently forced hopes,
And, worse than all, a treasonable growth
Of indecisive judgements that impaired   215
And shook the mind's simplicity. And yet
This was a gladsome time. Could I behold –
Who less insensible than sodden clay
On a sea-river's bed at ebb of tide
Could have beheld – with undelighted heart   220
So many happy youths, so wide and fair
A congregation in its budding-time
Of health, and hope, and beauty, all at once
So many divers samples of the growth
Of life's sweet season, could have seen unmoved   225
That miscellaneous garland of wild flowers
Upon the matron temples of a place
So famous through the world? To me at least
It was a goodly prospect; for, through youth,
Though I had been trained up to stand unpropped,   230
And independent musings pleased me so
That spells seemed on me when I was alone,
Yet could I only cleave to solitude
In lonesome places – if a throng was near
That way I leaned by nature, for my heart   235
Was social and loved idleness and joy.

FROM BOOK IV:
SUMMER VACATION

A freshness also found I at this time
In human life, the life I mean of those
Whose occupations really I loved.
The prospect often touched me with surprize:
Crowded and full, and changed, as seemed to me,   185
Even as a garden in the heat of spring
After an eight-days' absence. For – to omit
The things which were the same and yet appeared
So different – amid this solitude,
The little vale where was my chief abode,   190
'Twas not indifferent to a youthful mind
To note, perhaps, some sheltered seat in which
An old man had been used to sun himself,
Now empty; pale-faced babes whom I had left
In arms, known children of the neighbourhood,   195
Now rosy prattlers, tottering up and down;
And growing girls whose beauty, filched away
With all its pleasant promises, was gone
To deck some slighted playmate's homely cheek.

    Yes, I had something of another eye,   200
And often looking round was moved to smiles
Such as a delicate work of humour breeds.
I read, without design, the opinions, thoughts,
Of those plain-living people, in a sense
Of love and knowledge: with another eye   205
I saw the quiet woodman in the woods,
The shepherd on the hills. With new delight,
This chiefly, did I view my grey-haired dame,
Saw her go forth to church, or other work
Of state, equipped in monumental trim –   210
Short velvet cloak, her bonnet of the like,
A mantle such as Spanish cavaliers
Wore in old time. Her smooth domestic life –
Affectionate without uneasiness –
Her talk, her business, pleased me; and no less   215

Her clear though shallow stream of piety,
That ran on sabbath days a fresher course.
With thoughts unfelt till now I saw her read
Her bible on the Sunday afternoons,
And loved the book when she had dropped asleep   220
And made of it a pillow for her head.

   Nor less do I remember to have felt
Distinctly manifested at this time,
A dawning, even as of another sense,
A human-heartedness about my love   225
For objects hitherto the gladsome air
Of my own private being, and no more –
Which I had loved, even as a blessèd spirit
Or angel, if he were to dwell on earth,
Might love in individual happiness.   230
But now there opened on me other thoughts,
Of change, congratulation and regret,
A new-born feeling. It spread far and wide:
The trees, the mountains shared it, and the brooks,
The stars of heaven, now seen in their old haunts –   235
White Sirius glittering o'er the southern crags,
Orion with his belt, and those fair Seven,
Acquaintances of every little child,
And Jupiter, my own belovèd star.
Whatever shadings of mortality   240
Had fallen upon these objects heretofore
Were different in kind: not tender – strong,
Deep, gloomy were they, and severe, the scatterings
Of childhood, and moreover, had given way
In later youth to beauty and to love   245
Enthusiastic, to delight and joy.

   As one who hangs down-bending from the side
Of a slow-moving boat upon the breast
Of a still water, solacing himself
With such discoveries as his eye can make   250
Beneath him in the bottom of the deeps,
Sees many beauteous sights – weeds, fishes, flowers,
Grots, pebbles, roots of trees – and fancies more,

Yet often is perplexed, and cannot part
The shadow from the substance, rocks and sky,   255
Mountains and clouds, from that which is indeed
The region, and the things which there abide
In their true dwelling; now is crossed by gleam
Of his own image, by a sunbeam now,
And motions that are sent he knows not whence,   260
Impediments that make his task more sweet;
Such pleasant office have we long pursued
Incumbent o'er the surface of past time –
With like success. Nor have we often looked
On more alluring shows – to me at least –   265
More soft, or less ambiguously descried,
Than those which now we have been passing by,
And where we still are lingering. Yet in spite
Of all these new employments of the mind
There was an inner falling off. I loved,   270
Loved deeply, all that I had loved before,
More deeply even than ever; but a swarm
Of heady thoughts jostling each other, gawds
And feast and dance and public revelry
And sports and games – less pleasing in themselves   275
Than as they were a badge, glossy and fresh,
Of manliness and freedom – these did now
Seduce me from the firm habitual quest
Of feeding pleasures, from that eager zeal,
Those yearnings which had every day been mine,   280
A wild, unworldly-minded youth, given up
To Nature and to books, or, at the most,
From time to time by inclination shipped
One among many, in societies
That were, or seemed, as simple as myself.   285
But now was come a change – it would demand
Some skill, and longer time than may be spared,
To paint even to myself these vanities,
And how they wrought – but sure it is that now
Contagious air did oft environ me,   290
Unknown among these haunts in former days.
The very garments that I wore appeared
To prey upon my strength, and stopped the course
And quiet stream of self-forgetfulness.

Something there was about me that perplexed   295
Th' authentic sight of reason, pressed too closely
On that religious dignity of mind
That is the very faculty of truth,
Which wanting – either, from the very first
A function never lighted up, or else   300
Extinguished – man, a creature great and good,
Seems but a pageant plaything with vile claws,
And this great frame of breathing elements
A senseless idol.

        This vague heartless chace
Of trivial pleasures was a poor exchange   305
For books and Nature at that early age.
'Tis true, some casual knowledge might be gained
Of character or life; but at that time,
Of manners put to school I took small note,
And all my deeper passions lay elsewhere –   310
Far better had it been to exalt the mind
By solitary study, to uphold
Intense desire by thought and quietness.
And yet, in chastisement of these regrets,
The memory of one particular hour   315
Doth here rise up against me. In a throng,
A festal company of maids and youths,
Old men and matrons, staid, promiscuous rout,
A medley of all tempers, I had passed
The night in dancing, gaiety and mirth –   320
With din of instruments, and shuffling feet,
And glancing forms, and tapers glittering,
And unaimed prattle flying up and down,
Spirits upon the stretch, and here and there
Slight shocks of young love-liking interspersed   325
That mounted up like joy into the head,
And tingled through the veins. Ere we retired
The cock had crowed, the sky was bright with day;
Two miles I had to walk along the fields
Before I reached my home. Magnificent   330
The morning was, a memorable pomp,
More glorious than I ever had beheld.
The sea was laughing at a distance; all

The solid mountains were as bright as clouds,
Grain-tinctured, drenched in empyrean light;   335
And in the meadows and the lower grounds
Was all the sweetness of a common dawn –
Dews, vapours, and the melody of birds,
And labourers going forth into the fields.
Ah, need I say, dear friend, that to the brim   340
My heart was full? I made no vows, but vows
Were then made for me: bond unknown to me
Was given, that I should be – else sinning greatly –
A dedicated spirit. On I walked
In blessedness, which even yet remains.   345

*   *   *

   While thus I wandered, step by step led on,   400
It chanced a sudden turning of the road
Presented to my view an uncouth shape,
So near that, slipping back into the shade
Of a thick hawthorn, I could mark him well,
Myself unseen. He was of stature tall,   405
A foot above man's common measure tall,
Stiff in his form, and upright, lank and lean –
A man more meagre, as it seemed to me,
Was never seen abroad by night or day.
His arms were long, and bare his hands; his mouth   410
Shewed ghastly in the moonlight; from behind,
A milestone propped him, and his figure seemed
Half sitting, and half standing. I could mark
That he was clad in military garb,
Though faded yet entire. He was alone,   415
Had no attendant, neither dog, nor staff,
Nor knapsack; in his very dress appeared
A desolation, a simplicity
That seemed akin to solitude. Long time
Did I peruse him with a mingled sense   420
Of fear and sorrow. From his lips meanwhile
There issued murmuring sounds, as if of pain
Or of uneasy thought; yet still his form
Kept the same steadiness, and at his feet
His shadow lay, and moved not. In a glen   425

Hard by, a village stood, whose roofs and
    doors
Were visible among the scattered trees,
Scarce distant from the spot an arrow's flight.
I wished to see him move, but he remained
Fixed to his place, and still from time to time   430
Sent forth a murmuring voice of dead complaint,
Groans scarcely audible. Without self-blame
I had not thus prolonged my watch; and now,
Subduing my heart's specious cowardice,
I left the shady nook where I had stood   435
And hailed him. Slowly from his resting-place
He rose, and with a lean and wasted arm
In measured gesture lifted to his head
Returned my salutation, then resumed
His station as before. And when erelong   440
I asked his history, he in reply
Was neither slow nor eager, but, unmoved,
And with a quiet uncomplaining voice,
A stately air of mild indifference,
He told in simple words a soldier's tale: 445
That in the tropic islands he had served,
Whence he had landed scarcely ten days past –
That on his landing he had been dismissed,
And now was travelling to his native home.
At this I turned and looked towards the village,   450
But all were gone to rest, the fires all out,
And every silent window to the moon
Shone with a yellow glitter. 'No one there,'
Said I, 'is waking; we must measure back
The way which we have come. Behind yon wood   455
A labourer dwells, and, take it on my word,
He will not murmur should we break his rest,
And with a ready heart will give you food
And lodging for the night.' At this he stooped,
And from the ground took up an oaken staff   460
By me yet unobserved, a traveller's staff
Which I suppose from his slack hand had
    dropped,
And lain till now neglected in the grass.

    Towards the cottage without more delay
We shaped our course. As it appeared to me   465
He travelled without pain, and I beheld
With ill-suppressed astonishment his tall
And ghastly figure moving at my side;
Nor while we journeyed thus could I forbear
To question him of what he had endured   470
From hardship, battle, or the pestilence.
He all the while was in demeanor calm,
Concise in answer. Solemn and sublime
He might have seemed, but that in all he said
There was a strange half-absence, and a tone   475
Of weakness and indifference, as of one
Remembering the importance of his theme
But feeling it no longer. We advanced
Slowly, and ere we to the wood were come
Discourse had ceased. Together on we passed   480
In silence through the shades, gloomy and dark;
Then, turning up along an open field,
We gained the cottage. At the door I knocked,
Calling aloud, 'My friend, here is a man
By sickness overcome. Beneath your roof   485
This night let him find rest, and give him food
If food he need, for he is faint and tired.'
Assured that now my comrade would repose
In comfort, I entreated that henceforth
He would not linger in the public ways,   490
But ask for timely furtherance, and help
Such as his state required. At this reproof,
With the same ghastly mildness in his look,
He said, 'My trust is in the God of Heaven,
And in the eye of him that passes me.'   495
The cottage door was speedily unlocked,
And now the soldier touched his hat again
With his lean hand, and in a voice that seemed
To speak with a reviving interest,
Till then unfelt, he thanked me; I returned   500
The blessing of the poor unhappy man,
And so we parted. Back I cast a look,
And lingered near the door a little space,
Then sought with quiet heart my distant home.

FROM BOOK V:
BOOKS

A thought is with me sometimes, and I say,
'Should earth by inward throes be wrenched throughout,
Or fire be sent from far to wither all   30
Her pleasant habitations, and dry up
Old Ocean in his bed, left singed and bare,
Yet would the living presence still subsist
Victorious; and composure would ensue,
And kindlings like the morning – presage sure,   35
Though slow perhaps, of a returning day.'
But all the meditations of mankind,
Yea, all the adamantine holds of truth
By reason built, or passion (which itself
Is highest reason in a soul sublime),   40
The consecrated works of bard and sage,
Sensuous or intellectual, wrought by men,
Twin labourers and heirs of the same hopes –
Where would they be? Oh, why hath not the mind
Some element to stamp her image on   45
In nature somewhat nearer to her own?
Why, gifted with such powers to send abroad
Her spirit, must it lodge in shrines so frail?

   One day, when in the hearing of a friend
I had given utterance to thoughts like these,   50
He answered with a smile that in plain truth
'Twas going far to seek disquietude –
But on the front of his reproof confessed
That he at sundry seasons had himself
Yielded to kindred hauntings, and, forthwith,   55
Added that once upon a summer's noon
While he was sitting in a rocky cave
By the seaside, perusing as it chanced,
The famous history of the errant knight
Recorded by Cervantes, these same thoughts   60
Came to him, and to height unusual rose
While listlessly he sate, and, having closed
The book, had turned his eyes towards the sea.

On poetry and geometric truth
(The knowledge that endures) upon these two,   65
And their high privilege of lasting life
Exempt from all internal injury,
He mused – upon these chiefly – and at length,
His senses yielding to the sultry air,
Sleep seized him and he passed into a dream.   70
He saw before him an Arabian waste,
A desart, and he fancied that himself
Was sitting there in the wide wilderness
Alone upon the sands. Distress of mind
Was growing in him when, behold, at once   75
To his great joy a man was at his side,
Upon a dromedary mounted high.
He seemed an arab of the Bedouin tribes;
A lance he bore, and underneath one arm
A stone, and in the opposite hand a shell   80
Of a surpassing brightness. Much rejoiced
The dreaming man that he should have a guide
To lead him through the desert; and he thought,
While questioning himself what this strange freight
Which the newcomer carried through the waste   85
Could mean, the arab told him that the stone –
To give it in the language of the dream –
Was *Euclid's Elements*. 'And this,' said he,
'This other,' pointing to the shell, 'this book
Is something of more worth.' 'And, at the word,   90
The stranger,' said my friend continuing,
'Stretched forth the shell towards me, with command
That I should hold it to my ear. I did so
And heard that instant in an unknown tongue,
Which yet I understood, articulate sounds,   95
A loud prophetic blast of harmony,
An ode in passion uttered, which foretold
Destruction to the children of the earth
By deluge now at hand. No sooner ceased
The song, but with calm look the arab said   100
That all was true, that it was even so
As had been spoken, and that he himself
Was going then to bury those two books –
The one that held acquaintance with the stars,

And wedded man to man by purest bond   105
Of nature, undisturbed by space or time;
Th' other that was a god, yea many gods,
Had voices more than all the winds, and was
A joy, a consolation, and a hope.'
My friend continued, 'Strange as it may seem   110
I wondered not, although I plainly saw
The one to be a stone, th' other a shell,
Nor doubted once but that they both were books,
Having a perfect faith in all that passed.
A wish was now engendered in my fear   115
To cleave unto this man, and I begged leave
To share his errand with him. On he passed
Not heeding me; I followed, and took note
That he looked often backward with wild look,
Grasping his twofold treasure to his side.   120
Upon a dromedary, lance in rest,
He rode, I keeping pace with him; and now
I fancied that he was the very knight
Whose tale Cervantes tells, yet not the knight,
But was an arab of the desert too,   125
Of these was neither, and was both at once.
His countenance meanwhile grew more disturbed,
And looking backwards when he looked I saw
A glittering light, and asked him whence it came.
"It is," said he, "the waters of the deep   130
Gathering upon us." Quickening then his pace
He left me; I called after him aloud;
He heeded not, but with his twofold charge
Beneath his arm – before me full in view –
I saw him riding o'er the desert sands   135
With the fleet waters of the drowning world
In chace of him; whereat I waked in terror,
And saw the sea before me, and the book
In which I had been reading at my side.'

        Full often, taking from the world of sleep   140
This arab phantom which my friend beheld,
This semi-Quixote, I to him have given
A substance, fancied him a living man –
A gentle dweller in the desert, crazed

By love, and feeling, and internal thought   145
Protracted among endless solitudes –
Have shaped him, in the oppression of his brain,
Wandering upon this quest and thus equipped.
And I have scarcely pitied him, have felt
A reverence for a being thus employed,   150
And thought that in the blind and awful lair
Of such a madness reason did lie couched.
Enow there are on earth to take in charge
Their wives, their children, and their virgin loves,
Or whatsoever else the heart holds dear –   155
Enow to think of these – yea, will I say,
In sober contemplation of the approach
Of such great overthrow, made manifest
By certain evidence, that I methinks
Could share that maniac's anxiousness, could go   160
Upon like errand. Oftentimes at least
Me hath such deep entrancement half-possessed
When I have held a volume in my hand –
Poor earthly casket of immortal verse –
Shakespeare or Milton, labourers divine.   165

FROM BOOK VI:
CAMBRIDGE AND THE ALPS

Whate'er in this wide circuit we beheld
Or heard was fitted to our unripe state   470
Of intellect and heart. By simple strains
Of feeling, the pure breath of real life,
We were not left untouched. With such a book
Before our eyes we could not chuse but read
A frequent lesson of sound tenderness,   475
The universal reason of mankind,
The truth of young and old. Nor, side by side
Pacing, two brother pilgrims, or alone
Each with his humour, could we fail to abound –
Craft this which hath been hinted at before –   480
In dreams and fictions pensively composed:
Dejection taken up for pleasure's sake,
And gilded sympathies, the willow wreath,
Even among those solitudes sublime,

And sober posies of funereal flowers,   485
Culled from the gardens of the Lady Sorrow,
Did sweeten many a meditative hour.

    Yet still in me, mingling with these delights,
Was something of stern mood, an under-thirst
Of vigour, never utterly asleep.   490
Far different dejection once was mine –
A deep and genuine sadness then I felt –
The circumstances I will here relate
Even as they were. Upturning with a band
Of travellers, from the Valais we had clomb   495
Along the road that leads to Italy;
A length of hours, making of these our guides,
Did we advance, and, having reached an inn
Among the mountains, we together ate
Our noon's repast, from which the travellers rose   500
Leaving us at the board. Erelong we followed,
Descending by the beaten road that led
Right to a rivulet's edge, and there broke off;
The only track now visible was one
Upon the further side, right opposite,   505
And up a lofty mountain. This we took,
After a little scruple and short pause,
And climbed with eagerness – though not, at length,
Without surprize and some anxiety
On finding that we did not overtake   510
Our comrades gone before. By fortunate chance,
While every moment now encreased our doubts,
A peasant met us, and from him we learned
That to the place which had perplexed us first
We must descend, and there should find the road   515
Which in the stony channel of the stream
Lay a few steps, and then along its banks –
And further, that thenceforward all our course
Was downwards with the current of that stream.
Hard of belief, we questioned him again,   520
And all the answers which the man returned
To our inquiries, in their sense and substance
Translated by the feelings which we had,
Ended in this – that we had crossed the Alps.

Imagination! – lifting up itself   525
Before the eye and progress of my song
Like an unfathered vapour, here that power,
In all the might of its endowments, came
Athwart me. I was lost as in a cloud,
Halted without a struggle to break through,   530
And now, recovering, to my soul I say
'I recognise thy glory.' In such strength
Of usurpation, in such visitings
Of awful promise, when the light of sense
Goes out in flashes that have shewn to us   535
The invisible world, doth greatness make abode,
There harbours whether we be young or old.
Our destiny, our nature, and our home,
Is with infinitude – and only there;
With hope it is, hope that can never die,   540
Effort, and expectation, and desire,
And something evermore about to be.
The mind beneath such banners militant
Thinks not of spoils or trophies, nor of aught
That may attest its prowess, blest in thoughts   545
That are their own perfection and reward –
Strong in itself, and in the access of joy
Which hides it like the overflowing Nile.

The dull and heavy slackening which ensued
Upon those tidings by the peasant given   550
Was soon dislodged; downwards we hurried fast,
And entered with the road which we had missed
Into a narrow chasm. The brook and road
Were fellow-travellers in this gloomy pass,
And with them did we journey several hours   555
At a slow step. The immeasurable height
Of woods decaying, never to be decayed,
The stationary blasts of waterfalls,
And everywhere along the hollow rent
Winds thwarting winds, bewildered and forlorn,   560
The torrents shooting from the clear blue sky,
The rocks that muttered close upon our ears –
Black drizzling crags that spake by the wayside
As if a voice were in them – the sick sight

And giddy prospect of the raving stream,   565
The unfettered clouds and region of the heavens,
Tumult and peace, the darkness and the light,
Were all like workings of one mind, the features
Of the same face, blossoms upon one tree,
Characters of the great apocalypse,   570
The types and symbols of eternity,
Of first, and last, and midst, and without end.

FROM BOOK VII:
RESIDENCE IN LONDON

But foolishness, and madness in parade,
Though most at home in this their dear domain,   590
Are scattered everywhere, no rarities,
Even to the rudest novice of the schools.
O friend, one feeling was there which belonged
To this great city by exclusive right:
How often in the overflowing streets   595
Have I gone forwards with the crowd, and said
Unto myself, 'The face of every one
That passes by me is a mystery.'
Thus have I looked, nor ceased to look, oppressed
By thoughts of what, and whither, when and how,   600
Until the shapes before my eyes became
A second-sight procession, such as glides
Over still mountains, or appears in dreams,
And all the ballast of familiar life –
The present, and the past, hope, fear, all stays,   605
All laws of acting, thinking, speaking man –
Went from me, neither knowing me, nor known.
And once, far travelled in such mood, beyond
The reach of common indications, lost
Amid the moving pageant, 'twas my chance   610
Abruptly to be smitten with the view
Of a blind beggar, who, with upright face,
Stood propped against a wall, upon his chest
Wearing a written paper, to explain
The story of the man, and who he was.   615
My mind did at this spectacle turn round
As with the might of waters, and it seemed

To me that in this label was a type
Or emblem of the utmost that we know
Both of ourselves and of the universe,   620
And on the shape of this unmoving man,
His fixèd face and sightless eyes, I looked,
As if admonished from another world.

  Though reared upon the base of outward things,
These chiefly are such structures as the mind   625
Builds for itself. Scenes different there are –
Full-formed – which take, with small internal help,
Possession of the faculties: the peace
Of night, for instance, the solemnity
Of Nature's intermediate hours of rest   630
When the great tide of human life stands still,
The business of the day to come unborn,
Of that gone by locked up as in the grave;
The calmness, beauty, of the spectacle,
Sky, stillness, moonshine, empty streets, and sounds   635
Unfrequent as in desarts; at late hours
Of winter evenings when unwholesome rains
Are falling hard, with people yet astir,
The feeble salutation from the voice
Of some unhappy woman now and then   640
Heard as we pass, when no one looks about,
Nothing is listened to. But these I fear
Are falsely catalogued: things that are, are not,
Even as we give them welcome, or assist –
Are prompt, or are remiss. What say you then   645
To times when half the city shall break out
Full of one passion – vengeance, rage, or fear –
To executions, to a street on fire,
Mobs, riots, or rejoicings? From those sights
Take one, an annual festival, the fair   650
Holden where martyrs suffered in past time,
And named of St Bartholomew, there see
A work that's finished to our hands, that lays,
If any spectacle on earth can do,
The whole creative powers of man asleep.   655
For once the Muse's help will we implore,
And she shall lodge us – wafted on her wings

Above the press and danger of the crowd –
Upon some showman's platform. What a hell
For eyes and ears, what anarchy and din   660
Barbarian and infernal – 'tis a dream
Monstrous in colour, motion, shape, sight, sound.
Below, the open space, through every nook
Of the wide area, twinkles, is alive
With heads; the midway region and above   665
Is thronged with staring pictures and huge scrolls,
Dumb proclamations of the prodigies;
And chattering monkeys dangling from their poles,
And children whirling in their roundabouts;
With those that stretch the neck, and strain the eyes,   670
And crack the voice in rivalship, the crowd
Inviting; with buffoons against buffoons
Grimacing, writhing, screaming; him who grinds
The hurdy-gurdy, at the fiddle weaves,
Rattles the salt-box, thumps the kettle-drum,   675
And him who at the trumpet puffs his cheeks,
The silver-collared negro with his timbrel,
Equestrians, tumblers, women, girls, and boys,
Blue-breeched, pink-vested, and with towering plumes.
All moveables of wonder from all parts   680
Are here, albinos, painted Indians, dwarfs,
The horse of knowledge, and the learned pig,
The stone-eater, the man that swallows fire,
Giants, ventriloquists, the invisible girl,
The bust that speaks and moves its goggling eyes,   685
The waxwork, clockwork, all the marvellous craft
Of modern Merlins, wild beasts, puppet-shows,
All out-o'-th'-way, far-fetched, perverted things,
All freaks of Nature, all Promethean thoughts
Of man – his dulness, madness, and their feats,   690
All jumbled up together to make up
This parliament of monsters. Tents and booths
Meanwhile – as if the whole were one vast mill –
Are vomiting, receiving, on all sides,
Men, women, three-years' children, babes in arms.   695

    O, blank confusion, and a type not false
Of what the mighty city is itself

To all, except a straggler here and there –
To the whole swarm of its inhabitants –
An undistinguishable world to men,   700
The slaves unrespited of low pursuits,
Living amid the same perpetual flow
Of trivial objects, melted and reduced
To one identity by differences
That have no law, no meaning, and no end –   705
Oppression under which even highest minds
Must labour, whence the strongest are not free.
But though the picture weary out the eye,
By nature an unmanageable sight,
It is not wholly so to him who looks   710
In steadiness, who hath among least things
An under-sense of greatest, sees the parts
As parts, but with a feeling of the whole.
This, of all acquisitions first, awaits
On sundry and most widely different modes   715
Of education – nor with least delight
On that through which I passed. Attention comes,
And comprehensiveness and memory,
From early converse with the works of God
Among all regions, chiefly where appear   720
Most obviously simplicity and power.
By influence habitual to the mind
The mountain's outline and its steady form
Gives a pure grandeur, and its presence shapes
The measure and the prospect of the soul   725
To majesty: such virtue have the forms
Perennial of the ancient hills – nor less
The changeful language of their countenances
Gives movement to the thoughts, and multitude,
With order and relation. This (if still,   730
As hitherto, with freedom I may speak,
And the same perfect openness of mind,
Not violating any just restraint,
As I would hope, of real modesty),
This did I feel in that vast receptacle.   735
The spirit of Nature was upon me here,
The soul of beauty and enduring life
Was present as a habit, and diffused –

Through meagre lines and colours, and the press
Of self-destroying, transitory things —   740
Composure and ennobling harmony.

FROM BOOK VIII:
RETROSPECT: LOVE OF NATURE LEADING TO
LOVE OF MANKIND

With deep devotion, Nature, did I feel
In that great city what I owed to thee:
High thoughts of God and man, and love of man,
Triumphant over all those loathsome sights   65
Of wretchedness and vice, a watchful eye,
Which, with the outside of our human life
Not satisfied, must read the inner mind.
For I already had been taught to love
My fellow-beings, to such habits trained   70
Among the woods and mountains, where I found
In thee a gracious guide to lead me forth
Beyond the bosom of my family,
My friends and youthful playmates. 'Twas thy power
That raised the first complacency in me,   75
And noticeable kindliness of heart,
Love human to the creature in himself
As he appeared, a stranger in my path,
Before my eyes a brother of this world —
Thou first didst with those motions of delight   80
Inspire me. I remember, far from home
Once having strayed while yet a very child,
I saw a sight — and with what joy and love!
It was a day of exhalations spread
Upon the mountains, mists and steam-like fogs   85
Redounding everywhere, not vehement,
But calm and mild, gentle and beautiful,
With gleams of sunshine on the eyelet spots
And loopholes of the hills, wherever seen,
Hidden by quiet process, and as soon   90
Unfolded, to be huddled up again —
Along a narrow valley and profound
I journeyed, when aloft above my head,
Emerging from the silvery vapours, lo,

A shepherd and his dog, in open day.   95
Girt round with mists they stood, and looked about
From that enclosure small, inhabitants
Of an aërial island floating on,
As seemed, with that abode in which they were,
A little pendant area of grey rocks,   100
By the soft wind breathed forward. With delight
As bland almost, one evening I beheld –
And at as early age (the spectacle
Is common, but by me was then first seen) –
A shepherd in the bottom of a vale,   105
Towards the centre standing, who with voice,
And hand waved to and fro as need required,
Gave signal to his dog, thus teaching him
To chace along the mazes of steep crags
The flock he could not see. And so the brute –   110
Dear creature – with a man's intelligence,
Advancing, or retreating on his steps,
Through every pervious strait, to right or left,
Thridded a way unbaffled, while the flock
Fled upwards from the terror of his bark   115
Through rocks and seams of turf with liquid gold
Irradiate – that deep farewell light by which
The setting sun proclaims the love he bears
To mountain regions.

                    *   *   *

                    A rambling schoolboy, thus   390
Have I beheld him; without knowing why,
Have felt his presence in his own domain
As of a lord and master, or a power,
Or genius, under Nature, under God,
Presiding – and severest solitude   395
Seemed more commanding oft when he was there.
Seeking the raven's nest and suddenly
Surprized with vapours, or on rainy days
When I have angled up the lonely brooks,
Mine eyes have glanced upon him, few steps off,   400
In size a giant, stalking through the fog,
His sheep like Greenland bears. At other times,

When round some shady promontory turning,
His form hath flashed upon me glorified
By the deep radiance of the setting sun;   405
Or him have I descried in distant sky,
A solitary object and sublime,
Above all height, like an aërial cross,
As it is stationed on some spiry rock
Of the Chartreuse, for worship. Thus was man   410
Ennobled outwardly before mine eyes,
And thus my heart at first was introduced
To an unconscious love and reverence
Of human nature; hence the human form
To me was like an index of delight,   415
Of grace and honour, power and worthiness.
Meanwhile, this creature – spiritual almost
As those of books, but more exalted far,
Far more of an imaginative form –
Was not a Corin of the groves, who lives   420
For his own fancies, or to dance by the hour
In coronal, with Phyllis in the midst,
But, for the purposes of kind, a man
With the most common – husband, father – learned,
Could teach, admonish, suffered with the rest   425
From vice and folly, wretchedness and fear.
Of this I little saw, cared less for it,
But something must have felt.

                            Call ye these appearances
Which I beheld of shepherds in my youth,
This sanctity of Nature given to man,   430
A shadow, a delusion? – ye who are fed
By the dead letter, not the spirit of things,
Whose truth is not a motion or a shape
Instinct with vital functions, but a block
Or waxen image which yourselves have made,   435
And ye adore. But blessèd be the God
Of Nature and of man that this was so,
That men did at the first present themselves
Before my untaught eyes thus purified,
Removed, and at a distance that was fit.   440
And so we all of us in some degree

Are led to knowledge, whencesoever led,
And howsoever – were it otherwise,
And we found evil fast as we find good
In our first years, or think that it is found,   445
How could the innocent heart bear up and live?
But doubly fortunate my lot: not here
Alone, that something of a better life
Perhaps was round me than it is the privilege
Of most to move in, but that first I looked   450
At man through objects that were great and fair,
First communed with him by their help. And thus
Was founded a sure safeguard and defence
Against the weight of meanness, selfish cares,
Coarse manners, vulgar passions, that beat in   455
On all sides from the ordinary world
In which we traffic. Starting from this point,
I had my face towards the truth, began
With an advantage, furnished with that kind
Of prepossession without which the soul   460
Receives no knowledge that can bring forth good –
No genuine insight ever comes to her –
Happy in this, that I with Nature walked,
Not having a too early intercourse
With the deformities of crowded life,   465
And those ensuing laughters and contempts
Self-pleasing, which if we would wish to think
With admiration and respect of man
Will not permit us, but pursue the mind
That to devotion willingly would be raised,   470
Into the temple and the temple's heart.

                    *   *   *

   But when that first poetic faculty
Of plain imagination and severe –
No longer a mute influence of the soul,
An element of the nature's inner self –
Began to have some promptings to put on   515
A visible shape, and to the works of art,
The notions and the images of books,
Did knowingly conform itself (by these

Enflamed, and proud of that her new delight),
There came among these shapes of human life   520
A wilfulness of fancy and conceit
Which gave them new importance to the mind –
And Nature and her objects beautified
These fictions, as, in some sort, in their turn
They burnished her. From touch of this new power   525
Nothing was safe: the elder-tree that grew
Beside the well-known charnel-house had then
A dismal look, the yew-tree had its ghost
That took its station there for ornament.
Then common death was none, common mishap,   530
But matter for this humour everywhere,
The tragic super-tragic, else left short.
Then, if a widow staggering with the blow
Of her distress was known to have made her way
To the cold grave in which her husband slept,   535
One night, or haply more than one – through pain
Or half-insensate impotence of mind –
The fact was caught at greedily, and there
She was a visitant the whole year through,
Wetting the turf with never-ending tears,   540
And all the storms of heaven must beat on her.

                    *   *   *

    Preceptress stern, that didst instruct me next,
London, to thee I willingly return.
Erewhile my verse played only with the flowers   680
Enwrought upon thy mantle, satisfied
With this amusement, and a simple look
Of childlike inquisition now and then
Cast upwards on thine eye to puzzle out
Some inner meanings which might harbour there.   685
Yet did I not give way to this light mood
Wholly beguiled, as one incapable
Of higher things, and ignorant that high things
Were round me. Never shall I forget the hour,
The moment rather say, when, having thridded   690
The labyrinth of suburban villages,
At length I did unto myself first seem
To enter the great city. On the roof

Of an itinerant vehicle I sat,
With vulgar men about me, vulgar forms   695
Of houses, pavement, streets, of men and things,
Mean shapes on every side; but, at the time,
When to myself it fairly might be said
(The very moment that I seemed to know)
'The threshold now is overpast', great God!   700
That aught *external* to the living mind
Should have such mighty sway, yet so it was:
A weight of ages did at once descend
Upon my heart – no thought embodied, no
Distinct remembrances, but weight and power,   705
Power growing with the weight. Alas, I feel
That I am trifling. 'Twas a moment's pause:
All that took place within me came and went
As in a moment, and I only now
Remember that it was a thing divine.   710

     As when a traveller hath from open day
With torches passed into some vault of earth,
The grotto of Antiparos, or the den
Of Yordas among Craven's mountain tracts,
He looks and sees the cavern spread and grow,   715
 Widening itself on all sides, sees, or thinks
He sees, erelong, the roof above his head,
Which instantly unsettles and recedes –
Substance and shadow, light and darkness, all
Commingled, making up a canopy   720
Of shapes, and forms, and tendencies to shape,
That shift and vanish, change and interchange
Like spectres – ferment quiet and sublime,
Which, after a short space, works less and less
Till, every effort, every motion gone,   725
The scene before him lies in perfect view
Exposed, and lifeless as a written book.
But let him pause awhile and look again,
And a new quickening shall succeed, at first
Beginning timidly, then creeping fast   730
Through all which he beholds: the senseless mass,
In its projections, wrinkles, cavities,
Through all its surface, with all colours streaming,

Like a magician's airy pageant, parts,
Unites, embodying everywhere some pressure   735
Or image, recognised or new, some type
Or picture of the world – forests and lakes,
Ships, rivers, towers, the warrior clad in mail,
The prancing steed, the pilgrim with his staff,
The mitred bishop and the thronèd king –   740
A spectacle to which there is no end.

*   *   *

   And is not, too, that vast abiding-place
Of human creatures, turn where'er we may,
Profusely sown with individual sights
Of courage, and integrity, and truth,   840
And tenderness, which, here set off by foil,
Appears more touching? In the tender scenes
Chiefly was my delight, and one of these
Never will be forgotten. 'Twas a man,
Whom I saw sitting in an open square   845
Close to the iron paling that fenced in
The spacious grass-plot: on the corner-stone
Of the low wall in which the pales were fixed
Sate this one man, and with a sickly babe
Upon his knee, whom he had thither brought   850
For sunshine, and to breathe the fresher air.
Of those who passed, and me who looked at him,
He took no note; but in his brawny arms
(The artificer was to the elbow bare,
And from his work this moment had been stolen)   855
He held the child, and, bending over it
As if he were afraid both of the sun
And of the air which he had come to seek,
He eyed it with unutterable love.

FROM BOOK IX:
RESIDENCE IN FRANCE

   A knot of military officers
That to a regiment appertained which then
Was stationed in the city were the chief

Of my associates; some of these wore swords   130
Which had been seasoned in the wars, and all
Were men well-born, at least laid claim to such
Distinction, as the chivalry of France.
In age and temper differing, they had yet
One spirit ruling in them all – alike   135
(Save only one, hereafter to be named)
Were bent upon undoing what was done.
This was their rest, and only hope; therewith
No fear had they of bad becoming worse,
For worst to them was come – nor would have stirred,   140
Or deemed it worth a moment's while to stir,
In any thing, save only as the act
Looked thitherward. One, reckoning by years,
Was in the prime of manhood, and erewhile
He had sate lord in many tender hearts,   145
Though heedless of such honours now, and changed:
His temper was quite mastered by the times,
And they had blighted him, had eat away
The beauty of his person, doing wrong
Alike to body and to mind. His port,   150
Which once had been erect and open, now
Was stooping and contracted, and a face
By nature lovely in itself, expressed,
As much as any that was ever seen,
A ravage out of season, made by thoughts   155
Unhealthy and vexatious. At the hour,
The most important of each day, in which
The public news was read, the fever came,
A punctual visitant, to shake this man,
Disarmed his voice and fanned his yellow cheek   160
Into a thousand colours. While he read,
Or mused, his sword was haunted by his touch
Continually, like an uneasy place
In his own body. 'Twas in truth an hour
Of universal ferment – mildest men   165
Were agitated, and commotions, strife
Of passion and opinion, filled the walls
Of peaceful houses with unquiet sounds.
The soil of common life was at that time
Too hot to tread upon. Oft said I then,   170

And not then only, 'What a mockery this
Of history, the past and that to come!
Now do I feel how I have been deceived,
Reading of nations and their works in faith –
Faith given to vanity and emptiness –   175
Oh, laughter for the page that would reflect
To future times the face of what now is!'
The land all swarmed with passion, like a plain
Devoured by locusts – Carra, Gorsas – add
A hundred other names, forgotten now,   180
Nor to be heard of more; yet were they powers,
Like earthquakes, shocks repeated day by day,
And felt through every nook of town and field.

                    *   *   *

              . . . where hope is, there love will be   510
For the abject multitude. And when we chanced
One day to meet a hunger-bitten girl
Who crept along fitting her languid self
Unto a heifer's motion – by a cord
Tied to her arm, and picking thus from the lane   515
Its sustenance, while the girl with her two hands
Was busy knitting in a heartless mood
Of solitude – and at the sight my friend
In agitation said, ''Tis against that
Which we are fighting', I with him believed   520
Devoutly that a spirit was abroad
Which could not be withstood, that poverty,
At least like this, would in a little time
Be found no more, that we should see the earth
Unthwarted in her wish to recompense   525
The industrious, and the lowly child of toil,
All institutes for ever blotted out
That legalized exclusion, empty pomp
Abolished, sensual state and cruel power,
Whether by edict of the one or few –   530
And finally, as sum and crown of all,
Should see the people having a strong hand
In making their own laws, whence better days
To all mankind. But, these things set apart,

Was not the single confidence enough   535
To animate the mind that ever turned
A thought to human welfare? – that henceforth
Captivity by mandate without law
Should cease, and open accusation lead
To sentence in the hearing of the world,   540
And open punishment, if not the air
Be free to breathe in, and the heart of man
Dread nothing.

FROM BOOK X:
RESIDENCE IN FRANCE AND FRENCH REVOLUTION

This was the time in which, enflamed with hope,
To Paris I returned. Again I ranged,
More eagerly than I had done before,   40
Through the wide city, and in progress passed
The prison where the unhappy monarch lay,
Associate with his children and his wife
In bondage, and the palace, lately stormed
With roar of cannon and a numerous host.   45
I crossed – a black and empty area then –
The square of the Carousel, few weeks back
Heaped up with dead and dying, upon these
And other sights looking as doth a man
Upon a volume whose contents he knows   50
Are memorable but from him locked up,
Being written in a tongue he cannot read,
So that he questions the mute leaves with pain,
And half upbraids their silence. But that night
When on my bed I lay, I was most moved   55
And felt most deeply in what world I was;
My room was high and lonely, near the roof
Of a large mansion or hotel, a spot
That would have pleased me in more quiet times –
Nor was it wholly without pleasure then.   60
With unextinguished taper I kept watch,
Reading at intervals. The fear gone by
Pressed on me almost like a fear to come.
I thought of those September massacres,
Divided from me by a little month,   65

And felt and touched them, a substantial dread
(The rest was conjured up from tragic fictions,
And mournful calendars of true history,
Remembrances and dim admonishments):
'The horse is taught his manage, and the wind   70
Of heaven wheels round and treads in his own steps;
Year follows year, the tide returns again,
Day follows day, all things have second birth;
The earthquake is not satisfied at once' –
And in such way I wrought upon myself,   75
Until I seemed to hear a voice that cried
To the whole city, 'Sleep no more!' To this
Add comments of a calmer mind – from which
I could not gather full security –
But at the best it seemed a place of fear,   80
Unfit for the repose of night,
Defenceless as a wood where tigers roam.

                *   *   *

    Such was my then belief – that there was one,
And only one, solicitude for all.
And now the strength of Britain was put forth
In league with the confederated host;   230
Not in my single self alone I found,
But in the minds of all ingenuous youth,
Change and subversion from this hour. No shock
Given to my moral nature had I known
Down to that very moment – neither lapse   235
Nor turn of sentiment – that might be named
A revolution, save at this one time:
All else was progress on the self-same path
On which with a diversity of pace
I had been travelling; this, a stride at once   240
Into another region. True it is,
'Twas not concealed with what ungracious eyes
Our native rulers from the very first
Had looked upon regenerated France;
Nor had I doubted that this day would come –   245
But in such contemplation I had thought
Of general interests only, beyond this

Had never once foretasted the event.
Now had I other business, for I felt
The ravage of this most unnatural strife   250
In my own heart; there lay it like a weight,
At enmity with all the tenderest springs
Of my enjoyments. I, who with the breeze
Had played, a green leaf on the blessed tree
Of my beloved country – nor had wished   255
For happier fortune than to wither there –
Now from my pleasant station was cut off,
And tossed about in whirlwinds. I rejoiced,
Yes, afterwards, truth painful to record,
Exulted in the triumph of my soul   260
When Englishmen by thousands were o'erthrown,
Left without glory on the field, or driven,
Brave hearts, to shameful flight. It was a grief –
Grief call it not, 'twas any thing but that –
A conflict of sensations without name,   265
Of which he only who may love the sight
Of a village steeple as I do can judge,
When in the congregation, bending all
To their great Father, prayers were offered up
Or praises for our country's victories,   270
And, 'mid the simple worshippers perchance
I only, like an uninvited guest
Whom no one owned, sate silent – shall I add,
Fed on the day of vengeance yet to come!

   Oh, much have they to account for, who could tear   275
By violence at one decisive rent
From the best youth in England their dear pride,
Their joy, in England. This, too, at a time
In which worst losses easily might wear
The best of names; when patriotic love   280
Did of itself in modesty give way
Like the precursor when the deity
Is come, whose harbinger he is – a time
In which apostacy from ancient faith
Seemed but conversion to a higher creed;   285
Withal a season dangerous and wild –
A time in which Experience would have plucked

Flowers out of any hedge to make thereof
A chaplet, in contempt of his grey locks.

    Ere yet the fleet of Britain had gone forth   290
On this unworthy service, whereunto
The unhappy counsel of a few weak men
Had doomed it, I beheld the vessels lie —
A brood of gallant creatures — on the deep
I saw them in their rest, a sojourner   295
Through a whole month of calm and glassy days
In that delightful island which protects
Their place of convocation. There I heard
Each evening, walking by the still sea-shore,
A monitory sound which never failed —   300
The sunset cannon. When the orb went down
In the tranquillity of Nature, came
That voice — ill requiem — seldom heard by me
Without a spirit overcast, a deep
Imagination, thought of woes to come,   305
And sorrow for mankind, and pain of heart.

    In France, the men who for their desperate ends
Had plucked up mercy by the roots were glad
Of this new enemy. Tyrants, strong before
In devilish pleas, were ten times stronger now,   310
And thus beset with foes on every side,
The goaded land waxed mad; the crimes of few
Spread into madness of the many; blasts
From hell came sanctified like airs from heaven.
The sternness of the just, the faith of those   315
Who doubted not that Providence had times
Of anger and of vengeance, theirs who throned
The human understanding paramount
And made of that their god, the hopes of those
Who were content to barter short-lived pangs   320
For a paradise of ages, the blind rage
Of insolent tempers, the light vanity
Of intermeddlers, steady purposes
Of the suspicious, slips of the indiscreet,
And all the accidents of life, were pressed   325
Into one service, busy with one work.

The Senate was heart-stricken, not a voice
Uplifted, none to oppose or mitigate.
Domestic carnage now filled all the year
With feast-days: the old man from the chimney-nook,   330
The maiden from the bosom of her love,
The mother from the cradle of her babe,
The warrior from the field – all perished, all –
Friends, enemies, of all parties, ages, ranks,
Head after head, and never heads enough   335
For those who bade them fall. They found their joy,
They made it, ever thirsty, as a child –
If light desires of innocent little ones
May with such heinous appetites be matched –
Having a toy, a windmill, though the air   340
Do of itself blow fresh and makes the vane
Spin in his eyesight, he is not content,
But with the plaything at arm's length he sets
His front against the blast, and runs amain
To make it whirl the faster.   345

                  In the depth
Of these enormities, even thinking minds
Forgot at seasons whence they had their being –
Forgot that such a sound was ever heard
As Liberty upon earth – yet all beneath
Her innocent authority was wrought,   350
Nor could have been, without her blessèd name.
The illustrious wife of Roland, in the hour
Of her composure, felt that agony
And gave it vent in her last words. O friend,
It was a lamentable time for man,   355
Whether a hope had e'er been his or not;
A woeful time for them whose hopes did still
Outlast the shock; most woeful for those few –
They had the deepest feeling of the grief –
Who still were flattered, and had trust in man.   360
Meanwhile the invaders fared as they deserved:
The herculean Commonwealth had put forth her arms,
And throttled with an infant godhead's might
The snakes about her cradle – that was well,
And as it should be, yet no cure for those   365

Whose souls were sick with pain of what would be
Hereafter brought in charge against mankind.
Most melancholy at that time, O friend,
Were my day-thoughts, my dreams were miserable;
Through months, through years, long after the last beat   370
Of those atrocities (I speak bare truth,
As if to thee alone in private talk)
I scarcely had one night of quiet sleep,
Such ghastly visions had I of despair,
And tyranny, and implements of death,   375
And long orations which in dreams I pleaded
Before unjust tribunals, with a voice
Labouring, a brain confounded, and a sense
Of treachery and desertion in the place
The holiest that I knew of – my own soul.   380

                    *   *   *

     This was the time when, all things tending fast   805
To depravation, the philosophy
That promised to abstract the hopes of man
Out of his feelings, to be fixed thenceforth
For ever in a purer element,
Found ready welcome. Tempting region that   810
For zeal to enter and refresh herself,
Where passions had the privilege to work,
And never hear the sound of their own names –
But, speaking more in charity, the dream
Was flattering to the young ingenuous mind   815
Pleased with extremes, and not the least with that
Which makes the human reason's naked self
The object of its fervour. What delight! –
How glorious! – in self-knowledge and self-rule
To look through all the frailties of the world,   820
And, with a resolute mastery shaking off
The accidents of nature, time, and place,
That make up the weak being of the past,
Build social freedom on its only basis:
The freedom of the individual mind,   825
Which, to the blind restraint of general laws
Superior, magisterially adopts

One guide – the light of circumstances, flashed
Upon an independent intellect.

                    *   *   *

   Enough, no doubt, the advocates themselves
Of ancient institutions had performed   850
To bring disgrace upon their very names;
Disgrace of which custom, and written law,
And sundry moral sentiments, as props
And emanations of these institutes,
Too justly bore a part. A veil had been   855
Uplifted. Why deceive ourselves? – 'twas so,
'Twas even so – and sorrow for the man
Who either had not eyes wherewith to see,
Or seeing hath forgotten. Let this pass,
Suffice it that a shock had then been given   860
To old opinions, and the minds of all men
Had felt it – that my mind was both let loose,
Let loose and goaded. After what hath been
Already said of patriotic love,
And hinted at in other sentiments,   865
We need not linger long upon this theme,
This only may be said, that from the first
Having two natures in me (joy the one,
The other melancholy), and withal
A happy man, and therefore bold to look   870
On painful things – slow, somewhat, too, and stern
In temperament – I took the knife in hand,
And, stopping not at parts less sensitive,
Endeavoured with my best of skill to probe
The living body of society   875
Even to the heart. I pushed without remorse
My speculations forward, yea, set foot
On Nature's holiest places.

                       Time may come
When some dramatic story may afford
Shapes livelier to convey to thee, my friend,   880
What then I learned – or think I learned – of truth,
And the errors into which I was betrayed

By present objects, and by reasonings false
From the beginning, inasmuch as drawn
Out of a heart which had been turned aside   885
From Nature by external accidents,
And which was thus confounded more and more,
Misguiding and misguided. Thus I fared,
Dragging all passions, notions, shapes of faith,
Like culprits to the bar, suspiciously   890
Calling the mind to establish in plain day
Her titles and her honours, now believing,
Now disbelieving, endlessly perplexed
With impulse, motive, right and wrong, the ground
Of moral obligation – what the rule,   895
And what the sanction – till, demanding proof,
And seeking it in every thing, I lost
All feeling of conviction, and, in fine,
Sick, wearied out with contrarieties,
Yielded up moral questions in despair.   900

*   *   *

FROM BOOK XI:
IMAGINATION, HOW IMPAIRED AND RESTORED

Oh mystery of man, from what a depth
Proceed thy honours! I am lost, but see
In simple childhood something of the base   330
On which thy greatness stands – but this I feel,
That from thyself it is that thou must give,
Else never canst receive. The days gone by
Come back upon me from the dawn almost
Of life; the hiding-places of my power   335
Seem open, I approach, and then they close;
I see by glimpses now, when age comes on
May scarcely see at all; and I would give
While yet we may, as far as words can give,
A substance and a life to what I feel: 340
I would enshrine the spirit of the past
For future restoration.

*   *   *

FROM BOOK XII:
SAME SUBJECT (CONTINUED)

I love a public road: few sights there are   145
That please me more – such object hath had power
O'er my imagination since the dawn
Of childhood, when its disappearing line
Seen daily afar off, on one bare steep
Beyond the limits which my feet had trod,   150
Was like a guide into eternity,
At least to things unknown and without bound.
Even something of the grandeur which invests
The mariner who sails the roaring sea
Through storm and darkness, early in my mind   155
Surrounded too the wanderers of the earth –
Grandeur as much, and loveliness far more.
Awed have I been by strolling bedlamites;
From many other uncouth vagrants, passed
In fear, have walked with quicker step – but why   160
Take note of this? When I began to inquire,
To watch and question those I met, and held
Familiar talk with them, the lonely roads
Were schools to me in which I daily read
With most delight the passions of mankind,   165
There saw into the depth of human souls –
Souls that appear to have no depth at all
To vulgar eyes. And now, convinced at heart
How little that to which alone we give
The name of education hath to do   170
With real feeling and just sense, how vain
A correspondence with the talking world
Proves to the most – and called to make good search
If man's estate, by doom of Nature yoked
With toil, is therefore yoked with ignorance,   175
If virtue be indeed so hard to rear,
And intellectual strength so rare a boon –
I prized such walks still more; for there I found
Hope to my hope, and to my pleasure peace
And steadiness, and healing and repose   180
To every angry passion. There I heard,

From mouths of lowly men and of obscure,
A tale of honour – sounds in unison
With loftiest promises of good and fair.

There are who think that strong affections, love   185
Known by whatever name, is falsely deemed
A gift (to use a term which they would use)
Of vulgar Nature – that its growth requires
Retirement, leisure, language purified
By manners thoughtful and elaborate –   190
That whoso feels such passion in excess
Must live within the very light and air
Of elegances that are made by man.
True is it, where oppression worse than death
Salutes the being at his birth, where grace   195
Of culture hath been utterly unknown,
And labour in excess and poverty
From day to day pre-occupy the ground
Of the affections, and to Nature's self
Oppose a deeper nature – there indeed   200
Love cannot be; nor does it easily thrive
In cities, where the human heart is sick,
And the eye feeds it not, and cannot feed:
Thus far, no further, is that inference good.

Yes, in those wanderings deeply did I feel   205
How we mislead each other, above all
How books mislead us – looking for their fame
To judgements of the wealthy few, who see
By artificial lights – how they debase
The many for the pleasure of those few,   210
Effeminately level down the truth
To certain general notions for the sake
Of being understood at once, or else
Through want of better knowledge in the men
Who frame them, flattering thus our self-conceit   215
With pictures that ambitiously set forth
The differences, the outside marks by which
Society has parted man from man,
Neglectful of the universal heart.

*   *   *

                Thus haply shall I teach,
Inspire, through unadulterated ears
Pour rapture, tenderness, and hope, my theme
No other than the very heart of man   240
As found among the best of those who live
Not unexalted by religious faith,
Nor uninformed by books (good books, though few),
In Nature's presence — thence may I select
Sorrow that is not sorrow but delight,   245
And miserable love that is not pain
To hear of, for the glory that redounds
Therefrom to human-kind and what we are.
Be mine to follow with no timid step
Where knowledge leads me: it shall be my pride   250
That I have dared to tread this holy ground,
Speaking no dream but things oracular,
Matter not lightly to be heard by those
Who to the letter of the outward promise
Do read the invisible soul, by men adroit   255
In speech and for communion with the world
Accomplished, minds whose faculties are then
Most active when they are most eloquent,
And elevated most when most admired.
Men may be found of other mold than these,   260
Who are their own upholders, to themselves
Encouragement, and energy, and will,
Expressing liveliest thoughts in lively words
As native passion dictates. Others, too,
There are among the walks of homely life   265
Still higher, men for contemplation framed,
Shy, and unpractised in the strife of phrase,
Meek men, whose very souls perhaps would sink
Beneath them, summoned to such intercourse:
Theirs is the language of the heavens, the power,   270
The thought, the image, and the silent joy;
Words are but under-agents in their souls —
When they are grasping with their greatest strength
They do not breathe among them. This I speak
In gratitude to God, who feeds our hearts   275
For his own service, knoweth, loveth us,
When we are unregarded by the world.

                *   *   *

                    Dearest friend,
Forgive me if I say that I, who long
Had harboured reverentially a thought   300
That poets, even as prophets, each with each
Connected in a mighty scheme of truth,
Have each for his peculiar dower a sense
By which he is enabled to perceive
Something unseen before – forgive me, friend,   305
If I, the meanest of this band, had hope
That unto me had also been vouchsafed
An influx, that in some sort I possessed
A privilege, and that a work of mine,
Proceeding from the depth of untaught things,   310
Enduring and creative, might become
A power like one of Nature's.

                    To such mood,
Once above all – a traveller at that time
Upon the plain of Sarum – was I raised:
There on the pastoral downs without a track   315
To guide me, or along the bare white roads
Lengthening in solitude their dreary line,
While through those vestiges of ancient times
I ranged, and by the solitude o'ercome,
I had a reverie and saw the past,   320
Saw multitudes of men, and here and there
A single Briton in his wolf-skin vest,
With shield and stone-ax, stride across the wold;
The voice of spears was heard, the rattling spear
Shaken by arms of mighty bone, in strength   325
Long mouldered, of barbaric majesty.
I called upon the darkness, and it took –
A midnight darkness seemed to come and take –
All objects from my sight; and lo, again
The desart visible by dismal flames!   330
It is the sacrificial altar, fed
With living men – how deep the groans! – the voice
Of those in the gigantic wicker thrills
Throughout the region far and near, pervades
The monumental hillocks, and the pomp   335
Is for both worlds, the living and the dead.

At other moments, for through that wide waste
Three summer days I roamed, when 'twas my chance
To have before me on the downy plain
Lines, circles, mounts, a mystery of shapes   340
Such as in many quarters yet survive,
With intricate profusion figuring o'er
The untilled ground (the work, as some divine,
Of infant science, imitative forms
By which the Druids covertly expressed   345
Their knowledge of the heavens, and imaged forth
The constellations), I was gently charmed,
Albeit with an antiquarian's dream,
And saw the bearded teachers, with white wands
Uplifted, pointing to the starry sky,   350
Alternately, and plain below, while breath
Of music seemed to guide them, and the waste
Was cheered with stillness and a pleasant sound.

FROM BOOK XIII:
CONCLUSION

In one of these excursions, travelling then
Through Wales on foot and with a youthful friend,
I left Bethkelet's huts at couching-time,
And westward took my way to see the sun
Rise from the top of Snowdon. Having reached   5
The cottage at the mountain's foot, we there
Rouzed up the shepherd who by ancient right
Of office is the stranger's usual guide,
And after short refreshment sallied forth.

    It was a summer's night, a close warm night,   10
Wan, dull, and glaring, with a dripping mist
Low-hung and thick that covered all the sky,
Half threatening storm and rain; but on we went
Unchecked, being full of heart and having faith
In our tried pilot. Little could we see,   15
Hemmed round on every side with fog and damp,
And, after ordinary travellers' chat
With our conductor, silently we sunk
Each into commerce with his private thoughts.

Thus did we breast the ascent, and by myself   20
Was nothing either seen or heard the while
Which took me from my musings, save that once
The shepherd's cur did to his own great joy
Unearth a hedgehog in the mountain-crags,
Round which he made a barking turbulent.   25
This small adventure – for even such it seemed
In that wild place and at the dead of night –
Being over and forgotten, on we wound
In silence as before. With forehead bent
Earthward, as if in opposition set   30
Against an enemy, I panted up
With eager pace, and no less eager thoughts;
Thus might we wear perhaps an hour away,
Ascending at loose distance each from each,
And I, as chanced, the foremost of the band –   35
When at my feet the ground appeared to
        brighten,
And with a step or two seemed brighter still;
Nor had I time to ask the cause of this,
For instantly a light upon the turf
Fell like a flash. I looked about, and lo,   40
The moon stood naked in the heavens at height
Immense above my head, and on the shore
I found myself of a huge sea of mist,
Which meek and silent rested at my feet.
A hundred hills their dusky backs upheaved   45
All over this still ocean, and beyond,
Far, far beyond, the vapours shot themselves
In headlands, tongues, and promontory shapes,
Into the sea, the real sea, that seemed
To dwindle and give up its majesty,   50
Usurped upon as far as sight could reach.
Meanwhile, the moon looked down upon this shew
In single glory, and we stood, the mist
Touching our very feet; and from the shore
At distance not the third part of a mile   55
Was a blue chasm, a fracture in the vapour,
A deep and gloomy breathing-place, through which
Mounted the roar of waters, torrents, streams
Innumerable, roaring with one voice.

The universal spectacle throughout   60
Was shaped for admiration and delight,
Grand in itself alone, but in that breach
Through which the homeless voice of waters rose,
That dark deep thoroughfare, had Nature lodged
The soul, the imagination of the whole.   65

    A meditation rose in me that night
Upon the lonely mountain when the scene
Had passed away, and it appeared to me
The perfect image of a mighty mind,
Of one that feeds upon infinity,   70
That is exalted by an under-presence,
The sense of God, or whatsoe'er is dim
Or vast in its own being – above all,
One function of such mind had Nature there
Exhibited by putting forth, and that   75
With circumstance most awful and sublime:
That domination which she oftentimes
Exerts upon the outward face of things,
So moulds them, and endues, abstracts, combines,
Or by abrupt and unhabitual influence   80
Doth make one object so impress itself
Upon all others, and pervades them so,
That even the grossest minds must see and hear,
And cannot chuse but feel. The power which these
Acknowledge when thus moved, which Nature thus   85
Thrusts forth upon the senses, is the express
Resemblance – in the fullness of its strength
Made visible – a genuine counterpart
And brother of the glorious faculty
Which higher minds bear with them as their own.   90
This is the very spirit in which they deal
With all the objects of the universe:
They from their native selves can send abroad
Like transformation, for themselves create
A like existence, and, whene'er it is   95
Created for them, catch it by an instinct.
Them the enduring and the transient both
Serve to exalt. They build up greatest things
From least suggestions, ever on the watch,

Willing to work and to be wrought upon.   100
They need not extraordinary calls
To rouze them – in a world of life they live,
By sensible impressions not enthralled,
But quickened, rouzed, and made thereby more fit
To hold communion with the invisible world.   105
Such minds are truly from the Deity,
For they are powers; and hence the highest bliss
That can be known is theirs – the consciousness
Of whom they are, habitually infused
Through every image, and through every thought,   110
And all impressions; hence religion, faith,
And endless occupation for the soul,
Whether discursive or intuitive;
Hence sovereignty within and peace at will,
Emotion which best foresight need not fear,   115
Most worthy then of trust when most intense;
Hence chearfulness in every act of life;
Hence truth in moral judgements; and delight
That fails not, in the external universe.

     Oh, who is he that hath his whole life long   120
Preserved, enlarged, this freedom in himself? –
For this alone is genuine liberty.
Witness, ye solitudes, where I received
My earliest visitations (careless then
Of what was given me), and where now I roam,   125
A meditative, oft a suffering man,
And yet I trust with undiminished powers;
Witness – whatever falls my better mind,
Revolving with the accidents of life,
May have sustained – that, howsoe'er misled,   130
I never in the quest of right and wrong
Did tamper with myself from private aims;
Nor was in any of my hopes the dupe
Of selfish passions; nor did wilfully
Yield ever to mean cares and low pursuits;   135
But rather did with jealousy shrink back
From every combination that might aid
The tendency, too potent in itself,
Of habit to enslave the mind – I mean

Oppress it by the laws of vulgar sense, 140
And substitute a universe of death,
The falsest of all worlds, in place of that
Which is divine and true. To fear and love
(To love as first and chief, for there fear ends)
Be this ascribed, to early intercourse 145
In presence of sublime and lovely forms
With the adverse principles of pain and joy –
Evil as one is rashly named by those
Who know not what they say. From love, for
    here
Do we begin and end, all grandeur comes, 150
All truth and beauty – from pervading love –
That gone, we are as dust. Behold the fields
In balmy springtime, full of rising flowers
And happy creatures; see that pair, the lamb
And the lamb's mother, and their tender ways 155
Shall touch thee to the heart; in some green
    bower
Rest, and be not alone, but have thou there
The one who is thy choice of all the world –
There linger, lulled, and lost, and rapt away –
Be happy to thy fill; thou call'st this love, 160
And so it is, but there is higher love
Than this, a love that comes into the heart
With awe and a diffusive sentiment.
Thy love is human merely: this proceeds
More from the brooding soul, and is divine. 165
   This love more intellectual cannot be
Without imagination, which in truth
Is but another name for absolute strength
And clearest insight, amplitude of mind,
And reason in her most exalted mood. 170
This faculty hath been the moving soul
Of our long labour: we have traced the stream
From darkness, and the very place of birth
In its blind cavern, whence is faintly heard
The sound of waters; followed it to light 175
And open day, accompanied its course
Among the ways of Nature, afterwards
Lost sight of it bewildered and engulphed,

Then given it greeting as it rose once more
With strength, reflecting in its solemn breast   180
The works of man, and face of human life;
And lastly, from its progress have we drawn
The feeling of life endless, the one thought
By which we live, infinity and God.

    Imagination having been our theme,   185
So also hath that intellectual love,
For they are each in each, and cannot stand
Dividually. Here must thou be, O man,
Strength to thyself – no helper hast thou here –
Here keepest thou thy individual state: 190
No other can divide with thee this work,
No secondary hand can intervene
To fashion this ability. 'Tis thine,
The prime and vital principle is thine
In the recesses of thy nature, far   195
From any reach of outward fellowship,
Else 'tis not thine at all. But joy to him,
O, joy to him who here hath sown – hath laid
Here the foundations of his future years –
For all that friendship, all that love can do,   200
All that a darling countenance can look
Or dear voice utter, to complete the man,
Perfect him, made imperfect in himself,
All shall be his. And he whose soul hath risen
Up to the height of feeling intellect   205
Shall want no humbler tenderness, his heart
Be tender as a nursing mother's heart;
Of female softness shall his life be full,
Of little loves and delicate desires,
Mild interests and gentlest sympathies.   210

From

POEMS IN TWO VOLUMES

1807

Louisa

I met Louisa in the shade,
And, having seen that lovely maid,
Why should I fear to say
That she is ruddy, fleet, and strong,
And down the rocks can leap along,   5
Like rivulets in May?

And she hath smiles to earth unknown:
Smiles, that with motion of their own
Do spread, and sink, and rise,
That come and go with endless play,   10
And ever, as they pass away,
Are hidden in her eyes.

She loves her fire, her cottage-home,
Yet o'er the moorland will she roam
In weather rough and bleak;   15
And when against the wind she strains,
Oh! might I kiss the mountain rains
That sparkle on her cheek.

Take all that's mine 'beneath the moon',
If I with her but half a noon   20
May sit beneath the walls
Of some old cave, or mossy nook,
When up she winds along the brook
To hunt the waterfalls.

'She was a phantom of delight'

She was a phantom of delight
When first she gleamed upon my sight:
A lovely apparition, sent
To be a moment's ornament;

Her eyes as stars of twilight fair;   5
Like twilight's, too, her dusky hair;
But all things else about her drawn
From May-time and the cheerful dawn:
A dancing shape, an image gay,
To haunt, to startle, and way-lay.   10

I saw her upon nearer view,
A spirit, yet a woman too!
Her household motions light and free,
And steps of virgin liberty;
A countenance in which did meet   15
Sweet records, promises as sweet;
A creature not too bright or good
For human nature's daily food,
For transient sorrows, simple wiles,
Praise, blame, love, kisses, tears, and smiles.   20

And now I see with eye serene
The very pulse of the machine:
A being breathing thoughtful breath,
A traveller betwixt life and death;
The reason firm, the temperate will,   25
Endurance, foresight, strength and skill —
A perfect woman, nobly planned
To warn, to comfort, and command;
And yet a spirit still, and bright
With something of an angel light.   30

Character of the Happy Warrior

Who is the happy warrior? Who is he
Whom every man in arms should wish to be?
— It is the generous spirit, who, when brought
Among the tasks of real life, hath wrought
Upon the plan that pleased his childish thought;   5
Whose high endeavours are an inward light
That make the path before him always bright;
Who, with a natural instinct to discern
What knowledge can perform, is diligent to learn;

Abides by this resolve, and stops not there,   10
But makes his moral being his prime care;
Who, doomed to go in company with pain,
And fear, and bloodshed, miserable train!
Turns his necessity to glorious gain;
In face of these doth exercise a power   15
Which is our human-nature's highest dower –
Controls them and subdues, transmutes, bereaves
Of their bad influence, and their good receives;
By objects, which might force the soul to abate
Her feeling, rendered more compassionate;   20
Is placable because occasions rise
So often that demand such sacrifice;
More skilful in self-knowledge, even more pure,
As tempted more; more able to endure,
As more exposed to suffering and distress;   25
Thence, also, more alive to tenderness.
'Tis he whose law is reason; who depends
Upon that law as on the best of friends;
Whence, in a state where men are tempted still
To evil for a guard against worse ill,   30
And what in quality or act is best
Doth seldom on a right foundation rest,
He fixes good on good alone, and owes
To virtue every triumph that he knows;
– Who, if he rise to station of command,   35
Rises by open means, and there will stand
On honourable terms, or else retire,
And in himself possess his own desire;
Who comprehends his trust, and to the same
Keeps faithful with a singleness of aim,   40
And therefore does not stoop, nor lie in wait
For wealth, or honours, or for worldly state,
Whom they must follow – on whose head must fall
Like showers of manna, if they come at all;
Whose powers shed round him in the common strife,   45
Or mild concerns of ordinary life,
A constant influence, a peculiar grace;
But who, if he be called upon to face
Some awful moment to which heaven has joined
Great issues, good or bad for human-kind,   50

Is happy as a lover, and attired
With sudden brightness like a man inspired;
And through the heat of conflict keeps the law
In calmness made, and sees what he foresaw;
Or if an unexpected call succeed,   55
Come when it will, is equal to the need;
— He who, though thus endued as with a sense
And faculty for storm and turbulence,
Is yet a soul whose master bias leans
To home-felt pleasures and to gentle scenes —   60
Sweet images! which, wheresoe'er he be,
Are at his heart, and such fidelity
It is his darling passion to approve;
More brave for this, that he hath much to love;
'Tis finally the man who, lifted high,   65
Conspicuous object in a nation's eye,
Or left unthought-of in obscurity,
Who, with a toward or untoward lot,
Prosperous or adverse, to his wish or not,
Plays, in the many games of life, that one   70
Where what he most doth value must be won;
Whom neither shape of danger can dismay,
Nor thought of tender happiness betray;
Who, not content that former worth stand fast,
Looks forward, persevering to the last,   75
From well to better, daily self-surpassed;
Who, whether praise of him must walk the earth
For ever, and to noble deeds give birth,
Or he must go to dust without his fame,
And leave a dead unprofitable name,   80
Finds comfort in himself and in his cause;
And, while the mortal mist is gathering, draws
His breath in confidence of heaven's applause.
This is the happy warrior; this is he
Whom every man in arms should wish to be.   85

To H.C., Six Years Old

O thou! whose fancies from afar are brought,
Who of thy words dost make a mock apparel,
And fittest to unutterable thought
The breeze-like motion and the self-born carol;
Thou faery voyager! that dost float   5
In such clear water, that thy boat
May rather seem
To brood on air than on an earthly stream—
Suspended in a stream as clear as sky,
Where earth and heaven do make one imagery;   10
O blessed vision! happy child!
That art so exquisitely wild,
I think of thee with many fears
For what may be thy lot in future years.

I thought of times when pain might be thy guest,   15
Lord of thy house and hospitality;
And grief, uneasy lover! never rest
But when she sat within the touch of thee.
Oh! too industrious folly!
Oh! vain and causeless melancholy!   20
Nature will either end thee quite,
Or, lengthening out thy season of delight,
Preserve for thee, by individual right,
A young lamb's heart among the full-grown flocks.
What hast thou to do with sorrow,   25
Or the injuries of tomorrow?
Thou art a dew-drop, which the morn brings forth,
Not doomed to jostle with unkindly shocks,
Or to be trailed along the soiling earth:
A gem that glitters while it lives,   30
And no forewarning gives,
But at the touch of wrong, without a strife,
Slips in a moment out of life.

'I travelled among unknown men'

I travelled among unknown men
   In lands beyond the sea;
Nor England! did I know till then
   What love I bore to thee.

'Tis past, that melancholy dream!   5
   Nor will I quit thy shore
A second time, for still I seem
   To love thee more and more.

Among thy mountains did I feel
   The joy of my desire,   10
And she I cherished turned her wheel
   Beside an English fire.

Thy mornings showed, thy nights concealed
   The bowers where Lucy played,
And thine is, too, the last green field   15
   Which Lucy's eyes surveyed!

Ode to Duty

Stern daughter of the voice of God!
O Duty! if that name thou love
Who art a light to guide, a rod
To check the erring, and reprove;
Thou who art victory and law   5
When empty terrors overawe;
From vain temptations dost set free –
From strife and from despair – a glorious ministry.

There are who ask not if thine eye
Be on them: who, in love and truth,   10
Where no misgiving is, rely
Upon the genial sense of youth –
Glad hearts! without reproach or blot,
Who do thy work, and know it not.

May joy be theirs while life shall last!   15
And thou, if they should totter, teach them to stand fast!

Serene will be our days and bright,
And happy will our nature be
When love is an unerring light,
And joy its own security.   20
And blessed are they who in the main
This faith, even now, do entertain —
Live in the spirit of this creed —
Yet find that other strength, according to their need.

I, loving freedom, and untried,   25
No sport of every random gust,
Yet being to myself a guide,
Too blindly have reposed my trust:
Resolved that nothing e'er should press
Upon my present happiness,   30
I shoved unwelcome tasks away;
But thee I now would serve more strictly, if I may.

Through no disturbance of my soul,
Or strong compunction in me wrought,
I supplicate for thy control;   35
But in the quietness of thought,
Me this unchartered freedom tires;
I feel the weight of chance desires;
My hopes no more must change their name:
I long for a repose which ever is the same.   40

Yet not the less would I throughout
Still act according to the voice
Of my own wish, and feel past doubt
That my submissiveness was choice;
Not seeking in the school of pride   45
For 'precepts over dignified',
Denial and restraint I prize
No farther than they breed a second will more wise.

Stern lawgiver! yet thou dost wear
The Godhead's most benignant grace;   50
Nor know we any thing so fair
As is the smile upon thy face:
Flowers laugh before thee on their beds,
And fragrance in thy footing treads;
Thou dost preserve the stars from wrong,   55
And the most ancient heavens through thee are fresh
          and strong.

To humbler functions, awful power!
I call thee: I myself commend
Unto thy guidance from this hour;
Oh! let my weakness have an end!   60
Give unto me, made lowly wise,
The spirit of self-sacrifice;
The confidence of reason give,
And in the light of truth, thy bondman let me live!

Beggars

She had a tall man's height, or more;
No bonnet screened her from the heat;
A long drab-coloured cloak she wore,
A mantle reaching to her feet;
What other dress she had I could not know,   5
Only she wore a cap that was as white as snow.

In all my walks through field or town,
Such figure had I never seen:
Her face was of Egyptian brown –
Fit person was she for a queen   10
To head those ancient Amazonian files,
Or ruling bandit's wife, among the Grecian isles.

Before me begging did she stand,
Pouring out sorrows like a sea –
Grief after grief; on English land   15
Such woes I knew could never be,
And yet a boon I gave her, for the creature
Was beautiful to see – a weed of glorious feature!

I left her and pursued my way,
And soon before me did espy   20
A pair of little boys at play,
Chasing a crimson butterfly;
  The taller followed with his hat in hand,
Wreathed round with yellow flow'rs – the gayest of the land.

The other wore a rimless crown,   25
With leaves of laurel stuck about,
And they both followed up and down,
Each whooping with a merry shout;
  Two brothers seemed they, eight and ten years old,
And like that woman's face as gold is like to gold.   30

They bolted on me thus, and lo!
Each ready with a plaintive whine;
Said I, 'Not half an hour ago
Your mother has had alms of mine.'
  'That cannot be,' one answered, 'she is dead.'   35
'Nay but I gave her pence, and she will buy you bread.'

'She has been dead, sir, many a day.'
'Sweet boys, you're telling me a lie;
It was your mother, as I say –'
And in the twinkling of an eye,   40
  'Come, come!' cried one, and without more ado,
Off to some other play they both together flew.

Resolution and Independence

There was a roaring in the wind all night;
The rain came heavily and fell in floods;
But now the sun is rising calm and bright;
The birds are singing in the distant woods;
Over his own sweet voice the stock-dove broods;   5
The jay makes answer as the magpie chatters,
And all the air is filled with pleasant noise of waters.

All things that love the sun are out of doors;
The sky rejoices in the morning's birth;
The grass is bright with rain-drops; on the moors   10
The hare is running races in her mirth,
And with her feet, she from the plashy earth
Raises a mist, which, glittering in the sun,
Runs with her all the way, wherever she doth run.

I was a traveller then upon the moor;   15
I saw the hare that raced about with joy;
I heard the woods and distant waters roar,
Or heard them not, as happy as a boy;
The pleasant season did my heart employ;
My old remembrances went from me wholly,   20
And all the ways of men, so vain and melancholy.

But, as it sometimes chanceth, from the might
Of joy in minds that can no farther go,
As high as we have mounted in delight
In our dejection do we sink as low;   25
To me that morning did it happen so,
And fears, and fancies, thick upon me came –
Dim sadness, and blind thoughts I knew not, nor could name.

I heard the skylark singing in the sky,
And I bethought me of the playful hare: 30
Even such a happy child of earth am I;
Even as these blissful creatures do I fare;
Far from the world I walk, and from all care,
But there may come another day to me –
Solitude, pain of heart, distress, and poverty.   35

My whole life I have lived in pleasant thought,
As if life's business were a summer mood,
As if all needful things would come unsought
To genial faith, still rich in genial good;
But how can he expect that others should   40
Build for him, sow for him, and at his call
Love him, who for himself will take no heed at all?

I thought of Chatterton, the marvellous boy,
The sleepless soul that perished in its pride;
Of him who walked in glory and in joy   45
Behind his plough, upon the mountain-side;
By our own spirits are we deified;
We poets in our youth begin in gladness,
But thereof comes in the end despondency and madness.

Now, whether it were by peculiar grace –   50
A leading from above, a something given –
Yet it befell that in this lonely place,
When up and down my fancy thus was driven,
And I with these untoward thoughts had striven,
I saw a man before me unawares: 55
The oldest man he seemed that ever wore grey hairs.

My course I stopped as soon as I espied
The old man in that naked wilderness:
Close by a pond, upon the further side,
He stood alone. A minute's space I guess   60
I watched him, he continuing motionless:
To the pool's further margin then I drew,
He being all the while before me full in view.

As a huge stone is sometimes seen to lie
Couched on the bald top of an eminence –   65
Wonder to all who do the same espy
By what means it could thither come, and whence,
So that it seems a thing endued with sense:
Like a sea-beast crawled forth, which on a shelf
Of rock or sand reposeth, there to sun itself.   70

Such seemed this man, not all alive nor dead,
Nor all asleep, in his extreme old age;
His body was bent double, feet and head
Coming together in their pilgrimage,
As if some dire constraint of pain, or rage   75
Of sickness felt by him in times long past,
A more than human weight upon his frame had cast.

Himself he propped, his body, limbs, and face,
Upon a long grey staff of shaven wood,
And, still as I drew near with gentle pace   80
Beside the little pond or moorish flood,
Motionless as a cloud the old man stood
That heareth not the loud winds when they call,
And moveth altogether, if it move at all.

At length, himself unsettling, he the pond   85
Stirred with his staff, and fixedly did look
Upon the muddy water, which he conned
As if he had been reading in a book;
And now such freedom as I could I took,
And drawing to his side, to him did say,   90
'This morning gives us promise of a glorious day.'

A gentle answer did the old man make,
In courteous speech which forth he slowly drew,
And him with further words I thus bespake,
'What kind of work is that which you pursue?   95
This is a lonesome place for one like you.'
He answered me with pleasure and surprise,
And there was while he spake a fire about his eyes.

His words came feebly, from a feeble chest,
Yet each in solemn order followed each,   100
With something of a lofty utterance dressed:
Choice word, and measured phrase, above the reach
Of ordinary men – a stately speech!
Such as grave livers do in Scotland use,
Religious men, who give to God and man their dues.   105

He told me that he to this pond had come
To gather leeches, being old and poor –
Employment hazardous and wearisome!
And he had many hardships to endure;
From pond to pond he roamed, from moor to moor,   110
Housing, with God's good help, by choice or chance,
And in this way he gained an honest maintenance.

The old man still stood talking by my side,
But now his voice to me was like a stream
Scarce heard, nor word from word could I divide;   115
And the whole body of the man did seem
Like one whom I had met with in a dream,
Or like a man from some far region sent
To give me human strength, and strong admonishment.

My former thoughts returned: the fear that kills,   120
The hope that is unwilling to be fed;
Cold, pain, and labour, and all fleshly ills,
And mighty poets in their misery dead.
And now, not knowing what the old man had said,
My question eagerly did I renew: 125
'How is it that you live, and what is it you do?'

He with a smile did then his words repeat,
And said that gathering leeches, far and wide
He travelled, stirring thus about his feet
The waters of the ponds where they abide.   130
'Once I could meet with them on every side,
But they have dwindled long by slow decay;
Yet still I persevere, and find them where I may.'

While he was talking thus, the lonely place,
The old man's shape and speech, all troubled me: 135
In my mind's eye I seemed to see him pace
About the weary moors continually,
Wandering about alone and silently.
While I these thoughts within myself pursued,
He, having made a pause, the same discourse renewed.   140

And soon with this he other matter blended,
Cheerfully uttered, with demeanour kind,
But stately in the main; and when he ended,
I could have laughed myself to scorn to find
In that decrepit man so firm a mind.   145
'God,' said I, 'be my help and stay secure;
I'll think of the leech-gatherer on the lonely moor.'

'Nuns fret not at their convent's narrow room'

Nuns fret not at their convent's narrow room,
And hermits are contented with their cells,
And students with their pensive citadels;
Maids at the wheel, the weaver at his loom,
Sit blithe and happy; bees that soar for bloom,   5
High as the highest peak of Furness Fells,
Will murmur by the hour in foxglove bells.
In truth, the prison, unto which we doom
Ourselves, no prison is; and hence to me,
In sundry moods, 'twas pastime to be bound   10
Within the sonnet's scanty plot of ground –
Pleased if some souls (for such there needs must be),
Who have felt the weight of too much liberty,
Should find short solace there, as I have found.

Composed after a Journey across the Hamilton Hills, Yorkshire

Ere we had reached the wished-for place, night fell;
We were too late at least by one dark hour,
And nothing could we see of all that power
Of prospect, whereof many thousands tell.
The western sky did recompense us well   5
With Grecian temple, minaret, and bower;
And, in one part, a minster with its tower
Substantially distinct – a place for bell
Or clock to toll from. Many a glorious pile
Did we behold, sights that might well repay   10
All disappointment! – and, as such, the eye
Delighted in them; but we felt, the while,
We should forget them: they are of the sky,
And from our earthly memory fade away.

From the Italian of Michael Angelo

Yes! hope may with my strong desire keep pace,
And I be undeluded, unbetrayed;
For if of our affections none find grace
In sight of heaven, then, wherefore hath God made
The world which we inhabit? Better plea   5
Love cannot have, than that in loving thee
Glory to that eternal peace is paid,
Who such divinity to thee imparts
As hallows and makes pure all gentle hearts.
His hope is treacherous only whose love dies   10
With beauty, which is varying every hour;
But, in chaste hearts uninfluenced by the power
Of outward change, there blooms a deathless flower,
That breathes on earth the air of paradise.

Written in very early Youth

Calm is all Nature as a resting wheel.
The kine are couched upon the dewy grass;
The horse alone, seen dimly as I pass,
Is up, and cropping yet his later meal.
Dark is the ground; a slumber seems to steal   5
O'er vale, and mountain, and the starless sky.
Now, in this blank of things, a harmony
Home-felt and home-created seems to heal
That grief for which the senses still supply
Fresh food; for only then, when memory   10
Is hushed, am I at rest. My friends, restrain
Those busy cares that would allay my pain:
Oh! leave me to myself, nor let me feel
The officious touch that makes me droop again.

Composed Upon Westminster Bridge,
Sept. 3, 1803

Earth has not any thing to show more fair;
Dull would he be of soul who could pass by
A sight so touching in its majesty.
This city now doth like a garment wear
The beauty of the morning; silent, bare,   5
Ships, towers, domes, theatres, and temples lie
Open unto the fields, and to the sky,
All bright and glittering in the smokeless air.
Never did sun more beautifully steep
In his first splendour valley, rock, or hill;   10
Ne'er saw I, never felt, a calm so deep!
The river glideth at his own sweet will;
Dear God! the very houses seem asleep,
And all that mighty heart is lying still!

'Methought I saw the footsteps of a throne'

Methought I saw the footsteps of a throne
Which mists and vapours from mine eyes did shroud,
Nor view of him who sat thereon allowed;
But all the steps and ground about were strown
With sights the ruefullest that flesh and bone   5
Ever put on: a miserable crowd,
Sick, hale, old, young, who cried before that cloud,
'Thou art our king, O Death! to thee we groan.'
I seemed to mount those steps; the vapours gave
Smooth way, and I beheld the face of one   10
Sleeping alone within a mossy cave,
With her face up to heaven, that seemed to have
Pleasing remembrance of a thought forgone:
A lovely beauty in a summer grave!

'The world is too much with us'

The world is too much with us; late and soon,
Getting and spending, we lay waste our powers:
Little we see in nature that is ours;
We have given our hearts away, a sordid boon!
This sea that bares her bosom to the moon,   5
The winds that will be howling at all hours
And are up-gathered now like sleeping flowers:
For this, for every thing, we are out of tune;
It moves us not – Great God! I'd rather be
A pagan suckled in a creed outworn;   10
So might I, standing on this pleasant lea,
Have glimpses that would make me less forlorn:
Have sight of Proteus coming from the sea,
Or hear old Triton blow his wreathed horn.

'It is a beauteous evening, calm and free'

It is a beauteous evening, calm and free;
The holy time is quiet as a nun
Breathless with adoration; the broad sun
Is sinking down in its tranquillity;
The gentleness of heaven is on the sea.   5
Listen! the mighty being is awake
And doth with his eternal motion make
A sound like thunder – everlastingly.
Dear child! dear girl! that walkest with me here,
If thou appear'st untouched by solemn thought,   10
Thy nature is not therefore less divine:
Thou liest in Abraham's bosom all the year,
And worship'st at the temple's inner shrine,
God being with thee when we know it not.

'I grieved for Buonaparte'

I grieved for Buonaparte, with a vain
And an unthinking grief! The vital blood
Of that man's mind what can it be? What food
Fed his first hopes? What knowledge could *he* gain?
'Tis not in battles that from youth we train   5
The governor who must be wise and good,
And temper with the sternness of the brain
Thoughts motherly, and meek as womanhood.
Wisdom doth live with children round her knees;
Books, leisure, perfect freedom, and the talk   10
Man holds with week-day man in the hourly walk
Of the mind's business: these are the degrees
By which true sway doth mount; this is the stalk
True power doth grow on, and her rights are these.

On the Extinction of the Venetian Republic

Once did she hold the gorgeous East in fee,
And was the safeguard of the West; the worth
Of Venice did not fall below her birth –
Venice, the eldest child of Liberty.
She was a maiden city, bright and free;   5
No guile seduced, no force could violate;
And when she took unto herself a mate,
She must espouse the everlasting sea.
And what if she had seen those glories fade,
Those titles vanish, and that strength decay,   10
Yet shall some tribute of regret be paid
When her long life hath reached its final day;
Men are we, and must grieve when even the shade
Of that which once was great is passed away.

To Toussaint L'Ouverture

Toussaint, the most unhappy man of men!
Whether the rural milk-maid by her cow
Sing in thy hearing, or thou liest now
Alone in some deep dungeon's earless den,
O miserable chieftain! where and when   5
Wilt thou find patience? Yet die not; do thou
Wear rather in thy bonds a cheerful brow:
Though fallen thyself, never to rise again,
Live, and take comfort. Thou hast left behind
Powers that will work for thee — air, earth, and skies;   10
There's not a breathing of the common wind
That will forget thee; thou hast great allies:
Thy friends are exultations, agonies,
And love, and man's unconquerable mind.

September, 1802

Inland within a hollow vale I stood,
And saw, while sea was calm and air was clear,
The coast of France, the coast of France how near! —
Drawn almost into frightful neighbourhood.
I shrank, for verily the barrier flood   5
Was like a lake, or river bright and fair —
A span of waters; yet what power is there!
What mightiness for evil and for good!
Even so doth God protect us if we be
Virtuous and wise. Winds blow and waters roll   10
Strength to the brave, and power, and deity,
Yet in themselves are nothing! One decree
Spake laws to *them*, and said that by the soul
Only the nations shall be great and free.

Thought of a Briton on the Subjugation of Switzerland

Two voices are there; one is of the sea,
One of the mountains: each a mighty voice;
In both from age to age thou didst rejoice –
They were thy chosen music, Liberty!
There came a tyrant, and with holy glee   5
Thou fought'st against him, but hast vainly striven;
Thou from thy Alpine holds at length art driven,
Where not a torrent murmurs heard by thee.
Of one deep bliss thine ear hath been bereft;
Then cleave, O cleave to that which still is left!   10
For, high-souled maid, what sorrow would it be
That mountain floods should thunder as before,
And ocean bellow from his rocky shore,
And neither awful voice be heard by thee!

Written in London, September, 1802

O friend! I know not which way I must look
For comfort, being as I am, oppressed,
To think that now our life is only dressed
For show – mean handiwork of craftsman, cook,
Or groom! We must run glittering like a brook   5
In the open sunshine, or we are unblest;
The wealthiest man among us is the best;
No grandeur now in nature or in book
Delights us. Rapine, avarice, expense:
This is idolatry, and these we adore;   10
Plain living and high thinking are no more;
The homely beauty of the good old cause
Is gone; our peace, our fearful innocence,
And pure religion breathing household laws.

London, 1802

Milton! thou should'st be living at this hour:
England hath need of thee; she is a fen
Of stagnant waters: altar, sword and pen,
Fireside, the heroic wealth of hall and bower,
Have forfeited their ancient English dower 5
Of inward happiness. We are selfish men;
Oh! raise us up, return to us again,
And give us manners, virtue, freedom, power.
Thy soul was like a star and dwelt apart:
Thou hadst a voice whose sound was like the sea, 10
Pure as the naked heavens, majestic, free;
So didst thou travel on life's common way
In cheerful godliness, and yet thy heart
The lowliest duties on itself did lay.

'Great men have been among us'

Great men have been among us; hands that penned
And tongues that uttered wisdom, better none:
The later Sidney, Marvel, Harrington,
Young Vane, and others who called Milton friend.
These moralists could act and comprehend: 5
They knew how genuine glory was put on,
Taught us how rightfully a nation shone
In splendour, what strength was, that would not bend
But in magnanimous meekness. France, 'tis strange,
Hath brought forth no such souls as we had then. 10
Perpetual emptiness! unceasing change!
No single volume paramount, no code,
No master spirit, no determined road,
But equally a want of books and men!

'There is a bondage which is worse to bear'

There is a bondage which is worse to bear
Than his who breathes by roof, and floor, and wall –
Pent in, a tyrant's solitary thrall;
'Tis his who walks about in the open air,
One of a nation who, henceforth, must wear   5
Their fetters in their souls. For who could be,
Who, even the best, in such condition, free
From self-reproach, reproach which he must share
With human nature? Never be it ours
To see the sun how brightly it will shine,   10
And know that noble feelings, manly powers,
Instead of gathering strength must droop and pine,
And earth with all her pleasant fruits and flowers
Fade, and participate in man's decline.

The Solitary Reaper

Behold her, single in the field,
Yon solitary Highland lass!
Reaping and singing by herself;
Stop here, or gently pass!
Alone she cuts and binds the grain,   5
And sings a melancholy strain;
O listen! for the vale profound
Is overflowing with the sound.

No nightingale did ever chaunt
So sweetly to reposing bands   10
Of travellers in some shady haunt
Among Arabian sands;
No sweeter voice was ever heard
In spring-time from the cuckoo-bird,
Breaking the silence of the seas   15
Among the farthest Hebrides.

Will no one tell me what she sings?
Perhaps the plaintive numbers flow
For old, unhappy, far-off things,
And battles long ago;   20
Or is it some more humble lay,
Familiar matter of today?
Some natural sorrow, loss, or pain,
That has been, and may be again?

Whate'er the theme, the maiden sang   25
As if her song could have no ending;
I saw her singing at her work,
And o'er the sickle bending;
I listened till I had my fill,
And as I mounted up the hill,   30
The music in my heart I bore
Long after it was heard no more.

Stepping Westward

While my fellow-traveller and I were walking by the side of Loch Ketterine, one fine evening after sun-set in our road to a hut where in the course of our tour we had been hospitably entertained some weeks before, we met, in one of the loneliest parts of that solitary region, two well dressed women, one of whom said to us by way of greeting, 'What, you are stepping westward?'

'What, you are stepping westward?' – 'Yea.'
— 'Twould be a wildish destiny,
If we, who thus together roam
In a strange land, and far from home,
Were in this place the guests of chance;   5
Yet who would stop, or fear to advance,
Though home or shelter he had none,
With such a sky to lead him on?

The dewy ground was dark and cold;
Behind, all gloomy to behold;   10
And stepping westward seemed to be
A kind of *heavenly* destiny;
I liked the greeting: 'twas a sound
Of something without place or bound,
And seemed to give me spiritual right   15
To travel through that region bright.

The voice was soft, and she who spake
Was walking by her native lake;
The salutation had to me
The very sound of courtesy.   20
Its power was felt, and while my eye
Was fixed upon the glowing sky,
The echo of the voice enwrought
A human sweetness with the thought
Of travelling through the world that lay   25
Before me in my endless way.

To a Highland Girl

(AT INVERSNEYDE, UPON LOCH LOMONDE)

Sweet Highland girl, a very shower
Of beauty is thy earthly dower!
Twice seven consenting years have shed
Their utmost bounty on thy head;
And these grey rocks, this household lawn, 5
These trees – a veil just half withdrawn –
This fall of water that doth make
A murmur near the silent lake,
This little bay, a quiet road
That holds in shelter thy abode: 10
In truth together ye do seem
Like something fashioned in a dream –
Such forms as from their covert peep
When earthly cares are laid asleep!
Yet, dream and vision as thou art, 15
I bless thee with a human heart:
God shield thee to thy latest years!
I neither know thee nor thy peers,
And yet my eyes are filled with tears.

With earnest feeling I shall pray 20
For thee when I am far away,
For never saw I mien or face
In which more plainly I could trace
Benignity and home-bred sense
Ripening in perfect innocence. 25
Here, scattered like a random seed,
Remote from men, thou dost not need
The embarrassed look of shy distress,
And maidenly shamefacedness –
Thou wear'st upon thy forehead clear 30
The freedom of a mountaineer.
A face with gladness overspread!
Sweet looks, by human kindness bred!
And seemliness complete, that sways
Thy courtesies, about thee plays 35

With no restraint, but such as springs
From quick and eager visitings
Of thoughts that lie beyond the reach
Of thy few words of English speech:
A bondage sweetly brooked — a strife   40
That gives thy gestures grace and life!
So have I, not unmoved in mind,
Seen birds of tempest-loving kind
Thus beating up against the wind.

What hand but would a garland cull   45
For thee who art so beautiful?
O happy pleasure! here to dwell
Beside thee in some heathy dell;
Adopt your homely ways and dress,
A shepherd, thou a shepherdess!   50
But I could frame a wish for thee
More like a grave reality:
Thou art to me but as a wave
Of the wild sea, and I would have
Some claim upon thee, if I could,   55
Though but of common neighbourhood.
What joy to hear thee, and to see!
Thy elder brother I would be,
Thy father, any thing to thee!

Now thanks to heaven, that of its grace   60
Hath led me to this lonely place.
Joy have I had, and going hence
I bear away my recompense.
In spots like these it is we prize
Our memory, feel that she hath eyes;   65
Then, why should I be loth to stir?
I feel this place was made for her,
To give new pleasure like the past,
Continued long as life shall last.
Nor am I loth, though pleased at heart,   70
Sweet Highland girl! from thee to part,
For I, methinks, till I grow old,
As fair before me shall behold,
As I do now, the cabin small,

The lake, the bay, the waterfall,   75
And thee, the spirit of them all!

To a Butterfly

Stay near me – do not take thy flight!
A little longer stay in sight!
Much converse do I find in thee,
Historian of my infancy!
Float near me; do not yet depart!   5
Dead times revive in thee:
Thou bring'st, gay creature as thou art!
A solemn image to my heart,
My father's family!

Oh! pleasant, pleasant were the days,   10
The time, when in our childish plays
My sister Emmeline and I
Together chased the butterfly!
A very hunter did I rush
Upon the prey; with leaps and springs   15
I followed on from brake to bush;
But she, God love her! feared to brush
The dust from off its wings.

'My heart leaps up'

My heart leaps up when I behold
    A rainbow in the sky:
So was it when my life began;
So is it now I am a man;
So be it when I shall grow old,   5
    Or let me die!
The child is father of the man,
And I could wish my days to be
Bound each to each by natural piety.

'I wandered lonely as a cloud'

I wandered lonely as a cloud
That floats on high o'er vales and hills,
When all at once I saw a crowd –
A host of dancing daffodils:
Along the lake, beneath the trees,   5
Ten thousand dancing in the breeze.

The waves beside them danced, but they
Outdid the sparkling waves in glee;
A poet could not but be gay
In such a laughing company.   10
I gazed – and gazed – but little thought
What wealth the show to me had brought.

For oft when on my couch I lie
In vacant or in pensive mood,
They flash upon that inward eye   15
Which is the bliss of solitude;
And then my heart with pleasure fills,
And dances with the daffodils.

To the Cuckoo

O blithe new-comer! I have heard,
I hear thee and rejoice;
O cuckoo! shall I call thee bird,
Or but a wandering voice?

While I am lying on the grass,   5
I hear thy restless shout:
From hill to hill it seems to pass,
About, and all about!

To me, no babbler with a tale
Of sunshine and of flowers;   10
Thou tellest, cuckoo! in the vale
Of visionary hours.

Thrice welcome, darling of the spring!
Even yet thou art to me
No bird, but an invisible thing –
A voice, a mystery.

The same whom in my school-boy days
I listened to: that cry
Which made me look a thousand ways
In bush, and tree, and sky.

To seek thee did I often rove
Through woods and on the green,
And thou wert still a hope, a love,
Still longed for, never seen!

And I can listen to thee yet –
Can lie upon the plain
And listen, till I do beget
That golden time again.

O blessed bird! the earth we pace
Again appears to be
An unsubstantial, faery place
That is fit home for thee!

To a Butterfly

I've watched you now a full half hour,
Self-poised upon that yellow flower;
And, little butterfly! indeed
I know not if you sleep, or feed.
How motionless! not frozen seas
More motionless! and then
What joy awaits you, when the breeze
Hath found you out among the trees,
And calls you forth again!

This plot of orchard-ground is ours;
My trees they are, my sister's flowers;
Stop here whenever you are weary,
And rest as in a sanctuary!

Come often to us; fear no wrong;
Sit near us on the bough!   15
We'll talk of sunshine and of song,
And summer days when we were young,
Sweet childish days, that were as long
        As twenty days are now!

Star Gazers

What crowd is this? what have we here? we must not pass it
        by –
A telescope upon its frame, and pointed to the sky;
Long is it as a barber's poll, or mast of little boat,
Some little pleasure-skiff, that doth on Thames's waters float.

The showman chooses well his place – 'tis Leicester's busy
        square,   5
And he's as happy in his night, for the heavens are blue and fair;
Calm though impatient is the crowd; each is ready with the fee,
And envies him that's looking – what an insight must it be!

Yet, showman, where can lie the cause? Shall thy implement
        have blame,
A boaster, that when he is tried, fails, and is put to shame?   10
Or is it good as others are, and be their eyes in fault?
Their eyes, or minds? or finally, is this resplendent vault?

Is nothing of that radiant pomp so good as we have here?
Or gives a thing but small delight that never can be dear?
The silver moon with all her vales, and hills of mightiest fame, 15
Do they betray us when they're seen? and are they but a name?

Or is it rather that conceit rapacious is and strong,
And bounty never yields so much but it seems to do her wrong?
Or is it, that when human souls a journey long have had,
And are returned into themselves, they cannot but be sad?   20

Or must we be constrained to think that these spectators rude,
Poor in estate, of manners base, men of the multitude,
Have souls which never yet have ris'n, and therefore prostrate
        lie?
No, no, this cannot be – men thirst for power and majesty!

Does, then, a deep and earnest thought the blissful mind
      employ   25
Of him who gazes, or has gazed? – a grave and steady joy
That doth reject all show of pride, admits no outward sign,
Because not of this noisy world, but silent and divine!

Whatever be the cause, 'tis sure that they who pry and pore
Seem to meet with little gain, seem less happy than before: 30
One after one they take their turns, nor have I one espied
That doth not slackly go away, as if dissatisfied.

A Complaint

    There is a change, and I am poor;
    Your love hath been, nor long ago,
    A fountain at my fond heart's door,
    Whose only business was to flow;
    And flow it did, not taking heed   5
    Of its own bounty, or my need.

    What happy moments did I count!
    Blessed was I then all bliss above!
    Now, for this consecrated fount
    Of murmuring, sparkling, living love,   10
    What have I? shall I dare to tell?
    A comfortless, and hidden well.

    A well of love – it may be deep –
    I trust it is, and never dry;
    What matter if the waters sleep   15
    In silence and obscurity?
    – Such change, and at the very door
    Of my fond heart, hath made me poor.

'I am not one who much or oft delight'

I am not one who much or oft delight
To season my fireside with personal talk
About friends, who live within an easy walk,
Or neighbours, daily, weekly, in my sight;

And, for my chance-acquaintance, ladies bright,   5
Sons, mothers, maidens withering on the stalk,
These all wear out of me, like forms with chalk
Painted on rich men's floors, for one feast-night.
Better than such discourse doth silence long –
Long, barren silence – square with my desire: 10
To sit without emotion, hope, or aim,
By my half-kitchen and half-parlour fire,
And listen to the flapping of the flame,
Or kettle, whispering its faint undersong.

'Yet life,' you say, 'is life; we have seen and see,   15
And with a living pleasure we describe,
And fits of sprightly malice do but bribe
The languid mind into activity.
Sound sense, and love itself, and mirth and glee,
Are fostered by the comment and the gibe.'   20
Even be it so; yet still among your tribe,
Our daily world's true worldlings, rank not me!
Children are blest, and powerful; their world lies
More justly balanced – partly at their feet,
And part far from them; sweetest melodies   25
Are those that are by distance made more sweet;
Whose mind is but the mind of his own eyes
He is a slave, the meanest we can meet!

Wings have we, and as far as we can go
We may find pleasure. Wilderness and wood,   30
Blank ocean and mere sky, support that mood
Which with the lofty sanctifies the low;
Dreams, books, are each a world, and books, we know,
Are a substantial world, both pure and good:
Round these, with tendrils strong as flesh and blood,   35
Our pastime and our happiness will grow.
There do I find a never-failing store
Of personal themes, and such as I love best –
Matter wherein right voluble I am.
Two will I mention, dearer than the rest: 40
The gentle lady, married to the Moor;
And heavenly Una with her milk-white lamb.

Nor can I not believe but that hereby
Great gains are mine, for thus I live remote
From evil-speaking; rancour, never sought,   45
Comes to me not; malignant truth, or lie.
Hence have I genial seasons, hence have I
Smooth passions, smooth discourse, and joyous thought,
And thus from day to day my little boat
Rocks in its harbour, lodging peaceably.   50
Blessings be with them, and eternal praise,
Who gave us nobler loves, and nobler cares –
The poets, who on earth have made us heirs
Of truth and pure delight by heavenly lays!
Oh! might my name be numbered among theirs,   55
Then gladly would I end my mortal days.

Lines Composed at Grasmere

*During a walk, one evening, after a stormy day: the author
having just read in a newspaper that the dissolution of Mr Fox
was hourly expected.*

Loud is the vale! the voice is up
With which she speaks when storms are gone –
A mighty unison of streams!
Of all her voices, one!

Loud is the vale; this inland depth   5
In peace is roaring like the sea;
Yon star upon the mountain-top
Is listening quietly.

Sad was I, ev'n to pain depressed,
Importunate and heavy load!   10
The comforter hath found me here,
Upon this lonely road;

And many thousands now are sad,
Wait the fulfilment of their fear;
For he must die who is their stay,   15
Their glory disappear.

A power is passing from the earth
To breathless Nature's dark abyss;
But when the mighty pass away,
What is it more than this,   20

That man, who is from God sent forth,
Doth yet again to God return? –
Such ebb and flow must ever be,
Then wherefore should we mourn?

Elegiac Stanzas

Suggested by a picture of Peele Castle, in a storm, painted by
Sir George Beaumont.

I was thy neighbour once, thou rugged pile!
Four summer weeks I dwelt in sight of thee;
I saw thee every day, and all the while
Thy form was sleeping on a glassy sea.

So pure the sky, so quiet was the air!   5
So like, so very like, was day to day!
Whene'er I looked, thy image still was there;
It trembled, but it never passed away.

How perfect was the calm! It seemed no sleep,
No mood, which season takes away, or brings: 10
I could have fancied that the mighty deep
Was even the gentlest of all gentle things.

Ah! then, if mine had been the painter's hand,
To express what then I saw, and add the gleam,
The light that never was on sea or land,   15
The consecration, and the poet's dream,

I would have planted thee, thou hoary pile!
Amid a world how different from this!
Beside a sea that could not cease to smile,
On tranquil land, beneath a sky of bliss.   20

Thou shouldst have seemed a treasure-house, a mine
Of peaceful years, a chronicle of heaven;
Of all the sunbeams that did ever shine
The very sweetest had to thee been given.

A picture had it been of lasting ease,   25
Elysian quiet, without toil or strife;
No motion but the moving tide, a breeze,
Or merely silent Nature's breathing life.

Such, in the fond delusion of my heart,
Such picture would I at that time have made,   30
And seen the soul of truth in every part –
A faith, a trust, that could not be betrayed.

So once it would have been; 'tis so no more:
I have submitted to a new control;
A power is gone, which nothing can restore;   35
A deep distress hath humanised my soul.

Not for a moment could I now behold
A smiling sea and be what I have been:
The feeling of my loss will ne'er be old;
This, which I know, I speak with mind serene.   40

Then, Beaumont, friend! who would have been the friend,
If he had lived, of him whom I deplore,
This work of thine I blame not, but commend –
This sea in anger, and that dismal shore.

Oh 'tis a passionate work! – yet wise and well;   45
Well chosen is the spirit that is here:
That hulk which labours in the deadly swell,
This rueful sky, this pageantry of fear!

And this huge castle, standing here sublime,
I love to see the look with which it braves,   50
Cased in the unfeeling armour of old time,
The light'ning, the fierce wind, and trampling waves.

Farewell, farewell the heart that lives alone,
Housed in a dream, at distance from the Kind!
Such happiness, wherever it be known,   55
Is to be pitied, for 'tis surely blind.

But welcome fortitude, and patient cheer,
And frequent sights of what is to be borne!
Such sights, or worse, as are before me here —
Not without hope we suffer and we mourn.   60

Ode

Paulò majora canamus

There was a time when meadow, grove, and stream,
The earth, and every common sight,
          To me did seem
          Apparelled in celestial light —
The glory and the freshness of a dream.   5
It is not now as it has been of yore;
          Turn wheresoe'er I may,
              By night or day,
The things which I have seen I now can see no more.

          The rainbow comes and goes,   10
          And lovely is the rose;
          The moon doth with delight
     Look round her when the heavens are bare;
          Waters on a starry night
          Are beautiful and fair;   15
     The sunshine is a glorious birth;
     But yet I know, where'er I go,
That there hath passed away a glory from the earth.

     Now, while the birds thus sing a joyous song,
          And while the young lambs bound   20
              As to the tabor's sound,
     To me alone there came a thought of grief;
     A timely utterance gave that thought relief,
          And I again am strong.

The cataracts blow their trumpets from the steep;   25
No more shall grief of mine the season wrong;
I hear the echoes through the mountains throng;
The winds come to me from the fields of sleep,
    And all the earth is gay;
      Land and sea   30
  Give themselves up to jollity,
    And with the heart of May
  Doth every beast keep holiday;
    Thou child of joy,
Shout round me, let me hear thy shouts, thou happy   35
    shepherd boy!

Ye blessed creatures, I have heard the call
  Ye to each other make; I see
The heavens laugh with you in your jubilee;
  My heart is at your festival,
    My head hath its coronal,   40
The fullness of your bliss, I feel—I feel it all.
    Oh evil day! if I were sullen
    While the earth herself is adorning
      This sweet May-morning,
    And the children are pulling,   45
      On every side,
    In a thousand valleys far and wide,
    Fresh flowers; while the sun shines warm,
And the babe leaps up on his mother's arm—
    I hear, I hear, with joy I hear!   50
  —But there's a tree, of many one,
A single field which I have looked upon,
Both of them speak of something that is gone;
    The pansy at my feet
    Doth the same tale repeat: 55
Whither is fled the visionary gleam?
Where is it now, the glory and the dream?

Our birth is but a sleep and a forgetting;
The soul that rises with us, our life's star,
    Hath had elsewhere its setting,   60
    And cometh from afar;
    Not in entire forgetfulness,
    And not in utter nakedness,

But trailing clouds of glory do we come
    From God, who is our home; 65
Heaven lies about us in our infancy!
Shades of the prison-house begin to close
    Upon the growing boy,
But he beholds the light, and whence it flows,
    He sees it in his joy; 70
The youth, who daily farther from the East
  Must travel, still is Nature's priest,
    And by the vision splendid
    Is on his way attended;
At length the man perceives it die away, 75
And fade into the light of common day.

Earth fills her lap with pleasures of her own;
Yearnings she hath in her own natural kind,
And, even with something of a mother's mind,
    And no unworthy aim, 80
  The homely nurse doth all she can
To make her foster-child, her inmate man,
  Forget the glories he hath known,
And that imperial palace whence he came.

Behold the child among his new-born blisses, 85
A four years' darling of a pigmy size!
See, where mid work of his own hand he lies,
Fretted by sallies of his mother's kisses,
With light upon him from his father's eyes!
See, at his feet, some little plan or chart, 90
Some fragment from his dream of human life,
Shaped by himself with newly-learned art;
    A wedding or a festival,
    A mourning or a funeral;
    And this hath now his heart, 95
    And unto this he frames his song;
    Then will he fit his tongue
To dialogues of business, love, or strife;
    But it will not be long
    Ere this be thrown aside, 100
    And with new joy and pride
The little actor cons another part,

Filling from time to time his 'humorous stage'
With all the persons, down to palsied Age,
That life brings with her in her equipage —   105
    As if his whole vocation
    Were endless imitation.

Thou, whose exterior semblance doth belie
    Thy soul's immensity —
Thou best philosopher, who yet dost keep   110
Thy heritage, thou eye among the blind,
That, deaf and silent, read'st the eternal deep,
Haunted for ever by the eternal mind —
    Mighty prophet! Seer blest!
    On whom those truths do rest   115
Which we are toiling all our lives to find;
Thou, over whom thy immortality
Broods like the day, a master o'er a slave,
A presence which is not to be put by;
    To whom the grave   120
Is but a lonely bed without the sense or sight
    Of day or the warm light,
A place of thought where we in waiting lie;
Thou little child, yet glorious in the might
Of untamed pleasures, on thy being's height,   125
Why with such earnest pains dost thou provoke
The years to bring the inevitable yoke,
Thus blindly with thy blessedness at strife?
Full soon thy soul shall have her earthly freight,
And custom lie upon thee with a weight   130
Heavy as frost, and deep almost as life!

    O joy! that in our embers
    Is something that doth live,
    That nature yet remembers
    What was so fugitive!   135
The thought of our past years in me doth breed
Perpetual benedictions: not indeed
For that which is most worthy to be blest —
Delight and liberty, the simple creed
Of childhood, whether fluttering or at rest,   140
With new-born hope for ever in his breast —

          Not for these I raise
            The song of thanks and praise,
          But for those obstinate questionings
          Of sense and outward things,   145
            Fallings from us, vanishings;
            Blank misgivings of a creature
Moving about in worlds not realised –
High instincts, before which our mortal nature
Did tremble like a guilty thing surprised;   150
          But for those first affections,
            Those shadowy recollections,
              Which, be they what they may,
Are yet the fountain light of all our day,
Are yet a master light of all our seeing,   155
            Uphold us, cherish us, and make
Our noisy years seem moments in the being
Of the eternal silence: truths that wake
              To perish never;
Which neither listlessness, nor mad endeavour,   160
            Nor man nor boy,
Nor all that is at enmity with joy,
Can utterly abolish or destroy!
          Hence, in a season of calm weather,
            Though inland far we be,   165
Our souls have sight of that immortal sea
            Which brought us hither,
            Can in a moment travel thither,
And see the children sport upon the shore,
And hear the mighty waters rolling evermore.   170

Then, sing ye birds, sing, sing a joyous song!
          And let the young lambs bound
            As to the tabor's sound!
        We in thought will join your throng,
            Ye that pipe and ye that play,   175
            Ye that through your hearts to-day
            Feel the gladness of the May!
What though the radiance which was once so bright
Be now for ever taken from my sight,
          Though nothing can bring back the hour   180
Of splendour in the grass, of glory in the flower,

We will grieve not, rather find
Strength in what remains behind –
In the primal sympathy
Which having been must ever be,   185
In the soothing thoughts that spring
Out of human suffering,
In the faith that looks through death,
In years that bring the philosophic mind.

And oh ye fountains, meadows, hills, and groves,   190
Think not of any severing of our loves!
Yet in my heart of hearts I feel your might:
I only have relinquished one delight
To live beneath your more habitual sway.
I love the brooks which down their channels fret   195
Even more than when I tripped lightly as they;
The innocent brightness of a new-born day
      Is lovely yet;
The clouds that gather round the setting sun
Do take a sober colouring from an eye   200
That hath kept watch o'er man's mortality;
Another race hath been, and other palms are won.
Thanks to the human heart by which we live,
Thanks to its tenderness, its joys, and fears,
To me the meanest flower that blows can give   205
Thoughts that do often lie too deep for tears.

St Paul's

Pressed with conflicting thoughts of love and fear
I parted from thee, friend! and took my way
Through the great city, pacing with an eye
Downcast, ear sleeping, and feet masterless
That were sufficient guide unto themselves,   5
And step by step went pensively. Now, mark!—
Not how my trouble was entirely hushed,
(That might not be) but how by sudden gift,
Gift of Imagination's holy power,
My soul in her uneasiness received   10
An anchor of stability. It chanced
That while I thus was pacing, I raised up
My heavy eyes and instantly beheld—
Saw at a glance in that familiar spot—
A visionary scene: a length of street   15
Laid open in its morning quietness,
Deep, hollow, unobstructed, vacant, smooth,
And white with winter's purest white—as fair,
As fresh and spotless as he ever sheds
On field or mountain. Moving form was none,   20
Save here and there a shadowy passenger—
Slow, shadowy, silent, dusky, and beyond
And high above this winding length of street,
This noiseless and unpeopled avenue,
Pure, silent, solemn, beautiful, was seen   25
The huge majestic temple of St Paul
In awful sequestration, through a veil,
Through its own sacred veil of falling snow.

From

POEMS
1815

Characteristics of a Child three years old

Loving she is, and tractable, though wild,
And innocence hath privilege in her
To dignify arch looks and laughing eyes,
And feats of cunning, and the pretty round
Of trespasses affected to provoke   5
Mock-chastisement and partnership in play.
And, as a faggot sparkles on the hearth –
Not less if unattended and alone
Than when both young and old sit gathered round
And take delight in its activity –   10
Even so this happy creature of herself
Is all sufficient: solitude to her
Is blithe society, who fills the air
With gladness and involuntary songs.
Light are her sallies as the tripping fawn's,   15
Forth-startled from the fern where she lay couched –
Unthought-of, unexpected as the stir
Of the soft breeze ruffling the meadow flowers,
Or from before it chasing wantonly
The many-coloured images impressed   20
Upon the bosom of a placid lake.

'Surprised by joy, impatient as the wind'

Surprised by joy, impatient as the wind,
I wished to share the transport – oh! with whom
But thee, long buried in the silent tomb,
That spot which no vicissitude can find?
Love, faithful love, recalled thee to my mind,   5
But how could I forget thee? Through what power,
Even for the least division of an hour,
Have I been so beguiled as to be blind
To my most grievous loss? That thought's return
Was the worst pang that sorrow ever bore,   10
Save one – one only – when I stood forlorn,
Knowing my heart's best treasure was no more:
That neither present time, nor years unborn
Could to my sight that heavenly face restore.

Yarrow Visited

SEPTEMBER, 1814

And is this Yarrow? *This* the stream
Of which my fancy cherished,
So faithfully, a waking dream? –
An image that hath perished!
O that some minstrel's harp were near   5
To utter notes of gladness,
And chase this silence from the air
That fills my heart with sadness!

Yet why? – a silvery current flows
With uncontrolled meanderings;   10
Nor have these eyes by greener hills
Been soothed, in all my wanderings.
And, through her depths, Saint Mary's Lake
Is visibly delighted,
For not a feature of those hills   15
Is in the mirror slighted.

A blue sky bends o'er Yarrow vale,
Save where that pearly whiteness
Is round the rising sun diffused –
A tender, hazy brightness: 20
Mild dawn of promise! that excludes
All profitless dejection,
Though not unwilling here to admit
A pensive recollection.

Where was it that the famous flower   25
Of Yarrow vale lay bleeding?
His bed perchance was yon smooth mound
On which the herd is feeding,
And haply from this crystal pool,
Now peaceful as the morning,   30
The water-wraith ascended thrice –
And gave his doleful warning.

Delicious is the lay that sings
The haunts of happy lovers,
The path that leads them to the grove,   35
The leafy grove that covers;
And pity sanctifies the verse
That paints, by strength of sorrow,
The unconquerable strength of love:
Bear witness, rueful Yarrow!   40

But thou, that didst appear so fair
To fond imagination,
Dost rival in the light of day
Her delicate creation;
Meek loveliness is round thee spread,   45
A softness still and holy,
The grace of forest charms decayed,
And pastoral melancholy.

That region left, the vale unfolds
Rich groves of lofty stature,   50
With Yarrow winding through the pomp
Of cultivated nature;
And, rising from those lofty groves,
Behold a ruin hoary!
The shattered front of Newark's towers,   55
Renowned in Border story.

Fair scenes for childhood's opening bloom,
For sportive youth to stray in,
For manhood to enjoy his strength,
And age to wear away in!   60
Yon cottage seems a bower of bliss –
It promises protection
To studious ease and generous cares,
And every chaste affection!

How sweet, on this autumnal day,   65
The wild wood's fruits to gather,
And on my true-love's forehead plant
A crest of blooming heather!
And what if I enwreathed my own?

'Twere no offence to reason;   70
The sober hills thus deck their brows
To meet the wintry season.

I see, but not by sight alone,
Loved Yarrow, have I won thee;
A ray of fancy still survives –   75
Her sunshine plays upon thee!
Thy ever-youthful waters keep
A course of lively pleasure,
And gladsome notes my lips can breathe,
Accordant to the measure.   80

The vapours linger round the heights –
They melt, and soon must vanish;
One hour is theirs, not more is mine –
Sad thought, which I would banish,
But that I know, where'er I go   85
Thy genuine image, Yarrow!
Will dwell with me to heighten joy,
And cheer my mind in sorrow.

'Say, what is honour?'

Say, what is honour? – 'Tis the finest sense
Of *justice* which the human mind can frame,
Intent each lurking frailty to disclaim,
And guard the way of life from all offence
Suffered or done. When lawless violence   5
A kingdom doth assault, and in the scale
Of perilous war her weightiest armies fail,
Honour is hopeful elevation – whence
Glory, and triumph. Yet with politic skill
Endangered states may yield to terms unjust,   10
Stoop their proud heads – but not unto the dust –
A foe's most favourite purpose to fulfil!
Happy occasions oft by self-mistrust
Are forfeited, but infamy doth kill.

'The power of armies is a visible thing'

The power of armies is a visible thing –
Formal, and circumscribed in time and place.
But who the limits of that power can trace
Which a brave people into light can bring
Or hide at will – for freedom combating,   5
By just revenge enflamed? No foot can chase,
No eye can follow to a *fatal* place
That power, that spirit, whether on the wing
Like the strong wind, or sleeping like the wind
Within its awful caves. From year to year   10
Springs this indigenous produce far and near;
No craft this subtle element can bind,
Rising like water from the soil to find
In every nook a lip that it may cheer.

Peter Bell, A Tale in Verse

There's something in a flying horse,
And something in a huge balloon,
But through the clouds I'll never float
Until I have a little boat
Whose shape is like the crescent-moon.   5

And now I *have* a little boat,
In shape a very crescent-moon:
Fast through the clouds my boat can sail,
But if perchance your faith should fail,
Look up, and you shall see me soon!   10

The woods, my friends, are round you roaring,
Rocking and roaring like a sea;
The noise of danger fills your ears,
And ye have all a thousand fears
Both for my little boat and me!   15

Meanwhile I from the helm admire
The pointed horns of my canoe,
And, did not pity touch my breast
To see how ye are all distressed,
Till my ribs ached, I'd laugh at you!   20

Away we go, my boat and I –
Frail man ne'er sat in such another;
Whether among the winds we strive,
Or deep into the heavens we dive,
Each is contented with the other.   25

Away we go – and what care we
For treasons, tumults, and for wars?
We are as calm in our delight
As is the crescent-moon so bright
Among the scattered stars.   30

Up goes my boat between the stars
Through many a breathless field of light,
Through many a long blue field of ether,
Leaving ten thousand stars beneath her,
Up goes my little boat so bright!   35

The Crab – the Scorpion – and the Bull –
We pry among them all, have shot
High o'er the red-haired race of Mars
Covered from top to toe with scars:
Such company I like it not!   40

The towns in Saturn are ill-built,
But proud let *him* be who has seen them;
The Pleiads, that appear to kiss
Each other in the vast abyss,
With joy I sail between them!   45

Swift Mercury resounds with mirth,
Great Jove is full of stately bowers,
But these, and all that they contain,
What are they to that tiny grain,
That darling speck of ours!   50

Then back to earth, the dear green earth;
Whole ages if I here should roam,
The world for my remarks and me
Would not a whit the better be;
I've left my heart at home.   55

And there it is, the matchless earth!
There spreads the famed Pacific ocean!
Old Andes thrusts yon craggy spear
Through the grey clouds; the Alps are here
Like waters in commotion!   60

Yon tawny slip is Libya's sands –
That silver thread the river Dnieper –
And look, where clothed in brightest green
Is a sweet isle, of isles the queen –
Ye fairies from all evil keep her!   65

And see the town where I was born!
Around those happy fields we span
In boyish gambols; I was lost
Where I have been, but on this coast
I feel I am a man.　　　　　　　　　　　　　　70

Never did fifty things at once
Appear so lovely – never, never –
How tunefully the forests ring!
To hear the earth's soft murmuring
Thus could I hang for ever!　　　　　　　　　75

'Shame on you,' cried my little boat,
'Was ever such a heartless loon
Within a living boat to sit,
And make no better use of it –
A boat twin-sister of the crescent-moon!　　　80

Out – out – and like a brooding hen,
Beside your sooty hearth-stone cower;
Go, creep along the dirt, and pick
Your way with your good walking-stick,
Just three good miles an hour!　　　　　　　85

Ne'er in the breast of full-grown poet
Fluttered so faint a heart before –
Was it the music of the spheres
That overpowered your mortal ears?
Such din shall trouble them no more.　　　　90

These nether precincts do not lack
Charms of their own; then come with me –
I want a comrade, and for you
There's nothing that I would not do;
Nought is there that you shall not see.　　　95

Haste! and above Siberian snows
We'll sport amid the boreal morning,
Will mingle with her lustres gliding
Among the stars, the stars now hiding
And now the stars adorning.　　　　　　　100

I know the secrets of a land
Where human foot did never stray:
Fair is the land as evening skies,
And cool, though in the depth it lies
Of burning Africa.   105

Or we'll into the realm of faery,
Among the lovely shades of things:
The shadowy forms of mountains bare,
And streams, and bowers, and ladies fair,
The shades of palaces and kings!   110

Or, if you thirst with hardy zeal
Less quiet regions to explore,
Prompt voyage shall to you reveal
How earth and heaven are taught to feel
The might of magic lore!'   115

'My little vagrant form of light,
My gay and beautiful canoe,
Well have you played your friendly part;
As kindly take what from my heart
Experience forces – then adieu!   120

Temptation lurks among your words;
But, while these pleasures you're pursuing
Without impediment or let,
My radiant pinnace, you forget
What on the earth is doing.   125

There was a time when all mankind
Did listen with a faith sincere
To tuneful tongues in mystery versed;
Then poets fearlessly rehearsed
The wonders of a wild career.   130

Go – but the world's a sleepy world,
And 'tis, I fear, an age too late;
Take with you some ambitious youth,
For I myself, in very truth,
Am all unfit to be your mate.   135

Long have I loved what I behold –
The night that calms, the day that cheers;
The common growth of mother earth
Suffices me – her tears, her mirth,
Her humblest mirth and tears.   140

The dragon's wing, the magic ring,
I shall not covet for my dower
If I along that lowly way
With sympathetic heart may stray
And with a soul of power.   145

These given, what more need I desire
To stir, to soothe, or elevate?
What nobler marvels than the mind
May in life's daily prospect find –
May find or there create?   150

A potent wand doth sorrow wield;
What spell so strong as guilty fear?
Repentance is a tender sprite:
If aught on earth have heavenly might,
'Tis lodged within her silent tear.   155

But grant my wishes – let us now
Descend from this ethereal height;
Then take thy way, adventurous skiff,
More daring far than Hippogriff,
And be thy own delight!   160

To the stone-table in my garden,
Loved haunt of many a summer hour,
The squire is come; his daughter Bess
Beside him in the cool recess
Sits blooming like a flower.   165

With these are many more convened;
They know not I have been so far –
I see them there in number nine
Beneath the spreading Weymouth pine –
I see them – there they are!   170

There sits the vicar, and his dame,
And there my good friend, Stephen Otter;
And, ere the light of evening fail,
To them I must relate the tale
Of Peter Bell the potter.'   175

Off flew my sparkling boat in scorn,
Yea in a trance of indignation!
And I, as well as I was able,
On two poor legs, to my stone-table
Limped on with some vexation.   180

'O, here he is!' cried little Bess —
She saw me at the garden door —
'We've waited anxiously and long,'
They cried, and all around me throng:
Full nine of them, or more!   185

'Reproach me not — your fears be still —
Be thankful we again have met;
Resume, my friends! within the shade
Your seats, and promptly shall be paid
The well-remembered debt.'   190

Breath failed me as I spoke, but soon
With lips, no doubt, and visage pale,
And sore too from a slight contusion,
Did I, to cover my confusion,
Begin the promised tale.   195

PART FIRST

'All by the moonlight river side
It gave three miserable groans;
"'Tis come then to a pretty pass,"
Said Peter to the groaning ass,
"But I will bang your bones!"'   200

'Good sir!' the vicar's voice exclaimed,
'You rush at once into the middle,'
And little Bess, with accent sweeter,
Cried, 'O dear sir! but who is Peter?'
Said Stephen, ''Tis a downright riddle!'   205

The squire said, 'Sure as paradise
Was lost to man by Adam's sinning,
This leap is for us all too bold;
Who Peter was, let that be told,
And start from the beginning.'   210

'A potter, sir, he was by trade,'
Said I, becoming quite collected,
'And wheresoever he appeared,
Full twenty times was Peter feared
For once that Peter was respected.   215

He two and thirty years or more
Had been a wild and woodland rover;
Had heard the Atlantic surges roar
On farthest Cornwall's rocky shore,
And trod the cliffs of Dover.   220

And he had seen Caernarvon's towers,
And well he knew the spire of Sarum,
And he had been where Lincoln bell
Flings o'er the fen its ponderous knell –
Its far-renowned alarum!   225

At Doncaster, at York, and Leeds,
And merry Carlisle had he been,
And all along the Lowlands fair,
All through the bonny shire of Ayr,
And far as Aberdeen.   230

And he had been at Inverness,
And Peter, by the mountain rills,
Had danced his round with Highland lasses,
And he had lain beside his asses
On lofty Cheviot Hills;   235

And he had trudged through Yorkshire dales,
Among the rocks and winding scars,
Where deep and low the hamlets lie
Beneath their little patch of sky
And little lot of stars;   240

And all along the indented coast,
Bespattered with the salt-sea foam,
Where'er a knot of houses lay,
On headland, or in hollow bay,
Sure never man like him did roam!   245

As well might Peter, in the Fleet,
Have been fast bound, a begging debtor;
He travelled here, he travelled there,
But not the value of a hair
Was heart or head the better.   250

He roved among the vales and streams,
In the green wood and hollow dell;
They were his dwellings night and day,
But Nature ne'er could find the way
Into the heart of Peter Bell.   255

In vain through every changeful year
Did Nature lead him as before –
A primrose by a river's brim
A yellow primrose was to him,
And it was nothing more.   260

Small change it made in Peter's heart
To see his gentle panniered train
With more than vernal pleasure feeding,
Where'er the tender grass was leading
Its earliest green along the lane.   265

In vain through water, earth, and air
The soul of happy sound was spread
When Peter, on some April morn,
Beneath the broom or budding thorn,
Made the warm earth his lazy bed.   270

At noon, when by the forest's edge
He lay beneath the branches high,
The soft blue sky did never melt
Into his heart – he never felt
The witchery of the soft blue sky!   275

On a fair prospect some have looked
And felt, as I have heard them say,
As if the moving time had been
A thing as steadfast as the scene
On which they gazed themselves away.   280

With Peter Bell, I need not tell
That this had never been the case;
He was a carl as wild and rude
As ever hue-and-cry pursued,
As ever ran a felon's race.   285

Of all that lead a lawless life,
Of all that love their lawless lives
In city or in village small,
He was the wildest far of all;
He had a dozen wedded wives.   290

Nay start not! – wedded wives – and twelve!
But how one wife could e'er come near him,
In simple truth I cannot tell,
For be it said of Peter Bell
To see him was to fear him.   295

Though Nature could not touch his heart
By lovely forms and silent weather
And tender sounds, yet you might see
At once that Peter Bell and she
Had often been together.   300

A savage wildness round him hung
As of a dweller out of doors;
In his whole figure and his mien
A savage character was seen,
Of mountains and of dreary moors.   305

To all the unshaped half-human thoughts
Which solitary Nature feeds
'Mid summer storms or winter's ice,
Had Peter joined whatever vice
The cruel city breeds.   310

His face was keen as is the wind
That cuts along the hawthorn fence;
Of courage you saw little there,
But, in its stead, a medley air
Of cunning and of impudence.   315

He had a dark and sidelong walk,
And long and slouching was his gait;
Beneath his looks so bare and bold
You might perceive his spirit cold
Was playing with some inward bait.   320

His forehead wrinkled was and furred –
A work one half of which was done
By thinking of his *whens* and *hows*,
And half by knitting of his brows
Beneath the glaring sun.   325

There was a hardness in his cheek,
There was a hardness in his eye,
As if the man had fixed his face
In many a solitary place
Against the wind and open sky!   330

One night (and now, my little Bess,
We've reached at last the promised tale),
One beautiful November night,
When the full moon was shining bright
Upon the rapid river Swale,   335

Along the river's winding banks
Peter was travelling all alone –
Whether to buy or sell, or led
By pleasure running in his head,
To me was never known.   340

He trudged along through copse and brake,
He trudged along o'er hill and dale;
Nor for the moon cared he a tittle,
And for the stars he cared as little,
And for the murmuring river Swale.   345

But chancing to espy a path
That promised to cut short the way,
As many a wiser man hath done,
He left a trusty guide for one
That might his steps betray.   350

To a thick wood he soon is brought
Where cheerfully his course he weaves,
And whistling loud may yet be heard,
Though often buried, like a bird
Darkling among the boughs and leaves.   355

But quickly Peter's mood is changed,
And on he drives with cheeks that burn
In downright fury and in wrath –
There's little sign the treacherous path
Will to the road return!   360

The path grows dim, and dimmer still,
Now up, now down, the rover wends
With all the sail that he can carry,
Till he is brought to an old quarry,
And there the pathway ends.   365

"What! would'st thou daunt me, grisly den?
Back must I, having come so far?
Stretch as thou wilt thy gloomy jaws,
I'll on, nor would I give two straws
For lantern or for star!"   370

And so, where on the huge rough stones
The black and massy shadows lay,
And through the dark, and through the cold,
And through the yawning fissures old,
Did Peter boldly press his way   375

Right through the quarry; and behold
A scene of soft and lovely hue!
Where blue, and grey, and tender green
Together made as sweet a scene
As ever human eye did view.   380

Beneath the clear blue sky he saw
A little field of meadow ground,
But field or meadow name it not;
Call it of earth a small green plot,
With rocks encompassed round.   385

The Swale flowed under the grey rocks,
But he flowed quiet and unseen –
You need a strong and stormy gale
To bring the noises of the Swale
To that green spot, so calm and green!   390

Now you'll suppose that Peter Bell
Felt small temptation here to tarry,
And so it was, but I must add,
His heart was not a little glad
When he was out of the old quarry.   395

And is there no one dwelling here,
No hermit with his beads and glass?
And does no little cottage look
Upon this soft and fertile nook?
Does no one live near this green grass?   400

Across that deep and quiet spot
Is Peter driving through the grass,
And now he is among the trees,
When, turning round his head, he sees
A solitary ass.   405

"No doubt I'm foundered in these woods;
For once," quoth he, "I will be wise –
With better speed I'll back again,
And lest the journey should prove vain,
Will take yon ass, my lawful prize!"   410

Off Peter hied; "A comely beast!
Though not so plump as he might be;
My honest friend, with such a platter,
You should have been a little fatter,
But come, sir, come with me!"   415

But first doth Peter deem it fit
To spy about him far and near;
There's not a single house in sight,
No woodman's hut, no cottage light –
Peter, you need not fear!   420

There's nothing to be seen but woods
And rocks that spread a hoary gleam,
And this one beast that from the bed
Of the green meadow hangs his head
Over the silent stream.   425

His head is with a halter bound;
The halter seizing, Peter leapt
Upon the ass's back, and plied
With ready heel the creature's side,
But still the ass his station kept.   430

"What's this!" cried Peter, brandishing
A new-peeled sapling white as cream;
The ass knew well what Peter said,
But, as before, hung down his head
Over the silent stream.   435

Then Peter gave a sudden jerk –
A jerk that from a dungeon floor
Would have pulled up an iron ring –
But still the heavy-headed thing
Stood just as he had stood before!   440

Quoth Peter, leaping from his seat,
"There is some plot against me laid";
Once more the little meadow ground
And all the hoary cliffs around
He cautiously surveyed.   445

All, all is silent; rocks and woods,
All still and silent, far and near;
Only the ass, with motion dull,
Upon the pivot of his skull
Turns round his long left ear.   450

Thought Peter, What can mean all this? —
Some ugly witchcraft must be here!
Once more the ass, with motion dull,
Upon the pivot of his skull
Turned round his long left ear.   455

"I'll cure you of these desperate tricks" —
And, with deliberate action slow,
His staff high-raising, in the pride
Of skill, upon the ass's hide
He dealt a sturdy blow.   460

What followed? — yielding to the shock
The ass, as if to take his ease,
In quiet uncomplaining mood
Upon the spot where he had stood
Dropped gently down upon his knees.   465

And then upon his side he fell
And by the river's brink did lie,
And, as he lay like one that mourned,
The patient beast on Peter turned
His shining hazel eye.   470

'Twas but one mild, reproachful look,
A look more tender than severe;
And straight in sorrow, not in dread,
He turned the eye-ball in his head
Towards the river deep and clear.   475

Upon the beast the sapling rings;
Heaved his lank sides, his limbs they stirred;
He gave a groan, and then another,
Of that which went before the brother,
And then he gave a third.   480

All by the moonlight river-side
He gave three miserable groans;
" 'Tis come then to a pretty pass,"
Said Peter to the groaning ass,
"But I will bang your bones!"   485

And Peter halts to gather breath,
And now full clearly was it shown
(What he before in part had seen)
How gaunt was the poor ass and lean,
Yea wasted to a skeleton!   490

With legs stretched out and stiff he lay;
No word of kind commiseration
Fell at the sight from Peter's tongue;
With hard contempt his heart was wrung –
With hatred and vexation.   495

The meagre beast lay still as death,
And Peter's lips with fury quiver;
Quoth he, "You little mulish dog,
I'll fling your carcase like a log
Head foremost down the river!"   500

An impious oath confirmed the threat,
But while upon the ground he lay,
To all the echoes, south and north,
And east and west, the ass sent forth
A loud and piteous bray!   505

This outcry, on the heart of Peter,
Seems like a note of joy to strike;
Joy on the heart of Peter knocks,
But in the echo of the rocks
Was something Peter did not like.   510

Whether to cheer his coward breast,
Or that he could not break the chain
In this serene and solemn hour
Twined round him by demoniac power,
To the blind work he turned again.   515

Among the rocks and winding crags,
Among the mountains far away,
Once more the ass did lengthen out
More ruefully an endless shout –
The long dry see-saw of his horrible bray!   520

What is there now in Peter's heart?
Or whence the might of this strange sound?
The moon uneasy looked and dimmer,
The broad blue heavens appeared to glimmer,
And the rocks staggered all around.   525

From Peter's hand the sapling dropped!
Threat has he none to execute –
"If any one should come and see
That I am here, they'll think," quoth he,
"I'm helping this poor dying brute."   530

He scans the ass from limb to limb,
And Peter now uplifts his eyes;
Steady the moon doth look and clear,
And like themselves the rocks appear,
And tranquil are the skies.   535

Whereat, in resolute mood, once more
He stoops the ass's neck to seize –
Foul purpose, quickly put to flight!
For in the pool a startling sight
Meets him, beneath the shadowy trees.   540

Is it the moon's distorted face?
The ghost-like image of a cloud?
Is it a gallows there portrayed?
Is Peter of himself afraid?
Is it a coffin, or a shroud?   545

A grisly idol hewn in stone?
Or imp from witch's lap let fall?
Or a gay ring of shining fairics,
Such as pursue their brisk vagaries
In sylvan bower, or haunted hall?   550

Is it a fiend that to a stake
Of fire his desperate self is tethering?
Or stubborn spirit doomed to yell
In solitary ward or cell,
Ten thousand miles from all his brethren?   555

Is it a party in a parlour,
Crammed just as they on earth were crammed?
Some sipping punch, some sipping tea,
But, as you by their faces see,
All silent and all damned!   560

A throbbing pulse the gazer hath —
Puzzled he was, and now is daunted;
He looks, he cannot choose but look,
Like one intent upon a book —
A book that is enchanted.   565

Ah, well-a-day for Peter Bell!
He will be turned to iron soon,
Meet statue for the court of Fear!
His hat is up, and every hair
Bristles and whitens in the moon!   570

He looks, he ponders, looks again;
He sees a motion, hears a groan;
His eyes will burst, his heart will break,
He gives a loud and frightful shriek,
And drops, a senseless weight, as if his life were flown! 575

PART SECOND

We left our hero in a trance,
Beneath the alders, near the river;
The ass is by the river-side,
And, where the feeble breezes glide,
Upon the stream the moon-beams quiver.   580

A happy respite! but he wakes,
And feels the glimmering of the moon,
And to stretch forth his hands is trying;
Sure, when he knows where he is lying,
He'll sink into a second swoon.   585

He lifts his head, he sees his staff,
He touches — 'tis to him a treasure!
Faint recollection seems to tell
That he is yet where mortals dwell —
A thought received with languid pleasure!   590

His head upon his elbow propped,
Becoming less and less perplexed,
Sky-ward he looks to rock and wood,
And then upon the placid flood
His wandering eye is fixed.   595

Thought he, that is the face of one
In his last sleep securely bound!
So, faltering not in *this* intent,
He makes his staff an instrument
The river's depth to sound.   600

Now like a tempest-shattered bark
That overwhelmed and prostrate lies,
And in a moment to the verge
Is lifted of a foaming surge,
Full suddenly the ass doth rise!   605

His staring bones all shake with joy,
And close by Peter's side he stands;
While Peter o'er the river bends,
The little ass his neck extends,
And fondly licks his hands.   610

Such life is in the ass's eyes,
Such life is in his limbs and ears
That Peter Bell, if he had been
The veriest coward ever seen,
Must now have thrown aside his fears.   615

The ass looks on, and to his work
Is Peter quietly resigned;
He touches here, he touches there,
And now among the dead man's hair
His sapling Peter has entwined.   620

He pulls and looks, and pulls again,
And he whom the poor ass had lost –
The man who had been four days dead –
Head foremost from the river's bed
Uprises like a ghost!   625

And Peter draws him to dry land,
And through the brain of Peter pass
Some poignant twitches, fast and faster:
"No doubt," quoth he, "he is the master
Of this poor miserable ass!"   630

The meagre shadow all this while –
What aim is his? what is he doing?
His sudden fit of joy is flown:
He on his knees hath laid him down,
As if he were his grief renewing.   635

That Peter on his back should mount
He shows a wish, well as he can,
"I'll go, I'll go, whate'er betide –
He to his home my way will guide,
The cottage of the drowned man."   640

This uttered, Peter mounts forthwith
Upon the pleased and thankful ass,
And then, without a moment's stay,
The earnest creature turned away,
Leaving the body on the grass.   645

Intent upon his faithful watch
The beast four days and nights had passed;
A sweeter meadow ne'er was seen,
And there the ass four days had been,
Nor ever once did break his fast!   650

Yet firm his step, and stout his heart;
The mead is crossed – the quarry's mouth
Is reached – but there the trusty guide
Into a thicket turns aside,
And takes his way towards the south.   655

When hark, a burst of doleful sound!
And Peter honestly might say
The like came never to his ears
Though he has been full thirty years
A rover night and day!   660

'Tis not a plover of the moors,
'Tis not a bittern of the fen,
Nor can it be a barking fox,
Nor night-bird chambered in the rocks,
Nor wild-cat in a woody glen!   665

The ass is startled, and stops short
Right in the middle of the thicket,
And Peter, wont to whistle loud
Whether alone or in a crowd,
Is silent as a silent cricket.   670

What ails you now, my little Bess?
Well may you tremble and look grave!
This cry that rings along the wood,
This cry that floats adown the flood,
Comes from the entrance of a cave.   675

I see a blooming wood-boy there,
And if I had the power to say
How sorrowful the wanderer is,
Your heart would be as sad as his
Till you had kissed his tears away!   680

Holding a hawthorn branch in hand,
All bright with berries ripe and red,
Into the cavern's mouth he peeps —
Thence back into the moon-light creeps;
What seeks the boy? — the silent dead!   685

His father! Him doth he require,
Whom he hath sought with fruitless pains
Among the rocks, behind the trees,
Now creeping on his hands and knees,
Now running o'er the open plains.   690

And hither is he come at last,
When he through such a day has gone,
By this dark cave to be distressed
Like a poor bird — her plundered nest
Hovering around with dolorous moan!   695

Of that intense and piercing cry
The listening ass doth rightly spell;
Wild as it is he there can read
Some intermingled notes that plead
With touches irresistible;   700

But Peter, when he saw the ass
Not only stop but turn, and change
The cherished tenor of his pace
That lamentable noise to chase,
It wrought in him conviction strange: 705

A faith that, for the dead man's sake
And this poor slave who loved him well,
Vengeance upon his head will fall –
Some visitation worse than all
Which ever till this night befell.   710

Meanwhile the ass to gain his end
Is striving stoutly as he may,
But, while he climbs the woody hill,
The cry grows weak and weaker still,
And now at last it dies away!   715

So with his freight the creature turns
Into a gloomy grove of beech,
Along the shade with footstep true
Descending slowly, till the two
The open moonlight reach.   720

And there, along a narrow dell,
A fair smooth pathway you discern –
A length of green and open road –
As if it from a fountain flowed,
Winding away between the fern.   725

The rocks that tower on either side
Build up a wild fantastic scene:
Temples like those among the Hindoos,
And mosques, and spires, and abbey windows,
And castles all with ivy green!   730

And, while the ass pursues his way
Along this solitary dell,
As pensively his steps advance,
The mosques and spires change countenance,
And look at Peter Bell!   735

That unintelligible cry
Hath left him high in preparation,
Convinced that he, or soon or late,
This very night will meet his fate,
And so he sits in expectation!   740

The verdant pathway, in and out,
Winds upwards like a straggling chain,
And, when two toilsome miles are past,
Up through the rocks it leads at last
Into a high and open plain.   745

The strenuous animal hath clomb
With the green path, and now he wends
Where, shining like the smoothest sea,
In undisturbed immensity
The level plain extends.   750

How blank! But whence this rustling sound
Which, all too long, the pair hath chased?
A dancing leaf is close behind,
Light plaything for the sportive wind
Upon that solitary waste.   755

When Peter spies the withered leaf,
It yields no cure to his distress —
"Where there is not a bush or tree,
The very leaves they follow me —
So huge hath been my wickedness!"   760

To a close lane they now are come,
Where as before the enduring ass
Moves on without a moment's stop,
Nor once turns round his head to crop
A bramble leaf or blade of grass.   765

Between the hedges as they go
The white dust sleeps upon the lane,
And Peter, ever and anon
Back-looking, sees upon a stone
Or in the dust, a crimson stain.   770

A stain as of a drop of blood
By moonlight made more faint and wan –
Ha! why this comfortless despair?
He knows not how the blood comes there,
And Peter is a wicked man.   775

At length he spies a bleeding wound
Where he had struck the ass's head;
He sees the blood, knows what it is –
A glimpse of sudden joy was his,
But then it quickly fled.   780

Of him whom sudden death had seized
He thought – of thee, O faithful ass!
And once again those darting pains,
As meteors shoot through heaven's wide plains,
Pass through his bosom and repass!   785

PART THIRD

I've heard of one, a gentle soul,
Though given to sadness and to gloom,
And for the fact will vouch – one night
It chanced that by a taper's light
This man was reading in his room;   790

Reading, as you or I might read
At night in any pious book,
When sudden blackness overspread
The snow-white page on which he read,
And made the good man round him look.   795

The chamber walls were dark all round,
And to his book he turned again;
The light had left the good man's taper,
And formed itself upon the paper
Into large letters, bright and plain!   800

The godly book was in his hand,
And on the page more black than coal
Appeared, set forth in strange array,
A word, which to his dying day
Perplexed the good man's gentle soul.   805

The ghostly word, which thus was framed,
Did never from his lips depart,
But he hath said, poor gentle wight!
It brought full many a sin to light
Out of the bottom of his heart.   810

Dread Spirits! to torment the good
Why wander from your course so far,
Disordering colour, form, and stature?
Let good men feel the soul of Nature,
And see things as they are.   815

I know you, potent spirits! well —
How with the feeling and the sense
Playing, ye govern foes or friends,
Yoked to your will, for fearful ends —
And this I speak in reverence!   820

But might I give advice to you,
Whom in my fear I love so well:
From men of pensive virtue go,
Dread beings! and your empire show
On hearts like that of Peter Bell.   825

Your presence I have often felt
In darkness and the stormy night,
And well I know, if need there be,
Ye can put forth your agency
When earth is calm, and heaven is bright.   830

Then, coming from the wayward world,
That powerful world in which ye dwell,
Come, spirits of the mind! and try
To-night, beneath the moonlight sky,
What may be done with Peter Bell!   835

O, would that some more skilful voice
My further labour might prevent!
Kind listeners, that around me sit,
I feel that I am all unfit
For such high argument.   840

I've played and danced with my narration –
I loitered long ere I began;
Ye waited then on my good pleasure –
Pour out indulgence still, in measure
As liberal as ye can!   845

Our travellers, ye remember well,
Are thridding a sequestered lane,
And Peter many tricks is trying,
And many anodynes applying,
To ease his conscience of its pain.   850

By this his heart is lighter far,
And finding that he can account
So clearly for that crimson stain,
His evil spirit up again
Does like an empty bucket mount.   855

And Peter is a deep logician
Who hath no lack of wit mercurial;
"Blood drops, leaves rustle, yet," quoth he,
"This poor man never, but for me,
Could have had Christian burial.   860

And, say the best you can, 'tis plain
That here hath been some wicked dealing;
No doubt the devil in me wrought –
I'm not the man who could have thought
An ass like this was worth the stealing!"   865

So from his pocket Peter takes
His shining horn tobacco-box,
And in a light and careless way,
As men who with their purpose play,
Upon the lid he knocks.   870

Let them whose voice can stop the clouds,
Whose cunning eye can see the wind,
Tell to a curious world the cause
Why, making here a sudden pause,
The ass turned round his head – and *grinned*.   875

Appalling process! – I have marked
The like on heath, in lonely wood,
And, verily, have seldom met
A spectacle more hideous – yet
It suited Peter's present mood.   880

And, grinning in his turn, his teeth
He in jocose defiance showed,
When, to confound his spiteful mirth,
A murmur, pent within the earth,
In the dead earth beneath the road,   885

Rolled audibly! It swept along,
A muffled noise, a rumbling sound!
'Twas by a troop of miners made,
Plying with gunpowder their trade,
Some twenty fathoms under ground.   890

Small cause of dire effect! for surely,
If ever mortal, king or cotter,
Believed that earth was charged to quake
And yawn for his unworthy sake,
'Twas Peter Bell the potter!   895

But, as an oak in breathless air
Will stand though to the centre hewn,
Or as the weakest things, if frost
Have stiffened them, maintain their post,
So he, beneath the gazing moon!   900

But now the pair have reached a spot
Where, sheltered by a rocky cove,
A little chapel stands alone,
With greenest ivy overgrown,
And tufted with an ivy grove.   905

Dying insensibly away
From human thoughts and purposes,
The building seems — wall, roof, and tower —
To bow to some transforming power,
And blend with the surrounding trees.   910

Deep sighing as he passed along,
Quoth Peter, "In the shire of Fife,
'Mid such a ruin, following still
From land to land a lawless will,
I married my sixth wife!"   915

The unheeding ass moves slowly on,
And now is passing by an inn
Brim-full of a carousing crew,
Making, with curses not a few,
An uproar and a drunken din.   920

I cannot well express the thoughts
Which Peter in those noises found;
A stifling power compressed his frame,
As if confusing darkness came
Over that dull and dreary sound.   925

For well did Peter know the sound;
The language of those drunken joys
To him, a jovial soul I ween,
But a few hours ago had been
A gladsome and a welcome noise.   930

Now, turned adrift into the past,
He finds no solace in his course;
Like planet-stricken men of yore
He trembles, smitten to the core
By strong compunction and remorse.   935

But more than all, his heart is stung
To think of one, almost a child –
A sweet and playful Highland girl,
As light and beauteous as a squirrel,
As beauteous and as wild!   940

A lonely house her dwelling was,
A cottage in a heathy dell,
And she put on her gown of green,
And left her mother at sixteen,
And followed Peter Bell.   945

But many good and pious thoughts
Had she, and in the kirk to pray,
Two long Scotch miles, through rain or snow,
To kirk she had been used to go,
Twice every sabbath-day.   950

And when she followed Peter Bell,
It was to lead an honest life,
For he, with tongue not used to falter,
Had pledged his troth before the altar
To love her as his wedded wife.   955

A mother's hope is hers, but soon
She drooped and pined like one forlorn;
From scripture she a name did borrow –
Benoni, or the child of sorrow,
She called her babe unborn.   960

For she had learned how Peter lived,
And took it in most grievous part;
She to the very bone was worn,
And, ere that little child was born,
Died of a broken heart.   965

And now the spirits of the mind
Are busy with poor Peter Bell;
Distraction reigns in soul and sense,
And reason drops in impotence
From her deserted pinnacle!   970

Close by a brake of flowering furze
(Above it shivering aspins play)
He sees an unsubstantial creature,
His very self in form and feature,
Not four yards from the broad highway.   975

And stretched beneath the furze he sees
The Highland girl – it is no other –
And hears her crying, as she cried
The very moment that she died,
"My mother! oh my mother!"   980

The sweat pours down from Peter's face,
So grievous is his heart's contrition;
With agony his eye-balls ache
While he beholds by the furze-brake
This miserable vision!   985

Calm is the well-deserving brute,
His peace hath no offence betrayed;
But now, while down that slope he wends,
A voice to Peter's ears ascends,
Resounding from the woody glade: 990

Though clamorous as a hunter's horn
Re-echoed from a naked rock,
'Tis from that tabernacle – list!
Within, a fervent Methodist
Is preaching to no heedless flock.   995

"Repent! repent!" he cries aloud,
"While yet ye may find mercy; strive
To love the Lord with all your might;
Turn to him, seek him day and night,
And save your souls alive!   1000

Repent! repent! though ye have gone
Through paths of wickedness and woe
After the Babylonian harlot,
And though your sins be red as scarlet
They shall be white as snow!"   1005

Even as he passed the door, these words
Did plainly come to Peter's ears,
And they such joyful tidings were –
The joy was more than he could bear –
He melted into tears.   1010

Sweet tears of hope and tenderness!
And fast they fell, a plenteous shower;
His nerves, his sinews seemed to melt;
Through all his iron frame was felt
A gentle, a relaxing power!   1015

Each fibre of his frame was weak;
Weak all the animal within,
But in its helplessness grew mild
And gentle as an infant child –
An infant that has known no sin.   1020

'Tis said that through prevailing grace
He not unmoved did notice now
The cross upon thy shoulders scored,
Meek beast! in memory of the Lord
To whom all human-kind shall bow –   1025

In memory of that solemn day
When Jesus humbly deigned to ride,
Entering the proud Jerusalem,
By an immeasurable stream
Of shouting people deified!   1030

Meanwhile the persevering ass
Towards a gate in open view
Turns up a narrow lane; his chest
Against the yielding gate he pressed,
And quietly passed through.   1035

And up the stony lane he goes;
No ghost more softly ever trod;
Among the stones and pebbles, he
Sets down his hoofs inaudibly,
As if with felt his hoofs were shod.   1040

Along the lane the trusty ass
Had gone two hundred yards, not more,
When to a lonely house he came;
He turned aside towards the same
And stopped before the door.　　　　　　　　1045

Thought Peter, 'tis the poor man's home!
He listens; not a sound is heard
Save from the trickling household rill,
But, stepping o'er the cottage-sill,
Forthwith a little girl appeared.　　　　　　1050

She to the meeting-house was bound
In hope some tidings there to gather –
No glimpse it is, no doubtful gleam –
She saw, and uttered with a scream,
"My father! here's my father!"　　　　　　1055

The very word was plainly heard,
Heard plainly by the wretched mother;
Her joy was like a deep affright,
And forth she rushed into the light,
And saw it was another!　　　　　　　　1060

And instantly, upon the earth
Beneath the full-moon shining bright,
Close at the ass's feet she fell;
At the same moment Peter Bell
Dismounts in most unhappy plight.　　　　1065

What could he do? The woman lay
Breathless and motionless; the mind
Of Peter sadly was confused;
But, though to such demands unused,
And helpless almost as the blind,　　　　　1070

He raised her up, and while he held
Her body propped against his knee,
The woman waked, and when she spied
The poor ass standing by her side,
She moaned most bitterly.　　　　　　　1075

"Oh! God be praised! – my heart's at ease –
For he is dead – I know it well!"
At this she wept a bitter flood,
And, in the best way that he could,
His tale did Peter tell.   1080

He trembles; he is pale as death;
His voice is weak with perturbation;
He turns aside his head; he pauses;
Poor Peter from a thousand causes
Is crippled sore in his narration.   1085

At length she learned how he espied
The ass in that small meadow ground,
And that her husband now lay dead
Beside that luckless river's bed
In which he had been drowned.   1090

A piercing look the sufferer cast
Upon the beast that near her stands;
She sees 'tis he, that 'tis the same;
She calls the poor ass by his name,
And wrings and wrings her hands.   1095

"O wretched loss! – untimely stroke!
If he had died upon his bed!
He knew not one forewarning pain –
He never will come home again –
Is dead – for ever dead!"   1100

Beside the woman Peter stands;
His heart is opening more and more;
A holy sense pervades his mind:
He feels what he for human kind
Had never felt before.   1105

At length, by Peter's arm sustained,
The woman rises from the ground;
"Oh mercy! something must be done –
My little Rachel, you must run –
Some willing neighbour must be found.   1110

Make haste, my little Rachel, do!
The first you meet with bid him come;
Ask him to lend his horse to-night,
And this good man, whom heaven requite,
Will help to bring the body home."   1115

Away goes Rachel weeping loud;
An infant, waked by her distress,
Makes in the house a piteous cry,
And Peter hears the mother sigh,
"Seven are they, and all fatherless!"   1120

And now is Peter taught to feel
That man's heart is a holy thing,
And Nature, through a world of death,
Breathes into him a second breath,
More searching than the breath of spring.   1125

Upon a stone the woman sits
In agony of silent grief;
From his own thoughts did Peter start;
He longs to press her to his heart
From love that cannot find relief.   1130

But roused, as if through every limb
Had passed a sudden shock of dread,
The mother o'er the threshold flies,
And up the cottage stairs she hies,
And to the pillow gives her burning head.   1135

And Peter turns his steps aside
Into a shade of darksome trees
Where he sits down, he knows not how,
With his hands pressed against his brow,
And resting on his tremulous knees.   1140

There, self-involved, does Peter sit
Until no sign of life he makes —
As if his mind were sinking deep
Through years that have been long asleep!
The trance is passed away — he wakes,   1145

He turns his head – and sees the ass
Yet standing in the clear moonshine;
"When shall I be as good as thou?
Oh! would, poor beast, that I had now
A heart but half as good as thine!" 1150

But he who deviously hath sought
His father through the lonesome woods,
Hath sought, proclaiming to the ear
Of night his inward grief and fear –
He comes, escaped from fields and floods, 1155

With weary pace is drawing nigh;
He sees the ass, and nothing living
Had ever such a fit of joy
As had this little orphan boy,
For he has no misgiving! 1160

Towards the gentle ass he springs,
And up about his neck he climbs;
In loving words he talks to him,
He kisses, kisses face and limb –
He kisses him a thousand times! 1165

This Peter sees, while in the shade
He stood beside the cottage door;
And Peter Bell, the ruffian wild,
Sobs loud, he sobs even like a child,
"Oh! God, I can endure no more!" 1170

Here ends my tale, for in a trice
Arrived a neighbour with his horse;
Peter went forth with him straightway,
And, with due care, ere break of day
Together they brought back the corse. 1175

And many years did this poor ass,
Whom once it was my luck to see
Cropping the shrubs of Leming-Lane,
Help by his labour to maintain
The widow and her family. 1180

And Peter Bell, who till that night
Had been the wildest of his clan,
Forsook his crimes, repressed his folly,
And, after ten months' melancholy,
Became a good and honest man.'   1185

LATER POEMS

Sequel to [Beggars]

Where are they now, those wanton boys
For whose free range the daedal earth
Was filled with animated toys
And implements of frolic mirth,
With tools for ready wit to guide,   5
And ornaments of seemlier pride
More fresh, more bright, than princes wear?
For what one moment flung aside,
Another could repair;
What good or evil have they seen   10
Since I their pastime witnessed here –
Their daring wiles, their sportive cheer?
I ask – but all is dark between!

Spirits of beauty and of grace!
Associates in that eager chase!   15
Ye, by a course to nature true,
The sterner judgement can subdue,
And waken a relenting smile
When she encounters fraud or guile;
And sometimes ye can charm away   20
The inward mischief, or allay –
Ye, who within the blameless mind
Your favourite seat of empire find!

They met me in a genial hour,
When universal nature breathed   25
As with the breath of one sweet flower;
A time to overrule the power
Of discontent, and check the birth
Of thoughts with better thoughts at strife –
The most familiar bane of life   30
Since parting innocence bequeathed
Mortality to earth!
Soft clouds, the whitest of the year,
Sailed through the sky; the brooks ran clear;
The lambs from rock to rock were bounding;   35

With songs the budded groves resounding;
And to my heart is still endeared
The faith with which it then was cheered –
The faith which saw that gladsome pair
Walk through the fire with unsinged hair.   40
Or, if such thoughts must needs deceive,
Kind spirits! may we not believe
That they, so happy and so fair,
Through your sweet influence, and the care
Of pitying heaven, at least were free   45
From touch of *deadly* injury?
Destined, whate'er their earthly doom,
For mercy and immortal bloom!

Ode, Composed upon an Evening of Extraordinary Splendour and Beauty

I

Had this effulgence disappeared
With flying haste, I might have sent
Among the speechless clouds a look
Of blank astonishment;
But 'tis endued with power to stay   5
And sanctify one closing day,
That frail mortality may see
What is? – ah no, but what *can* be!
Time was when field and watery cove
With modulated echoes rang,   10
While choirs of fervent angels sang
Their vespers in the grove,
Or, ranged like stars along some sovereign height,
Warbled, for heaven above and earth below,
Strains suitable to both. Such holy rite,   15
Methinks, if audibly repeated now
From hill or valley, could not move
Sublimer transport, purer love,
Than doth this silent spectacle – the gleam,
The shadow, and the peace supreme!   20

II

No sound is uttered, but a deep
And solemn harmony pervades
The hollow vale from steep to steep,
And penetrates the glades.
Far-distant images draw nigh,   25
Called forth by wond'rous potency
Of beamy radiance, that imbues
Whate'er it strikes with gem-like hues!
In vision exquisitely clear,
Herds range along the mountain side,   30
And glistening antlers are descried,
And gilded flocks appear.
Thine is the tranquil hour, purpureal eve!
But long as god-like wish or hope divine
Informs my spirit, ne'er can I believe   35
That this magnificence is wholly thine!
From worlds not quickened by the sun
A portion of the gift is won;
An intermingling of heaven's pomp is spread
On ground which British shepherds tread!   40

III

And if there be whom broken ties
Afflict, or injuries assail,
Yon hazy ridges to their eyes
Present a glorious scale,
Climbing suffused with sunny air   45
To stop – no record hath told where!
And tempting fancy to ascend,
And with immortal spirits blend!
Wings at my shoulder seem to play,
But rooted here, I stand and gaze   50
On those bright steps that heaven-ward raise
Their practicable way.
Come forth, ye drooping old men, look abroad
And see to what fair countries ye are bound!
And if some traveller, weary of his road,   55
Hath slept since noon-tide on the grassy ground,

Ye Genii! to his covert speed,
And wake him with such gentle heed
As may attune his soul to meet the dow'r
Bestowed on this transcendent hour!   60

IV

Such hues from their celestial urn
Were wont to stream before my eye
Where'er it wandered in the morn
Of blissful infancy.
This glimpse of glory, why renewed?   65
Nay, rather speak with gratitude,
For if a vestige of those gleams
Survived, 'twas only in my dreams.
Dread power! whom peace and calmness serve
No less than Nature's threatening voice,   70
If aught unworthy be my choice –
From Thee if I would swerve –
O, let thy grace remind me of the light,
Full early lost and fruitlessly deplored,
Which at this moment on my waking sight   75
Appears to shine, by miracle restored!
My soul, though yet confined to earth,
Rejoices in a second birth;
'Tis past; the visionary splendour fades,
And night approaches with her shades.   80

'Hopes, what are they?'

Hopes, what are they? – beads of morning
Strung on slender blades of grass,
Or a spider's web adorning
In a strait and treacherous pass.

What are fears but voices airy? –   5
Whispering harm where harm is not,
And deluding the unwary
Till the fatal bolt is shot.

What is glory? – in the socket
See how dying tapers fare!
What is pride? – a whizzing rocket
That would emulate a star.   10

What is friendship? – do not trust her,
Nor the vows which she has made;
Diamonds dart their brightest lustre   15
From a palsy-shaken head.

What is truth? – a staff rejected;
Duty? – an unwelcome clog;
Joy? – a dazzling moon reflected
In a swamp or watery bog;   20

Bright, as if through ether steering,
To the traveller's eye it shone:
He hath hailed it re-appearing,
And as quickly it is gone;

Gone, as if for ever hidden,   25
Or misshapen to the sight,
And by sullen weeds forbidden
To resume its native light.

What is youth? – a dancing billow,
Winds behind, and rocks before!   30
Age? – a drooping, tottering willow
On a flat and lazy shore.

What is peace? – when pain is over,
And love ceases to rebel,
Let the last faint sigh discover   35
That precedes the passing knell!

The River Duddon

I thought of thee, my partner and my guide,
As being passed away. Vain sympathies!
For, *backward*, Duddon! as I cast my eyes,
I see what was, and is, and will abide.
Still glides the stream, and shall for ever glide;   5
The form remains, the function never dies,
While *we*, the brave, the mighty, and the wise,
We men, who in our morn of youth defied
The elements, must vanish. Be it so!
Enough, if something from our hands have power   10
To live, and act, and serve the future hour;
And if, as tow'rd the silent tomb we go,
Thro' love, thro' hope, and faith's transcendent dower,
We feel that we are greater than we know.

Mutability

From low to high doth dissolution climb,
And sinks from high to low along a scale
Of awful notes, whose concord shall not fail –
A musical but melancholy chime,
Which they can hear who meddle not with crime,   5
Nor avarice, nor over-anxious care.
Truth fails not, but her outward forms that bear
The longest date do melt like frosty rime
That in the morning whitened hill and plain
And is no more – drop like the tower sublime   10
Of yesterday, which royally did wear
Its crown of weeds, but could not even sustain
Some casual shout that broke the silent air,
Or the unimaginable touch of time.

Steamboats, Viaducts, and Railways

Motions and means, on land and sea at war
With old poetic feeling: not for this
Shall ye, by poets even, be judged amiss.
Nor shall your presence, howsoe'er it mar
The loveliness of Nature, prove a bar   5
To the mind's gaining that prophetic sense
Of future change, that point of vision whence
May be discovered what in soul ye are.
In spite of all that beauty may disown
In your harsh features, Nature doth embrace   10
Her lawful offspring in man's art, and Time,
Pleased with your triumphs o'er his brother Space,
Accepts from your bold hands the proffered crown
Of hope, and smiles on you with cheer sublime.

Extempore Effusion upon the Death of James Hogg

When first, descending from the moorlands,
I saw the stream of Yarrow glide
Along a bare and open valley,
The Ettrick Shepherd was my guide.

When last along its banks I wandered,   5
Through groves that had begun to shed
Their golden leaves upon the pathways,
My steps the Border Minstrel led.

The mighty minstrel breathes no longer,
'Mid mouldering ruins low he lies,   10
And death upon the braes of Yarrow
Has closed the shepherd-poet's eyes.

Nor has the rolling year twice measured,
From sign to sign, its steadfast course,
Since every mortal power of Coleridge   15
Was frozen at its marvellous source—

The rapt one, of the godlike forehead,
The heaven-eyed creature sleeps in earth,
And Lamb, the frolic and the gentle,
Has vanished from his lonely hearth.　　　　　　　　　20

Like clouds that rake the mountain-summits,
Or waves that own no curbing hand,
How fast has brother followed brother
From sunshine to the sunless land!

Yet I, whose lids from infant slumbers　　　　　　　　25
Were earlier raised, remain to hear
A timid voice, that asks in whispers,
'Who next will drop and disappear?'

Our haughty life is crowned with darkness,
Like London with its own black wreath,　　　　　　　30
On which with thee, O Crabbe! forth-looking,
I gazed from Hampstead's breezy heath.

As if but yesterday departed,
Thou too art gone before; but why,
O'er ripe fruit, seasonably gathered,　　　　　　　　35
Should frail survivors heave a sigh?

Mourn rather for that holy spirit,
Sweet as the spring, as ocean deep;
For her who, ere her summer faded,
Has sunk into a breathless sleep.　　　　　　　　　40

No more of old romantic sorrows,
For slaughtered youth or love-lorn maid!
With sharper grief is Yarrow smitten,
And Ettrick mourns with her their Poet dead.

November, 1836

Even so for me a vision sanctified
The sway of death, long ere mine eyes had seen
Thy countenance – the still rapture of thy mien –
When thou, dear sister! wert become Death's bride;
No trace of pain or languor could abide   5
That change: age on thy brow was smoothed; thy cold
Wan cheek at once was privileged to unfold
A loveliness to living youth denied.
Oh! if within me hope should ere decline,
The lamp of faith, lost friend! too faintly burn,   10
Then may that heaven-revealing smile of thine –
The bright assurance – visibly return,
And let my spirit in that power divine
Rejoice, as through that power it ceased to mourn.

NOTES

(I.F. refers to notes Wordsworth dictated to Isabella Fenwick in 1843)

From *An Evening Walk*, 1793 (p. 3)

Serious composition probably began during the summer vacation, 1788. Possibly completed by early 1792. Published with *Descriptive Sketches* in 1793. The subtitle runs – *An Evening Walk: An Epistle in Verse, addressed to a Young Lady, from the Lakes of the North of England*. The 'Young Lady' is Dorothy Wordsworth.

'There is not an image in it which I have not observed, and now, in my seventy-third year, I recollect the time and place where most of them were noticed . . . The plan [of the poem] has not been confined to a particular walk or an individual place: a proof . . . of my unwillingness to submit the poetic spirit to the chains of fact and real circumstance. The country is idealized, rather than described in any one of its local aspects.' (I.F.)

It was *An Evening Walk* and *Descriptive Sketches* that first brought Wordsworth, as a talented writer in the eighteenth-century genre of topographical poetry, to the attention of Coleridge at Cambridge, two years before they met. In 1801, W referred to both poems as 'juvenile productions, inflated and obscure', but he thought highly of his achievement in both poems, which he saw as containing 'many new images, and vigorous lines', and kept on revising them. The notes to both poems will reveal W's poetic debt to other writers.

l.3   wizard course: Cp Milton's *Lycidas*, l.55.
l.19   Cp Charlotte Smith, *Elegiac Sonnets*, V, 'To the South Downs', l.1.
l.26   W's note: 'In the beginning of winter, these mountains, in the moonlight nights, are covered with immense quantities of woodcocks, which, in the dark nights, retire into the woods.'
ll.27–30 Quoted in the *Monthly Review*, October 1793, with the comment: 'Life *rearing* up the sun! Transport kissing away an *April* tear and *rocking* the year as in a dream! Would the cradle had been specified! Seriously, these are figures which no poetical licence can justify.'
l.29   Cp Lady Winchilsea, 'Life's Progress', l.22.
l.30   Cp Milton's *Areopagitica*: 'There be delights . . . that will fetch the day about from sun to sun, and rock the tedious year as in a delightful dream.'
ll.37–42 A prose draft lies behind the lines: 'Human life is like the [?] of

a dial: hope brightens the future, reflection the hour that is past, but the present is always marked with a shadow.'

l.47   The grammatical subject of the line is 'the ray . . . of morning'.

l.114   W's note: '"Vivid rings of green." – Greenwood's Poem on Shooting.'

l.116   W's note: '"Down the rough slope the pondrous waggon rings." Beattie [*The Minstrel*, I, 39].'

l.117   W's note: 'These rude structures, to protect the flocks, are frequent in this country . . .'

l.124   Cp *Paradise Lost*, II, 476–7.

l.129   W's note: '"Dolcemente feroce" – Tasso [*Gerusalemme Liberata*, I, 58]. In this description of the cock, I remembered a spirited one of the same animal in the l'Agriculture, ou Les Géorgiques Françoises, of M. Rossuet.'

l.146   Cp *Paradise Lost*, II, 592.

l.153   aegis: like a shield.

l.158   'prospect all on fire': from Moses Browne's 'Sunday Thoughts', which W read in John Scott's *Critical Essays* (1785) – an analysis of nine seventeenth- and eighteenth-century poems including *Lycidas* and *The Deserted Village*.

ll.165–8   'I was an eye-witness of this for the first time while crossing the pass of Dunmail Raise.' (I.F.)

l.171   W's note: 'Not far from Broughton is a Druid monument, of which I do not recollect that any tour . . . makes mention.'

ll.173–4   Cp Thomson, *The Seasons*, 'Summer', ll.1627–9. W's note acknowledges his debt.

ll.179–90   W's note: 'See a description of an appearance of this kind in Clark's "Survey of the Lakes", accompanied with vouchers of its veracity that may amuse the reader.'

ll.241–56   See Mary Jacobus, *Tradition and Experiment in Wordsworth's Lyrical Ballads, 1798* (Oxford, 1976), p.144. Compare this passage with W's account of the 'tragic super-tragic' in *The Prelude*, VIII, 550–9, where he has these lines in mind as he writes with a hint of self-parody. Compare ll.241–300 with the story of Margaret in *The Ruined Cottage*.

l.254   The battle of Bunker Hill was fought during the American Revolution.

l.256   Cp *Ecclesiastes* 12:6 – 'or the pitcher be broken at the fountain', *Descriptive Sketches*, l.741, and *The Ruined Cottage*, ll.82–91.

l.258   Cp Gray's 'Elegy written in a country Churchyard', l.18.

l.263   her elder grief: the 1836 version makes the sense clear – 'her elder child'.

l.268   Cp Milton, *Samson Agonistes*, l.89.

l.278   'Green radiance' was borrowed and acknowledged by Coleridge in 'Lines written at Shurton Bars'.

l.333   W's note draws the reader's attention to lines from Spenser's *The Faerie Queene*, I, Canto 3, 4.

l.361   W's note cites Young's *Night Thoughts*, V, 1042.

l.378   W's note: ' "Charming the night-calm with her powerful song". A line of one of our older poets.' The line, slightly misquoted by W, is from Drayton's 'The Owl', ll.221–2.

From *Descriptive Sketches*, 1793 (p.10)

Most of the drafting done in France between early December 1791 and Autumn, 1792. Nearing completion on 3 September 1792. The full title reads – *Descriptive Sketches, in Verse, taken during a Pedestrian Tour in the Italian, Grison, Swiss, and Savoyard Alps.*

To the great chagrin of his family, the twenty-year-old W left Cambridge for a walking tour of the Continent in the company of a fellow student, Robert Jones, in the summer of 1790. The Bastille had fallen only the previous year. For fourteen weeks they travelled through France, northern Italy, and Switzerland, and saw the Alps. Not merely a loco-descriptive poem, *Descriptive Sketches* is a highly politicised work.

'Much of the greatest part of this poem was composed during my walks upon the banks of the Loire . . . I will only notice that the description of the valley filled with mist, beginning "In solemn shapes", was taken from that beautiful region of which the principal features are Lungarn and Sarnen. Nothing that I ever saw in nature left a more delightful impression on my mind than that which I have attempted, alas, how feebly! to convey to others in these lines . . .' (I.F.)

In *Biographia Literaria*, Chapter IV, Coleridge recalls that with the publication of *An Evening Walk* and *Descriptive Sketches*, 'seldom, if ever, was the emergence of an original poetic genius above the literary horizon more evidently announced . . . The language was not only peculiar and strong, but at times knotty and contorted, as by its own impatient strength . . . It not seldom therefore justified the complaint of obscurity.' The charge of obscurity was also levelled against the poem by contemporary reviewers – the *Critical Review* and the *Monthly Review* regarding many passages as 'unintelligible'.

l.130   Cp *The Prelude*, 1805, VI, 561.

l.151   young desire: Cp Gray, 'The Progress of Poesy', ll.40–1.

ll.164–5   W's note acknowledges his debt to two lines of Petrarch.

l.179   W's note: 'The river along whose banks you descend in crossing the Alps by the Sempion pass. From the striking contrast of its features, this pass I should imagine to be the most interesting among the Alps.'

l.209   W's note: 'Most of the bridges among the Alps are of wood and covered; these bridges have a heavy appearance, and rather injure the effect of the scenery in some places.'

l.213   W's note: '"Red came the river down, and loud, and oft/The angry Spirit of the water shriek'd". Home's *Douglas*.'

l.215   Cp *The Prelude*, VI, 549 – 'The dull and heavy slackening that ensued' – where W is describing his feelings on having crossed the Alps without knowing it.

ll.241–2   It is the 'babe's small cry' that 'scatters wild dismay'.

l.249   Cp *The Prelude*, VI, 563.

l.253   W's note: 'The Catholic religion prevails here; these cells are . . . planted, like the Roman tombs, along the road side.'

l.256   W's note: 'Crosses commemorative of the deaths of travellers by the fall of snow and other accidents very common along this dreadful road.'

ll.332–47   W's note: 'I had once given to these sketches the title of the Picturesque, but the Alps are insulted in applying to them that term. Whoever . . . should confine himself to the cold rules of painting would give his reader but a very imperfect idea of those emotions which they have the irresistible power of communicating to the most impassive imaginations . . . I consulted nature and my feelings. The ideas excited by the stormy sunset . . . owed their sublimity to that deluge of light, or rather of fire, in which nature had wrapped the immense forms around me.' Note in these words W's strong emphasis on the poetic mind's *subjective response* to the sublimity of the scene.

ll.494–511   Cp the Ascent of Snowdon passage in *The Prelude*, XIII, 36–65, and Beattie's *Minstrel*, I, XXI, 181–9. See also *Paradise Lost*, VII, 285–7 (on which W drew for the Snowdon lines) and XI, 826–8. 'He' (l.511) refers to a Swiss shepherd.

ll.520–35   As de Selincourt notes, Beatty in *Representative Poems of Wordsworth* points out that W took 'the thesis that Switzerland is the representative of primeval man, who is free, independent, hospitable – at least so far as the herdsmen and hunters are concerned' from Ramond de Carbonnières' translation of William Coxe's *Sketches of the Natural, Civil, and Political State of Swisserland* (1779).

ll.526–7   Cp *Paradise Lost*, IV, 291–3.

ll.535   W misquotes slightly from Smollett's 'Ode to Leven-water', ll.27–8.

l.539   W's note: 'Alluding to several battles which the Swiss in very small numbers have gained over their oppressors, the House of Austria, and in particular, to one fought at Naeffels near Glarus, where three hundred and thirty men defeated an army of between fifteen and twenty thousand Austrians.'

l.543   Cp some of W's later statements on the relationship between the living and the dead, especially the memorable lines from *The Convention of Cintra* (1809): 'Here then they, with whom I *hope*, take their stand.

There is a spiritual community binding together the living and the dead . . .
We would not be rejected from this community, and therefore do we hope.'
See also W's essays *Upon Epitaphs*.

l.569   Two years after *Descriptive Sketches*, Coleridge, in the third of his
Lectures on Revealed Religion, was to speak of 'private attachment',
'universal philanthropy', and *widening* circles: 'Jesus knew our nature,
and that expands like the circles of a lake: the love of our friends, parents,
and neighbours lead[s] us to the love of our country to the love of all
mankind.'

l.704   delicious vale: the vale of Chamouny.

l.706   W's note: 'It is scarce necessary to observe that these lines were
written before the emancipation of Savoy [by French annexation, 1793–
4].' In the 'Argument' to *Descriptive Sketches*, W indicates that these lines
refer to the 'slavery of Savoy' under the Austrians.

ll.706–8   Cp *Paradise Lost*, XI, 881–3.

l.741   See note to *An Evening Walk*, l.256.

l.746   W's note: 'This, as may be supposed, was written before France
became the seat of war.'

l.755   W's note: 'An insect so called, which emits a short, melancholy
cry . . .'

l.767   See note to *An Evening Walk*, l.30.

l.779   Cp Milton, *Il Penseroso*, ll.74–6.

ll.782–8   W might be echoing Virgil's famous, and famously prophetic,
fourth eclogue – 'Iam redit et virgo, redeunt Saturnia regna'. For the
conclusion to W's poem, see the end of Pope's 'Windsor Forest', also
indebted to Virgil.

ll.792–5   Obscurely pseudo-Miltonic. I interpret 792–4 thus: W asks
God to endow Freedom's waves with the power to 'ride sublime o'er
Conquest' etc., and to *break*, as cleansing breakers, on the land where
Death 'scours' the vales with Famine.

l.805   Cp Gray, 'The Alliance of Education and Government', ll.101 and
103.

ll.810–13   Cp the conclusion to *Paradise Lost*.

Salisbury Plain (p.20)

Composed summer 1793 to May 1794. It was revised and expanded in
1795 as 'Adventures on Salisbury Plain' (the didactic and moralistic
authorial commentary giving way to a dramatised presentation of the
tragedy of individuals), and finally published in 1842, revised again, as
'Guilt and Sorrow, or Incidents upon Salisbury Plain'. Lines 226–324
and 352–94 were published, slightly altered, as part of 'The Female
Vagrant' in *Lyrical Ballads*, 1798. From the heroic couplets of the two
early poems, W has moved on in this poem to the Spenserian stanza.

Separated from Annette and Caroline by the war between France and England (declared in February 1793), disillusioned with England's foreign and domestic policy, appalled by the plight of the poor, and having seen the English fleet gathering near the Isle of Wight, W walked over Salisbury Plain, largely without food, in the summer of 1793. His mind was in a state of heightened imaginative sensitivity. See *The Prelude* accounts of the experience – X, 229–74, and XII, 312–53 – together with the notes to 'Tintern Abbey'. The war referred to in the poem is the American War of Independence.

Coleridge admired the poem's 'union of deep feeling with profound thought'.

l.92   Stonehenge, where in 1793, W, 'overcome with heat and fatigue', 'took [his] siesta' (Letter to Kenyon, 1838).

l.258   W's note in the *Lyrical Ballads*, 1798: 'Several of the lakes in the north of England are let out to different fishermen, in parcels marked out by imaginary lines drawn from rock to rock.'

l.306   devoted: 'doomed to destruction'.

ll.424–7   It was believed, erroneously, that sacrificial victims were placed by the Druids in wicker effigies and burned alive.

l.509   Lifted from Milton's sonnet 'On the Lord General Fairfax at the siege of Colchester', l.10.

ll.541–9   'Error's monster race' did not 'start at the light with pain/And die' so easily. The war with France continued; 1794 brought the Treason Trials, and suspension of Habeas Corpus persisted.

Argument for Suicide (p.37)

From Dove Cottage MS 13. Probably written between 24 October 1796 and 25 February 1797. Never published by W.

The Baker's Cart [fragment] (p.37)

From Dove Cottage MS 13. Probably composed Spring 1797. Never published by W.

This poem appears in the MS on a leaf preceding a version of *The Ruined Cottage*, and some of the elements of the longer poem are present in this fragment: the mother, who remains nameless, living in penury, with a 'sick and extravagant' cast of mind. Her pitcher also points forward to the story of Margaret in *The Ruined Cottage*.

ll.1–4   Cp W's play *The Borderers*, ll.1333–6:

> I have heard
> The boisterous carman, in the miry road,
> Crack his loud whip and hail us with mild voice,
> And speak with milder voice to his poor beasts.

l.13   W left the MS blank here for a name he did not later supply.

'Are there no groans, no breeze or wind?'(p.38)

From Dove Cottage MS 14. Composed at Alfoxden, probably around 19 March 1798, or between 20 April and 16 May 1798. Never published by W.

l.6   loophole: the word in the MS is difficult to decipher; it seems more like 'loophole' to me than 'lamphole' – the reading offered by Butler and Green in *Lyrical Ballads and Other Poems, 1797–1800* (Cornell University Press, 1992). 'Loophole' also seems to fit more comfortably with the image of the eye that follows.

'Away, away, it is the air' (p.38)

From Dove Cottage MS 14. Composed at Alfoxden, probably between 20 April and 16 May 1798. Never published by W.

De Selincourt in the *Poetical Works* (V, p.470) describes these lines as 'a curious survival of W's earlier and more "romantic" taste'. Together with 'Are there no groans . . . ?', these lines have also been seen as an attempt to record feelings of personal anguish and disillusionment – as a survival of the emotional trauma of earlier experience in the 1790s – or as in some way related to the anguish of Martha Ray in 'The Thorn'.

The Ruined Cottage (p.39) and *The Pedlar* (p.54)

The version of *The Ruined Cottage* used is that of MS D of *The Excursion*; the text of *The Pedlar* is that of the poem as first separated from *The Ruined Cottage* in Dove Cottage MS 16.

These two works are here presented as two separate poems, but the history of their composition links them together. *The Ruined Cottage* was composed April–June 1797 and January–March 1798. It was revised and developed from 1802–4 and published, revised further, as Book I of *The Excursion* (1814). During February–March 1798, W added considerably to *The Ruined Cottage*, writing a life-history of the narrator of the main tale, the Pedlar. Dorothy on 5 March 1798 could state that 'the Pedlar's character makes a very, perhaps the *most*, considerable part of the poem'. These additions, in which W was for the first time drawing on childhood experience in a sustained piece of writing, focused on the pedlar's philosophical ideas and his reaction to the tragedy of Margaret. It is significant that at this time W was inspired by philosophical discussions with Coleridge, which developed his own ideas about man's relationship with Nature, and that March 1798 saw the birth of the idea for the great philosophical poem *The Recluse* (see notes to *Home at Grasmere* and the 'Prospectus' to *The Recluse*). It is this interest in philosophical ideas and the development of the mind that makes *The Ruined Cottage* and *The Pedlar* so different, and it is hardly surprising that the major statements of *The Pedlar* were incorporated into *The Prelude*, and given the autobiographical 'I'.

   The Pedlar was initially inserted into *The Ruined Cottage*, but in 1799 it was excerpted, and it became a separate poem, both on paper and, most probably, in W's mind. But in late 1803 *The Pedlar* was inserted into *The Ruined Cottage* at a time when *The Ruined Cottage* was seen by W as part of the scheme for *The Excursion*.

The Ruined Cottage (p.39)

' . . . for several passages describing the employment and demeanour of Margaret during her affliction I was indebted to observations made in Dorsetshire and afterwards at Alfoxden in Somersetshire . . . several of the most touching things which she is represented as saying and doing are taken from actual observation of the distresses and trials under which different persons were suffering − some of them strangers to me, and others daily under my notice . . . the state in which I represent Robert's mind to be I had frequent opportunities of observing at the commencement of our rupture with France in [17]93.' (I.F. note to *The Excursion*.) The hardships W mentions are actual: the harvest of 1794 was bad, and the winter one of the worst on record; there were bread riots in 1795; and the war with France was a further cause of misery.

l.53   The MSS are defective at this point.
ll.88–91   Cp note to *An Evening Walk*, l.256.
l.98   passenger: a passer-by.
ll.104–8   Cp Goldsmith's *Deserted Village* (1770), ll.47–8.
l.107   tricked: covered.
ll.133–8   W has the bad harvests of 1794–5 in mind as well as the war with France. The war was being fought as he was writing the poem, but the story is located at the time of the American war, which ended in 1783.
l.144   Cp *Paradise Lost*, VII, 144, Psalm 103:16 and Job 7:10.
l.232   Cp 'Hart-Leap Well', l.97 and *Othello*, I, iii, 135.
l.264   A purse of gold: In order to buy the services of much-needed militiamen, the British army offered a bounty of ten guineas.

l.295   The quotation is from Burns's poem 'To W. Simpson, Ochiltree', st.xv, l.3. MS B of *The Ruined Cottage* carries a significant epigraph from Burns's 'Epistle to J. Lapraik' – 'Give me a spark of nature's fire,/'Tis the best learning I desire;/My Muse, though homely in attire,/May touch the heart'.

ll.330–6   Inspired by Dorothy's *Journal* entry for 4 February 1798.

ll.455–92   Coleridge asked Dorothy to transcribe these lines for him. He sent them in a letter of 10 June 1797 to John Prior Estlin.

ll.520–4   Cp lines 413–19 of Coleridge's *Religious Musings*, which W has in mind.

ll.526–38   Cp concluding lines of Milton's *Lycidas*.

The Pedlar (p.54)

. . . had I been born in a class which would have deprived me of what is called a liberal education, it is not unlikely that . . . I should have taken to a way of life such as that in which my Pedlar passed the greater part of his days . . . the character I have represented in his person is chiefly an idea of what I fancied my own character might have become in his circumstances. Nevertheless much of what he says and does has an external existence that fell under my youthful and subsequent observation . . . An individual named Patrick, by birth and education a Scotchman, followed this humble occupation . . . He married a kinswoman of my wife's, and her sister Sarah was brought up . . . under this good man's eye. My own imaginations I was happy to find clothed in reality and fresh ones suggested by what she reported of this man's tenderness of heart, history and pure imagination, and his solid attainments in literature chiefly religious . . . At Hawkshead also . . . there occasionally resided a Packman . . . with whom I had frequent conversations upon what had befallen him and what he had observed during his wandering life . . .' (I.F. note to *The Excursion*.)

For W's great lines on the pantheist One Life in *The Pedlar*, see Coleridge's 'Aeolian Harp' and his *Religious Musings*. ''Tis the sublime of man,/Our noontide majesty', Coleridge declares in *Religious Musings* (1794–6), 'to know ourselves/Parts and proportions of one wond'rous whole/ . . . But 'tis God/Diffused through all, that doth make all one whole.' The notion of God as the 'impulse of all to all', as a pervasive life-force, and of the universal harmony of animated life, was something W was drawn to towards the end of 1797. But these notions were not taken over wholesale from Coleridge; in April 1794 W held the belief that the physical world was a world of feeling and of life – a Priestleyan notion current among Unitarians of the 1790s.

ll.39–43   The child compares the actual landscape of his memory with 'ideal' representations of landscape that he has created in his mind by a process of intense 'brooding'. Cp the thought of 'Tintern Abbey'.

ll.52–4   a peculiar eye: penetrating observation; creative feeling over-borne: creative, imaginative sympathy; predominance of thought oppressed: cerebral response.

ll.55–7   What lies behind the lines is the Berkeleyan notion of Nature as the symbolic language of God.

ll.95–114   W has in mind Coleridge's 'Reflections on having left a place of Retirement'.

ll.204–22   These great pantheist lines were incorporated into the 2-part *Prelude* in Autumn 1799. See 1799, II, 446–64.

ll.239–45   The lines point forward to the nature of the poetry of the *Lyrical Ballads*.

l.320   The reference to Burns, the poet of ordinary life, is significant.

ll.324–56   Adapted for *The Prelude* as W worked towards a third book. See *The Prelude*, 1805, III, 82 and 122–67.

l.334   The Pedlar ascribes feeling and life to the physical world – believing in the doctrine of Animism.

l.347   shades of difference: Jonathan Wordsworth offers an explanation – 'minute underlying differences that shade into one another and are thus perceptible only to an unusually penetrating mind'.

'Not useless do I deem' (p.63)

The lines are a discarded passage from a MS B draft conclusion to *The Ruined Cottage*. A version of the passage was finally incorporated into *The Excursion*, Book IV.

See Coleridge's letter of 10 March 1798 to George Coleridge – 'I love fields and woods and mounta[ins] with almost a visionary fondness . . . ' where he quotes the first eighteen lines.

From *Lyrical Ballads*, 1798

The order of the poems selected follows that of the 1798 *Lyrical Ballads*.

Lines left upon a Seat in a Yew-Tree which stands near the Lake of Esthwaite (p.69)

A few lines were perhaps composed as early as 1786 or 1787; main composition between 8 February and July 1797.

In the Fenwick note, W states that 'the individual whose habits and character are here given, was a gentleman of the neighbourhood, a man of talent and learning, who had been educated at one of our Universities, and returned to pass his time in seclusion on his own estate. He died a bachelor in middle age'. This was a Rev. William Braithwaite of Satterhow, who despite W's statement in line 43 was still alive at the time of writing. Robert Woof, however, has argued against too precise an identification of the poetic character with a real person.

Implicit in this study of the disappointed, solipsistic recluse is W's rejection of the arrogant self-sufficiency of Godwinian philosophy. Disillusioned retreat from the world is no answer: the recluse is depriving himself of a larger life of joy and love. The statement that true dignity 'abides with him' who 'can still suspect, and still revere himself/In lowliness of heart' seems to refute the Godwinian position that vice proceeds not from the individual *per se*, but from contact with society. Coleridge has the poem in mind when in a letter of around 17 July 1797 he writes, 'I am as much a Pangloss as ever – only less *contemptuous* than I used to be, when I argue how unwise it is to feel contempt for any living thing.'

l.24   Charles Lamb lamented the excision of this line in 1815, describing is as 'a line quite alive'.
ll.32–3   Cp Dorothy's *Journal* entry for 26 February 1798: 'We lay sidelong upon the turf, and gazed on the landscape till it melted into more than natural loveliness.'

Goody Blake and Harry Gill (p.70)

Composed around 7–13 March 1798.

W's 'advertisement' to the 1798 edition informs the reader that the poem is 'founded on a well-authenticated fact which happened in Warwickshire'. The poem is based on a story in Erasmus Darwin's *Zoönomia, or the Laws of Organic Life* (1794–6), which W borrowed from the publisher Cottle in March 1798: 'A young farmer in War- wickshire, finding his hedges broke, and the sticks carried away during a frosty season, determined to watch for the thief. He lay many cold hours under a haystack, and at length an old woman . . . approached, and began to pull up the hedge . . . Springing from his concealment, he seized his prey with violent threats . . . She kneeled upon her bundle of sticks, and, raising her arms to heaven beneath the bright moon then at the full, spoke to the farmer . . . "Heaven grant, that thou mayest never know again the blessing to be warm." He complained of cold all the next day . . . [and] kept his bed above twenty years for fear of the cold air, till at length he died.'

See Dorothy's letter of 30 November 1795: 'The peasants are miserably poor; their cottages are shapeless structures (I may almost say) of wood or clay – indeed they are not at all beyond what might be expected in savage life.'

l.39   canty: dialect word in the north of England – 'cheerful', 'lively', 'active'.

ll.124–5   A possible echo of *King Lear*, III, iv, 147 and IV, i, 52.

Lines written at a small distance from my House (p.74)

Composed 1–9 March 1798. The poem was given the short title of 'To my Sister' from 1845.

'Composed in front of Alfoxden House. My little boy messenger on this occasion was the son of Basil Montagu. The larch mentioned in the first stanza was standing when I revisited the place in May 1841, more than forty years after . . . ' (I.F.) Montagu's son, also called Basil, appears again in 'Anecdote for Fathers'. Mary Moorman states that this lyric is probably the ' "singular but fine poem of Wordsworth's" ' which, says James Losh, Southey repeated to him in Bath' (*William Wordsworth: A Biography; The Early Years, 1770–1803*, p. 379).

Simon Lee, the old Huntsman (p.76)

Written in short ballad metre and composed between early March and *c.* 16 May 1798. Subsequently much revised.

·   The 1800 Preface to the *Lyrical Ballads* declares that W's aim in writing the poem was to place the reader 'in the way of receiving from ordinary moral sensations another and more salutary impression than we are accustomed to receive from them'.

'This old man had been huntsman to the Squires of Alfoxden . . . It is unnecessary to add, the fact was as mentioned in the poem; and I have, after an interval of 45 years, the image of the old man as fresh before my eyes as if I had seen him yesterday. The expression when the hounds were out, "I dearly love their voices" was word for word from his own lips.' (I.F.)

The poem seems to have an anti-Godwinian drive: it was Godwin's belief in *Political Justice* that 'if by gratitude we understand a system of preference which I entertain towards another, upon the ground of my having been subject of his benefits, it is no part of justice or virtue'.

l.22   As Peter Bement has observed, W, referring to the empty 'Hall of Ivor' in the 'sweet shire of Cardigan', may have in mind the ruins of the hall of the fourteenth-century Welsh lord Ifor ap Llywelyn in Monmouthshire, famously lamented by the Welsh poet Evan Evans (a native of Cardiganshire): 'Llys Ifor hael – gwael yw'r gwedd . . . ' ('The court of Ifor the generous – a sorry sight . . . '). W might have been attracted by the Welsh background since Ifor was the patron of the great

Welsh medieval poet, Dafydd ap Gwilym. He might even have seen
Evans's English translation of his own poem in manuscript.

l.74   silent thought: Cp Shakespeare, Sonnet XXX: 'When to the
sessions of sweet silent thought . . . '

ll.101–4   A possible echo of Burns's 'Man was made to mourn', lines
55–6: 'Man's inhumanity to man/Makes countless thousands mourn'.

Anecdote for Fathers (p.79)

Composed between early March or early April and *c.* 16 May 1798.

'The name of Kilve is from a village on the Bristol Channel, about a
mile from Alfoxden, and the name of Liswyn Farm was taken from a
beautiful spot on the Wye.' (I.F.)

The young child of the poem is Basil Montagu jnr, whom the Ws
looked after both at Racedown and at Alfoxden. 'He is my perpetual
pleasure,' Dorothy once stated, but W on 7 March 1796 remarked that
'Basil is quite well quant au physique mais pour le moral il-y-a bien à
craindre. Among other things he lies like a little devil.'

The aim of the poem is to 'point out the injurious effects of putting
inconsiderate questions to children, and urging them to give answers
upon matters either uninteresting to them or upon which they had no
decided opinion' (*The Letters of William and Dorothy Wordsworth: The
Later Years*, ed. de Selincourt, rev. Hill, Part I, p.486). The point made in
the poem is illuminated by the 1845 omission of the subtitle and the
insertion of a quotation from Eusebius (it is the Delphic Oracle that
speaks): 'Retine vim istam: falso enim dicam, si coges' ('Restrain your
force, for if you coerce me, I shall tell you lies'). What the poem
emphasises, refuting Godwin's claim that children are not naturally liars,
is that lying is not merely a consequence of contact with a corrupt society.

We are seven (p.81)

Composed between early March and *c.* 16 May 1798.

'The little girl who is the heroine I met within the area of Goodrich
Castle in the year 1793 . . . ' (I.F.) This Fenwick note describes the setting
up of the scheme for the *Lyrical Ballads* with Coleridge. The first stanza
of the poem is Coleridge's: 'When it was all but finished', W recalls, 'I
came in . . . and said "A prefatory stanza must be added" . . . and
Coleridge immediately threw off the stanza thus:

>   A little child, dear brother Jem –'

W changed 'little child' to 'simple child', and in 1815 omitted 'dear
brother Jem' from the first line. W stated in the 1800 Preface that the aim
of the poem is to reveal 'the perplexity and obscurity which in childhood

attend our notion of death, or rather our utter inability to admit that notion'. The revised first stanza of the poem is quoted in the Fenwick note to 'Ode: Intimations of Immortality', which should be consulted in relation to this poem.

Lines written in early spring (p.83)

Composed between early March or early April and *c.* 16 May 1798.

'Actually composed while I was sitting by the side of the brook that runs down from the comb, in which stands the village of Alford, through the grounds of Alfoxden. It was a chosen resort of mine.' (I.F.) See also the similar themes of 'Lines written at a small distance from my House', 'Expostulation and Reply', and 'The Tables Turned'.

ll.7–8   See note to 'Simon Lee', ll.101–4.

The Thorn (p.84)

Composed between 19 March and 20 April or 16 May 1798.

'[The poem] arose out of my observing, on the ridge of Quantock Hill, on a stormy day, a thorn which I had often passed in calm and bright weather without noticing it. I said to myself, "Cannot I by some invention do as much to make this thorn an impressive object as the storm has made it to my eyes at this moment [?]"' (I.F.)

The 'Advertisement' to the 1798 *Lyrical Ballads* stated that the poem 'is not supposed to be spoken in the author's own person: the character of the loquacious narrator will sufficiently show itself in the course of the story'. W included a long note on the poem in the 1800 edition, identifying the speaker as 'a Captain of a small trading vessel . . . who being past the middle age of life, had retired upon an annuity . . . to some village or country town . . . such men having little to do become credulous and talkative from indolence . . .' One of his aims in the poem, W declares, is to adhere to the linguistic style such characters might use while ensuring that 'words, which in their minds are impregnated with passion, should likewise convey passion to Readers who are not accustomed to sympathise with men feeling in that manner or using such language'. Taking issue with W's theory of language as put forward in the Preface to the 1800 *Lyrical Ballads*, Coleridge in Chapter XVII of *Biographia Literaria* perceptively remarks on the 'sinkings' and 're-elevations' of the poem's different voices, also stating that 'it is not possible to imitate truly a dull and garrulous discourser, without repeating the effects of dulness and garrulity'.

l.116   Martha Ray was the name of Basil Montagu's grandmother.

The Idiot Boy (p.92)

Composed between early March and *c.* 16 May 1798. W continued to have a high regard for the poem. See *The Prelude*, XIII, 399–402.

'The last stanza – "The cocks did crow to-whoo, to-whoo, and the sun did shine so cold" – was the foundation of the whole. The words were reported to me by my dear friend Thomas Poole, but I have since heard the same repeated of other idiots. Let me add that this long poem was composed in the groves of Alfoxden . . . I never wrote anything with so much glee.' (I.F.)

See Southey's attack on the poem in the *Critical Review*, October 1798: '[The poem] resembles a Flemish picture in the worthlessness of its design and the excellence of its execution', together with Coleridge's strictures in *Biographia Literaria* – 'the mother's character is not so much a real and native product of a "situation where the essential passions of the heart find a better soil in which they can attain their maturity and speak a plain and more emphatic language", as it is an impersonation of an instinct abandoned by judgement . . . the author has not . . . taken sufficient care to preclude from the reader's fancy the disgusting images of *ordinary morbid idiocy* . . . the idiocy of the *boy* is so evenly balanced by the folly of the *mother*, as to present to the general reader . . . a laughable burlesque on the blindness of anile dotage . . . '

Defending the poem against some of the criticisms of the 17-year-old John Wilson (Wilson's letter to W is otherwise something of a eulogy) W stated memorably: 'Few ever consider books but with reference to their power of pleasing . . . men of a higher rank; few descend lower, among cottages and fields, and among children. A man must have done this habitually before his judgment on "The Idiot Boy" would be in any way decisive with me . . . I have often applied to idiots . . . that sublime expression of Scripture, that *their life is hidden with God* . . . I have indeed often looked upon the conduct of fathers and mothers of the lower classes of society towards idiots as the great triumph of the human heart.'

ll.116 and 359   Echoes of *King Lear*, IV, vi, 26–7 – lines spoken by Edgar, who has been feigning madness in a play in which, significantly, the fool plays a prominent part.

Lines written near Richmond, upon the Thames (p.105)

Begun perhaps as early as 1788–91; bulk of composition early 1797, and complete by March 1797.

The 'Lines' were printed as two separate poems in the 1800 edition of *Lyrical Ballads*.

ll.17–24   A strong echo of Denham's *Cooper's Hill* (1642), ll.189–92.

l.30   W's note in 1798: 'Collins's Ode on the death of Thomson, the last written, I believe, of the poems that were published during his life-time. This Ode is also alluded to in the next stanza.'
ll.31–2   recall ll.21–3 of Collins's poem while ll.34–5 recall ll.13–16.

Expostulation and Reply (p.106)

Composed on 23 May 1798.

The 'Advertisement' to the 1798 *Lyrical Ballads* declares that this poem and 'The Tables Turned' 'arose out of conversation with a friend who was somewhat unreasonably attached to modern books of moral philosophy' – most probably William Hazlitt, who was writing his *Essay on the Principles of Human Action* at the time. In his famous essay, 'On my first Acquaintance with Poets', Hazlitt recalls that during his visit to Alfoxden in May–June 1798, he 'got into a metaphysical argument with Wordsworth . . . in which neither of us succeeded in making ourselves intelligible'. For the identity of Matthew here, see notes to 'Lines written on a Tablet in a School'.

The poem is not declaring hostility to books and literature generally, but rather to books or systems of moral philosophy (Godwin's in particular) that ignore or depreciate the primary emotions of the human heart. W's *Essay on Morals*, begun in September 1798, articulates a similar argument.

The Tables Turned (p.107)

Date as for the above, to which this poem is a companion-piece.

The theme of this poem – Nature as teacher – is central to W's thinking. How to educate a young child's mind was not merely an abstract issue for W at this time. The Ws were looking after little Basil Montagu, and, as Dorothy states in a letter of 19 March 1797, educating him in a system 'so simple that in this age of systems you will hardly be likely to follow it. We teach him nothing at present but what he learns from the evidence of his senses . . . [his] insatiable curiosity . . . is directed to everything he sees – the sky, the fields, trees, shrubs, corn, the making of tools, carts, etc. . . . ' In 1797 it had been suggested that W take part in Thomas Wedgwood's rather disturbing educational scheme designed to nurture a genius by controlling sensory experience. See Mary Moorman, *William Wordsworth: A Biography; The Early Years* (Oxford, 1957), pp.332–7, and *The Prelude*, 1805, V, 290–449 for W's passage on the infant prodigy.

Old Man Travelling (p.109)

Composed between the latter part of 1796 and early June 1797.

'If I recollect right these verses were an overflowing from "The Old Cumberland Beggar".' (I.F.)

'The present poem has split off [from 'The Old Cumberland Beggar'] as a study of the inward state of the Old Man expressed in his outward form: "resigned to quietness" in the margin of ll.7–8 [in MS] expresses the spiritual core of it' (*Poetical Works*, IV, 448). After 1805, ll.15–20 were omitted (possibly because they were too close to ll.18–21 of Southey's 'The Sailor's Mother'), and in 1800 the subtitle became the title.

ll.11–12   Cp Lear's famous request – *King Lear*, II, iv, 274.

The Complaint of a forsaken Indian Woman (p.110)

Composed between early March and *c.* 16 May 1798.

'Written at Alfoxden in 1798, where I read Hearne's Journey [*A Journey from Prince of Wales's Fort in Hudson's Bay to the Northern Ocean*, 1795] with deep interest.' (I.F.) The 1800 Preface declares that it is the poem's aim to 'follow the fluxes and refluxes of the mind when agitated by the great and simple affections of our nature', and to describe 'the last struggles of a human being at the approach of death, cleaving in solitude to life and society'.

The Convict (p.112)

Composed between 21 March and early October 1796. Finished by 14 December 1797 and published under the pseudonym 'Mortimer' – the name of the character duped by Rivers in W's play *The Borderers* – in the *Morning Post* of 14 December 1797, soon after Covent Garden had rejected W's play.

See the poem's companion piece in the 1798 *Lyrical Ballads*, Coleridge's 'The Dungeon'. Both poems express the need (more directly stated in Coleridge's poem) to allow *Nature* to reform the offender. Both are statements of faith in Nature's healing ministrations. W's poem, however, expresses greater interest in the prisoner's psychological state; Coleridge's is a poem of explicit social comment: 'And this place our forefathers made for man! . . . /Is this the only cure?'

W's desire to see a change in the penal laws, in the nature of state punishment, clearly has a Godwinian base. See Godwin on 'Crimes and Punishment', Book VII of *Political Justice* (third edition).

Lines written a few miles above Tintern Abbey (p.114)

Composed 11–13 July 1798.

'No poem of mine was composed under circumstances more pleasant for me to remember than this. I began it upon leaving Tintern, after crossing the Wye, and concluded it just as I was entering Bristol in the evening . . .' (I.F.)

A letter of September 1848 from the Duke of Argyle to T. S. Howson, describing W's impassioned reading of the poem, notes a sad change: 'The strong emphasis that he put on the words addressed personally to the person to whom the poem is addressed struck me as almost unnatural at the time – "My dear, *dear* friend" ran the words – "in thy wild eyes". It was not till after the reading was over that we found out that the old paralytic and *doited* woman we had seen in the morning was the sister to whom T.A. was addressed . . . it was melancholy to think that the vacant silly stare which we had seen . . . was from the "wild eyes" of 1798.'

l.1   W first visited Tintern Abbey, South Wales, in August 1793 on a journey from the Isle of Wight to North Wales, and revisited the spot on 10–13 July 1798.

ll.8 and 18–19   Cp William Gilpin, *Observations on the River Wye* (1782): 'Many of the furnaces on the banks of the river consume charcoal . . . the smoke which is frequently seen issuing from the sides of the hills . . . beautifully breaks their lines, and unites them with the sky.'

l.25   See W's remarks on a blind man's capacity to describe 'appearances' in the 'Essay, supplementary to the Preface' (1815).

l.34   that best portion of a good man's life: Cp Milton's preface to *The Judgment of Martin Bucer concerning Divorce*: ' . . . good men in the best portion of their lives . . . are compelled to civil indignities'.

l.39   the burthen of the mystery: explained in the next two lines. Life itself is burdensome in its often being unintelligible, a mystery.

ll.42–50   Cp *The Prelude*, 1799, Pt II, 397–440.

ll.53–4   A possible echo of *Hamlet*, I, ii, 133–4.

ll.71–3   A reference to W's first visit to Tintern. A short while before he arrived at Tintern, W had seen the British fleet gathering in the Solent off the Isle of Wight in preparation for war with France, where his political sympathy and private attachment (Annette and his child Caroline) lay. He had reached Tintern exhausted, having crossed Salisbury Plain with very little food.

ll.94–103   For this great statement of the pantheist One Life, see *The Pedlar*, ll.204–22, and the notes to that poem.

l.107   W's note acknowledges that he is *half*-remembering a line from Young's *Night Thoughts* (1742–5), VI, 427: 'And half-create the wondrous world they see'.

l.109   language of the sense: sense-impressions.

l.114   Jonathan Wordsworth has suggested that W has Milton's *Samson Agonistes*, ll.594–6, in mind.

l.115   Cp Psalm 23:4.

ll.123–4   Cp Coleridge's 'This Lime-Tree Bower my Prison', ll.59–60: 'Henceforth I shall know/That Nature ne'er deserts the wise and pure'.
l.129   Cp *Paradise Lost*, VII, 25–6.
l.153   W elaborates on this description of himself in a letter of January 1815 (*The Letters of William and Dorothy Wordsworth, The Middle Years*, ed. de Selincourt, rev. Moorman and Hill, Part II, p.188).

From *Lyrical Ballads*, 1800

As with *Lyrical Ballads*, 1798, and apart from the grouping together of the four 'Lucy' poems, the order of the poems follows that of the second volume of 1800.

Hart-Leap Well (p.121)

Composed early 1800; probably complete by 5 April.
   Compare *Home at Grasmere*, ll.236–56. The poem's main source is Bürger's *Der Wilde Jäger*. W had been reading Bürger in Germany.
   ' . . . having tired . . . myself with labouring at an awkward passage in "The Brothers", I started with a sudden impulse to this to get rid of the other, and finished it in a day or two. My sister and I had passed the place [on 17 December 1799] a few weeks before in our wild winter journey from Sockburn . . . to Grasmere. A peasant whom we met near the spot told us the story'. (I.F.)

ll.75–6   Two rivers in North Yorkshire.
ll.97–8   moving accident: Cp *Othello*, I, iii, 135: 'Of moving accidents by flood or field'. 'Freeze the blood' echoes *Hamlet*, I, v, 15–16.

'There was a boy' (p.126)

Written at Goslar, Germany, between 6 October and late November or early December 1798.
   In the Preface to *Poems*, 1815, W, referring to this poem, states that, 'guided by one of my own primary consciousnesses, I have represented a commutation and transfer of internal feelings, co-operating with external accidents, to plant, for immortality, images of sound and sight, in the celestial soil of the Imagination. The boy . . . is listening, with something of a feverish and restless anxiety, for the recurrence of the riotous sounds which he had previously excited; and, at the moment when the intenseness of his mind is beginning to remit, he is surprised into a

perception of the solemn and tranquillizing images which the poem describes.' The poem was later incorporated into *The Prelude*, 1805, V, 389–422.

'Strange fits of passion' (p.127)
Song ('She dwelt among th' untrodden ways') (p.128)
'A slumber did my spirit seal' (p.129)
'Three years she grew in sun and shower' (p.129)

The first versions of the first three poems were composed at Goslar between 6 October and 28 December 1798: 'Three years she grew' might have been written at the same time or in late February 1799.

These four poems, together with 'I travelled among unknown men' from *Poems in Two Volumes*, 1807 (originally intended for the *Lyrical Ballads*), are known as the 'Lucy' poems. The identity of Lucy is a matter of speculation – Dorothy, Mary Hutchinson, her sister Sara, Annette Vallon, and an early sweetheart of W's have all been suggested, as well as composites of these. 'Lucy', though, was a common enough name for a dead lover in eighteenth-century poetry. Coleridge, in a letter of 6 April 1799, states that 'some months ago, Wordsworth transmitted to me a most sublime epitaph ['A slumber . . .']; whether it had any reality, I cannot say. Most probably in some gloomier moment he had fancied the moment in which his sister might die.'

Lucy Gray (p.130)

Composed at Goslar between 6 October 1798 and 23 February 1799.

'It was founded on a circumstance told me by my sister of a little girl who, not far from Halifax in Yorkshire, was bewildered in a snowstorm. Her footsteps were traced by her parents to the middle of the lock of a canal. The way in which the incident was treated, and the spiritualising of the character, might furnish hints for contrasting the imaginative influences which I have endeavoured to throw over common life with Crabbe's matter-of-fact style of treating subjects of the same kind.' (I.F.) In 1816, Henry Crabb Robinson noted in his diary that W 'removed from [the poem] all that pertained to art, and it being his object to exhibit poetically entire *solitude*, he represents the child as observing the day-*moon* which no town or village girl would ever notice'. Later, the title of the poem was altered to 'Lucy Gray, or Solitude'.

''Tis said that some have died for love' (p.132)

First version composed perhaps at Goslar between 6 October and 28

December 1798; revised at Grasmere late 1799–summer 1800. 'Emma' is one of the names W often uses for his sister Dorothy.

ll.48–52   Cp 'Tintern Abbey', ll.147–50, in which W, addressing Dorothy, considers his own death and its effect on his sister.

Poor Susan (p.134)

Composed at Goslar between 6 October and 28 December 1798. The title was later altered to 'The Reverie of Poor Susan'.

'This arose out of my observation of the affecting music of these birds hanging in this way in the London streets during the freshness and stillness of the Spring morning.' (I.F.) The fifth stanza appeared only in the 1800 edition; it may have been dropped following Lamb's criticism that it 'threw a kind of dubiety upon Susan's moral conduct. Susan is a servant maid. I see her trundling her mop, and contemplating the whirling phenomenon through blurred optics; to term her a poor outcast seems as much as to say that poor Susan is no better than she should be, which I trust was not what you meant to say.' The metre of the poem is that of many contemporary street ballads.

To a Sexton (p.135)

Composed probably at Goslar between 6 October 1798 and 23 February 1799.

'A whirl-blast from behind the hill' (p.136)

First version composed 18 or 19 March 1798; revised 1 August 1800.

'Observed in the holly grove at Alfoxden . . . I had the pleasure of again seeing, with dear friends, this grove in unimpaired beauty, 41 years after.' (I.F.) Dorothy's *Journal* entry for 18 March 1798 reads: 'On our return, sheltered under the hollies, during a hail-shower. The withered leaves danced with the hailstones. William wrote a description of the storm.'

Song for the Wandering Jew (p.136)

Probably composed at Goslar between 6 October 1798 and 23 February 1799.

Dorothy's *Journal* entry for 30 September 1798 records that she and W saw a Jew mistreated and driven out of Hamburg. What lies behind the poem is the legend that the Jew who refused to let Christ rest on his way to

Golgotha is condemned to wander the earth until Christ's Second Coming.

Lines written on a Tablet in a School ('If Nature, for a favourite child') (p.137)

Composed at Goslar between 6 October and 28 December 1798. The title was altered to 'Matthew', 1836–7.

The poem refers to a tablet in Hawkshead School that displayed the names of past schoolmasters, not up-to-date during W's own time as a schoolboy. Matthew has been variously identified as William Taylor, W's Hawkshead schoolmaster, John Harrison, another teacher, John Gibson, an attorney, and Thomas Cowperthwaite, an ironmonger. The Fenwick note states that 'this and other poems connected with Matthew would not gain by a literal detail of facts. Like the Wanderer in *The Excursion*, [he] was made up of several both of his class and men of other occupations.' See T. W. Thompson, *Wordsworth's Hawkshead*, pp.151–66, for some detective work on the identity of Matthew.

The Two April Mornings (p.138)

Composed at Goslar between 6 October and 28 December 1798.
For the identity of Matthew, see the note to the above.

ll.59–60 Cp *The Merchant of Venice*, V, i, 9: 'In such a night/Stood Dido with a willow in her hand'.

The Fountain (p.140)

Composed at Goslar between 6 October and 28 December 1798. For the identity of Matthew, see note to 'Lines written on a Tablet in a School'.

ll.15–16 and 71–2 are possibly echoes of Crowe's *Lewesdon Hill*, l.441 – 'False-measured melody on crazy bells'.

Nutting (p.143)

First version composed at Goslar between 6 October and 28 December 1798.
'Nutting,' the Fenwick note states, was 'intended as part of a poem on my own life [*The Prelude*] but struck out as not being wanted there.'

W thought that 'To Joanna' and 'Nutting' 'show the greatest genius of any poems' in the second volume of the 1800 *Lyrical Ballads*; 'Michael', he thought, expressed his most important views.

l.10   frugal Dame: Ann Tyson, in whose house W lodged while at Hawkshead School.

The Old Cumberland Beggar (p.144)

Composed between the second half of 1796 and June 1797, and between 25 January and 5 March 1798.

'Observed, and with great benefit to my own heart, when I was a child . . . The political economists were about that time beginning their war upon mendacity in all its forms, and by implication, if not directly, on almsgiving also. This heartless process has been carried as far as it can go by the AMENDED poor law bill, tho' the inhumanity that prevails in this measure is somewhat disguised by the profession that one of its objects is to throw the poor upon the voluntary donations of their neighbours; that is . . . to force them into a condition between relief in the Union poor-house, and alms robbed of their Christian grace and spirit, as being *forced* rather from the benevolent than given to them . . .' (I.F.) As a consequence of the war with France and the bad harvests of 1794–5, the 1790s saw a dramatic increase in the number of beggars and vagrants. For the interest W shows here in the psychological mechanisms of benevolence, see Book IV, Chapter X, of the third edition of Godwin's *Political Justice*, 'Of Self-love and Benevolence'.

l.61   cottage curs: Cp Beattie's *Minstrel* (1771), I, 39, 'The cottage curs at early pilgrim bark'.
l.146   One of the great Wordsworthian statements. W quoted the line in a letter of 1835 to Henry Crabb Robinson: 'If my writings are to last, it will I myself believe, be mainly owing to this characteristic. They will please for the single cause, that we have all of us one human heart!' W wanted his poetry to be remembered primarily for this very human-heartedness.
ll.155 and 164   Cp *King Lear*, V, iii, 315–17.
l.172   House . . . of industry: workhouse.

A Poet's Epitaph (p.149)

Composed at Goslar between 6 October and 28 December 1798.

See the passage from the 1802 Preface to the *Lyrical Ballads* beginning 'Aristotle, I have been told, hath said that poetry is the most philosophic of all writing; it is so: its subject is truth . . . ' In a letter of 30 January

1801 Charles Lamb objected to the nature of some of the satire, calling it 'vulgar'.

l.11   Doctor: theologian.
l.18   Philosopher: natural philosopher – a scientist.
l.25   Moralist: moral philosopher.

From Poems on the Naming of Places: IV – 'A narrow girdle of rough stones and crags' (p.151)

Composed between 23 July and 6 November 1800.

This is the fourth in a series of poems 'On the Naming of Places'. The Fenwick note identifies the 'two beloved friends' as Coleridge and Dorothy.

In 1800, the five poems were introduced by an advertisement: 'By persons resident in the country . . . many places will be found unnamed or of unknown names, where little incidents will have occurred, or feelings been experienced, which will have given to such places a private and peculiar interest.'

On 23 July 1800 Coleridge wrote in his notebook: 'Poor fellow at a distance idle? in this haytime when wages are so high? Come near – thin, pale, can scarce speak – or throw out his fishing rod.'

l.38   Naid: A Naiad, a water-nymph in Greek mythology.

Michael: a Pastoral Poem (p.154)

Composed in 1800 between early October and 18 December. Fifteen lines of the poem (202–16), 'by a shameful negligence of the printer' (W to Thomas Poole, 9 April 1801), were omitted in the first edition.

'The sheepfold, on which so much of the poem turns, remains, or rather the ruins of it. The character and circumstances of Luke were taken from a family to whom had belonged, many years before, the house we lived in at Town End.' (I.F.)

W sent a copy of the 1800 edition of *Lyrical Ballads* to the Whig statesman Charles James Fox, and a letter of 14 January 1801 to Fox makes specific reference to 'The Brothers' and to 'Michael' – 'The two poems I have mentioned were written with a view to shew that men who do not wear fine clothes can feel deeply.' To Thomas Poole in the letter referred to above, W wrote, 'I have attempted to give a picture of a man of a strong mind and lively sensibility, agitated by two of the most powerful affections of the human heart – the parental affection, and the love of property, *landed* property, including the feelings of inheritance, home, and personal and family independence.'

l.2   Greenhead Gill: a stream to the north of Grasmere.

ll.10–12   Cp Dorothy's *Journal* entry for 11 October 1800: 'Kites sailing in the sky above our heads – sheep bleating and in lines and chains and patterns scattered over the mountains.'

l.33   See the opening of the 'Prospectus' to *The Recluse*, *Home at Grasmere*, l.959.

l.179   W's 1800 note: 'Clipping is the word used in the north of England for shearing.'

l.268   W's 1800 note: 'The story alluded to here is well known in the country. The chapel is called Ings chapel, and is on the right hand side of the road leading from Kendal to Ambleside.' The wealthy merchant Robert Bateman rebuilt the chapel in 1743.

l.334   W's 1800 note: 'It may be proper to inform some readers, that a sheep-fold in these mountains is an unroofed building of stone walls, with different divisions. It is generally placed by the side of a brook, for the convenience of washing the sheep, but it is also useful as a shelter for them.'

Home at Grasmere (and the 'Prospectus' to *The Recluse*) (p.167)

The text is that of MS B. Written March to early April 1800; revised late summer 1806, and described by W in 1806 as the first book of *The Recluse*.

Lines 959–1048 are known as the 'Prospectus' to *The Recluse* since they were printed in the preface to *The Excursion* (1814) as 'a kind of *prospectus* of the design and scope' of *The Recluse*.

Home at Grasmere, never published during W's lifetime, is his first major attempt to write the main philosophical section – the core – of his projected *magnum opus*, *The Recluse*, and the only part of that section to be completed. Indeed, it is the only part of the whole *Recluse* project to be completed, apart from *The Excursion*, which in 1814 was to be the second part of the as yet unwritten three-part *Recluse*. The plan for *The Recluse* was first broached in 1798, when Coleridge suggested that W compose a major philosophical poem and 'deliver upon authority a system of philosophy'. In March 1798, W wrote, 'I have written 1300 lines of a poem in which I contrive to convey most of the knowledge of which I am possessed. My object is to give pictures of Man, Nature, and Society. Indeed I know not anything which will not come within the scope of my plan.' These lines may comprise *The Ruined Cottage* and *The Pedlar*, 'The Old Cumberland Beggar' and an early draft of 'The

Discharged Soldier' (included here in an extract from *The Prelude*, Book IV). The beginning of the 'Prospectus' (line 959 here), echoing the wording of the plan for *The Recluse*, is obviously a start on what was later to be seen as the central section of the great (and ultimately inchoate) *Recluse*. In a slightly different form, the 'Prospectus' was written soon after the Ws arrived at Dove Cottage on 20 December 1799. It was probably first regarded as an introduction to *Home at Grasmere*, but it was later used to form the climax of the poem.

ll.171–9 Dorothy (Emma here) and W had been separated after the death of their parents. They were reunited in 1794.

ll.218–56 The Ws had travelled across Yorkshire to reach Grasmere.

ll.236–56 Cp 'Hart-Leap Well'.

l.864 a stranger: W's brother John. See note to 'Elegiac Stanzas'.

ll.869–70 sisters . . . a brother of our hearts: Mary Hutchinson (later W's wife), her sisters Sara and Joanna, and Coleridge.

ll.972–4 See *Paradise Lost*, VII, 1 and 30–1, together with W's review of possible poetic subjects in *The Prelude*, 1805, I, 169–234.

ll.980–4 Blake commented peevishly on these lines: 'Solomon when he married Pharaoh's daughter and became a convert to the heathen mythology talked exactly in this way of Jehovah as a very inferior object of man's contemplations; he also passed him by unalarmed.'

ll.1002–14 An important passage not present in the first draft of the 'Prospectus'.

l.1011 Blake commented again: 'You shall not bring me down to believe such fitting and fitted; I know better and please your Lordship.'

The Forsaken (p.193)

Composed probably between 1800 and early January 1807. Published in 1842.

'This was an overflow from "The Affliction of Margaret" . . . preserved in the faint hope that it may turn to account by restoring a shy lover to some forsaken damsel. My poetry has been complained of as deficient in interests of this sort.' (I.F.)

'These chairs, they have no words to utter' (p.193)

From Dove Cottage MS 41. Probably composed *c.* 22 April 1802. Never published by W.

Compare Dorothy's *Journal* entry for 29 April 1802: 'We then went to John's Grove, sate a while at first. Afterwards William lay, and I lay in the trench under the fence – he with his eyes shut and listening to the waterfalls and the birds . . . William heard me breathing and rustling now and then but we both lay still, and unseen by one another. He thought that it would be as sweet thus to lie so in the grave, to hear the *peaceful* sounds of the earth and just to know that our dear friends were near.' Quoting lines 120–3 of the 'Ode' ('Intimations of Immortality') in *Biographia Literaria*, Chapter XXII, Coleridge, considering W's thought on the subject of a child's notion of death, expresses his alarm at 'the frightful notion of lying awake in [the] grave' 'as in a place of thought'.

l.19   Cp Chaucer, *The Knight's Tale*, l.2779.

'I only looked for pain and grief' (p.194)

From Dove Cottage MS 57. Probably composed 8 June 1805. In revised form, the poem was published in 1842 entitled 'Elegiac Verses, in memory of my brother John Wordsworth'.

John (1772–1805) was drowned in his ship, *The Earl of Abergavenny*, on 5–6 February 1805. See also 'Elegiac Stanzas'.

l.41   Cp Dorothy's *Journal*, 29 September 1800: 'John left us. Wm. and I parted with him in sight of Ullswater.' In 1843 W could still locate the exact spot: 'The point is 2 or 3 yards below the outlet of Grisedale Tarn.' (I.F.)

The Prelude, 1799 (p.199)

During October–November 1798 in Goslar, Germany, the 1799 *Prelude* (never published in this form during W's lifetime) took shape as W asked himself a series of questions. With Coleridge, the plan for the great philosophical poem *The Recluse* had been decided upon earlier in the year, but that *magnum opus* was just not getting written, and the opening of the 1799 *Prelude* finds W considering whether, despite his formative years as a 'favoured being' amongst the mountains of Cumbria, amongst the ministering powers of Nature, he was not after all qualified or ready to write the great philosophical work. The poem then develops into an examination of the many forces that during infancy, childhood and adolescence had fitted him to become the poet of *The Recluse*. The celebrated 'Spots of Time' sequence in particular (First Part, lines 288–374, heralded by 258–87) memorably reveals the 'hiding places' of W's poetic vision, exploring the child's reaction to death and Nature in epiphanies of imaginative response. The poem was transcribed as a rounded composition at the beginning of December 1799, Part Two having been written back in England.

On 12 October 1799 Coleridge wrote to Wordsworth: 'I long to see what you have been doing. O let it be the tailpiece of the *Recluse*!' From the very beginning of the *Prelude*'s life, Coleridge was lamenting that the poem was not something else – *The Recluse*, or a (modest) part of it. *The Prelude* was to be seen by W in 1804 as one of the three sections of *The Recluse*, but the main philosophical section of that poem was never to be completed.

First Part

ll.1, 6, 17   'This' seems to refer to W's inability to get on with the philosophical *Recluse*.

l.8   The quotation is from Coleridge's 'Frost at Midnight', l.28. Coleridge is referring to his birth-place at Ottery St Mary, Devonshire, from which he went to Christ's Hospital, London, where, he states, he was denied the Wordsworthian childhood as a favoured being.

l.23   grunsel: ragwort.

l.34   springes: snares.

ll.89–90   Cp *Paradise Lost*, XII, 1–2.

ll.95–6   Cp Coleridge's *Ancient Mariner*, ll.265–6.

l.182   Cp another Goslar poem, 'A slumber did my spirit seal', ll.5–8.

ll.186–9   Cp *The Tempest*, V, i, 33.

l.194   characters: marks, handwriting.

ll.208–25   Cp Pope's mock-heroic game of ombre, *Rape of the Lock* (1717), III, 37–100. Lines 221–2 of W's poem recall William Cowper's 'The Winter Evening' (1785) in *The Task*, IV, 218–19: 'Ensanguin'd hearts, clubs typical of strife,/And spades, the emblem of untimely graves'.

l.210   A mock-heroic recasting of Milton's line 'With centric and eccentric scribbled o'er', in *Paradise Lost*, VIII, 83.

l.221   Ironic diamonds: 'ironic' because the cards are down-at-heel, the diamond a precious stone.

l.227   Cp Amiens' line, 'Thy tooth is not so keen' in the song 'Blow, blow, thou winter wind' (*As You Like It*, II, vii).

l.236   Cp another Goslar poem, 'Nutting'.

l.279   James Jackson, schoolmaster, was drowned while bathing in Esthwaite water, 18 June 1779. See *The Prelude*, V, 456–81.

ll.279–82   Cp *Othello*, I, iii, 134–5.

ll.288–374   were revised and expanded to form Book XI, 257–388 of the 1805 *Prelude*.

l.294   Cp 'Tintern Abbey', ll.40–2.

ll.302–3   'Honest James' was probably the servant of W's grandparents at Penrith.

l.310   W here conflates two murders: in 1767 Thomas Nicholson had murdered a butcher near Penrith and had been hanged there; in 1672

Thomas Lancaster had poisoned his wife and had been hung on a gibbet in the water-meadows near Hawkshead.

l.322   Cp Milton's oxymoron 'darkness visible'.

l.351   W's father died on 30 December 1783. W was 13.

l.375   Cp *Paradise Lost*, IX, 27–9, in which Milton defines what he *does not* choose to treat as poetic subjects – heroic and chivalric epic.

l.376   collateral: indirect.

l.383   Cp *Measure for Measure*, I, iv, 59.

l.385   intellectual: as invariably in *The Prelude*, 'spiritual'.

ll.405–8   These lines suggest David Hartley's theory of the 'association of ideas', presented in the *Observations on Man* (1749). Simply, Hartley argues that ideas that have occurred together or which have followed one another in the mind have a tendency to recall one another. Ideas, say, of pain or pleasure, become associated with certain sensations or actions. Hartley then follows the development of the higher pleasures out of the lower – a process of evolution that culminates in the loss of self in God and in the 'pure love of God'. It is Hartley's theory that underpins W's theory of language in the 1800 Preface to the *Lyrical Ballads*.

ll.429–31   Cp *The Pedlar*, ll.33–4.

l.453   W is referring to *The Recluse*, or more specifically, the writing of the philosophical section of that poem.

Second Part

ll.25–6   Cp 'Tintern Abbey', ll.44–6.

ll.79–81   W has the frugality of Horace on his Sabine farm in mind.

l.109   Furness Abbey near Barrow.

l.146   gavel: used in the north of England for 'gable'.

l.208   The 'minstrel' was Robert Greenwood, later Fellow of Trinity College, Cambridge, remembered by W's landlady at Hawkshead, Ann Tyson, as 't'lad wi' t'flute'.

ll.255–6   W is thinking of Coleridge's Unitarian beliefs – the basis of his vision of natural and spiritual harmony in a world animated by God.

l.262   Cp *Paradise Lost*, V, 564.

l.286   apprehensive habitude: a relationship conducive to learning.

ll.288–90   Cp 'Tintern Abbey', ll.101–2.

ll.291–4   The bond between the mother and the child is the basis of the bond between the individual and Nature and between the individual and society.

ll.300–5   For the creativity and receptivity of the child's mind, see *The Prelude*, 1805, VI, 525–48, and XIII, 53–119, together with Coleridge's definition of the godlike primary imagination in Chapters XII and XIII of *Biographia Literaria*.

l.344   Cp *Paradise Lost*, IX, 249: 'For solitude is sometimes best society'.

ll.351–71   These lines were written in February 1798 to describe the Pedlar.

l.392   Cp Thomson's *Seasons*, II, 1042: 'Sad on the jutting eminence he sits'.

l.411   plastic power: a characteristically Coleridgean phrase, referring to the shaping, creative imagination.

ll.446–64   These lines were written for *The Pedlar* (see ll.204–22) and incorporated here in autumn 1799. In order to accommodate this great declaration of pantheist faith, W altered the 'he' to 'I'. W is locating his awareness of the pantheist One Life back in 1786 and not at Alfoxden. *The Prelude* throughout shows W's willingness to disregard fact in the service of an imaginative re-ordering of experience.

ll.465–6   Cp 'Tintern Abbey', ll.50–8 and Shakespeare's Sonnet 116, 13.

ll.478–86   The passage takes its cue from a Coleridge letter to W of September 1799: 'I wish you would write a poem, in blank verse, addressed to those, who, in consequence of the complete failure of the French Revolution, have thrown up all hopes of the amelioration of mankind . . .'

ll.480–6   W has the political apostasy of such erstwhile radicals as James Mackintosh in mind.

ll.496–7   See Coleridge's 'Frost at Midnight', ll.51–2.

ll.501–5   Cp 'Tintern Abbey', ll.122–35.

l.509   The valediction: in November 1799 Coleridge had decided to go to London to pursue a career as a journalist. The Ws were about to establish themselves at Dove Cottage, Grasmere.

From *The Prelude*, 1805 and 1850 (p.227)

The attempt to expand the 1799 *Prelude* did not really begin until 1804. A five-book poem was in existence before March 1804 when W decided to extend the scope of the poem still further. By 19 May 1805, thirteen books had been written, and W was by this time adamant that the autobiographical poem would not be published during his lifetime unless the appearance of *The Recluse* (the main philosophical section in particular) could justify the intense autobiographical focus of *The Prelude*. However, *The Prelude* had also by this time increased in importance in W's mind in relation to *The Recluse*, and was seen as one of the three sections of the larger poem, whose scope was also to encompass a narrative poem, which became *The Excursion*. In the 1814 preface to *The Excursion*, W's plans appear to have changed, and *The Prelude* seems merely introductory – its relation to *The Recluse* being described as that between an 'ante-chapel' and the 'body of a Gothic church'. *The Prelude* was further revised up to 1839 and posthumously published in fourteen books in 1850.

Much of the most impressive verse of Books I, II and XI (the 'Spots of Time' in particular) will be found in its earlier form in the 1799 *Prelude*.

Book III: Residence at Cambridge (p.229)

W arrived at St John's College, Cambridge, in October 1787.

From 1850
ll.62–3   A late and impressive addition, drawing on Thomson's elegy on Newton, ll.125–8.

From 1805
l.65   J. Maxwell observes that W is punning on the Latin 'examen', 'a balance'.
l.76   W's family hoped that he would become a Fellow at St John's.
l.115   incumbences: 'spiritual brooding' (NED).
l.182   Cp *Paradise Lost*, IX, 28–9.
l.191   heartless: without hope or courage.

Book IV: Summer Vacation (p.233)

W describes his experiences having returned from Cambridge to his 'native hills' after 'nine months' of 'submissive idleness'.

l.199   Cp *Lycidas*, l.65.
l.208   W is referring to Ann Tyson, his landlady when he was at school. She died in 1796.
l.225   W locates the dawning of his human-heartedness here in 1788. 'Tintern Abbey', however, locates it post-1793 – the ability to hear the 'still, sad music of humanity' being in that poem only a recent acquisition.
l.239   W was born under Jupiter, on 7 April. The 'fair Seven': the Pleiades.
l.309   manners put to school: human behaviour observed.
l.318   promiscuous rout: varied gathering.
l.335   Cp *Paradise Lost*, V, 285.
l.338   Cp *Paradise Lost* VIII, 527–8.
ll.400–504   The 'Discharged Soldier' passage was written in early 1798 as a separate poem and as a companion-piece to 'The Old Cumberland Beggar'.
l.435   i.e., the cowardice of my specious heart.

Book V: Books (p.240)

l.60   Cervantes' *Don Quixote* (1605).

ll.71–139   The dream, which W in *1805* identified as that of a friend and in *1850* as his own, is a recasting of a dream experienced by Descartes in 1619.

l.88   Euclid: Greek mathematician of the third century BC. His *Elements* established the basis of geometry.

Book VI: Cambridge and the Alps (p.243)

l.478   The pilgrims are W and his Cambridge friend Robert Jones. They landed in France on 13 July 1790, on the eve of the first anniversary of the Fall of the Bastille. The Fête de la Fédération was celebrated the next day.

l.495   clomb: climbed.

ll.524–5   The transition between disappointment and celebratory exultation is striking, but the earliest draft of the lines shows that VIII, 711–27, originally separated the two moods.

l.572   Cp Milton's description of God in *Paradise Lost*, V, 165.

Book VII: Residence in London (p.246)

ll.597–8   Cp Book IV, 58–9, for a very different encounter: 'The face of every neighbour whom I met/Was as a volume to me'.

ll.595–8   The lines feed directly into the first section of T. S. Eliot's *The Waste Land*: 'A crowd flowed over London Bridge, so many/I had not thought death had undone so many'.

l.623   Cp the admonishment of the leech-gatherer in 'Resolution and Independence'.

l.634   Cp the vision of the sonnet 'Composed upon Westminster Bridge'.

l.652   St Bartholomew's Fair at Smithfield was held in W's time from 4–7 September. During Queen Mary's reign, Protestant martyrs were burned there. Charles Lamb took the Ws to see the fair in 1802.

l.675   salt-box: a crude musical instrument in which salt was rattled.

l.686   Madame Tussaud's collection.

l.689   Promethean: creative; Prometheus fashioned man out of clay. See *Paradise Lost*, II, 624–5.

ll.701–5   These lines were written in 1800 for 'Michael'.

Book VIII: Retrospect – Love of Nature leading to love of Mankind (p.250)

l.75   complacency: contentedness.

ll.78–9 Cp the impersonality of the encounter in the city, VII, 597–8.

l.391 him: W has been describing a 'sagacious' Cumbrian shepherd.

l.401 Cp Thomson's *Seasons*, III, 725–7.

ll.420–2 Corin and Phyllis: names common in pastoral poetry; coronal: a ring of dancers.

l.423 purposes of kind: by nature.

l.471 See *Home at Grasmere*, l.1028.

ll.511–41 W is considering the operations of the wilful fancy – a capricious thing later contrasted with the *unifying* imagination.

l.532 tragic super-tragic: The tragic, for the enflamed and fanciful young mind, had to be *super*-tragic to make any impression at all.

l.681 Cp *Lycidas*, ll.104–5.

ll.713–14 Antiparos: an Aegean island boasting a huge cavern. Yordas is a limestone cave in Yorkshire.

ll.716–17 Cp Virgil *The Aeneid*, VI, 454, and *Paradise Lost*, I, 783–4.

ll.711–27 In these lines W seeks to analyse his sense of disappointment at having crossed the Alps without knowing it. See note to VI, 524–5.

Book IX: Residence in France (p.256)

l.136 Michel Beaupuy, the French officer who exerted a formative influence on the mind of the young W.

l.179 Carra and Gorsas were members of the Girondin group, and were executed by Robespierre in October 1793. Carlyle tells how W informed him that he had seen the death of Gorsas, but it is doubtful whether W actually made this 'secret' trip to Paris.

l.538 The line refers to the 'lettres de cachets' – orders for incarceration without trial.

Book X: Residence in France and French Revolution (p.259)

l.48 Following the deposition of Louis XVI on 10 August 1792, an attack on the Palace of the Tuileries, Paris, left 600 defending Swiss guardsmen dead; 390 attackers were killed or wounded. The corpses were burned in the Place de la Carrousel.

l.64 During the massacres of 2–6 September 1792, half the prisoners in the jails of Paris were dragged from their cells and executed by the mob. 'A little month': *Hamlet*, I, ii, 147.

l.70 manage: the motions taught to a horse during training.

ll.70–4 Cp W. B. Yeats's apocalyptic poem, 'The Second Coming'.

l.77 Cp *Macbeth*, II, ii, 35–6.

l.230 France declared war on England on 1 February 1793. The 'confederated host': most importantly Prussia and Austria.

ll.240–1 Cp the 1842 published version of W's play *The Borderers*, ll.1817–18: 'I seemed a Being who had passed alone/Into a region of futurity'.

l.242–4 W is thinking primarily of the arguments of Burke's *Reflections on the Revolution in France* (1790).

l.269 Cp Coleridge's 'The Ancient Mariner', l.640.

ll.309–10 Cp *Paradise Lost*, IV, 394.

l.314 W has Robespierre's Reign of Terror in mind. Cp also *Hamlet*, I, iv, 41.

ll.317–19 In the autumn of 1793, Notre Dame was actually renamed 'The Temple of Reason'.

l.354 On the guillotine platform, Madame Roland, who was associated with the Girondin party, is reputed to have said, 'Oh Liberty, what crimes are committed in thy name!'

l.364 W uses the story of the infant Hercules' throttling of serpents sent by Hera to kill him in his cradle to figure the victories of France over invading armies and the suppression of counter-revolution in 1793–4.

l.806 The reference is to the philosophy of William Godwin as put forward in his *Enquiry concerning Political Justice*, which recommends the exercise of reason as a firmer ground of hope for British radicals – and mankind in general – than the emotions. Initially attracted by Godwin's ideas, W became disillusioned with them, and his 1796 moral and emotional crisis (l.900) had much to do with that disillusionment. This *Prelude* passage is a mocking commentary, and it is significant that in ll.828–9 W quotes from his own post-Godwinian play *The Borderers* in which Rivers succeeds in corrupting Mortimer by the exercise of reason.

l.879 W refers to the writing of what became *The Excursion*, the second part of *The Recluse*.

l.898 in fine: finally.

Book XI: Imagination, how Impaired and Restored (p.266)

ll.328–42 A passage of characteristically Wordsworthian notions. It functions as an important link here in a revised version of the 'Spots of Time' sequence.

ll.337–8 See the 'Ode: Intimations of Immortality'.

Book XII: Same Subject, Continued (p.267)

l.158 bedlamites: madmen, who were known by the name of London's Bethlehem ('Bedlam') Hospital.

l.271 W referred to his brother John as 'the silent poet'. He also has the response of his own poetic character Michael in mind.

l.274   'them' refers back to 'words'. The passage as a whole can be seen as a description of the nature of W's vision in the prefaces and poems of the *Lyrical Ballads*.
l.308   influx: inspiration.
l.314   See notes to *Salisbury Plain*.

Book XIII: Conclusion (p.271)

The ascent of Snowdon forms the climax to *The Prelude*. W climbed the Welsh mountain when he was 21.

l.2   The 'youthful friend' was the Welshman Robert Jones, with whom W made a walking-tour of North Wales in the summer of 1791.
l.3   couching-time: bed-time.
ll.36–65   Cp *Descriptive Sketches*, ll.492–509.
l.46   Cp *Paradise Lost*, VII, 285–7, in which Milton describes the Creation.
ll.84–96   W draws a parallel between Nature represented by the sea of mist and the workings of the Imagination, between the transformation effected by that 'usurping' sea and that produced by the power of the Imagination. Cp Coleridge's description in *Biographia Literaria*, XIII, of the secondary Imagination, which 'dissolves, diffuses, dissipates, in order to re-create'. The Imagination is both creative and receptive. See Coleridge's definition of the primary Imagination, as both 'the living power and prime agent of all human perception' and 'a repetition in the finite mind of the eternal act of creation in the Infinite I am'.
l.113   Cp *Paradise Lost*, V, 487–90.
l.141   A 'universe of death' would be one apprehended through merely ordinary sense-perception with a dearth of imaginative response.
l.186   intellectual love: uniting, spiritual love.

From *Poems in Two Volumes*, 1807

The order of the poems follows that in the 1807 volumes.

Volume I

Louisa (p.279)

Perhaps composed in 1802 between 23 and 27 January. Complete by February 1802.

Henry Crabb Robinson identified Louisa as Mary Hutchinson's sister Joanna – 'The very *beau ideal* of a stout-hearted and stout-bodied rustic

girl' – though de Selincourt states that it was Dorothy who was 'chiefly in
W's thoughts as he wrote'.

l.19   beneath the moon: Cp *King Lear*, IV, vi, 36–7.

'She was a phantom of delight' (p.279)

Probably composed between 14 October 1803 and 6 March 1804.

'The germ of this poem was four lines composed as a part of the verses
on the Highland Girl. Though beginning in this way, it was written from
my heart as is sufficiently obvious.' (I.F.) Christopher Wordsworth, in his
Memoirs of William Wordsworth, quotes Justice Coleridge's claim that
W had said the poem was written 'on his dear wife'.

Character of the Happy Warrior (p.280)

Probably composed between *c*. December 1805 and early January
1806.

'*Who is the happy warrior*. The course of the great war with the French
naturally fixed one's attention upon the military character . . . Lord
Nelson carried most of the virtues that the trials he was exposed to . . .
call forth . . . But his public life was stained with one great crime, so
that . . . I have not been able to connect his name with the poem as I could
wish . . . I will add that many of the elements of the character here
portrayed were found in my brother John who perished by shipwreck.'
(I.F.)

Lord Nelson died at Trafalgar, 21 October 1805. Captain John
Wordsworth drowned in his ship, *The Earl of Abergavenny*, 5–6
February 1805. The 'character' is also presumably indebted to Michel
Beaupuy, the French army captain who had a profound effect in 1792 on
the young W's mind.

ll.75–6   W's note:
> 'For Knightes ever should be preserving
> To seek honour without feintise or slouth
> Fro wele to better in all manner thing.
>   Chaucer, *The Floure and the Leaf*'

To H.C., Six Years Old (p.283)

Possibly composed between 27 March and 17 June 1802, or more
probably early 1804.

'H.C.' is Hartley Coleridge, S. T. Coleridge's first son. Quoting line 12,
Coleridge describes his son in a letter of 14 October 1803: 'Hartley is
what he always was – a strange, strange boy – "*exquisitely wild*"! An

utter visionary! Like the moon among thin clouds, he moves in a circle of light of his own making – he alone, in a light of his own.'

l.6   W's note refers the reader to Jonathan Carver's *Travels through the interior parts of North America* (1778). Carver describes his 'suspended' canoe: 'The water . . . was as pure and transparent as air, and my canoe seemed as if it hung suspended in that element.'

'I travelled among unknown men' (p.284)

Probably composed *c.* 29 April 1801.

W intended to include the poem in the 1802 edition of the *Lyrical Ballads*. With 'Song: she dwelt among the untrodden ways', 'Strange fits of passion', 'A slumber did my spirit seal' and 'Three years she grew in sun and shower', the poem forms a group known as the 'Lucy Poems' (see notes above).

Ode to Duty (p.284)

Largely composed, excluding stanza 1, by 6 March 1804. First stanza added between late March 1804 and early December 1806.

'This ode . . . is on the model of Gray's Ode to Adversity which is copied from Horace's Ode to Fortune. Many and many a time have I been twitted by my wife and sister for having forgotten this dedication of myself to the stern law-giver.' (I.F.)

l.1   Cp *Paradise Lost*, IX, 652–3.
l.46   See Milton's Dedication to *The Doctrine and Discipline of Divorce*: 'to enslave the dignity of man, to put a garrison upon his neck of empty and over-dignified precepts'.
ll.57–64   Introduced by W in the 'Reply to "Mathetes"' (1809–10): 'in his character of philosophical poet, having thought of morality as implying in its essence voluntary obedience, and producing the effect of order, he transfers, in the transport of imagination, the law of moral to physical natures, and having contemplated, through the medium of that order, all modes of existence as subservient to one spirit, concludes his address to the power of Duty in the following words [those of this final stanza]'.
l.61   lowly wise: Cp *Paradise Lost*, VII, 173–4.
l.63   confidence of reason: from Johnson's *Life of Addison*.

Beggars (p.286)

Composed 13 and 14 March 1802.

'Met and described by me to my sister near the quarry at the head of Rydal Lake – a place still a chosen resort of migrants travelling with their families.' (I.F.) Dorothy's *Journal* entry for 10 June 1800 describes the encounter. She read the account to W as he was composing the poem, 'and an unlucky thing it was', she states, 'for he could not escape from those very words, and so he could not write the poem'. W told Henry Crabb Robinson that the aim of the poem was to 'exhibit the power of physical beauty and health and vigour in childhood even in a state of moral depravity'.

Resolution and Independence (p.287)

First version composed 3–7 May 1802; revised 9 May and 14 June– early July 1802. The poem was known before publication as 'The Leech-Gatherer'.

'This old man I met a few hundred yards from my cottage at Town-End, Grasmere, and the account of him is taken from his own mouth. I was in the state of feeling described in the beginning of the poem . . . The image of the hare I then observed on a ridge of the fell.' (I.F.) Dorothy's *Journal* entry for 3 October 1800 also describes the encounter: 'we met an old man almost double . . . His face was interesting . . . He had had a wife "and a good woman and it pleased God to bless us with ten children" . . . His trade was to gather leeches, but now leeches are scarce and he had not strength for it. He lived by begging.' See W's letter to Sara Hutchinson, 14 June 1802: 'I describe myself as having been exalted to the highest pitch of delight by the joyousness and beauty of Nature, and then . . . overwhelmed by the thought of the miserable reverses which have befallen the happiest of all men, viz. poets . . . I was rescued from my dejection and despair almost as an interposition of Providence . . . What is brought forward? A lonely place, "a pond, by which an old man *was*" . . . not *stood*, not *sat*, but *was* – the figure presented in the most naked simplicity possible . . . I cannot conceive a figure more impressive than that of an old man like this . . . carrying with him his own fortitude and the necessities which an unjust state of society has entailed upon him.'

l.5   See W's Preface to *Poems*, 1815: 'by the intervention of the metaphor *broods*, the affections are called in by the imagination to assist in marking the manner in which the bird reiterates and prolongs her soft note, as if herself delighting to listen to it'.
l.43   The metre of the poem is in fact that of Thomas Chatterton's (1752–70) 'Excellent Ballade of Charitie'.
l.45   him: Robert Burns (1759–96), the ploughman-poet.

ll.59–63   Coleridge compares these lines in *Biographia Literaria*, Chapter XXII, with lines 80–4 to illustrate W's 'inconstancy' and 'incongruity' of style. He characterises lines such as 59–63 as being written in an idiom 'which is only proper in prose', and the style of lines 127–33 as 'not only unimpassioned but undistinguished'. W omitted lines 57–63 in 1820.

ll.64–72 and 82–4   In the Preface to *Poems*, 1815 W quotes these lines to show how, in the interplay of the images of stone, sea-beast and old man, 'the conferring, the abstracting, and the modifying powers of the Imagination, immediately and mediately acting, are all brought into conjunction'.

l.119   Cp *The Prelude*, VII, 623.

'Nuns fret not at their convent's narrow room' (p.292)

Possibly composed late 1802. This is the prefatory sonnet to a series of sonnets in the first volume.

For W and the sonnet form, see W's letter to Dyce of *c.* 22 April 1833.

l.6   Furness is the south-western area of the Lake Country.

Composed after a Journey across the Hamilton Hills, Yorkshire (p.292)

Probably composed on 4 October 1802.

'Composed . . . on a day memorable to me – the day of my marriage.' (I.F.) Dorothy describes the scene in a *Journal* entry for October 1802.

From the Italian of Michael Angelo (p.293)

Probably composed in 1805, by 24 August.

The poem is a translation of Sonnet LX, done at the request of Duppa who was writing a life of Michelangelo. It is the first of four sonnets in the volume translated from Michelangelo. In a letter of 17 October 1805 to Sir George Beaumont, W refers to the difficulties of translation: '[Michelangelo's poetry] is the most difficult to construe I ever met with . . . so much meaning has been put by [him] into so little room . . . that I found the difficulty of translating him insurmountable.'

Written in very early Youth (p.293)

The sonnet could have been composed as early as 1788–91, but also at any time up to 2 July 1797. It was first published in the *Morning Post*, 13 February 1802.

l.7   blank of things: Cp *Paradise Lost*, III, 48–9.
l.8   Home-felt: Cp Milton's *Comus*, 262.

Composed upon Westminster Bridge (p.294)

Begun possibly 31 July 1802; finished by 3 September. '1803' in the title was later corrected by W.

   'Composed on the roof of a coach, on my way to France, Sepbr. 1802.' (I.F.) See Dorothy's *Journal* entry for 31 July: 'It was a beautiful morning. The city, St Paul's, with the river and a multitude of little boats, made a most beautiful sight as we crossed Westminster Bridge . . . there was even something like the purity of one of nature's own grand spectacles.' See also 'St Paul's'.

'Methought I saw the footsteps of a throne (p.294)

Probably composed between 21 May and late 1802.

   'The latter part of [this poem] was a great favourite with my sister Sara Hutchinson.' (I.F.) See notes to 'November, 1836'.

l.1   Cp Milton's sonnnet 'Methought I saw my late espoused saint'.

'The world is too much with us' (p.295)

Probably composed between 21 May 1802 and 6 March 1804.

ll.11–14   See Spenser's 'Colin Clout's come home again', ll.245–8 and 281–3.
l.13   Cp *Paradise Lost*, III, 603–4.

'It is a beauteous evening, calm and free' (p.295)

Probably composed between 1 and 29 August 1802.

   'This was composed on the beach near Calais in the autumn of 1802.' (I.F.) The peace of Amiens enabled W to visit his nine-year-old daughter Caroline (line 9) and Annette Vallon at this time.
l.12   See Luke 16:22.

'I grieved for Buonaparte' (p.296)

Probably composed 21 May 1802.

This poem is the earliest of W's political sonnets – 'Sonnets dedicated to Liberty', as they are termed in the first volume of 1807. It was published in the *Morning Post*, 16 September 1802.

'In the cottage of Town End, one afternoon [in 1802], my sister read to me the sonnets of Milton. I had long been well acquainted with them, but I was particularly struck . . . with the dignified simplicity and majestic harmony that runs through most of them . . . I took fire . . . and produced three sonnets the same afternoon.' (I.F.) This sonnet was one of those three.

Napoleon Buonaparte (1769–1821): General-in-Chief of the French army from 1796–9; made First Consul in 1799 and crowned himself Emperor in 1804; defeated at Waterloo, 1815. W declared that 'after Buonaparte had violated Switzerland, my heart turned against him and the nation that could submit to be the instrument of such an outrage.'

On the Extinction of the Venetian Republic (p.296)

Probably composed between 21 May 1802 and early February 1807.

l.1   The Crusades of the twelfth century secured much land in the East for the great maritime power of Venice, and its wealth and power as a trade centre was strongly established in the fifteenth and sixteenth centuries.

l.2   Venice was 'the safeguard of the West' against the Turks after the fall of Constantinople in 1453.

ll.7–8   A ceremony was held in Venice on Ascension Day in which the Doge symbolically married the city and the Adriatic by dropping a ring into the sea.

l.12   Napoleon entered Venice on 16 May 1797, and the end of the Republic was proclaimed. In October 1797, he handed Venice over to Austria.

To Toussaint L'Ouverture (p.297)

Possibly composed between 1 and 29 August 1802, and first published in the *Morning Post* on 2 February 1803.

François Dominique Toussaint L'Ouverture (1743–1803) was the son of a negro slave. As Governor of Haiti, he resisted Napoleon's decree re-establishing slavery, and was imprisoned in Paris in June 1802. He died in prison in April 1803.

l.14   unconquerable mind: from Gray's *Progress of Poesy* (1757), l.65.

September, 1802 ('Inland within a hollow vale') (p.297)

Probably composed 30 August 1802.

ll.3–7   Cp Dorothy's *Journal* entry for that date: 'We both bathed and sat upon the Dover cliffs and looked upon France with many a melancholy and tender thought. We could see the shores almost as plain as if it were but an English lake.'

Thought of a Briton on the Subjugation of Switzerland (p.298)

Probably composed between 30 October 1806 and January 1807.

In 1808 W considered this the best sonnet he had written. Coleridge reprinted it in *The Friend*, describing it as 'one of the noblest sonnets in our language'. In *Descriptive Sketches*, W had celebrated the Swiss as symbolising Liberty; their country was invaded by the French in the spring of 1798.

Written in London, September, 1802 (p.298)

Composed in 1802, by 22 September.

'This was written immediately after my return from France to London, when I could not but be struck . . . with the vanity and parade of our own country, especially in great towns and cities, as contrasted with the quiet, and I may say the desolation, that the revolution had produced in France.' (I.F.)

l.9   Cp Milton, Sonnet 15, 'On the Lord General Fairfax at the siege of Colchester', ll.13–14.

London, 1802 (p.299)

Date as for the above.

Milton is invoked as the man and poet who can serve as an example to a selfish and vicious generation of godliness, virtue and simplicity. 'Milton's sonnets I think manly and dignified compositions,' W wrote in a letter of November 1802, 'distinguished by simplicity and unity of object and aim, and undisfigured by false or vicious ornaments.'

See the Fenwick note to the above for the thought of this sonnet.

'Great men have been among us' (p.299)

Probably written between 21 May and late 1802.

The sonnet refers to some great Puritan republicans of the Commonwealth: Algernon Sidney (born 1622, executed 1683), the author of *Discourse concerning Civil Government*; Andrew Marvell (1621–78), poet; James Harrington (1611–77), the author of the *Commonwealth of Oceana*; and Sir Henry Vane the younger (born 1613, executed 1662).

'There is a bondage which is worse to bear' (p.300)

Probably composed between 21 May 1802 and late 1802.

Volume II

The Solitary Reaper (p.301)

Probably composed 5 November 1805.

W's note: 'This poem was suggested by a beautiful sentence in a MS Tour in Scotland written by a friend, the last line being taken from it *verbatim*.'

The inspirational sentence is from Thomas Wilkinson's *Tours to the British Mountains* (1824) which W had seen in MS: 'Passed a female who was reaping alone; she sung in Erse as she bended over her sickle – the sweetest human voice I ever heard: her strains were tenderly melancholy, and felt delicious, long after they were heard no more.' Compare Dorothy's *Recollections of a Tour made in Scotland*: 'It was harvest time, and the fields were quietly – might I be allowed to say pensively? – enlivened by small companies of reapers. It is not uncommon in the more lonely parts of the Highlands to see a single person so employed.'

Stepping Westward (p.302)

Probably composed 3 June 1805.

In her *Recollections of a Tour made in Scotland*, Dorothy describes the encounter in terms similar to W's in the headnote.

l.1　Cp the *Recollections*: 'I cannot describe how affecting this simple expression was in that remote place, with the western sky in front, *yet* glowing with the departed sun.'
ll.25–6　Cp the conclusion to *Paradise Lost*.

To a Highland Girl (p.303)

Probably composed between 14 October 1803 and 6 March 1804.

'This delightful creature and her demeanour are particularly described in my sister's Journal. The sort of prophecy with which the verses conclude has through God's goodness been realized, and now approaching the close of my 73rd year I have a most vivid remembrance of her and the beautiful objects with which she was surrounded.' (I.F.)

To a Butterfly ('Stay near me – do not take thy flight!') (p.305)

Composed 14 March 1802.

'Written in the orchard . . . My sister and I were parted immediately after the death of our mother who died in 1778, both being very young.' (I.F.)

See 'To a Butterfly': 'I've watched you now a full half hour'. As de Selincourt observes, the two poems express two different moods, 'a fact which W emphasized . . . by placing one at the beginning and the other at the end of the section [in *Poems in Two Volumes*] entitled "Moods of my own Mind"'. Dorothy states: 'I told [W] that I used to chase them a little, but that I was afraid of brushing the dust off their wings. He told me how they used to kill all the white ones when he went to school because they were Frenchmen.'

'My heart leaps up' (p.305)

Probably composed 26 March 1802.

The final three lines were used in W's *Poems*, 1815, as an epigraph to the 'Ode: Intimations of Immortality'.

'I wandered lonely as a cloud' (p.306)

Probably composed between late March 1804 and early April 1807.

'The two best lines in it [15–16] are by Mary [Wordsworth]. The daffodils grew . . . on the margin of Ullswater and probably may be seen to this day as beautiful in the month of March nodding their golden heads beside the dancing and foaming waves.' (I.F.) See Dorothy's *Journal* description of 15 April 1802: '[The daffodils] tossed and reeled and danced, and seemed as if they verily laughed with the wind . . . they looked so gay, ever glancing, ever changing . . . ' See also W's letter of 4 November 1807 and his letter to Sir George Beaumont, February 1808.

To the Cuckoo (p.306)

Composed mainly 23–26 March 1802. Complete by early June.

Compare W's *Guide through the District of the Lakes*: 'there is also an imaginative influence in the voice of the cuckoo, when the voice has taken possession of a deep mountain valley.' See also the preface to *Poems*, 1815, in which W refers to lines 3–4: 'This concise interrogation characterises the seeming ubiquity of the voice of the cuckoo, and dispossesses the creature almost of a corporeal existence; the Imagination being tempted to this exertion of her power by a consciousness in the memory that the cuckoo is almost perpetually heard throughout the season of spring, but seldom becomes an object of sight.'

To a Butterfly ('I've watched you now a full half hour') (p.307)

Composed 20 April 1802.

See note to 'To a Butterfly': 'Stay near me – do not take thy flight!'

Star Gazers (p.308)

Probably composed between 4 April and 14 November 1806.

'Observed by me in Leicester Square as here described, 1806.' (I.F.)

ll.9–10   The question does not seem to connect with any viewpoint previously established in the poem. W is in fact referring (as will become clear in lines 29–32) to the London citizens' dissatisfaction with what they see through the showman's telescope.

A Complaint (p.309)

Probably composed between 30 October 1806 and early April 1807.

'Suggested by a change in the manner of a friend.' (I.F.) The 'friend' was most probably Coleridge, who had stayed with the Ws at Sir George Beaumont's from December 1806–January 1807. Coleridge's emotional distress (infatuation with Sara Hutchinson, W's sister-in-law, and his decision to separate from his wife) pained the Ws.

'I am not one who much or oft delight' (p.309)

Probably composed between 21 May 1802 and 6 March 1804.

l.6   A line 'stigmatised' by Isabella Fenwick as vulgar and 'worthy only of having been composed by a country Squire'. Cp *A Midsummer Night's Dream*, I, i, 76–8 and Milton's *Comus*, ll.743–4.
ll.25–6   Cp William Collins's ode. 'The Passions', l.60.
l.32   Cp Isaiah 2:12.

ll.41–2   W refers to Desdemona and Othello in Shakespeare's play (which he thought one of the 'most pathetic of human compositions'), and to Book I of Spenser's *The Faerie Queene*.
ll.51–6   Inscribed on W's statue in Westminster Abbey.

Lines Composed at Grasmere (p.311)

Probably composed around early September 1806.

The Whig statesman Charles James Fox, to whom W had sent a copy of the 1800 edition of the *Lyrical Ballads* (see note to 'Michael') died on 13 September 1806.

l.10   W's note refers the reader to the first line of Michelangelo's Sonnet 103, of which this line is a translation. W translated Michelangelo's sonnet twice.

Elegiac Stanzas (p.312)

Probably composed between *c.* 20 May and 27 June 1806.

Peele Castle is situated on a promontory off the coast of the Lake District opposite Rampside, where W stayed in 1794. W probably saw Sir George Beaumont's painting, *A Storm: Peele Castle*, to which the poem refers, at the Royal Academy on 2 May 1806. The painting was used as a frontispiece to the second volume of W's *Poems*, 1815.

W's poem confronts the pain and grief occasioned by the death of his brother John, who went down with his ship *The Earl of Abergavenny* on 5–6 February 1805. For the contrast in the poem between a calm and storm-tossed sea, compare W's essay *Upon Epitaphs* in *The Prose Works of William Wordsworth*, ed. Owen and Smyser, ii, pp.63–4.

Ode ('There was a time') (p.314)

Some or all of stanzas 1–4 composed 27 March 1802. Some of stanzas 5–8 composed 17 June 1802. Most of the final 7 stanzas composed, and the poem finished, by 6 March 1804. In 1815, the poem was given the title 'Ode: Intimations of Immortality from Recollections of early Childhood'.

'Nothing was more difficult for me in childhood than to admit the notion of death as a state applicable to my own being. I have said elsewhere [in 'We are Seven'] "a simple child that lightly draws its breath and feels its life in every limb, what should it know of death?", but it was not so much from [?] of animal vivacity that my difficulty came as from a sense of the indomitableness of the spirit within me . . . I was often unable to think of external things as having external existence, and I communed with all that I saw as something not apart from but inherent in my own immaterial nature. Many times while going to school have I grasped at a wall or tree to recall myself from this abyss of idealism to the reality. At that time I was afraid of such processes. In later periods of life I have deplored . . . a subjugation of an opposite character and have rejoiced over the remembrances as is expressed in the lines "obstinate questionings &c". To that dream-like vividness and splendour which invest objects of sight in childhood, every one, I believe . . . could bear testimony, and . . . in the poem [I have] regarded it as presumptive evidence of a prior state of existence . . . I took hold of the notion of pre-existence as having sufficient foundation in humanity for authorizing me to make for my purpose the best use of it I could as a poet.' (I.F.)

Compare W's 'Ode: Composed upon an Evening of Extraordinary Splendour and Beauty', the 'Reply to "Mathetes"', and the first of the essays Upon Epitaphs. Coleridge's 'Dejection: an Ode' (1802) forms a dialogue with stanzas 1–4, and the continuation of W's poem further expands that poetic dialogue.

W's epigraph to the poem 'Paulò majora canamus' ('Come, let us sing a somewhat loftier strain'), is from Virgil's Eclogues, IV, i. In 1815, the final three lines of 'My heart leaps up' were used as epigraph.

ll.1–9   Lamenting the passing away of the glory of the child's blessed and radiant vision of the world (a lament that continues through the first four stanzas), W's lines echo Coleridge's Mad Monk, ll.9–16: 'There was a time when earth, and sea, and skies . . . '
l.28   the fields of sleep: attempting to interpret the phrase, scholars have referred to the 'slumbering countryside', the 'wind from the sleepy fields', the blowing of the west wind (the west being associated with sunset and therefore with sleep) and to the more mysterious and shadowy areas of the soul at a remove from day-to-day consciousness.
l.41   Cp Coleridge's 'Dejection: an Ode', ll.37–8.
ll.58–84   The thought of the passage is Platonic. For ll.58–76, see Vaughan, 'The Retreate'. The soul of the child comes into the world from a blessed state of pre-existence, and is still 'attended' by a divine vision during childhood. But what W in The Prelude calls 'substantial life', the fetters of custom and of existence in the workaday world ('common day'), inevitably render the vision less radiant and immediate as the child grows up, until the man loses sight of it. What remains, and remains valuable, however, is the blessedness of memory (lines 132 onwards).
l.67   Cp Judges 16:25.
ll.85–9   W has Hartley Coleridge, Coleridge's first son, as well as himself in mind. Cp Coleridge's Christabel, ll.656–61.
l.103   W quotes from Samuel Daniel's dedicatory sonnet to Fulke Greville in Musophilus.

ll.110–19   See Coleridge's *Biographia Literaria*, Chapter XXII, where these lines are criticised as an example of 'mental bombast or thoughts and images too great for the subject'. 'In what sense,' Coleridge asks, 'is a child of that age a *philosopher*? In what sense does he *read* the eternal deep?'

ll.120–3   See note to 'These chairs, they have no words to utter'. Lines 121–4 were cut after 1815.

ll.144–8   Cp the letter from Professor Bonamy Price to William Knight, 21 April 1881: '[W] passed across me to a five-barred gate in the wall which bounded the road on the side of the lake. He clenched the top bar firmly with his right hand, pushed strongly against it, and then uttered these ever-memorable words: "There was a time in my life when I had to push against something that resisted, to be sure that there was anything outside me. I was sure of my own mind; everything else fell away, and vanished into thought." ' See Fenwick note above and Traherne's poem, 'My Spirit', for a similar thought.

l.150   Cp *Hamlet*, I, i, 148.

l.152   shadowy recollections: of a state of pre-natal existence.

l.163   Cp *Paradise Lost*, II, 92.

l.205   Cp Gray's 'Ode on the Pleasure arising from Vicissitude', l.49: 'The meanest floweret of the vale'.

St Paul's (p.320)

From Dove Cottage MS 65. Composed between 8 April and early autumn 1808. Never published by W.

The poem was written for the main philosophical section of the projected (and unfinished) philosophical work, *The Recluse*. It is one of W's few attempts after *Home at Grasmere* to get to grips with the philosophical core of the *magnum opus*.

To Sir George Beaumont, 8 April 1808, W wrote: 'Some of the imagery of London has . . . been more present to my mind than that of this noble vale. I left Coleridge [the 'friend' of line 2] at seven o'clock on Sunday morning, and walked towards the city in a very thoughtful and melancholy state of mind. I had passed through Temple Bar and St Dunstan's, noticing nothing . . . when, looking up, I saw before me the avenue of Fleet Street, silent, empty, and pure white, with a sprinkling of new fallen snow . . . beyond . . . was the huge and majestic form of St Paul's, solemnised by a thin veil of falling snow. I cannot say . . . what a blessing I felt there is in habits of exalted imagination. My sorrow was controlled, and my uneasiness of mind . . . seemed at once to receive . . . an anchor of security.'

From *Poems*, 1815

Poems, 1815 was Wordsworth's first collected edition.

Characteristics of a Child three years old (p.323)

Probably composed early 1813 and before 5 May 1814.

Compare 'Surprised by joy'. 'Picture of my daughter Catherine.' (I.F.) Catherine Wordsworth was born on 6 September 1808 and died on 4 June 1812.

ll.12–13   Cp *Paradise Lost*, IX, 429: 'For solitude sometimes is best society'.

'Surprised by joy, impatient as the wind' (p.323)

Composed a considerable time after 14 June 1812 and before late October 1814.

'This was in fact suggested by my daughter Catherine long after her death.' (I.F.) Dorothy said of Catherine that 'she had a temper never ruffled – there seemed no seed of evil in her and she was so loving that the smallest notice or kindness shown to her . . . used to draw from her the fondest caress and expressions of love' (letter to Catherine Clarkson, 23 June 1812).

Yarrow Visited (p.324)

Composed between 1 September 1814 and mid-September; revised between that date and late October.

'As mentioned in my verses on the death of the Ettrick shepherd [James Hogg – see W's 'Extempore Effusion'] my first visit to Yarrow [1 September 1814] was in his company.' (I.F.)

This is the second of three 'Yarrow' poems; the other two are 'Yarrow Unvisited' and 'Yarrow Revisited'. W wrote to Robert Gillies, 23 November 1814: 'Second parts, if much inferior to the first, are always disgusting, and as I had succeeded in "Yarrow Unvisited", I was anxious that there should be no falling off; but that was unavoidable, perhaps from the subject, as imagination almost always transcends the reality.' Cp *The Prelude*, VI, 452–61.

ll.25–32   W draws on two ballads in this stanza: William Hamilton's 'The Braes of Yarrow', in which a young man is pierced by a rival's spear on the banks of the river; and John Logan's poem of the same title, in

which a young man drowns in the river. In the latter, a 'water-wraith' –
the young man's ghost – rising from the water, appears to his lover.
ll.41–8   Lamb told W that 'no lovelier stanza can be found in the wide
world of poetry'.
ll.55–6   See Scott's *Lay of the Last Minstrel*.

'Say, what is honour?' (p.326)

Composed perhaps November–December 1808.
  Lines 9–12 of the poem glance at Spain's subservience to Napoleon in
accepting his brother, Joseph Buonaparte, as king, mid-1808.

ll.13–14   A possible reference to the failure of British forces to pursue
the French after the battle of Vimeiro in late August 1808.

'The power of armies is a visible thing' (p.327)

Composed 1811, probably after the end of March.
  Speaking of the Hessians in America, W states in his pamphlet *The
Convention of Cintra* (1809) that 'the force with which these troops
would attack was gross – tangible – and might be calculated; but the
spirit of resistance, which their presence would create, was subtle –
ethereal – mighty – and incalculable.'

Peter Bell, A Tale in Verse (p.328)

Composed April–May 1798. Published, after revision, in 1819. The
text is that of the first published version.
  'Founded upon an anecdote, which I read in a newspaper, of an ass
being found hanging his head over a canal in a wretched posture. Upon
examination a dead body was found in the water . . . The countenance,
gait, and figure of Peter were taken from a wild rover with whom I walked
from Builth, on the river Wye, downwards nearly as far as the town of
Hay. He told me strange stories . . . ' (I.F.)
  The 1819 dedication to Southey recalls the description, in *Biographia
Literaria*, Chapter XIV, of the nature of the joint plan for the *Lyrical
Ballads*, in which Coleridge was to choose as poetic subjects 'persons and
characters supernatural', while W was to 'give the charm of novelty to
things of every day' and 'excite a feeling analogous to the supernatural'.
  The dedication states that *Peter Bell* was composed 'under a belief that
the Imagination not only does not require for its exercise the intervention
of supernatural agency, but that . . . the faculty may be called forth as

imperiously, and for kindred results of pleasure, by incidents . . . in the humblest departments of daily life'.

J. H. Reynolds, a week before the publication of *Peter Bell*, picked up on the publishers' advertisement announcing the forthcoming W poem to offer an 'anticipated parody'. Shelley's more famous demonic parody, *Peter Bell the Third*, was also written in 1819. Henry Crabb Robinson saw in *Peter Bell* 'a great deal of profound psychology interspersed with exquisite description, psychological and natural'.

l.159   Hippogriff: a griffin-like beast with the body of a horse.
ll.623–5   Cp the description in *The Prelude*, 1799, Part One, of the drowned man being raised from Esthwaite lake (ll.263–79).
l.959   W states in the Fenwick note: 'Benoni, or the child of sorrow I knew when I was a school-boy. His mother had been deserted by a gentleman of the neighbourhood . . . The circumstances of her story were told me by my dear old Dame, Ann Tyson, who was her confidante.'
l.1178   Leming-Lane: Leeming Lane, a village in Yorkshire, where the Ws stayed in October 1802.

Later Poems

Sequel to ['Beggars'] (p.365)

Composed 1817 and published 1827.

The poem is a sequel to 'Beggars' (see *Poems in Two Volumes*), which was printed before this later poem in the 1827 edition of the *Poetical Works*.

l.1   Cp *King Lear*, IV, i, 38.
l.2   'daedal': 'adorned with natural wonders'. Cp *The Faerie Queene*, IV, x, 45.

Ode, Composed upon an Evening of Extraordinary Splendour and Beauty (p.366)

Composed at the beginning of summer 1817, and not completed before December. Published in *The River Duddon*, 1820.

'Felt, and in a great measure composed, upon the little mount in front of our abode at Rydal.' (I.F.)

ll.49–60   W's note: 'The multiplication of mountain-ridges, described at the commencement of the third stanza of this ode as a kind of Jacob's

Ladder, leading to heaven, is produced either by watery vapours, or sunny haze . . . ' W also acknowledges the inspiration of Washington Allston's painting, *Jacob's Dream*, in the 1820 Collected Edition.
ll.61–80   Cp the 'Ode: Intimations of Immortality'.

'Hopes, what are they?' (p.368)

Composed early 1818 and published in *The River Duddon*, 1820.
   The piece is part of a series of poems articulating a disillusioned vision of the world entitled 'Inscriptions, supposed to be found in, and near, a hermit's cell'.

The River Duddon: Afterthought (p.370)

Composed 1818–20. The poem is the conclusion to the Duddon sonnet sequence.

l.5   Cp *Home at Grasmere*, ll.383–4. Cp Coleridge's description of a waterfall, 25 August 1802: 'the continual *change* of the *matter*, the perpetual *sameness* of the *form* – it is an awful image and shadow of God and the world.'
l.14   Cp *Paradise Lost*, VIII, 282: 'And feel that I am happier than I know'.

Mutability (p.370)

Composed 1821 and published 1822 in *Ecclesiastical Sketches*.
   W had used the final line in 1796 in the 'Gothic Tale' fragment: 'The unimaginable touch of time/Or shouldering rend had split with ruin deep/Those towers that stately stood'. For a possible influence on these lines and on lines 10–14 of the sonnet, see John Dyer's 'The Ruins of Rome' (1740) ll.41–5.

Steamboats, Viaducts, and Railways (p.371)

Written during, or shortly after, W's tour to the Isle of Man, Staffa and Iona in 1833. Published in *Yarrow Revisited and other Poems* (1835).
   W considers the march of the Industrial Revolution and the place of poetry in a mechanised world, producing a poem whose argument vis-à-vis the world of Nature might seem strangely un-Wordsworthian. See Turner's atmospheric painting, *Rain, Steam and Speed* (1844).

Extempore Effusion upon the Death of James Hogg (p.371)

Composed November 1835 and published 5 December in the *Newcastle Journal* and in *Poetical Works*, 1836–7.

'These verses were written extempore, immediately after reading a notice of the Ettrick shepherd's death . . . The persons lamented in these verses were all either of my friends or acquaintance.' (I.F.)

James Hogg, 'The Ettrick Shepherd', remembered for the *Private Memoirs and Confessions of a justified Sinner*, was born in 1770 and died on 21 November 1835. The other friends and acquaintances lamented are Sir Walter Scott (1771–1832), poet and novelist; S. T. Coleridge (1771–1834); Charles Lamb (1775–1834), author of the *Essays of Elia* ; George Crabbe (1754–1832), author of *The Village* and *The Borough*, and Felicia Hemans (1793–1835), the best-selling poetess.

ll.1–8 Hogg had accompanied W when they visited Yarrow on 1 September 1814 (see 'Yarrow Visited'). On 20 September 1831, when W revisited the place, Scott was his travelling companion.
l.10 Scott was buried in Dryburgh Abbey.
l.12 Hogg in youth had been a shepherd.
l.19 In line 28 of 'This Lime-tree Bower my Prison' (1797), Coleridge had referred to Lamb as 'gentle-hearted' – an appellation Lamb objected to. See Lamb's letter of 14 August 1800.

November, 1836 (p.373)

Composed at that date and published 1837.

It is printed facing 'Methought I saw', to which the opening lines refer. 'November 1836' was written after the death on 23 June 1835 of Sara Hutchinson, W's sister-in-law. The latter half of 'Methought I saw' was one of her favourite passages of W's verse. 'O my dear Southey,' W wrote to Robert Southey on 24 June 1835, 'we have lost a precious friend . . . I saw her within an hour after her decease, in the silence and peace of death, with as heavenly an expression on her countenance as ever human creature had. Surely there is food for faith in these appearances . . . I have passed a wakeful night, more in joy than sorrow, with that blessed face before my eyes perpetually.'

Popular in some degree from the first, [Young and Cowper] entered upon the inheritance of their fame almost at once. Far different was the fate of Wordsworth; for in poetry of this class, which appeals to what lies deepest in man, in proportion to the native power of the poet, and his fitness for permanent life, is the strength of resistance in the public taste. Whatever is too original will be hated at the first. It must slowly mould a public for itself, and the resistance of the early thoughtless judgements must be overcome by a counter resistance to itself, in a better audience slowly mustering against the first. Forty and seven years it is since William Wordsworth first appeared as an author. Twenty of those years he was the scoff of the world, and his poetry a by-word of scorn. Since then, and more than once, senates have rung with acclamations to the echo of his name. Now at this moment, whilst we are talking about him, he has entered upon his seventy-sixth year. For himself, according to the course of nature, he cannot be far from his setting; but his poetry is only now clearing the clouds that gathered about its rising.

De Quincey, 'On Wordsworth's Poetry', 1845

Contemporary Criticism, 1793–1831

FROM A REVIEW OF *DESCRIPTIVE SKETCHES*: THE *MONTHLY REVIEW* (OCTOBER 1793)

Though enthusiastically discussed in various literary groups, Wordsworth's *An Evening Walk* and *Descriptive Sketches* caused no great stir. Some reviews were polite, others quite favourable, but the obscurity of some passages inevitably invited censure.

More descriptive poetry! . . . Have we not yet enough? Must eternal changes be rung on uplands and lowlands, and nodding forests, and brooding clouds, and cells, and dells, and dingles? Yes; more, and yet more: so it is decreed.

Mr Wordsworth begins his descriptive sketches with the following exordium: [quotes lines 1–12]:

May we ask, how it is that rivers join the song of ev'n? or, in plain prose, the evening! but, if they do, is it not true that they equally join the song of morning, noon, and night? The *purple morning falling in flakes* of light is a bold figure: but we are told, it falls far and wide – Where? – On the mountain's *side*. We are sorry to see the purple morning confined so like a maniac in a straight waistcoat. What the night of wing of silence is, we are unable to comprehend: but the climax of the passage is, that, were there such a spot of holy ground as is here so sublimely described, *unfound* by Pain and her sad family, Nature's God had surely given that spot to man, though its *woods are undiscovered* – [quotes lines 13–28].

Here we find that *doubly* pitying Nature is very kind to the traveller, but that this traveller has a *wounded heart* and *plods* his road *forlorn*. In the next line but one we discover that – [quotes lines 17–18].

The flowers, though they have lost themselves, or are lost, exhale their idle sweets for him; the *spire peeps* for him; sod-seats, forests, clouds, nature's charities, and babbling brooks, all are to him luxury and friendship. He is the happiest of mortals, and plods, is forlorn, and has a wounded heart. How often shall we in vain advise those, who are so delighted with their own thoughts that they cannot forbear from putting them into ryhme [*sic*], to examine those thoughts till they themselves understand them? No man will ever be a poet, till his mind be sufficiently powerful to sustain this labour.

FROM A REVIEW OF THE *LYRICAL BALLADS*, 1798, BY CHARLES BURNEY: *MONTHLY REVIEW* (JUNE 1799)

When this review appeared, Southey had already written an un-favourable review of the *Lyrical Ballads*. Burney's review is less harsh and, though not rapturous, it does recognise the importance and success of the poetry.

The author of these ingenious compositions presents the major part of them as *experiments*; since they were written, as he informs us in the *advertisement* prefixed, 'chiefly with a view to ascertain how far the language of conversation in the middle and lower classes of society is adapted to the purposes of poetic pleasure'. Though we have been extremely entertained with the fancy, the facility and (in general) the sentiments, of these pieces, we cannot regard them as *poetry*, of a class to be cultivated at the expense of a higher species of versification, unknown in our language at the time when our elder writers, whom this author condescends to imitate wrote their ballads.

* * *

The Yew Tree seems a seat for Jean Jacques; while the reflections on the subject appear from a more pious pen.

*   *   *

Distress from poverty and want is admirably described in the true story of *Goody Blake and Harry Gill*: but are we to imagine that Harry was bewitched by Goody Blake? The hardest heart must be softened into pity for the poor old woman; and yet, if all the poor are to help, and supply their wants from the possessions of their neighbours, what imaginary wants and real anarchy would it not create? Goody Blake should have been relieved of the two millions annually allowed by the state to the poor of this country not by the plunder of an individual.

Lines on the first mild day of March abound with beautiful sentiments from a polished mind.

Simon Lee, the old Huntsman, is the portrait, admirably painted, of every huntsman who, by toil, age, and infirmities, is rendered unable to guide and govern his canine family.

Anecdote for Fathers. Of this, the dialogue is ingenious and natural: but the object of the child's choice, and the inferences, are not quite obvious.

We are Seven. – innocent and pretty infantine prattle.

On An Early Spring. – The first stanza of this poem seems unworthy of the rest, which contain reflections truly pious and philosophical.

The Thorn. – All our author's pictures, in colouring, are dark as those of Rembrandt . . .

*   *   *

The Idiot Boy leads the reader on from anxiety to distress, and from distress to terror, by incidents and alarms which, though of the most mean and ignoble kind, interest, frighten, and terrify, almost to torture, during the perusal of more than a hundred stanzas.

Lines written near Richmond. – Literally 'most musical, most melancholy'.

Expostulation and Reply. – These two pieces will afford our readers an opportunity of judging of the author's poetical talents, in a more modern and less gloomy style than his Ballads.

The Old Man Travelling, A Sketch. – Finely drawn, but the termination seems pointed against the war, from which, however, we are now no more able to separate ourselves, than Hercules was to free himself from the shirt of Nessus. The old traveller's son might have died by disease.

Each ballad is a tale of woe. The style and versification are those of our ancient ditties but much polished, and more constantly excellent. In old songs, we have only a fine line or stanza now and then; here we meet with few that are feeble; but it is *poesie larmoiante*. The author is more plaintive than Gray himself.

The Complaint of the Forsaken Indian Woman: another tale of woe of the most affecting and harrowing kind.

The Convict. – What a description! What misplaced commiseration! . . . We do not comprehend the drift of lavishing that tenderness and compassion on a criminal, which should be reserved for virtue in unmerited misery and distress, suffering untimely death from accident, injustice, or disease.

Lines written near Tintern Abbey. – The reflections of no common mind; poetical, beautiful, and philosophical: but somewhat tinctured with gloomy, narrow, and unsociable ideas of seclusion from the commerce of the world: as if men were born to live in woods and wilds, unconnected with each other . . . So much genius and originality are discovered in this publication, that we wish to see another from the same hand, written on more elevated subjects and in a more cheerful disposition.

FROM A REVIEW OF THE *LYRICAL BALLADS* (1800)
BY FRANCIS WRANGHAM, *BRITISH CRITIC* (FEBRUARY 1801)

Whatever may be thought of these poems, it is evident that they are not to be confounded with the flood of poetry which is poured forth in such profusion by the modern Bards of Science, or their Brethren, the Bards of Insipidity. The author has thought for himself; he has deeply studied human nature, in the book of human action; and he has adopted his language from the same sources as his feelings. Aware that his Poems are so materially different from those upon which general approbation is at present bestowed, he has now defended them in a Preface of some length; not with the foolish hope of reasoning his readers into the approbation of these particular Poems, but as a necessary justification of the species of poetry to which they belong. This Preface, though written in some parts with a degree of metaphysical obscurity, conveys much penetrating judicious observation . . . Perhaps it would be expecting too much from any one but Shakespeare, were we to demand that he should be the Poet of human nature. It would be no mean, it would indeed be a very lofty praise, to assert of a writer, that he is able to pour into other bosoms powerful feelings of a particular class, or belonging to a particular order of men. To this praise, Mr Wordsworth lays a well-supported claim.

WORDSWORTH: FROM THE PREFACE TO
THE *LYRICAL BALLADS* (1800 AND 1802)

Wordsworth's great poetic manifesto.

The First Volume of these Poems has already been submitted to general perusal. It was published, as an experiment which, I hoped, might be of some use to ascertain, how far, by fitting to metrical arrangement a selection of the real language of men in a state of vivid sensation, that sort of pleasure and that quantity of pleasure may be imparted, which a Poet may rationally endeavour to impart.

*   *   *

It is supposed, that by the act of writing in verse an Author makes a formal engagement that he will gratify certain known habits of association, that he not only thus apprizes the Reader that certain classes of ideas and expressions will be found in his book, but that others will be carefully excluded . . . I will not take upon me to determine the exact import of the promise which by the act of writing in verse an Author in the present day makes to his Reader; but I am certain it will appear to many persons that I have not fulfilled the terms of an engagement thus voluntarily contracted.

*   *   *

The principal object then which I proposed to myself in these Poems was to make the incidents of common life interesting by tracing in them, truly though not ostentatiously, the primary laws of our nature: chiefly as far as regards the manner in which we associate ideas in a state of excitement. Low and rustic life was generally chosen because in that situation the essential passions of the heart find a better soil in which they can attain their maturity, are less under restraint, and speak a plainer and more emphatic language; because in that situation our elementary feelings exist in a state of greater simplicity and consequently may be more accurately contemplated and more forcibly communicated; because the manners of rural life germinate from those elementary feelings; and from the necessary character of rural occupations are more easily comprehended; and are more durable; and lastly, because in that situation the passions of men are incorporated with the beautiful and permanent forms of nature. The language too of these men is adopted (purified indeed from what appear to be its real defects, from all lasting and rational causes of dislike or disgust) because such men hourly communicate with the best objects from which the best part of language is originally derived; and because, from their rank in society and the sameness and narrow circle of their intercourse, being less under the action of social vanity they convey their feelings and notions in simple and unelaborated expressions. Accordingly such a language arising out of repeated experience and regular feelings is a more permanent and a far more philosophical language than that which is frequently substituted for it by Poets, who think that they are conferring honour upon themselves and their art in proportion as they separate themselves from the sympathies of men, and indulge in arbitrary and capricious habits of expression in order to furnish food for fickle tastes and fickle appetites of their own creation.

I cannot be insensible of the present outcry against the triviality and meanness both of thought and language, which some of my contemporaries have occasionally introduced into their metrical compositions . . . From such verses the Poems in these volumes will be found distinguished at least by one mark of difference, that each of them has a worthy *purpose*. Not that I mean to say, that I always began to write with a distinct purpose formally conceived; but I believe that my habits of meditation have so formed my feelings, as that my descriptions of such objects as strongly excite those feelings, will be found to carry along with them a *purpose*. If in this opinion I am mistaken I can have little right to the name of a Poet. For all good poetry is the spontaneous overflow of powerful feelings; but though this be true, Poems to which any value can be attached, were never produced on any variety of subjects but by a man who being possessed of more than usual organic sensibility had also thought long and deeply.

*   *   *

. . . it is proper that I should mention one other circumstance which distinguishes these Poems from the popular Poetry of the day; it is this, that the feeling therein developed gives importance to the action and situation and not the action and situation to the feeling.

*   *   *

Except in a very few instances the Reader will find no personifications of abstract ideas in these volumes, not that I mean to censure such personifications: they may be well fitted for certain sorts of composition, but in these Poems I propose to myself to imitate, and, as far as possible, to adopt the very language of men, and I do not find that such personifications make any regular or natural part of that language. I wish to keep my Reader in the company of flesh and blood . . . There will also be found in these volumes little of what is usually called poetic diction; I have taken as much pains to avoid it as others ordinarily take to produce it; this I have done for the reason already alleged, to bring my language near to the language of men . . .

* * *

If in a Poem there should be found a series of lines, or even a single line, in which the language, though naturally arranged and according to the strict laws of metre, does not differ from that of prose, there is a numerous class of critics who, when they stumble upon these prosaisms as they call them, imagine that they have made a notable discovery, and exult over the Poet as over a man ignorant of his own profession. Now these men would establish a canon of criticism which the Reader will conclude he must utterly reject if he wishes to be pleased with these volumes.

* * *

Is there then, it will be asked, no essential difference between the language of prose and metrical composition? I answer that there neither is nor can be any essential difference.

* * *

I answer that the language of such Poetry as I am recommending is, as far as is possible, a selection of the language really spoken by men; that this selection, wherever it is made with true taste and feeling, will of itself form a distinction far greater than would at first be imagined, and will entirely separate the composition from the vulgarity and meanness of ordinary life; and, if metre be superadded thereto, I believe that a dissimilitude will be produced altogether sufficient for the gratification of a rational mind.

* * *

Taking up the subject, then, upon general grounds, I ask what is meant by the word Poet? What is a Poet? To whom does he address himself? And what language is to be expected from him? He is a man speaking to men: a man, it is true, endued with more lively sensibility, more enthusiasm and tenderness, who has a greater knowledge of human nature, and a more comprehensive soul, than are supposed to be common among mankind.

* * *

Aristotle, I have been told, hath said, that Poetry is the most philosophic of all writing: it is so: its object is truth, not individual and local, but general, and operative; not standing upon external testimony, but carried alive into the heart by passion; truth which is its own testimony, which gives strength and divinity to the tribunal to which it appeals, and receives them from the same tribunal. Poetry is the image of man and nature.

*   *   *

The knowledge both of the Poet and the Man of Science is pleasure; but the knowledge of the one cleaves to us as a necessary part of our existence, our natural and unalienable inheritance; the other is a personal and individual acquisition, slow to come to us, and by no habitual and direct sympathy connecting us with our fellow-beings. The Man of Science seeks truth as a remote and unknown benefactor; he cherishes and loves it in his solitude: the Poet, singing a song in which all human beings join with him, rejoices in the presence of truth as our visible friend and hourly companion. Poetry is the breath and finer spirit of all knowledge: it is the impassioned expression which is in the countenance of all Science. Emphatically may it be said of the Poet, as Shakespeare hath said of man, 'that he looks before and after'. He is the rock of defence of human nature; an upholder and preserver, carrying every where with him relationship and love . . . the Poet binds together by passion and knowledge the vast empire of human society, as it is spread over the whole earth, and over all time.

*   *   *

The Poet thinks and feels in the spirit of the passions of men. How, then, can his language differ in any material degree from that of all other men who feel vividly and see clearly? It might be *proved* that it is impossible. But supposing that this were not the case, the Poet might then be allowed to use a peculiar language when expressing his feelings for his own gratification, or that of men like himself. But Poets do not write for Poets alone, but for men.

*   *   *

I have said that Poetry is the spontaneous overflow of powerful feelings: it takes its origin from emotion recollected in tranquillity: the emotion is contemplated till by a species of reaction the tranquillity gradually disappears, and an emotion, similar to that which was before the subject of contemplation, is gradually produced, and does itself actually exist in the mind. In this mood successful composition generally begins, and in a mood similar to this it is carried on . . .

JOHN WILSON: FROM A LETTER TO WORDSWORTH
(24 MAY 1802)

That your poetry is the language of nature, in my opinion, admits of no doubt. Both the thoughts and expressions may be tried by that standard. You have seized upon those feelings that most deeply interest the heart, and that also come within the sphere of common observation. You do not write merely for the pleasure of philosophers and men of improved taste, but for all who think – for all who feel. If we have ever known the happiness arising from parental or fraternal love; if we have ever known that delightful sympathy of souls connecting persons of different sex; if we have ever dropped a tear at the death of friends, or grieved for the misfortunes of others; if, in short, we have ever felt the more amiable emotions of human nature – it is impossible to read *your* poems without being greatly interested and frequently in raptures; your sentiments, feelings and thoughts are therefore exactly such as ought to constitute the subject of poetry, and cannot fail of exciting interest in every heart . . . But your poems may not be considered merely in a philosophical light, or even as containing refined and natural feelings; they present us with a body of morality of the purest kind. They represent the enjoyment resulting from the cultivation of the social affections of our nature; they inculcate a conscientious regard to the rights of our fellow-men; they show that every creature on the face of the earth is entitled in some measure to our kindness. They prove that in every mind, *however* depraved, there exist some qualities deserving our esteem. They point out the proper way to happiness. They show that such a thing as perfect misery does not exist. They flash on our souls convictions of immortality. Considered therefore in this view, *Lyrical Ballads* is, to use your own words, the book which I value next to my Bible.

*   *   *

. . . in the execution of this design you have inadvertently fallen into an error, the effects of which are, however, exceedingly trivial. No feeling, no state of mind ought, in my opinion, to become the subject of poetry, that does not please . . . In a few cases, then, I think that even you have failed to excite interest. In the poem entitled *The Idiot Boy*, your intention, as you inform us in your preface, was to trace the maternal passion through its more subtle windings. This design is no doubt accompanied with much difficulty, but, if properly executed,

cannot fail of interesting the heart. But sir, in my opinion, the manner
in which you have executed this plan has frustrated the end you
intended to produce by it; the affection of Betty Foy has nothing in it to
excite interest. It exhibits merely the effects of that instinctive feeling
inherent in the constitution of every animal. The excessive fondness of
the mother disgusts us, and prevents us from sympathizing with her.
We are unable to enter into her feelings; we cannot conceive ourselves
actuated by the same feelings, and consequently take little or no
interest in her situation. The object of her affection is indeed her son,
and in that relation much consists, but then he is represented as totally
destitute of any attachment towards her; the state of his mind is
represented as perfectly deplorable, and, in short, to me it appears
almost unnatural that a person in a state of complete idiotism should
excite the warmest feelings of attachment in the breast even of his
mother.

WILLIAM WORDSWORTH: FROM A LETTER TO JOHN WILSON (7 JUNE 1802)

Wordsworth replies memorably to John Wilson's strictures and
discusses the vision on which an appreciative and informed reading
of 'The Idiot Boy' depends.

You begin what you say upon 'The Idiot Boy' with this observation,
that nothing is a fit subject for poetry which does not please. But here
follows a question, Does not please whom? Some have little know-
ledge of natural imagery of any kind, and, of course, little relish for it;
some are disgusted with the very mention of the words 'pastoral
poetry', 'sheep', or 'shepherds'; some cannot tolerate a poem with a
ghost or any supernatural agency in it; others would shrink from an
animated description of the pleasures of love, as from a thing carnal
and libidinous; some cannot bear to see delicate and refined feelings
ascribed to men in low conditions in society, because their vanity and
self-love tell them that these belong only to themselves and men like
themselves in dress, station, and way of life; others are disgusted with
the naked language of some of the most interesting passions of men,
because either it is indelicate, or gross, or vulgar . . .

I return then to [the] question, please whom? or what? I answer,
human nature, as it has been [and eve]r will be. But where are we to
find the best measure of this? I answer, [with]in; by stripping our own
hearts naked, and by looking out of ourselves to [me]n who lead the
simplest lives, and most according to nature; men who [ha]ve never
known false refinements, wayward and artificial desires, false
criti[ci]sms, effeminate habits of thinking and feeling, or who, having
known these [t]hings, have outgrown them . . . Whom do we generally

associate with? Gentlemen, persons of fortune, professional men, ladies, persons who can afford to buy, or can easily procure, books of half-a-guinea price, hot-pressed, and printed upon superfine paper. These persons are, it is true, a part of human nature, but we err lamentably if we suppose them to be fair representatives of the vast mass of human existence. And yet few ever consider books but with reference to their power of pleasing these persons and men of a higher rank; few descend lower, among cottages and fields, and among children. A man must have done this habitually before his judgment upon 'The Idiot Boy' would be in any way decisive with me. I *know* I have done this myself habitually . . . You have given me prais[e] for having reflected faithfully in my poems the feelings of human nature. I would fain hope that I have done so. But a great Poet ought to do more than this: he ought, to a certain degree, to rectify men's feelings, to give them new compositions of feeling, to render their feelings more sane, pure, and permanent, in short, more consonant to nature, that is, to eternal nature, and the great moving spirit of things. He ought to travel before men occasionally as well as at their sides . . . the loathing and disgust which many peo[ple] have at the sight of an idiot is a feeling which, though having som[e] foundation in human nature, is not necessarily attached to it in any vi[tal] degree, but is owing in a great measure to a false delicacy, and, if I [may] say it without rudeness, a certain want of comprehensiveness of think[ing] and feeling.

*   *   *

I have often applied to idiots, in my own mind, that sublime expression of Scripture, that *their life is hidden with God.*

DOROTHY WORDSWORTH: FROM A LETTER TO MARY AND SARA HUTCHINSON (14 JUNE 1802)

Dorothy seeks to educate Sara, who had been bored by 'Resolution and Independence', into an appreciative and correct response to her brother's poems. The tone of the final sentence about bread-baking shows that she had been ruffled by Sara's initial response.

Dear Sara

　　When you happen to be displeased with what you suppose to be the tendency or moral of any poem which William writes, ask yourself whether you have hit upon the real tendency and true moral, and above all never think that he writes for no reason but merely because a thing happened – and when you feel any poem of his to be tedious, ask yourself in what spirit it was written – whether merely to tell the tale and be through with it, or to illustrate a particular character or truth etc etc.

I am glad that you have found out how to bake bread in my way – we never want yeast now.

WORDSWORTH: FROM A LETTER TO LADY BEAUMONT (21 MAY 1807)

The things which I have taken, whether from within or without – what have they to do with routs, dinners, morning calls, hurry from door to door, from street to street, on foot or in carriage; with Mr Pitt or Mr Fox, Mr Paul or Sir Francis Burdett, the Westminster Election or the Borough of Honiton; in a word, for I cannot stop to make my way through the hurry of images that present themselves to me, what have they to do with endless talking about things nobody cares anything for except as far as their own vanity is concerned, and this with persons they care nothing for but as their vanity or *selfishness* is concerned; what have they to do (to say all at once) with a life without love? In such a life there can be no thought; for we have no thought (save thoughts of pain) but as far as we have love and admiration . . .

FRANCIS JEFFREY: FROM A REVIEW OF *POEMS IN TWO VOLUMES* (1807), *EDINBURGH REVIEW* (OCTOBER 1807)

One of the most damning and influential contemporary reviews of Wordsworth. Jeffrey's strictures here damaged both Wordsworth's poetic reputation and his sales.

One great beauty of diction exists only for those who have some degree of scholarship or critical skill. This is what depends on the exquisite *propriety* of the words employed, and the delicacy with which they are adapted to the meaning which is to be expressed.

*   *   *

From this great source of pleasure, we think the readers of Mr Wordsworth are in a great measure cut off. His diction has nowhere any pretensions to elegance or dignity; and he has scarcely ever condescended to give the grace of correctness or melody to his versification . . . in good truth, no man, nowadays, composes verse for publication with a slovenly neglect of their language. It is a fine and laborious manufacture, which can scarcely ever be made in a hurry; and the faults which it has, may, for the most part, be set down to bad taste or incapacity, rather than to carelessness or oversight. With Mr Wordsworth and his friends, it is plain that their peculiarities of diction are things of choice, and not of accident. They write as they do, upon principle and system; and it evidently costs them much pains to keep *down* to the standard which they have proposed to themselves.

*   *   *

Their peculiarities of diction alone, are enough, perhaps, to render them ridiculous; but the author before us really seems anxious to court this literary martyrdom by a device still more infallible – we mean, that of connecting his most lofty, tender, or impassioned conceptions, with objects and incidents, which the greater part of his readers will probably persist in thinking low, silly, or uninteresting. Whether this is done from affectation and conceit alone, or whether it may not arise, from the self-illusion of a mind of extraordinary sensibility, habituated to solitary meditation, we cannot undertake to determine. It is possible enough, we allow, that the sight of a friend's garden spade, or a sparrow's nest, or a man gathering leeches might really have suggested to such a mind a train of powerful impressions and interesting reflections; but it is certain, that, to most minds, such associations will always appear forced, strained and unnatural; and that the composition in which it is attempted to exhibit them will always have the air of parody, or ludicrous and affected singularity.

BYRON: FROM *ENGLISH BARDS AND SCOTCH REVIEWERS* (1809)

Referring to the *Lyrical Ballads*, Byron's satire on the literature of his day notes Wordsworth's poetic simplicity, and turns the author of 'The Idiot Boy' into the idiot Bard.

> The simple WORDSWORTH, framer of a lay
> As soft as evening in his favourite May;
> Who warns his friend 'to shake off toil and trouble,
> And quit his books, for fear of growing double';
> Who, both by precept and example, shows
> That prose is verse, and verse is merely prose,
> Convincing all by demonstration plain,
> Poetic souls delight in prose insane;
> And Christmas stories tortured into rhyme,
> Contain the essence of the true sublime:
> Thus when he tells the tale of Betty Foy,
> The idiot mother of 'an idiot Boy';
> A moon-struck silly lad who lost his way,
> And, like his Bard, confounded night with day,

> So close on each pathetic part he dwells,
> And each adventure so sublimely tells,
> That all who view the 'idiot in his glory',
> Conceive the Bard the hero of the story.

WILLIAM HAZLITT: FROM A REVIEW OF *THE EXCURSION*, IN *THE
EXAMINER* (21, 28 AUGUST, 2 OCTOBER 1814)

He may be said to create his own materials; his thoughts are his real
subjects. His understanding broods over that which is 'without form
and void' and 'makes it pregnant'. He sees all things in himself. He
hardly ever avails himself of remarkable objects or situations, but, in
general, rejects them as interfering with the workings of his own mind,
as disturbing the smooth, deep, majestic current of his own feelings.

*   *   *

In describing human nature, Mr Wordsworth equally shuns the
common vantage-grounds of popular story, of striking incident or
fatal catastrophe, as cheap and vulgar modes of producing an effect.
He scans the human race as the naturalist measures the earth's zone,
without attending to the picturesque points of view, the abrupt
inequalities of the surface. He contemplates the passions and habits of
men, not in their extremes but the first elements; their follies and vices,
not at their height, with all their embossed seeds upon their heads, but
as lurking in embryo, the seeds of the disorder inwoven with our very
constitution. He only sympathizes with those simple forms of feeling
which mingle at once with his own identity, or with the stream of
general humanity . . . An intense intellectual egotism swallows up
everything . . . the evident scope and tendency of Mr Wordsworth's
mind is the reverse of dramatic. It resists all change of character, all
variety of scenery, all the hustle, machinery, and pantomime of the
stage or of real life – whatever might relieve or relax or change the
direction of its own activity, jealous of all competition. The power of
his mind preys upon itself. It is as if there were nothing but himself and
the universe. He lives in the busy solitude of his own heart; in the deep
silence of thought. His imagination lends life and feeling only to the
'bare trees and mountains bare', peoples the viewless tracts of air, and
converses with the silent clouds.

*   *   *

We take Mr Wordsworth himself for a great poet, a fine moralist, and
a deep philosopher; but if he insists on introducing us to a friend of his,

a parish clerk or the barber of the village, who is as wise as himself, we must be excused if we draw back with some little want of cordial faith.

FRANCIS JEFFREY: FROM A REVIEW OF *THE EXCURSION*, *EDINBURGH REVIEW* (NOVEMBER 1814)

Jeffrey's is one of the most famous opening sentences in reviewing history. Again, as with his review of *Poems in Two Volumes* (1807), Jeffrey's criticism of *The Excursion* was influentially damning. He considers here what retreat and seclusion have done to Wordsworth's poetry.

This will never do.

*   *   *

Long habits of seclusion, and an excessive ambition of originality, can alone account for the disproportion which seems to exist between this author's taste and his genius; or for the devotion with which he has sacrificed so many precious gifts at the shrine of those paltry idols which he has set up for himself among his lakes and his mountains. Solitary musings, amidst such scenes, might no doubt be expected to nurse up the mind to the majesty of poetical conception – (though it is remarkable, that all the greater poets lived, or had lived, in the full current of society). – But the collision of equal minds – the admonition of prevailing impressions – seems necessary to reduce its redundancies, and repress that tendency to extravagance or puerility, into which the self-indulgence and self-admiration of genius is so apt to be betrayed, when it is allowed to wanton, without awe or restraint, in the triumph and delight of its own intoxication. That its flights should be graceful and glorious in the eyes of men, it seems almost to be necessary that they should be made in the consciousness that men's eyes are to behold them, and that the inward transport and vigour by which they are inspired, should be tempered by an occasional reference to what will be thought of them by those ultimate dispensers of glory . . . if Mr Wordsworth, instead of confining himself almost entirely to the society of the dalesmen and cottagers, and little children, who form the subjects of his book, had condescended to mingle a little more with the people that were to read and judge of it, we cannot help thinking, that its texture would have been considerably improved. At least it appears to us to be absolutely impossible, that any one who had lived or mixed familiarly with men of literature and ordinary judgement in poetry (of course we exclude the coadjutors and disciples of his own school), could ever have fallen into such gross faults, or so long mistaken them for beauties.

S. T. COLERIDGE: FROM *BIOGRAPHIA LITERARIA*,
CHAPTER XVII (1817)

Coleridge takes issue with Wordsworth's theory of poetic language.

My own differences from certain supposed parts of Mr Wordsworth's theory ground themselves on the assumption that his words had been rightly interpreted, as purporting that the proper diction for poetry in general consists altogether in a language taken, with due exceptions, from the mouths of men in real life, a language which actually constitutes the natural conversation of men under the influence of natural feelings. My objection is, first, that in any sense this rule is applicable only to certain classes of poetry; secondly, that even to these classes it is not applicable, except in such a sense as hath never by any one (as far as I know or have read) been denied or doubted; and, lastly, that as far as, and in that degree in which it is practicable, it is yet as a *rule* useless, if not injurious, and therefore either need not or ought not to be practised.

*   *   *

Now it is clear to me that in the most interesting of the poems in which the author is more or less dramatic, as the 'Brothers', 'Michael', 'Ruth', the 'Mad Mother', etc., the persons introduced are by no means taken from low or rustic life in the common acceptation of those words; and it is not less clear that the sentiments and language, as far as they can be conceived to have been really transferred from the minds and conversation of such persons, are attributable to causes and circumstances not necessarily connected with 'their occupations and abode'. The thoughts, feelings, language and manners of the shepherd-farmers in the vales of Cumberland and Westmoreland, as far as they are actually adopted in those poems, may be accounted for from causes which will and do produce the same results in every state of life, whether in town or country.

*   *   *

. . . a rustic's language, purified from all provincialism and grossness, and so far re-constructed as to be made consistent with the rules of grammar (which are in essence no other than the laws of universal logic applied to psychological materials), will not differ from the language of any other man of common-sense, however learned or refined he may be, except as far as the notions which the rustic has to convey are fewer and more indiscriminate. This will become still clearer if we add the consideration (equally important though less obvious) that the rustic, from the more imperfect development of his faculties and from the lower state of their cultivation, aims almost solely to convey insulated facts, either those of his scanty experience or his traditional belief; while the educated man chiefly seeks to discover and express those connections of things, or those relative bearings of fact to fact, from which some more or less general law is deducible.

*   *   *

As little can I agree with the assertion that from the objects with which the rustic hourly communicates the best part of language is formed. For first, if to communicate with an object implies such an acquaintance with it as renders it capable of being discriminately reflected on, the distinct knowledge of an uneducated rustic would furnish a very scanty vocabulary. The few things and modes of action requisite for his bodily conveniences would alone be individualized; while all the rest of nature would be expressed by a small number of confused general terms. Secondly, I deny that the words and combinations of words derived from the objects with which the rustic is familiar, whether with distinct or confused knowledge, can be justly said to form the best part of language. It is more than probable that many classes of the brute creation possess discriminating sounds by which they can convey to each other notices of such objects as concern their food, shelter or safety. Yet we hesitate to call the aggregate of such sounds a language otherwise than metaphorically. The best part of human language, properly so called, is derived from reflections on the acts of the mind itself. It is formed by a voluntary appropriation of fixed symbols to internal acts, to processes and results of imagination, the greater part of which have no place in the consciousness of uneducated man; though in civilized society, by imitation and passive remembrance of what they hear from their religious instructors and other superiors, the most uneducated share in the harvest which they neither sowed or reaped.

*   *   *

Here let me be permitted to remind the reader that the positions which I controvert are contained in the sentences – 'a selection of the real language of men'; – 'the language of these men (i.e. men in low and rustic life) I propose to myself to imitate, and as far as possible to adopt the very language of men'. 'Between the language of prose and that of metrical composition there neither is, nor can be any essential difference.' It is against these exclusively that my opposition is directed.

I object, in the very first instance, to an equivocation in the use of the word '*real*'. Every man's language varies according to the extent of his knowledge, the activity of his faculties and the depth or quickness of his feelings. Every man's language has, first, its individualities; secondly, the common properties of the class to which he belongs; and thirdly, words and phrases of universal use. The language of Hooker, Bacon, Bishop Taylor and Burke differs from the common language of the learned class only by the superior number and novelty of the thoughts and relations which they had to convey. The language of Algernon Sidney differs not at all from that which every well educated gentleman would wish to write . . . Neither one or the other differ half as much from the general language of cultivated society as the language of Mr Wordsworth's homeliest composition differs from that of a common peasant. For 'real' therefore we must substitute *ordinary*, or *lingua communis*. And this, we have proved, is no more to be found in the phraseology of low and rustic life than in that of any other class. Omit the peculiarities of each, and the result of course must be common to all. And assuredly the omissions and changes to be made in the language of rustics before it could be transferred to any species of poem, except the drama or other professed imitation, are at least as numerous and weighty as would be required in adapting to the same purpose the ordinary language of tradesmen and manufacturers. Not to mention that the language so highly extolled by Mr Wordsworth varies in every county, nay in every village, according to the accidental character of the clergyman, the existence or non-existence of schools; or even, perhaps, as the exciseman, publican or barber happen to be, or not to be, zealous politicians and readers of the weekly newspaper *pro bono publico*.

* * *

Neither is the case rendered at all more tenable by the addition of the words 'in a state of excitement'. For the nature of a man's words, when he is strongly affected by joy, grief or anger, must necessarily depend on the number and quality of the general truths, conceptions and images, and of the words expressing them, with which his mind had been previously stored.

S. T. COLERIDGE: FROM *BIOGRAPHIA LITERARIA*,
CHAPTER XXII (1817)

Coleridge considers the strengths and weaknesses of Wordsworth's poetry.

The first *characteristic, though only occasional* defect, which I appear to myself to find in these poems is the *inconstancy* of the *style*. Under this name I refer to the sudden and unprepared transitions from lines or sentences of peculiar felicity (at all events striking and original) to a style, not only unimpassioned but undistinguished. He sinks too often and too abruptly to that style, which I should place in the second division of language, dividing it into the three species; *first*, that which is peculiar to poetry; *second*, that which is only proper in prose; and *third*, the neutral or common to both . . .

*   *   *

The second defect I can generalize with tolerable accuracy, if the reader will pardon an uncouth and new coined word. There is, I should say, not seldom a *matter-of-factness* in certain poems. This may be divided into, *first*, a laborious minuteness and fidelity in the representation of objects, and their positions, as they appeared to the poet himself; *secondly*, the insertion of accidental circumstances, in order to the full explanation of his living characters, their dispositions and actions; which circumstances might be necessary to establish the probability of a statement in real life, where nothing is taken for granted by the hearer; but appear superfluous in poetry, where the reader is willing to believe for his own sake . . .

The second division respects an apparent minute adherence to *matter-of-fact* in character and incidents; *a biographical* attention to probability, and an *anxiety* of explanation and retrospect. Under this head I shall deliver, with no feigned diffidence, the results of my best reflection on the great point of controversy between Mr Wordsworth and his objectors; namely, on *the choice of his characters*. I have already declared, and, I trust justified, my utter dissent from the mode of argument which his critics have hitherto employed. To *their* question, – 'Why did you chuse such a character, or a character from such a rank of life?' – the poet might in my opinion fairly retort: 'Why with the conception of my character did you make wilful choice of mean or ludicrous associations not furnished by me, but supplied from your own sickly and fastidious feelings?' How was it, indeed, probable, that such arguments could have any weight with an author, whose plan, whose guiding principle, and main object it was to attack and subdue that state of association, which leads us to place the chief value on those things on which man *differs* from man, and to forget or disregard the high dignities, which belong to *Human Nature*, the sense and the feeling, which *may* be, and *ought* to be, found in *all* ranks?

*   *   *

But yet I object, nevertheless, and for the following reasons. First, because the object in view, as an *immediate* object, belongs to the moral philosopher, and would be pursued, not only more appropriately, but in my opinion with far greater probability of success, in sermons or moral essays, than in an elevated poem. It seems, indeed, to destroy the main fundamental distinction, not only between a *poem* and *prose*, but even between philosophy and works of fiction, inasmuch as it proposes *truth* for its immediate object, instead of *pleasure* . . .

Third; an undue predilection for the *dramatic* form in certain poems, from which one or other of two evils result. Either the thoughts and diction are different from that of the poet, and then there arises an incongruity of style; or they are the same and indistinguishable, and then it presents a species of ventriloquism, where two are represented as talking, while in truth one man only speaks.

The fourth class of defects is closely connected with the former . . . In this class, I comprise occasional prolixity, repetition, and an eddying, instead of progression, of thought.

*   *   *

Fifth and last; thoughts and images too great for the subject. This is an approximation to what might be called *mental* bombast, as distinguished from verbal: for, as in the latter there is a disproportion of the expressions to the thoughts, so in this there is a disproportion of thought to the circumstance and occasion.

*   *   *

The last instance of this defect, (for I know no other than these already cited) is from the Ode . . . where, speaking of a child, 'a six years' darling of a pigmy size', he thus addresses him [quotes lines 110–19 of the Ode ('There was a time')].

Now here, not to stop at the daring spirit of metaphor which connects the epithets 'deaf and silent', with the apostrophised *eye*: or (if we refer it to the preceding word, philosopher) the faulty and equivocal syntax of the passage; and without examining the propriety of making a 'master *brood* o'er a slave', or the *day* brood *at all*; we will merely ask, what does all this mean? In what sense is a child of that age a *philosopher*? In what sense does he *read* 'the eternal deep?' In what sense is he declared to be '*for ever haunted*' by the Supreme Being? or so inspired as to deserve the splendid titles of a *mighty prophet*, a *blessed seer*? By reflection? by knowledge? by conscious intuition? or by *any* form or modification of consciousness? These would be tidings indeed; but such as would pre-suppose an immediate revelation to the inspired communicator, and require miracles to authenticate his inspiration.

* * *

To these defects which, as appears by the extracts, are only occasional, I may oppose with far less fear of encountering the dissent of any candid and intelligent reader, the following (for the most part correspondent) excellencies. First, an austere purity of language both grammatically and logically; in short a perfect appropriateness of the words to the meaning.

* * *

In poetry, in which every line, every phrase, may pass the ordeal of deliberation and deliberate choice, it is possible, and barely possible, to attain that ultimatum which I have ventured to propose as the infallible test of a blameless style; namely; its *untranslatableness* in words of the same language without injury to the meaning. Be it observed, however, that I include in the *meaning* of a word not only its correspondent object, but likewise all the associations which it recalls. For language is framed to convey not the object alone, but likewise the character, mood and intentions of the person who is representing it.

* * *

The second characteristic excellence of Mr W's works is: a correspondent weight and sanity of the Thoughts and Sentiments, – won, not from books; but – from the poet's own meditative observation. They are *fresh* and have the dew upon them [quotes last 4 lines of 'Simon Lee'].

* * *

Third (and wherein he soars far above Daniel) the sinewy strength and originality of single lines and paragraphs: the frequent *curiosa felicitas* of his diction, of which I need not here give specimens, having anticipated them in a preceding page. This beauty, and as eminently characteristic of Wordsworth's poetry, his rudest assailants have felt themselves compelled to acknowledge and admire.

Fourth; the perfect truth of nature in his images and descriptions as taken immediately from nature, and proving a long and genial intimacy with the very spirit which gives the physiognomic expression to all the works of nature. Like a green field reflected in a calm and perfectly transparent lake, the image is distinguished from the reality only by its greater softness and lustre. Like the moisture or the polish on a pebble, genius neither distorts nor false-colours its objects; but on the contrary brings out many a vein and many a tint, which escape the eye of common observation, thus raising to the rank of gems, what had been often kicked away by the hurrying foot of the traveller on the dusty high road of custom.

*   *   *

Fifth: a meditative pathos, a union of deep and subtle thought with sensibility; a sympathy with man as man; the sympathy indeed of a contemplator, rather than a fellow-sufferer or co-mate, (spectator, *haud particeps*) but of a contemplator, from whose view no difference of rank conceals the sameness of the nature; no injuries of wind or weather, of toil, or even of ignorance, wholly disguise the human face divine. The superscription and the image of the Creator still remain legible to *him* under the dark lines, with which guilt or calamity had cancelled or cross-barred it. Here the man and the poet lose and find themselves in each other, the one as glorified, the latter as substantiated. In this mild and philosophic pathos, Wordsworth appears to me without a compeer. Such he *is*: so he *writes*.

*   *   *

Last, and pre-eminently, I challenge for this poet the gift of IMAGINATION in the highest and strictest sense of the word. In the play of *Fancy*, Wordsworth, to my feelings, is not always graceful, and sometimes *recondite*. The *likeness* is occasionally too strange, or demands too peculiar a point of view, or is such as appears the creature of predetermined research, rather than spontaneous presentation. Indeed his fancy seldom displays itself, as mere and unmodified fancy. But in imaginative power, he stands nearest of all modern writers to Shakespear and Milton; and yet in a kind perfectly unborrowed and his own.

JOHN KEATS: FROM A LETTER TO JOHN HAMILTON REYNOLDS (3 MAY 1818)

Keats considers the differences between Wordsworth and Milton.

... here I have nothing but surmises, from an uncertainty whether Milton's apparently less anxiety for Humanity proceeds from his seeing further or no than Wordsworth: And whether Wordsworth has in truth epic passion, and martyrs himself to the human heart, the main region of his song – In regard to his genius alone – we find what he says true as far as we have experienced and we can judge no further but by larger experience – for axioms in philosophy are not axioms until they are proved upon our pulses. We read fine things but never feel them to the full until we have gone the same steps as the Author . . .

I compare human life to a large Mansion of Many Apartments, two of which I can only describe, the doors of the rest being as yet shut upon me. The first we step into we call the infant or thoughtless Chamber, in which we remain as long as we do not think – We remain there a long while, and notwithstanding the doors of the second Chamber remain wide open, showing a bright appearance, we care not to hasten to it; but are at length imperceptibly impelled by the awakening of the thinking principle within us – we no sooner get into the second Chamber, which I shall call the Chamber of Maiden Thought, than we become intoxicated with the light and the atmosphere, we see nothing but pleasant wonders, and think of delaying there for ever in delight: However among the effects this breathing is father of is that tremendous one of sharpening one's vision into the heart and nature of Man – of convincing one's nerves that the world is full of Misery and Heartbreak, Pain, Sickness and oppression – whereby this Chamber of Maiden Thought becomes gradually darken'd and at the same time on all sides of it many *doors* are set open – but all dark – all leading to dark passages – We see not the balance of good and evil. We are in a Mist. *We* are now in that state – We feel the 'burden of the Mystery'. To this Point was Wordsworth come, as far as I can conceive when he wrote 'Tintern Abbey' and it seems to me that his Genius is explorative of those dark Passages. Now if we live, and go on thinking, we too shall explore them – he is a Genius and superior to us, in so far as he can, more than we, make discoveries, and shed a light in them – Here I must think Wordsworth is deeper than Milton – though I think it has depended more upon the general and gregarious advance of intellect, than individual greatness of Mind.

JOHN KEATS: FROM A LETTER TO RICHARD WOODHOUSE
(27 OCTOBER 1818)

In this famous letter, Keats considers the nature of 'the poetical character', contrasting the poet of 'the wordsworthian or egotistical sublime' (note the 'w' in the lower case) with the poet who allows his own identity to merge with, to invade, that of others and of other things.

The best answer I can give you is in a clerklike manner to make some observations on two principle points, which seem to point like indices into the midst of the whole pro and con, about genius, and views and atchievements and ambition and cœtera. 1st As to the poetical Character itself, (I mean that sort of which, if I am any thing, I am a Member; that sort distinguished from the wordsworthian or egotistical sublime; which is a thing per se and stands alone) it is not itself – it has no self – it is every thing and nothing – It has no character – it enjoys light and shade; it lives in gusto, be it foul or fair, high or low, rich or poor, mean or elevated – It has as much delight in conceiving an Iago as an Imogen. What shocks the virtuous philosopher, delights the camelion Poet. It does no harm from its relish of the dark side of things any more than from its taste for the bright one; because they both end in speculation. A Poet is the most unpoetical of any thing in existence; because he has no Identity – he is continually [informing] – and filling some other Body – The Sun, the Moon, the Sea and Men and Women who are creatures of impulse are poetical and have about them an unchangeable attribute – the poet has none; no identity – he is certainly the most unpoetical of all God's Creatures.

WILLIAM HAZLITT: FROM *LECTURES ON THE ENGLISH POETS* (1818)

Hazlitt's assessment of Wordsworth is appreciative, though Wordsworth is certainly not 'sacred from criticism'.

Mr Wordsworth is at the head of that which has been denominated the Lake school of poetry; a school which, with all my respect for it, I do not think sacred from criticism or exempt from faults . . . This school of poetry had its origin in the French revolution, or rather in those sentiments and opinions which produced that revolution . . . They founded the new school on a principle of sheer humanity, on pure nature void of art . . . They took the same method in their new-fangled 'metre ballad-mongering' scheme, which Rousseau did in his prose paradoxes – of exciting attention by reversing the established standards of opinion and estimation in the world. They were for bringing poetry back to its primitive simplicity and state of nature, as he was for bringing society back to the savage state . . . A thorough adept in this school of poetry and philanthropy is jealous of all excellence but his own. He does not even like to share his reputation with his subject; for he would have it all proceed from his own power and originality of mind. Such a one is slow to admire any thing that is admirable; feels no interest in what is most interesting to others, no grandeur in anything grand, no beauty in anything beautiful. He tolerates only what he himself creates; he sympathizes only with what can enter into no competition with him, with 'the bare trees and mountains bare, and grass in the green field'. He sees nothing but himself and the universe.

He hates all greatness and all pretensions to it, whether well or ill-founded. His egotism is in some respects a madness; for he scorns even the admiration of himself, thinking it a presumption in any one to suppose that he has taste or sense enough to understand him. He hates all science and all art; he hates chemistry, he hates conchology; he hates Voltaire; he hates Sir Isaac Newton; he hates wisdom; he hates wit; he hates mataphysics, which he says are unintelligible, and yet he would be thought to understand them; he hates prose; he hates all poetry but his own . . .

SHELLEY: FROM *PETER BELL THE THIRD* (COMPOSED 1819)

A demonic parody of Wordsworth's *Peter Bell*. For Peter, read Wordsworth.

PART THE FOURTH

SIN

Lo, Peter in Hell's Grosvenor Square,
   A footman in the Devil's service!
And the misjudging world would swear
That every man in service there
   To virtue would prefer vice.

But Peter, though now damned, was not
   What Peter was before damnation.
Men oftentimes prepare a lot
Which ere it finds them, is not what
   Suits with their genuine station.

All things that Peter saw and felt
   Had a peculiar aspect to him;
And when they came within the belt
Of his own nature, seemed to melt,
   Like cloud to cloud, into him.

And so the outward world uniting
   To that within him, he became
Considerably uninviting
To those who, meditation slighting,
   Were moulded in a different frame.

And he scorned them, and they scorned him
   And he scorned all they did; and they
Did all that men of their own trim
Are wont to do to please their whim,
   Drinking, lying, swearing, play.

*   *   *

He had a mind which was somehow
   At once circumference and centre
Of all he might or feel or know;
Nothing went ever out, although
   Something did ever enter.

He had as much imagination
   As a pint-pot; – he never could
Fancy another situation,
From which to dart his contemplation,
   Than that wherein he stood.

Yet his was individual mind,
   And new created all he saw
In a new manner, and refined
Those new creations, and combined
   Them, by a master-spirit's law.

Thus – though unimaginative –
   An apprehension clear, intense,
Of his mind's work, had made alive
The things it wrought on; I believe
   Wakening a sort of thought in sense.

But from the first 'twas Peter's drift
   To be a kind of moral eunuch,
He touched the hem of Nature's shift,
Felt faint – and never dared uplift
   The closest, all-concealing tunic.

*   *   *

At night he oft would start and wake
   Like a lover, and began
In a wild measure songs to make
On moor, and glen, and rocky lake,
   And on the heart of man–

And on the universal sky –
   And the wide earth's bosom green, –
And the sweet, strange mystery
Of what beyond these things may lie,
   And yet remain unseen.

For in his thoughts he visited
   The spots in which, ere dead and damned,
He his wayward life had led;
Yet knew not whence the thoughts were fed
   Which thus his fancy crammed.

And these obscure remembrances
   Stirred such harmony in Peter,
That, whensoever he should please,
He could speak of rocks and trees
   In poetic metre.

For though it was without a sense
   Of memory, yet he remembered well
Many a ditch and quick-set fence;
Of lakes he had intelligence,
   He knew something of heath and fell.

He had also dim recollections
   Of pedlars tramping on their rounds;
Milk-pans and pails; and odd collections
Of saws, and proverbs; and reflections
   Old parsons make in burying-grounds.

But Peter's verse was clear, and came
   Announcing from the frozen hearth
Of a cold age, that none might tame
The soul of that diviner flame
   It augured to the Earth:

Like gentle rains, on the dry plains,
   Making that green which late was gray,
Or like the sudden moon, that stains
Some gloomy chamber's window-panes
   With a broad light like day.

For language was in Peter's hand
    Like clay while he was yet a potter;
And he made songs for all the land,
Sweet both to feel and understand,
    As pipkins late to mountain Cotter.

*   *   *

When Peter's next new book found vent,
    The Devil to all the first Reviews
A copy of it slyly sent,
With five-pound note as compliment,
    And this short notice – 'Pray abuse.'

BYRON: FROM *DON JUAN*, CANTO III (1821)

Wordsworth's last quarto, by the way, is bigger
    Than any since the birthday of typography;
A drowsy frowzy poem, call'd the 'Excursion',
Writ in a manner which is my aversion.

95

He there builds up a formidable dyke
    Between his own and others' intellect;
But Wordsworth's poem, and his followers, like
    Joanna Southcote's Shiloh, and her sect,
Are things which in this century don't strike
    The public mind, so few are the elect;
And the new births of both their stale virginities
Have proved but dropsies, taken for divinities.

*   *   *

98

We learn from Horace, Homer sometimes sleeps;
    We feel without him: Wordsworth sometimes wakes,
To show with what complacency he creeps,
    With his dear '*Waggoners*', around his lakes;
He wishes for 'a boat' to sail the deeps –
    Of ocean? – No, of air; and then he makes
Another outcry for 'a little boat',
And drivels seas to set it well afloat.

*   *   *

100

'Pedlars', and 'boats', and 'waggons'! Oh! ye shades
    Of Pope and Dryden, are we come to this?
That trash of such sort not alone evades
    Contempt, but from the bathos' vast abyss
Floats scumlike uppermost, and these Jack Cades
    Of sense and song above your graves may hiss –
The 'little boatman' and his 'Peter Bell'
Can sneer at him who drew 'Achitophel'!

WILLIAM HAZLITT: FROM *THE SPIRIT OF THE AGE* (1825)

Mr Wordsworth's genius is a pure emanation of the Spirit of the Age. Had he lived in any other period of the world, he would never have been heard of.

*　　*　　*

It is one of the innovations of the time. It partakes of, and is carried along with, the revolutionary movement of our age: the political changes of the day were the model on which he formed and conducted his poetical experiments. His Muse (it cannot be denied, and without this we cannot explain its character at all) is a levelling one. It proceeds on a principle of equality, and strives to reduce all things to the same standard. It is distinguished by a proud humility. It relies upon its own resources, and disdains external show and relief. It takes the commonest events and objects, as a test to prove that nature is always interesting from its inherent truth and beauty, without any of the ornaments of dress or pomp of circumstances to set it off. Hence the unaccountable mixture of seeming simplicity and real abstruseness in the *Lyrical Ballads*. Fools have laughed at, wise men scarcely understand, them.

*　　*　　*

His popular, inartificial style gets rid (at a blow) of all the trappings of verse, of all the high places of poetry: 'the cloud-capt towers, the solemn temples, the gorgeous palaces', are swept to the ground, and 'like the baseless fabric of a vision, leave not a wreck behind'. All the traditions of learning, all the superstitions of age, are obliterated and effaced. We begin *de novo* on a *tabula rasa* of poetry.

*　　*　　*

There is a lofty philosophic tone, a thoughtful humanity, infused into his pastoral vein. Remote from the passions and events of the great world, he has communicated interest and dignity to the primal movements of the heart of man, and ingrafted his own conscious reflections on the casual thoughts of hinds and shepherds. Nursed amidst the grandeur of mountain scenery, he has stooped to have a nearer view of the daisy under his feet, or plucked a branch of white-thorn from the spray: but, in describing it, his mind seems imbued with the majesty and solemnity of the objects around him. The tall rock lifts its head in the erectness of his spirit; the cataract roars in the sound of his verse and in its dim and mysterious meaning, the mists seem to gather in the hollows of Helvellyn, and the forked Skiddaw hovers in the distance.

*   *   *

Lord Byron we have called, according to the old proverb, 'the spoiled child of fortune': Mr Wordsworth might plead, in mitigation of some peculiarities, that he is 'the spoiled child of disappointment'. We are convinced, if he had been early a popular poet, he would have borne his honours meekly, and would have been a person of great *bonhomie* and frankness of disposition. But the sense of injustice and of undeserved ridicule sours the temper and narrows the views. To have produced works of genius, and to find them neglected or treated with scorn, is one of the heaviest trials of human patience. We exaggerate our own merits when they are denied by others, and are apt to grudge and cavil at every particle of praise bestowed on those to whom we feel a conscious superiority. In mere self-defence we turn against the world when it turns against us.

LORD MACAULAY: FROM HIS ESSAY ON MOORE'S
LIFE OF BYRON (1831)

Lord Byron was . . . the mediator between two generations, between two hostile poetical sects. Though always sneering at Mr Words-worth, he was yet, though perhaps unconsciously, the interpreter between Mr Wordsworth and the multitude. In the *Lyrical Ballads* and the *Excursion* Mr Wordsworth appeared as the high priest of a worship, of which nature was the idol. No poems have ever indicated a more exquisite perception of the beauty of the outer world or a more passionate love and reverence for that beauty. Yet they were not popular; and it is not likely that they ever will be popular as the poetry of Sir Walter Scott is popular. The feeling which pervaded them was too deep for general sympathy. Their style was often too mysterious for general comprehension. They made a few esoteric disciples, and many scoffers. Lord Byron founded what may be called an exoteric Lake school; and all the readers of verse in England, we might say in Europe, hastened to sit at his feet. What Mr Wordsworth had said like a recluse, Lord Byron said like a man of the world, with less profound feeling, but with more perspicuity, energy, and conciseness. We would refer our readers to the last two cantos of *Childe Harold* and to *Manfred*, in proof of these observations.

Victorian Attitudes, 1836–1891

EDGAR ALLAN POE: FROM 'LETTER TO B—' (JULY 1836)

As to Wordsworth, I have no faith in him. That he had, in youth, the feelings of a poet I believe – for there are glimpses of extreme delicacy in his writings – (and delicacy is the poet's own kingdom – his *El Dorado*) – but they have the appearance of a better day recollected; and glimpses, at best, are little evidence of present poetic fire – we know that a few straggling flowers spring up daily in the crevices of the glacier.

He was to blame in wearing away his youth in contemplation with the end of poetizing in his manhood. With the increase of his judgment the light which should make it apparent has faded away. His judgment consequently is too correct.

*   *   *

The long wordy discussions by which he tries to reason us into admiration of his poetry, speak very little in his favor: they are full of such assertions as this – (I have opened one of his volumes at random) 'Of genius the only proof is the act of doing well what is worthy to be done, and what was never done before' – indeed! then it follows that in doing what is *un*worthy to be done, or what *has* been done before, no genius can be evinced: yet the picking of pockets is an unworthy act, pockets have been picked time immemorial, and Barrington, the pick-pocket, in point of genius, would have thought hard of a comparison with William Wordsworth, the poet.

Again – in estimating the merit of certain poems, whether they be Ossian's or M'Pherson's, can surely be of little consequence, yet, in order to prove their worthlessness, Mr W has expended many pages in the controversy . . . that he may bear down every argument in favor of these poems, he triumphantly drags forward a passage, in his abomination of which he expects the reader to sympathize. It is the beginning of the epic poem '*Temora*'. 'The blue waves of Ullin roll in light; the green hills are covered with day; trees shake their dusky

heads in the breeze.' And this – this gorgeous, yet simple imagery –
where all is alive and panting with immortality – this – William
Wordsworth, the author of Peter Bell, has *selected* for his contempt.
We shall see what better he, in his own person, has to offer . . .

> The dew was falling fast, the – stars began to blink,
> I heard a voice, it said – drink, pretty creature, drink;
> And looking o'er the hedge, be – fore me I espied
> A snow-white mountain lamb with a – maiden at its side,
> No other sheep were near, the lamb was all alone,
> And by a slender cord was – tether'd to a stone.

Now we have no doubt this is all true; we *will* believe it, indeed we will,
Mr W. Is it sympathy for the sheep you wish to excite? I love a sheep
from the bottom of my heart.

ROBERT BROWNING: FROM
DRAMATIC ROMANCES AND LYRICS (1845)

In 1813 Wordsworth became Distributor of Stamps for Westmore-
land – an employee of the government – and received a Civil List
Pension in 1842. The following year he was Poet Laureate. Here,
politics and poetry meet as Browning laments Wordsworth's political
'apostasy', the change from youth's revolutionary ardour to the
conservative stance of manhood and old age.

THE LOST LEADER

I

> Just for a handful of silver he left us,
>   Just for a riband to stick in his coat –
> Found the one gift of which fortune bereft us,
>   Lost all the others she lets us devote;
> They, with the gold to give, doled him out silver,
>   So much was theirs who so little allowed:
> How all our copper had gone for his service!
>   Rags – were they purple, his heart had been proud!
> We that had loved him so, followed him, honoured him,
>   Lived in his mild and magnificent eye,
> Learned his great language, caught his clear accents,
>   Made him our pattern to live and to die!
> Shakespeare was of us, Milton was for us,
>   Burns, Shelley, were with us, – they watch from their
>   graves!
> He alone breaks from the van and the freemen,
>   – He alone sinks to the rear and the slaves!

THOMAS DE QUINCEY: FROM HIS ESSAY 'ON WORDSWORTH'S POETRY' (1845)

De Quincey considers some of the problems associated with Wordsworth's theory of poetic diction.

... there is a challenge of a separate nature to the curiosity of the readers, in the remarkable contrast between the first stage of Wordsworth's acceptation with the public and that which he enjoys at present. One original obstacle to the favourable impression of the Wordsworthian poetry, and an obstacle purely self-created, was his theory of Poetic Diction. The diction itself, without the theory, was of less consequence; for the mass of readers would have been too blind or too careless to notice it. But the preface to the second edition of his Poems (2 vols. 1799–1800) compelled all readers to notice it. Nothing more injudicious was ever done by man. An unpopular truth would, at any rate, have been a bad inauguration for what, on *other* accounts, the author had announced as 'an experiment'. His poetry was already, and confessedly, an experiment as regarded the quality of the subjects selected, and as regarded the mode of treating them. That was surely trial enough for the reader's untrained sensibilities, without the unpopular novelty besides as to the quality of the diction. But, in the meantime, this novelty, besides being unpopular, was also in part false; it was true, and it was *not* true. And it was not true in a double way. Stating broadly, and allowing it to be taken for his meaning, that the diction of ordinary life (in his own words, 'the very language of men') was the proper diction for poetry, the writer meant no such thing; for only a *part* of this diction, according to his own subsequent restriction, was available for such a use. And, secondly, as his own subsequent practice showed, even this part was available only for peculiar classes of poetry. In his own exquisite '*Laodamia*', in his 'Sonnets', in his 'Excursion', few are his obligations to the idiomatic language of life, as distinguished from that of books, or of prescriptive usage. Coleridge remarked, justly, that the 'Excursion' bristles beyond most poems with what are called 'dictionary' words; that is, polysyllabic words of Latin or Greek origin. And so it must ever be in meditative poetry upon solemn philosophic themes.

*　　*　　*

In Pope, and sometimes in Dryden, there is much of the unfeeling and the prescriptive diction which Wordsworth denounced. During the eighty years between 1660 and 1740, grew up that scrofulous taint in our diction, which was denounced by Wordsworth, as technically received for 'poetic language' ... Spenser, Shakspere, the Bible of

1610, and Milton – how say you, William Wordsworth – are these sound and true as to diction, or are they not? If you say they *are*, then what is it that you are proposing to change? What room for a revolution? Would you, as Sancho says, have 'better bread than is made of wheat'? But, if you say *No*, they are *not* sound, then, indeed, you open a fearful range to your own artillery, but in a war greater than you could, by possibility, have contemplated. In the first case, that is, if the leading classics of the English literature are, in quality of diction and style, loyal to the canons of sound taste, then you cut away the *locus standi* for yourself as a reformer: the reformation applies only to secondary and recent abuses. In the second case, if they also are faulty, you undertake an *onus* of hostility so vast that you will be found fighting against stars.

MATTHEW ARNOLD: FROM 'MEMORIAL VERSES' (1850)

Like J. S. Mill (cited hereafter), Arnold in this poem, written at the time of Wordsworth's funeral, emphasises the 'healing powers' of Wordsworth's poetry.

> Goethe in Weimar sleeps, and Greece,
> Long since, saw Byron's struggle cease.
> But one such death remained to come;
> The last poetic voice is dumb –
> We stand to-day by Wordsworth's tomb.

> *   *   *

> And Wordsworth! – Ah, pale ghosts, rejoice!
> For never has such soothing voice
> Been to your shadowy world convey'd,
> Since erst, at morn, some wandering shade
> Heard the clear song of Orpheus come
> Through Hades, and the mournful gloom.
> Wordsworth has gone from us – and ye,
> Ah, may ye feel his voice as we!
> He too upon a wintry clime
> Had fallen – on this iron time
> Of doubts, disputes, distractions, fears.
> He found us when the age had bound
> Our souls in its benumbing round;
> He spoke, and loosed our heart in tears.
> He laid us as we lay at birth
> On the cool flowery lap of earth,
> Smiles broke from us and we had ease;
> The hills were round us, and the breeze

Went o'er the sun-lit fields again;
Our foreheads felt the wind and rain.
Our youth return'd; for there was shed
On spirits that had long been dead,
Spirits dried up and closely furled,
The freshness of the early world.

Ah! since dark days still bring to light
Man's prudence and man's fiery might,
Time may restore us in his course
Goethe's sage mind and Byron's force;
But where will Europe's latter hour
Again find Wordsworth's healing power?
Others will teach us how to dare,
And against fear our breast to steel;
Others will strengthen us to bear –
But who, ah! who, will make us feel?
The cloud of mortal destiny,
Others will front it fearlessly –
But who, like him, will put it by?

Keep fresh the grass upon his grave,
O Rotha, with thy living wave!
Sing him thy best! for few or none
Hears thy voice right, now he is gone.

R. W. EMERSON: FROM THE ESSAY 'LITERATURE' FROM *ENGLISH TRAITS* (1865)

The exceptional fact of the period is the genius of Wordsworth. He had no master but nature and solitude. 'He wrote a poem,' says Landor, 'without the aid of war.' His verse is the voice of sanity in a worldly and ambitious age. One regrets that his temperament was not more liquid and musical. He has written longer than he was inspired. But for the rest, he has no competitor.

ARTHUR HUGH CLOUGH: FROM 'LECTURE ON THE POETRY OF WORDSWORTH', *POETRY AND PROSE REMAINS* (1869)

Clough's lecture, not bowing to what one might call the Victorian Wordsworthian orthodoxy (which chose to ignore so many of the *problems* associated with an appraisal of the man and poet, focusing rather on the 'wisdom and truth' of his philosophy) emphasises some of the limitations of the poetry.

> Unless above himself he can
> Erect himself, how poor a thing is Man.

Unless above himself, how poor a thing; yet, if beyond and outside of his world, how useless and purposeless a thing. This also must be remembered. And I cannot help thinking that there is in Wordsworth's poems something of a spirit of withdrawal and seclusion from, and even evasion of, the actual world. In his own quiet rural sphere it is true he did fairly enough look at things as they were; he did not belie his own senses, nor pretend to recognize in outward things what really was not in them. But his sphere was a small one; the objects he lived among unimportant and petty. Retiring early from all conflict and even contact with the busy world, he shut himself from the elements which it was his business to encounter and master. This gives to his writings, compared with those of Scott and Byron, an appearance of sterility and unreality. He cannot indeed, be said, like Cowper, to be an indoors poet; but he is a poet rather of a country house or a picturesque tour, not of life and business, action and fact.

J. S. MILL: FROM HIS *AUTOBIOGRAPHY* (1873)

Mill charts his mental crisis of 1826, which resulted in a reconsideration of his own beliefs and those of the Benthamites, and describes the healing power he found in Wordsworth's *Poems*, 1815.

This state of my thoughts and feelings made the fact of my reading Wordsworth for the first time (in the autumn of 1828) an important event in my life . . . In the worst period of my depression I had read through the whole of Byron (then new to me) to try whether a poet, whose peculiar department was supposed to be that of the intenser feelings, could rouse any feeling in me. As might be expected, I got no good from this reading, but the reverse . . . But the miscellaneous poems, in the two-volume edition of 1815 (to which little of value was added in the latter part of the author's life), proved to be the precise thing for my mental wants at that particular juncture.

In the first place, these poems addressed themselves powerfully to one of the strongest of my pleasurable susceptibilities, the love of rural objects and natural scenery . . . But Wordsworth would never have had any great effect on me, if he had merely placed before me beautiful pictures of natural scenery. Scott does this still better than Wordsworth, and a very second-rate landscape does it more effectually than any poet. What made Wordsworth's poems a medicine for my state of mind, was that they expressed, not mere outward beauty, but states of feeling, and of thought coloured by feeling, under the excitement of beauty. They seemed to be the very culture of the feelings, which I was in quest of. In them I seemed to draw from a source of inward joy, of sympathetic and imaginative pleasure, which could be shared in by all human beings; which had no connexion with struggle or imperfection, but would be made richer by every improvement in the physical or social condition of mankind. From them I seemed to learn what would be the perennial sources of happiness, when all the greater evils of life shall have been removed. And I felt myself at once better and happier as I came under their influence . . . The result was that I gradually, but completely, emerged from my habitual depression, and was never again subject to it.

WALTER PATER: FROM 'WORDSWORTH', FORTNIGHTLY REVIEW (1874)

Pater sees Wordsworth's poetry as a 'continual protest' against the 'machinery' of existence. Pater writes thoughtfully, but his Wordsworth does have an element of blitheness about him.

. . . for most of us, the conception of means and ends covers the whole of life, and is the exclusive type or figure under which we represent our lives to ourselves. Such a figure, reducing all things to machinery, though it has on its side the authority of that old Greek moralist who has fixed for succeeding generations the outline of the theory of right living, is too like a mere picture or description of men's lives as we actually find them, to be the basis of the higher ethics. It covers the meanness of men's daily lives, and much of the dexterity and the vigour with which they pursue what may seem to them the good of themselves or of others; but not the intangible perfection of those whose ideal is rather in *being* than *doing* . . .

*   *   *

Against this predominance of machinery in our existence, Wordsworth's poetry, like all great art and poetry, is a continual protest. Justify rather the end by the means, it seems to say: whatever may become of the fruit, make sure of the flowers and leaves. It was justly said, therefore, by one who had meditated very profoundly on the true relation of means to ends in life, and on the distinction between what is desirable in itself and what is desirable only as machinery, that when the battle which he and his friends were waging had been won, the world would need more than ever those qualities which Wordsworth was keeping alive and nourishing.

*   *   *

Wordsworth, and other poets who have been like him in ancient or more recent times, are the masters, the experts, in this art of impassioned contemplation. Their work is, not to teach lessons, or enforce rules, or even to stimulate us to noble ends; but to withdraw the thoughts for a little while from the mere machinery of life, to fix them, with appropriate emotions, on the spectacle of those great facts in man's existence which no machinery affects, 'on the great and universal passions of men, the most general and interesting of their occupations and the entire world of nature', – on 'the operations of the elements and the appearances of the visible universe, on storm and sunshine, on the revolutions of the seasons, on cold and heat, on loss of friends and kindred, on injuries and resentments, on gratitude and hope, on fear and sorrow'.

LESLIE STEPHEN: FROM 'WORDSWORTH'S ETHICS', *HOURS IN A LIBRARY* (THIRD SERIES, 1879)

Stephen's paper focuses on the importance of Wordsworth's philosophy in a reading of the poetry. Here, he deals with the problems attendant on an analysis of Wordsworth's presentation of Nature, the opposition of Wordsworth's poetry to the 'modern' world's crushing of the individual, and the consoling strengths of the poetry.

The teaching, indeed, assumes that view of the universe which is implied in his pantheistic language. The Divinity really reveals Himself in the lonely mountains and the starry heavens. By contemplating them we are able to rise into that 'blessed mood' in which for a time the burden of the mystery is rolled off our souls, and we can 'see into the life of things'. And here we must admit that Wordsworth is not entirely free from the weakness which generally besets thinkers of this tendency. Like Shaftesbury in the previous century, who speaks of the universal harmony as emphatically though not as poetically as Wordsworth, he is tempted to adopt a too facile optimism. He seems at times to have overlooked that dark side of nature which is recognized in theological doctrines of corruption, or in the scientific theories about the fierce struggle for existence. Can we in fact say that these early instincts prove more than the happy constitution of the individual who feels them? Is there not a teaching of nature very apt to suggest horror and despair rather than a complacent brooding over soothing thoughts? Do not the mountains which Wordsworth loved so well, speak of decay and catastrophe in every line of their slopes? Do they not suggest the helplessness and narrow limitations of man, as forcibly as his possible exaltation?

*　　　*　　　*

To say that Wordsworth has not given a complete answer to such difficulties, is to say that he has not explained the origin of evil. It may be admitted, however, that he does to a certain extent show a narrowness of conception. The voice of nature, as he says, resembles an echo; but we 'unthinking creatures' listen to 'voices of two different natures'. We do not always distinguish between the echo of our lower passions and the 'echoes from beyond the grave'. Wordsworth sometimes fails to recognize the ambiguity of the oracle to which he appeals. The 'blessed mood' in which we get rid of the burden of the world, is too easily confused with the mood in which we simply refuse to attend to it. He finds lonely meditation so inspiring that he is too indifferent to the troubles of less self-sufficing or clear-sighted human beings. The ambiguity makes itself felt in the sphere of morality. The ethical doctrine that virtue consists in conformity to nature becomes ambiguous with him, as with all its advocates, when we ask for a precise definition of nature. How are we to know which natural forces make for us and which fight against us?

*　　*　　*

The division of labour, celebrated with such enthusiasm by Adam Smith, tends to crush all real life out of its victims. The soul of the political economist may rejoice when he sees a human being devoting his whole faculties to the performance of one subsidiary operation in the manufacture of a pin. The poet and the moralist must notice with anxiety the contrast between the old-fashioned peasant who, if he discharged each particular function clumsily, discharged at least many functions, and found exercise for all the intellectual and moral faculties of his nature, and the modern artisan doomed to the incessant repetition of one petty set of muscular expansions and contractions, and whose soul, if he has one, is therefore rather an incumbrance than otherwise. This is the evil which is constantly before Wordsworth's eyes, as it has certainly not become less prominent since his time. The danger of crushing the individual is a serious one according to his view; not because it implies the neglect of some abstract political rights, but from the impoverishment of character which is implied in the process. Give every man a vote, and abolish all interference with each man's private tastes, and the danger may still be as great as ever. The tendency to 'differentiation' – as we call it in modern phraseology – the social pulverization, the lowering and narrowing of the individual's sphere of action and feeling to the pettiest details, depends upon processes underlying all political changes. It cannot, therefore, be cured by any nostrum of constitution-mongers, or by the negative remedy of removing old barriers. It requires to be met by profounder moral and religious teaching.

*　　*　　*

Now Wordsworth's favourite lesson is the possibility of turning grief and disappointment into account. He teaches in many forms the necessity of 'transmuting' sorrow into strength. One of the great evils is a lack of power,

> An agonizing sorrow to transmute.

The Happy Warrior is, above all, the man who in face of all human miseries can

> Exercise a power
> Which is our human nature's highest dower;
> Controls them, and subdues, transmutes, bereaves
> Of their bad influence, and their good receives;

who is made more compassionate by familiarity with sorrow, more placable by contest, purer by temptation, and more enduring by distress. It is owing to the constant presence of this thought, to his sensibility to the refining influence of sorrow, that Wordsworth is the only poet who will bear reading in times of distress. Other poets mock us by an impossible optimism, or merely reflect the feelings which, however we may play with them in times of cheerfulness, have now become an intolerable burden. Wordsworth suggests the single topic which, so far at least as this world is concerned, can really be called 'consolatory'.

MATTHEW ARNOLD: FROM THE INTRODUCTION TO *POEMS OF WORDSWORTH* (1879)

Arnold's famous essay, which formed the introduction to his edition, *Poems of Wordsworth* (1879), asks us to be on our guard against those Wordsworthians who pay more attention to his philosophy than to his poetry. In this respect, the essay is a reply to Leslie Stephen. Poetry, Arnold argues, 'is at bottom a criticism of life . . . the greatness of a poet lies in his powerful and beautiful application of ideas to life – to the question: how to live'. The essay is also famous for its emphasis on the need to select what is of lasting value in the Wordsworth canon and relieve the poet from 'poetical baggage'.

Wordsworth composed verses during a space of some sixty years; and it is no exaggeration to say that within one single decade of those years, between 1798 and 1808, almost all his really first-rate work was produced. A mass of inferior work remains, work done before and after this golden prime, imbedding the first-rate work and clogging it, obstructing our approach to it, chilling, not unfrequently, the high-wrought mood with which we leave it. To be recognized far and wide as a great poet, to be possible and receivable as a classic, Wordsworth needs to be relieved of a great deal of the poetical baggage which now encumbers him.

*   *   *

When we come across a poet like Wordsworth, who sings,

> Of truth, of grandeur, beauty, love and hope,
> And melancholy fear subdued by faith,
> Of blessed consolations in distress,
> Of moral strength and intellectual power,
> Of joy in widest commonalty spread –

then we have a poet intent on 'the best and master thing', and who prosecutes his journey home. We say, for brevity's sake, that he deals with *life*, because he deals with that in which life really consists.

*   *   *

Burns, Keats, Heine, not to speak of others in our list, have this accent; who can doubt it? And at the same time they have treasures of humour, felicity, passion, for which in Wordsworth we shall look in vain. Where, then, is Wordsworth's superiority? It is here; he deals with more of *life* than they do; he deals with *life*, as a whole, more powerfully.

No Wordsworthian will doubt this. Nay, the fervent Wordsworthian will add, as Mr Leslie Stephen does, that Wordsworth's poetry is precious because his philosophy is sound; that his 'ethical system is as distinctive and capable of exposition as Bishop Butler's'; that his poetry is informed by ideas which 'fall spontaneously into a scientific system of thought'. But we must be on our guard against the Wordsworthians, if we want to secure for Wordsworth his due rank as a poet. The Wordsworthians are apt to praise him for the wrong things, and to lay far too much stress upon what they call his philosophy. His poetry is the reality, his philosophy, – so far, at least, as it may put on the form and habit of 'a scientific system of thought', and the more that it puts them on – is the illusion. Perhaps we shall one day learn to make this proposition general, and to say: Poetry is the reality, philosophy the illusion. But in Wordsworth's case, at any rate, we cannot do him justice until we dismiss his formal philosophy.

The Excursion abounds with philosophy, and therefore *The Excursion* is to the Wordsworthian what it never can be to the disinterested lover of poetry – a satisfactory work.

*   *   *

Even the 'intimations' of the famous Ode, those corner-stones of the supposed philosophic system of Wordsworth – the idea of the high instincts and affections coming out in childhood, testifying of a divine home recently left, and fading away as our life proceeds – this idea, of undeniable beauty as a play of fancy, has itself not the character of poetic truth of the best kind; it has no real solidity. The instinct of delight in Nature and her beauty had no doubt extraordinary strength in Wordsworth himself as a child. But to say that universally this instinct is mighty in childhood, and tends to die away afterwards, is to say what is extremely doubtful. In many people, perhaps with the majority of educated persons, the love of nature is nearly imperceptible at ten years old, but strong and operative at thirty. In general we may say of these high instincts of early childhood, the base of the alleged systematic philosophy of Wordsworth, what Thucydides says of the early achievements of the Greek race: 'It is impossible to speak with certainty of what is so remote; but from all that we can really investigate, I should say that they were no very great things.'

JOHN RUSKIN: FROM *FICTION, FAIR AND FOUL* (1880)

Wordsworth is simply a Westmorland peasant, with considerably less shrewdness than most border Englishmen or Scotsmen inherit; and no sense of humour: but gifted (in this singularly) with vivid sense of natural beauty, and a pretty turn for reflections, not always acute, but, as far as they reach, medicinal to the fever of the restless and corrupted life around him. Water to parched lips may be better than Samian wine, but do not let us therefore confuse the qualities of wine and water. I much doubt there being many inglorious Miltons in our country churchyards; but I am very sure there are many Wordsworths resting there, who were inferior to the renowned one only in caring less to hear themselves talk.

There are two Voices: one is of the deep;
It learns the storm-cloud's thundrous melody,
Now roars, now murmurs with the changing sea,
Now bird-like pipes, now closes soft in sleep.
And one is of an old half-witted sheep
Which bleats articulate monotony,
And indicates that two and one are three,
That grass is green, lakes damp, and mountains steep.
And, Wordsworth, both are thine . . .

Modern Criticism, 1909–Present Day

A. C. BRADLEY: FROM *OXFORD LECTURES ON POETRY* (1909)

Bradley's important essay focuses on the 'mystic strain', the mystic
strengths, of Wordsworth, at a remove from the 'ordinariness' of
many of his poetic subjects.

> However much Wordsworth was the poet of small and humble things,
> and the poet who saw his ideal realized, not in Utopia, but here and
> now before his eyes, he was, quite as much, what some would call a
> mystic. He saw everything in the light of 'the visionary power'. He
> was, for himself
>
> > The transitory being that beheld
> > This Vision.
>
> He apprehended all things, natural or human, as the expression of
> something which, while manifested in them, immeasurably transcends
> them. And nothing can be more intensely Wordsworthian than the
> poems and passages most marked by this visionary power and most
> directly issuing from this apprehension.

* * *

Arnold wished to make Wordsworth more popular; and so he was
tempted to represent Wordsworth's poetry as much more simple and
unambitious than it really was, and as much more easily apprehended
than it ever can be. He was also annoyed by attempts to formulate a
systematic Wordsworthian philosophy; partly, doubtless, because he
knew that, however great the value of a poet's ideas may be, it cannot

by itself determine the value of his poetry; but partly also because, having himself but little turn for philosophy, he was disposed to regard it as illusory; and further because, even in the poetic sphere, he was somewhat deficient in that kind of imagination which is allied to metaphysical thought.

*   *   *

Setting aside, then, any questions as to the ultimate import of the 'mystic' strain in Wordsworth's poetry, I intend only to call attention to certain traits in the kind of poetic experience which exhibits it most plainly. And we may observe at once that in this there is always traceable a certain hostility to 'sense'. I do not mean that hostility which is present in *all* poetic experience, and of which Wordsworth was very distinctly aware. The regular action of the senses on their customary material produces, in his view, a 'tyranny' over the soul. It helps to construct that everyday picture of the world, of sensible objects and events 'in disconnection dead and spiritless', which we take for reality. In relation to this reality we become passive slaves; it lies on us with a weight 'heavy as frost and deep almost as life' . . . On the other hand, in the kind of experience which forms our present subject, there is always some feeling of definite contrast with the limited sensible world. The arresting feature or object is felt in some way *against* this background, or even as in some way a denial of it. Sometimes it is a visionary unearthly light resting on a scene or on some strange figure. Sometimes it is the feeling that the scene or figure belongs to the world of dream. Sometimes it is an intimation of boundlessness, contradicting or abolishing the fixed limits of our habitual view. Sometimes it is the obscure sense of 'unknown modes of being', unlike the familiar modes. This kind of experience, further, comes often with a distinct shock, which may bewilder, confuse or trouble the mind. And, lastly, it is especially, though not invariably, associated with mountains, and again with solitude.

*   *   *

   the wind and sleety rain
And all the business of the elements,
The single sheep, and the one blasted tree,
And the bleak music from that old stone wall,
The noise of wood and water, and the mist
That on the line of each of those two roads
Advanced in such indisputable shapes.

Everything here is natural, but everything is apocalyptic. And we happen to know why. Wordsworth is describing the scene in the light of memory. In that eagerly expected holiday his father died; and that scene, as he recalled it, was charged with the sense of contrast between the narrow world of common pleasures and blind and easy hopes, and the vast unseen world which encloses it in beneficent yet dark and inexorable arms. The visionary feeling has here a peculiar tone; but always, openly or covertly, it is the intimation of something illimitable, over-arching or breaking into the customary 'reality'.

*   *   *

Solitude and solitariness were to him, in the main, one of these intimations. They had not for him merely the 'eeriness' which they have at times for everyone, though that was essential to some of the poems we have reviewed. They were the symbol of power to stand alone, to be 'self-sufficing', to dispense with custom and surroundings and aid and sympathy – a self-dependence at once the image and the communication of 'the soul of all the worlds'. Even when they were full of 'sounds and sweet airs that give delight and hurt not', the solitude of the Reaper or of Lucy, they so appealed to him. But they appealed also to that austerer strain which led him to love 'bare trees and mountains bare', and lonely places, and the bleak music of the old stone wall, and to dwell with awe, and yet with exultation, on the majesty of that 'unconquerable mind' which through long years holds its solitary purpose, sustains its solitary passion, feeds upon its solitary anguish.

ALDOUS HUXLEY: FROM 'WORDSWORTH IN THE TROPICS'
FROM *DO WHAT YOU WILL* (1931)

Wordsworth, as the poet of Nature, transplanted.

For good Wordsworthians – and most serious-minded people are now Wordsworthians, either by direct inspiration or at second hand – a walk in the country is the equivalent of going to church, a tour through Westmorland is as good as a pilgrimage to Jerusalem. To commune with the fields and waters, the woodlands and the hills, is to commune, according to our modern and northern ideas, with the visible manifestations of the 'Wisdom and Spirit of the Universe'.

The Wordsworthian who exports this pantheistic worship of Nature to the tropics is liable to have his religious convictions somewhat rudely disturbed. Nature, under a vertical sun, and nourished by the equatorial rains, is not at all like that chaste, mild deity who presides over the *Gemütlichkeit*, the prettiness, the cozy sublimities of the Lake District. The worst that Wordsworth's goddess ever did to him was to make him hear

> Low breathings coming after me, and sounds
> Of undistinguishable motion, steps
> Almost as silent as the turf they trod;

was to make him realize, in the shape of 'a huge peak, black and huge', the existence of 'unknown modes of being'. He seems to have imagined that this was the worst Nature *could* do. A few weeks in Malaya or Borneo would have undeceived him. Wandering in the hothouse darkness of the jungle, he would not have felt so serenely certain of those 'Presences of Nature', those 'Souls of Lonely Places', which he was in the habit of worshipping on the shores of Windermere and Rydal.

*   *   *

The Wordsworthian adoration of Nature has two principal defects. The first, as we have seen, is that it is only possible in a country where Nature has been nearly or quite enslaved to man. The second is that it is only possible for those who are prepared to falsify their immediate intuitions of Nature. For Nature, even in the temperate zone, is always alien and inhuman, and occasionally diabolic. Meredith explicitly invites us to explain any unpleasant experiences away. We are to interpret them, Pangloss fashion, in terms of a preconceived philosophy; after which, all will surely be for the best in the best of all possible Westermaines. Less openly, Wordsworth asks us to make the same falsification of immediate experience. It is only very occasionally that he admits the existence in the world around him of those 'unknown modes of being' of which our immediate intuitions of things make us so disquietingly aware. Normally what he does is to pump the dangerous Unknown out of Nature and refill the emptied forms of hills and woods, flowers and waters, with something more reassuringly familiar – with humanity, with Anglicanism.

T. S. ELIOT: FROM 'WORDSWORTH AND COLERIDGE' IN *THE USE OF POETRY AND THE USE OF CRITICISM* (1933)

Eliot contrasts the poetic natures of Wordsworth and Coleridge and focuses on Wordsworth's 'social interest' as that which underpins his theory of poetic language.

Wordsworth ... wrote his *Preface*, as I have said, while in the plenitude of his poetic powers and while his reputation was still only sustained by readers of discernment. And he was of an opposite poetic type to Coleridge. Whether the bulk of his genuine poetic achievement is so much greater than Coleridge's as it appears, is uncertain. Whether his power and inspiration remained with him to the end is, alas, not even doubtful. But Wordsworth had no ghastly shadows at his back, no Eumenides to pursue him; or if he did, he gave no sign and took no notice; and he went droning on the still sad music of infirmity to the verge of the grave. His inspiration never having been of that sudden, fitful and terrifying kind that visited Coleridge, he was never, apparently, troubled by the consciousness of having lost it. As André Gide's Prometheus said, in the lecture which he gave before a large audience in Paris: *Il faut avoir un aigle*. Coleridge remained in contact with his eagle. Neither in detail of life and interest were the two men similar – Wordsworth indifferent to books, Coleridge the voracious reader.

* * *

In [the] matter of poetic diction, it is at first very hard to understand what all the fuss is about. Wordsworth's poems had met with no worse reception than verse of such novelty is accustomed to receive. I myself can remember a time when some question of 'poetic diction' was in the air; when Ezra Pound issued his statement that 'poetry ought to be as well written as prose'; and when he and I and our colleagues were mentioned by a writer in the *Morning Post* as 'literary bolsheviks' . . . Wordsworth, when he said that his purpose was 'to imitate, and as far as possible, to adopt, the very language of men', was only saying in other words what Dryden had said, and fighting the battle which Dryden had fought . . . And on the other hand, as has also been pointed out, first by Coleridge himself in the *Biographia*, Wordsworth by no means worried himself to excess in observing his own principles . . . And Donne has seemed to us, in recent years, as striking a peculiarly conversational style; but did Wordsworth or Coleridge acclaim Donne? No, when it came to Donne – and Cowley – you will find that Wordsworth and Coleridge were led by the nose by Samuel Johnson; they were just as eighteenth century as anybody; except that where the eighteenth century spoke of lack of elegance the Lake poets found lack of passion. And much of the poetry of Wordsworth and Coleridge is just as turgid and artificial and elegant as any eighteenth century die-hard could wish.

* * *

But it is Wordsworth's social interest that inspires his own novelty of form in verse, and backs up his explicit remarks upon poetic diction;

and it is really this social interest which (consciously or not) the fuss was all about. It was not so much from lack of thought as from warmth of feeling that Wordsworth originally wrote the words 'the language of conversation in middle and lower class society'.

JAMES SMITH: FROM 'WORDSWORTH: A PRELIMINARY SURVEY', *SCRUTINY*, NO. 7 (1938)

An analysis of Wordsworth's rhetoric.

... we must take care not to be dazzled by his rhetorical skill – 'rhetorical' is a word with a number of senses, but I use it, I believe, in the best. It would be difficult to exaggerate this skill in Wordsworth, and the danger which results from it.

Nature, he seems to have thought, produces only the bare essence of poetry, to which man must fit an outer garment of words and metre; therefore a poet, if he would not be mute, must set himself to acquire the knack of metre, as he would any other accomplishment. Wordsworth laboured early and long for this end. 'I have bestowed great care upon my style,' he said, 'and yield to none in the love of my art.' From his use of the term elsewhere, it seems probable that by 'art' and 'style' he means the power simultaneously to observe the rules for lucid and grammatical English, and for any verse-form in which he happened to be working. He practised and attained proficiency in a great many: in the sonnet, and in the forms of Spenser, Milton, Pope, Hamilton, Burns and Scott.

The sort of merit which he thus brought within his reach, and which it is important to recognize and name lest, remarkable as it is, it be mistaken for something yet more remarkable, is fairly clearly illustrated by his poem *Yew-Trees*. This is familiar, if for no other reason, for being quoted as an example of the grand style outside Milton. It may be so; but I do not think we can call it anything more than an exercise in Miltonics.

> ... those fraternal Four of Borrowdale,
> Joined in one solemn and capacious grove;
> Huge trunks! and each particular trunk a growth
> Of intertwisted fibres serpentine
> Upcoiling, and inveterately convolved;
> Nor uninformed with Phantasy ...

A brilliant exercise, but only brilliant.

*   *   *

Mastery over metre qualifies him to be a conversational poet – the sort of poet, that is, who flourished in a number of countries during the Renaissance, and in England in the early eighteenth century. At these places and periods a firm tradition of poetic performance permitted the treatment of an unusually wide variety of subjects at least as efficiently in verse as in prose, and often with the urgency and vividness of verse. A number of passages in *The Prelude*, like the description of his dame at Hawkshead or of the sights of London, reach a high level of excellence in this way. One of them, on the Terror, suggests that he might have maintained himself fairly consistently at the highest level, if he had been more secure of an audience; for poetry of this kind, to persist, depends on a society whose members continually stimulate and restrain. But the audience was lacking, and for various reasons he gradually withdrew into a more and more remote exile. In consequence, some of his later verse, which has been praised for its technical perfection, is no more than scholarly, it is directed, that is, at a distant, almost a disembodied audience. And some of the rest suffers from a lack of focus, as though it were directed at two widely differing audiences at once. This is the fault of the didactic part of *The Prelude*, where Wordsworth seems unable to convince himself that what he has to say is of itself such as to interest the reader. Therefore, by means of orotundity and ornament he seeks to provide an elegant diversion, to combine, as it were, the roles of Lucretius and of Dyer in *The Fleece*.

* * *

[*The Prelude*, 1805 Book VI, lines 531–42]

Let me first note about this passage the ample warrant it provides for all that has been said about Wordsworth's skill in rhetoric. Like Milton, he knows how to draw out the sense variously from verse to verse; or, as he puts it to Klopstock, to secure 'an apt arrangement of pauses and cadences, and the sweep of whole paragraphs'. Secondly, the occasion seems not unsuitable for the display of such skill; an attempt, it seems, is to be made to communicate something by its nature difficult, if not incapable, of communication, upon which therefore only a number of sallies can be made. If each is doomed to be ineffectual, all of them together, and the variety of their points of departure and return, may be not wholly without effect. 'Strength of usurpation' and 'visitings of awful promise' corroborate each other; and if it is not clear exactly how, inevitable lack of clarity is part of what is to be conveyed. The figure of an invisible world made visible by a flash of light which thereby extinguishes itself, as though by a supreme effort, recommends for acceptance a difficulty for which, even when accepted, there can be no hope of solution. And as the passage goes on, a solution begins to appear less and less necessary: the metre becomes more regular, the difficulty is not at all impossible, it is even exhilarating to live with. The line 'With hope it is, hope that can never die' encourages to aspiration; 'Effort and expectation and desire' suggests an unremitting eagerness in the soul. The last line, 'And something evermore about to be', is the most regular of all.

The trouble is that it is too regular – too regular to be smooth. There is no peace about it, but a merciless beat; and with infinitude there should surely be peace. When we have reached this line the suspicion arises, I think, that Wordsworth is not in fact where a mystic should be – with infinitude, outside or above the world; but, rather, well within it. And, if so, some of the preceding lines need to be reconsidered, and our opinion on them to be revised. Aspiration can be unreservedly welcome only where, as with infinitude, there is certainty that it will be fulfilled; elsewhere 'hope that can never die' is but a euphemism for hope that has never lived. And elsewhere than with infinitude effort and expectation and desire are grim companions: that eagerness is unremitting is no guarantee that, in this world, it will not be baffled. If we turn our attention from the sound to the sense of the last line we see it to have the minimum of meaning: there is nothing in the future to which it will not apply. So far as we can talk of a future in eternity it is of a piece with the present and prophecy cannot arouse mistrust; but to a creature in time the mere idea of futurity cannot bring consolation, and confidence based upon it and nothing more is a poor thing. Loudly to proclaim such a confidence is a still poorer thing.

If we read over the passage with these and similar reflections in mind we discover I think that the rhetoric is not only skilful, it is too obviously skilful: it has no natural movement which, if we admire, we admire as concrete in the substance which moves; but rather a mechanical, to admire which we must abstract and even oppose it to the substance. 'How subtle the play of the levers!' we say, and all the time are thinking of the unexpectedness of such subtlety in dead matter. The poem is not alive, but an extremely cleverly constructed simulacrum; a robot put together, no doubt, for his purposes; but still not a poem.

HELEN DARBISHIRE: FROM *THE POET WORDSWORTH*
(THE CLARK LECTURES 1950)

'In thought,' Helen Darbishire states, 'the later *Prelude* records an inevitable change of mind.' Her essay focuses on the nature of Wordsworth's revisions of the 1805 *Prelude* – revisions which at times produce a radically different vision of human life.

Wordsworth's creed may be said in three words: God, Man, Nature. These three were divine: it might almost be said that they were one divinity. God was necessarily greatest, Man came next, and Nature, which had taught him to know the divinity in man, was last yet first, the source of his inspiration and first step in all his vital knowledge. When he first confessed his faith in *The Prelude* he had only to use these words, simply and passionately, and all his meaning was conveyed. He had only to speak, in the lines already quoted, of the soul that 'passing through all Nature rests with God', and he had uttered the first article of his creed. The words were charged with power. What greater things can be said than God, Man, Nature? But the middle-aged Wordsworth who revised *The Prelude* . . . was betrayed by the ineradicable weakness of civilized man; he had to explain, to rationalize, to moralize. Moreover, since he was not only a civilized, but a deeply religious man, and a devout adherent of the Anglican Church, he had to translate his thought into the terms of an orthodox Christian creed. Thus the phrase 'to think with admiration and respect of man' becomes

> to think
> With a due reverence of earth's rightful lord
> Here placed to be the inheritor of heaven.

'God and Nature's single sovereignty' is amplified to

> presences of God's mysterious power
> Made manifest in Nature's sovereignty.

'Great God!' gives place to 'Power supreme!' and in another context, ludicrously and lamentably, to 'How strange!' 'Living God!', simplest sublime address to the Deity, becomes 'Righteous Heaven!' At the time when he wrote *The Prelude* Wordsworth's faith, in one aspect a simple form of pantheism, in another a Hegelian belief in the power of the human mind, bore little, if any, trace of dogmatic Christianity. If he gave it afterwards a carefully Christian colouring, was this only, to use his own phrase of a famous expunction in *Peter Bell*, 'not to offend the pious'? Or did it portend some vital change of mind?

   To answer that question we must examine some of the patched places in *The Prelude* text.

   In the early version of Book V, lines 11–18 ran:

> Hitherto,
> In progress through this Verse, my mind hath look'd
> Upon the speaking face of earth and heaven
> As her prime Teacher, intercourse with man
> Established by the sovereign Intellect,
> Who through that bodily Image hath diffus'd
> A soul divine which we participate,
> A deathless spirit.

In revising this, he cut out the line which holds the essence of his meaning, 'A soul divine which we participate', and substituted an apologetic phrase to fill the gap, so that the triumphant passage now ends lamely thus:

> Who through that bodily image hath diffused,
> As might appear to the eye of fleeting time,
> A deathless spirit.

Again his apostrophe in Book X:

> Great God!
> Who send'st thyself into this breathing world
> Through Nature and through every kind of life,
> And mak'st man what he is, Creature divine,

is reworded:

> O Power Supreme!
> Without Whose care this world would cease to breathe,
> Who from the fountain of Thy grace doth fill
> The veins that branch through every frame of life,
> Making man what he is, creature divine.

The early versions here show a vital difference in thought, not only in expression. The great God who sends Himself into the world through Nature, who diffuses through her 'a soul divine which we participate', is more like the God of Spinoza than the God of Dr Watts. What Wordsworth has ejected in the process of revision is the naked fact of the soul of man meeting God in Nature.

One more passage will throw light. He altered the lines

> The feeling of life endless, the great thought
> By which we live, infinity and God,

to

> Faith in life endless, the sustaining thought
> Of human being, eternity and God.

The verbal change is slight, but its import great. 'The feeling of life endless', his own personal intuition, comes to be called 'Faith in life endless', a faith which he shares with the Christian Church; the great thought by which we live, infinity and God, becomes the Christian thought of human immortality. Strange that the words 'infinity' and 'eternity' should mean the same thing with such a difference.

* * *

[*The Prelude*, 1805 Book III, lines 81–93]

The meaning of these lines is unequivocal. The holy powers in which he exulted were the powers of his own mind freely communicating with Nature and drawing thence mysterious strength. They had nothing to do with intellectual training or moral worth, still less with religion in the orthodox sense, which he does not so much as refer to.

The passage appears in our known text shorn of all its daring, and deliberately touched with Christian thought:

> But wherefore be cast down?
> For (not to speak of Reason and her pure
> Reflective acts to fix the moral law
> Deep in the conscience, nor of Christian Hope,
> Bowing her head before her sister Faith
> As one far mightier), hither I had come,
> Bear witness, Truth, endowed with holy powers
> And faculties, whether to work or feel.

Hope bows before Faith: both are expressly Christian. Reason is tied to a moral function. Majesty, dignity, sovereignty, freedom, give place to a studious humility of mind. And here once more we touch a radical change in Wordsworth's thought. The pressure of the years and crushing personal sorrows had taught him the inherent weakness of human nature, a weakness from which neither mind nor spirit was exempt. When we find him after a magnificent eulogy of man, 'as of all visible natures crown', adding the words 'though born of dust and kindred to the worm', we are put out by what seems an irrelevant concession. But the words, out of key as they are with his earlier mood, were strictly relevant to his later position. They stand for something not only sincerely thought, but passionately felt.

DONALD DAVIE: FROM 'DICTION AND INVENTION: WORDSWORTH', *PURITY OF DICTION IN ENGLISH VERSE* (1952)

A consideration of Wordsworth's diction.

Now Wordsworth is a conspicuous example of a poet in whom invention is so powerful that diction hardly ever matters. De Quincey said as much in a fine passage when he hailed Wordsworth as above all a discoverer of new or forgotten truths. And of no part of Wordsworth's work is this so true as of *Lyrical Ballads*. Wordsworth was technically incompetent at least until 1801, when he seems to have put himself to school with Chaucer, Shakespeare and Milton. By luck or genius (they amount to the same thing) he had before that hit upon some primitive forms which could just sustain what he had to say; and what he had found to say before that was so novel and surprising that it could carry the day. Even *The Brothers* and *Michael* are great in spite of, not because of, their language. And even so, luck failed him on occasions; for instance *The Two Thieves* of 1800 displays a nobly poetical conception (similar to *The Old Cumberland Beggar*) thrown away in an inappropriate form. The early poems, when they succeed, do so by virtue of invention; the language is as nearly irrelevant as it can be in poetry.

After the turn of the century Wordsworth emerges, through some uncomfortable experiments, as a highly accomplished poet. He creates not one style, but many, according to what he needs to do. There is the style of the political sonnets; the style of *The Prelude*; and the style of the Immortality Ode. There are others, but these are the most important. And each of these styles can be called a 'diction', in the sense of a private language, a distinctive vocabulary and turn of phrase. Wordsworth's own criticism had paved the way for this loose usage. And the shift in meaning is further obscured for us by the circumstance that some later poets, such as Arnold, made use of one or other of the Wordsworthian styles; so that we detect 'Wordsworthian diction' in other poets.

But this use of diction, to mean a private language, is the very opposite of the older one, by which it was 'the perfection of a common language'. It is only the latter of which one can say that it is pure or impure. And this is a diction which hardly ever appears in Wordsworth's work. The question of purity does not arise. Almost to the end what matters in Wordsworth is his invention, his astonishing discoveries about human sentiments. As he pieced his discoveries together into systems, he had to learn his trade and master techniques more elaborate and sophisticated than those which had served him in *Lyrical Ballads*. But at no time does the question of pure or impure diction enter into the matter.

After all, how could it? A pure diction embodies urbanity; a vicious diction offers to do that, and fails. But Wordsworth was not interested in urbanity, and had no faith in it; he pledged himself to its opposite, a determined provincialism. He spoke as a solitary, not as a spokesman; urbanity was none of his business, nor diction either. It is one way of explaining what went wrong with Wordsworth's poetry, in his later life, to say that as recognition came to him, he saw himself more and more as, after all, a spokesman of national sentiment. No poet was less fitted, by training and temperament, for such a role; and no poet's art was so unsuitable for carrying it.

F. W. BATESON: FROM *WORDSWORTH: A RE-INTERPRETATION*
(SECOND EDITION, 1956)

Bateson's is something of a notorious book, (in)famous for its thesis that the poetry can be interpreted in relation to Wordsworth's incestuous feelings for Dorothy. As a piece of biographical criticism, it is valuable in that it links Wordsworth's emotional imbalances to the *kind* of poetry he wrote and felt he needed to write.

Why did he write? In the complex of conscious and semi-conscious motives, was there one that can be distinguished as the efficient cause of Wordsworth's poetry?

Wordsworth's stock answer, repeated with greater and greater emphasis as his youth receded, was that he was a teacher, and that he wrote his poetry primarily in order to provide his readers with moral instruction. This is certainly the gist of the long letter that he wrote to John Wilson . . .

* * *

If we can trust the letter to Wilson the central doctrine preached in the earlier poems is egalitarianism . . . With these convictions Wordsworth's poetic mission-field as the prophet of nature was necessarily in the towns. It was the townsman and not the countryman who in fact read his poems, and to whom they are obviously primarily addressed. Unfortunately, however, as an early critic pointed out, the prolonged access which they prescribe to nature in its grandest and wildest forms was only possible in the nineteenth century to the townsman with a large income. The urban rich could save their souls, the urban poor couldn't – a conclusion that is hardly compatible with the enthusiastic egalitarianism of the letter to Wilson.

Wordsworth never succeeded in resolving this logical contradiction between his belief in equality and his belief in the spiritual benefits to be obtained from an intimate communion with wild nature. When it was proposed to extend the railway line from Kendal to Windermere he resisted the proposal with all the eloquence he could then command (1844) in both verse and prose. But to the advocates of the extension who pointed out that the new railway would now enable the poor to enjoy the scenery of the Lake District he could only reply (in a letter to the *Morning Post*): 'Rocks and mountains, torrents and wide-spread waters, and all those features of nature which go to the composition of such scenes as this part of England is distinguished for, cannot, in their finer relations to the human mind, be comprehended, or even very imperfectly conceived, without processes of culture or opportunities of observation in some degree habitual.' The admission, however, is fatal to a central thesis of *The Prelude* – that the basis of the good life is *unconscious* intercourse with natural beauty. Moreover the townsman who has to undergo preliminary 'processes of culture' and be provided with appropriate 'opportunities of observation' will at best only turn into another connoisseur of Picturesque Beauty, like the Reverend William Gilpin.

The honest answer to the projectors of the Kendal and Windermere Railway – that the privacy of the Lake District was a necessity for his own mental health – was one that Wordsworth himself could not give. It is not that he was a hypocrite, but he was a man exceptionally unaware of his own motives. At this very time, when by opposing the railway he was strenuously denying the poor opportunities already available to the rich, he used to hold forth 'with great animation' at Ambleside tea-parties, we are told, 'of the unfortunate separation between the rich and the poor in this country'. Nor was this an isolated sentimentality; the long 'Postscript' that he added to the Prefaces of his poems in 1835 contains a thoroughly sensible and humane attack upon the New Poor Law. But Wordsworth's right hand did not know, and so could not understand, what his left hand was doing.

It will be apparent that this contradiction between the 'messages' Wordsworth meant his poetry to convey is one more example of the incompatibility of the Two Voices . . . To overcome the contradiction it is necessary to go behind Wordsworth's various pronouncements about the function of his poetry to the personal motives, of which he himself was often only partly conscious, out of which all that is most genuine and original in it really emerges. In other words, if we are to look for an efficient cause of his poetry, the ultimate explanation for its being written at all, the place where we may hope to find it is not in his Prefaces, or in semi-public letters like those to Wilson or Fox, but in the recesses of his personality, the dark corners that were only partly explored even in *The Prelude*.

∗   ∗   ∗

The failure of his own plans and ambitions, his unintended desertion of Annette and Caroline, the war with France, and the degeneration of revolutionary idealism into Robespierre's Reign of Terror had combined to deprive him not only of a social function for himself but of a content to the very concept of society. And the return to sanity was by a process of sympathetic self-identification with other social outcasts. In the anti-social nightmare he was still able from time to time to 'grasp' the basic human traits exhibited by such companions in his misfortune as Peter Bell's original or the heroine of 'We are Seven'. It cannot be an accident that, with only one or two important exceptions, all the poems Wordsworth wrote during the five years between the summer of 1793 and the summer of 1798 are concerned with social outcasts and misfits, whose natural goodness and purity are contrasted with the treatment they receive from an indifferent and inhuman social order. By identifying himself subjectively with *dramatis personæ* as objectively different from himself as the hero and heroine of *Salisbury Plain*, the Margaret of *The Ruined Cottage*, the Cumberland Beggar, Poor Susan, Goody Blake, Simon Lee and the others he was able to overcome in himself the temptations to moral nihilism represented by Oswald in *The Borderers* and the wicked mother in 'The Three Graves'. In the process of understanding them he was learning to understand and accept his own position in an ideal society.

*   *   *

Why did he write? The question has now received a partial answer. The efficient cause, so far as the poetry had a single originating source, was the impelling need Wordsworth felt to integrate the more subjective or inward-looking and the more objective or outward-looking aspects of his personality. The poetry, it turns out, was not so much autobiography as a technique of self-preservation and self-recreation.

*   *   *

So far from surrendering to the neurotic elements in his personality, as so many Romantic poets have done, Wordsworth's early life was one long desperate struggle against them. And whatever one's reservations about this or that poem the general direction of the poetry is undoubtedly towards sanity, sincerity, sympathy, gaiety – in a word, the humane virtues. What makes their successful realisation in Wordsworth's best poems so exhilarating to the modern reader is his continuous consciousness of how hardly the successes have been won, how precarious the achievement is. There were no easy victories for him either as a man or a poet. The failures on the other hand, and there were plenty of them, are refreshingly obvious and blatant.

Wordsworth achieves greatness because his private struggles towards psychic integration have a representative quality. The poems generalise themselves, as they are read, into the reactions of the human individual fighting for its spiritual survival in a society that seems to have no place for it. And this makes him, with Blake, the first specifically modern English poet.

JOHN JONES: FROM *THE EGOTISTICAL SUBLIME* (1954)

Jones considers the implications of Wordsworth's famous statement that language is not the dress of thought but its incarnation.

When he was confronted with the vulgar eighteenth-century definition of language as the clothing of thought, Wordsworth replied that language is not thought's dress but its incarnation. His more specific remarks about language are nearly always consistent with this statement of general principle, as, for example, his protest against the Augustan element in Byron's poetry:

> the sentiment by being expressed in an antithetical manner, is taken out of the Region of high and imaginative feeling, to be placed in that of point and epigram. To illustrate my meaning and for no other purpose I refer to my own Lines on the Wye *Tintern Abbey*, where you will find the same sentiment not formally put as it is here, but ejaculated as it were fortuitously in the musical succession of preconceived feelings.

Wordsworth rejects the notion that poets, or other men, think a thought and then look for an attractive way of presenting it. Language is not like that. What then, of the distinction between knowing what you think and knowing how to say it? Implicit in his remarks about language, and especially, in his reckless commendations of spontaneous utterance, is the will to free the activity of thinking from association with the concept thought.

*   *   *

He dislikes the dress metaphor because it suggests that language is independent of other things in a way that is untrue. It goes wrong at the start by implying that there are naked thoughts. However importunate the hubbub of life below the level of expression, only error can result from talking of thoughts arising, like Venus, from the sea of brute experience; for the false dichotomy of thought and word is immediately encouraged. This is partly a matter of chronology, of Wordsworth's testifying, as other artists have done, that although you cannot start work until you know what you want to do, it is equally the case that you do not know what you want to do until you have done it: so the thought has no priority in time. But more important is his objection to the analogy of the body and its dress. Even if Venus-Thoughts were described as emerging fully clothed, he would still have been unsatisfied. You can do what you like with clothes, tell any story you please, and if language is a kind of clothing, all use of language is a playing with words.

As always, Wordsworth's ultimate problem is a moral and aesthetic complex. Language is moral because of the way in which it is bound to life: it is poetic for the same reason. His quarrel with the dress metaphor affords an introduction to this complex since the status of language is endangered in both connections when it is associated with adornment or even with working clothes. A moral-poetic responsibility is evaded by those who think of something ready made, waiting to be assumed. And so he challenged the divorce of language and life, the whole idea of poetic diction, the principles involved in Gray's famous statement that there is one language for art and another for nature. He believed in a single language, no further from the living heart of things than the breath that bears it.

* * *

Thought incarnate is not thought expressed, or there would be no need to distinguish the word and the mathematical symbol; but when he refuses to allow that thoughts are clothed in words, he fears not so much a direct confusion with mathematics as the reducing of language to a conceptual instrument, external to those who use it. Language must have a corresponding inwardness in order to enact the reciprocity of nature.

ROBERT MAYO: FROM 'THE CONTEMPORANEITY OF THE *LYRICAL BALLADS*', *PMLA*, VOL. 69 (1954)

Mayo examines the ways in which the *Lyrical Ballads*, 1798 – 'too exclusively' regarded as a revolutionary volume – connects with, rather than breaks away from, contemporary verse.

A fruitful but unfrequented approach to the *Lyrical Ballads* is through the poetry of the magazines. The volume unquestionably belongs to 1798, and seen in relation to the popular verse of that day, its contemporaneous features are very striking. We have been asked to consider too exclusively the revolutionary aspects of the *Lyrical Ballads*. Revolutionary they unquestionably were, but not in every respect. Except that they were much better than other poems published in 1798, the *Ballads* were not such a 'complete change' as some writers would have us believe. Even their eccentricity has been exaggerated. Actually, there is a conventional side to the *Lyrical Ballads*, although it is usually overlooked.

* * *

In general, the drift is in several directions only – towards 'nature' and 'simplicity', and towards humanitarianism and sentimental morality. Without discriminating too precisely between these categories, the reader of that day would tend to construe most of the contents of the

Lyrical Ballads in terms of these modes of popular poetry, with which he was already familiar.

He would, for example, if the poetry departments of the magazines are any index, regard as perfectly normal a miscellany of ballads on pastoral subjects (treated both sentimentally and jocularly), moral and philosophic poems inspired by physical nature, and lyrical pieces in a variety of kinds describing rural scenes, the pleasures of the seasons, flora and fauna, and a simple life in the out-of-doors. Subjects drawn from 'nature', including both landscape and rural life, as many writers have pointed out, were commonplace in the minor verse of the last years of the eighteenth century. Viewed in relation to this considerable body of writing, poems like *Lines Written in Early Spring, Lines Left upon a Seat in a Yew-Tree, Lines Written near Richmond* and *The Nightingale* are obviously not experimental in subject; nor in *form* either, as a matter of fact. Considered as a species of poetry, the 'nature' poems of the *Lyrical Ballads* were anything but surprising in 1798. Novelty, of course, is a very complex and ephemeral quality in any poem or collection of poems, extremely difficult to isolate. It depends upon a thousand particulars, now vanished, which were once an unmistakable part of the literary climate. But the more one reads the popular poetry of the last quarter of the eighteenth century the more he is likely to feel that the really surprising feature of these poems in the *Lyrical Ballads* (as well as of many of the others) – apart from sheer literary excellence – is their intense fulfillment of an already stale convention, and not their discovery of an interest in rivers, valleys, groves, lakes and mountains, flowers and budding trees, the changing seasons, sunsets, the freshness of the morning and the songs of birds. This fact is a commonplace. Yet it is astonishing how often responsible Wordsworthians go astray in this respect, and tend to view Wordsworth and Coleridge as reacting with a kind of totality against contemporary fashions in verse. The question is not whether the *Ballads* were altogether conventional, which no one would attempt to affirm, but whether they were completely out of touch with popular taste. This was certainly the nineteenth century conception of Wordsworth, who was viewed as a kind of prophet writing in the wilderness; and it is evidently still the view of some present-day critics and historians, who, struck by the phenomenal literary quality of the *Ballads*, tend to confuse one kind of change with another. They have perhaps been misled by the ambiguities of the Advertisement of 1798, which seems to claim more than it actually does.

*   *   *

However much they may be rendered fresh and new by poetic treatment, it must be recognized that most of the objects of sympathy in

the volume belong to an order of beings familiar to every reader of
magazine poetry – namely, bereaved mothers and deserted females,
mad women and distracted creatures, beggars, convicts and prisoners,
and old people of the depressed classes, particularly peasants. For
nearly every character, portrait or figure, there is some seasoned
counterpart in contemporary poetry. It is true that there were other
species of unfortunates and social outcasts being similarly favoured
in the literature of the 1790s – namely, negro slaves, blind men,
prostitutes, exiles, foundlings and natural children. Nevertheless,
although the two poets avoid some, they do not avoid all the way-
worn paths of literary convention.

JOHN DANBY: FROM *THE SIMPLE WORDSWORTH* (1960)

Wordsworth is still in the great Renaissance tradition which saw in
the poet a responsible human spokesman. As against the eighteenth
century he must insist on a reconstitution of 'the truth'. His view of
what is to be inculcated will be different from that of a poet like
Thomson, but poetry, he will agree, must continue to be both moral
and didactic. Moral edification, however, is not now with him a matter
of verbal precept. Rather, it is the embodiment of living occasions in
words, the admission of the reader through words into the remoulding
experience. It is in fact poems: poems 'proper', as poems, after the
romantics, will be considered to be. A new standard of actuality in
poetry is insisted upon, a new conception of what poets should be,
a new understanding of how their words actually work upon their
audience. The poet is responsible in a new way to his world, to himself,
and to his readers.

'Under-agents of the soul' – once words are seen in this light a fresh
approach can be made both to the Wordsworthian revolution and to
the general problem of simplicity in poetry which it forces forward.
Simplicity is Wordsworth's main concern.

*   *   *

Poetry for Wordsworth is the utterance, ideally, of a responsive
sensibility and a securely grounded judgement, acting together.
Spontaneity in itself can be the rash-like irruption of trivialities. The
poet's claim to attention is his practical acquaintance with what for
men is important or unimportant. Ultimately the poet will be capable,
owing to the discipline of habit, of only a special kind of spontaneity:
most especially, of 'those thoughts and feelings which, by his own
choice, or from the structure of his own mind, arise in him without
immediate external excitement'.

Wordsworth is describing a process of disciplined self-integration which his best poetry, in fact, exemplifies. There is a poetry of simplicity, however, different from this, and different altogether from the other kinds already indicated. In this 'simplicity' all the effects ascribable to the arduous training of thought, feeling, and choice seem to be effortlessly brought off as if by an angelic intelligence, a 'schöne Seele', careless and undeliberating and unerringly right.

* * *

When a poet breaks with a way of writing he is also breaking, as Wordsworth said, with 'pre-established codes of decision'. Such a break pushes the poet at once into the region of the 'extrinsic'. His only recourse is to the simple and non-literary – or, rather, because no poet can be pushed outside the sphere of words, into modes of communication that are not part of the established codes: the poet might go back to a former tradition, or he might strive to create a new one. In asking readers to divest themselves of all their usual literary habits – habits which Wordsworth felt were in his time already degenerate and likely for various social reasons to deteriorate further – the poet is asking for a new nakedness of relation. Of course the user of words cannot step outside words. Nor can the 'man speaking to men' step outside what men know or are willing to be interested in. Simplicity, that is, sets up a much more 'general' context for communication, and makes special because unprecedented demands on the reader. Wordsworth was queerly aware of this new relation. Writing of the new kind of poet he had in mind, he insisted:

> And you must love him e'er to you
> He will seem worthy of your love.

This awareness of the need for an initial indulgence is the obverse of the egotism which makes its peremptory demands in the *Advertisement*.

Breaking with 'pre-established codes of decision' and breaking with a literary language are the same thing: Wordsworth objected as much to the matter of the eighteenth-century poet as to his manner, and was aware of a false cult of simplicity fashionable in his own time. To break into 'simplicity' meant rejecting the system whereby eighteenth-century poetry managed its internal verbal economy. Bare language will now have to carry the poem, mediating situation, and plot, and tone, until such time as the poet, creating the taste by which he will be appreciated, has established new habits in the reader, and opened a way for new intrinsic verbal relations (those, in Wordsworth's case, that have to do with 'coadunation') to be accepted as the norm of the poetic. The simplicity is an invitation to a new intimacy, a new discipline, and a new complexity. The rhythm of the revolutionary in literature – it is a sufficiently commonplace observation – is to break with the intrinsic, to call in the extrinsic, and thereafter gradually to develop new intrinsic codes, of symbol or diction, which are then handed on to the extenders or degenerators who follow.

GEOFFREY HARTMAN: FROM *WORDSWORTH'S POETRY*, *1787–1814* (1964)

Hartman considers Wordsworth's 'conversion to himself' at Alfoxden, his 'consciousness of self', and focuses on a series of blank verse fragments written from July 1797 to July 1798.

Wordsworth called Alfoxden the turning point in his career as a poet. What occurred must have been like a conversion, though it was in the making since 1793 and heralded by the intense poetic activity at Racedown in the spring of 1797. It is a self-discovery – a conversion to himself – and leads beyond 'The Ruined Cottage' to a poem on Wordsworth's own mind. Not that things will suddenly cease to be problematic; on the contrary, Wordsworth is not completely happy with his best subject, himself. He keeps running after the false fire of an epic theme. Yet the promise of Alfoxden is never extinguished, and it takes him far beyond the simple conviction that the past is redeemable.

*   *   *

Wordsworth does not believe in single, independent things, yet the 'I' he uses freely, and without which *The Prelude* could not have been written, expresses a consciousness of self clearly distinguished from consciousness of nature. It is not, however, a persona-consciousness, for a persona dramatizes an attitude or a public presence while Wordsworth's 'I' represents itself only. There are glimpses, of course, of a more public and prophetic voice, yet in these fragments the first person is usually an immediate construct answering immediate feelings, as if mood and person were born simultaneously and sustained each other's life. An inner confidence allows him to meet nature, or his own emotions, without a persona, and the energy of this blank verse (an idling energy of extraordinary power) also reflects this confidence. Because Alfoxden has removed the terror of discontinuity, the poet threads past, present, and future:

Along the mazes of this song I go
As inward motions of the wandering thought
Lead me, or outward circumstance impels.
Thus do I urge a never-ending way
Year after year, with many a sleep between,
Through joy and sorrow; if my lot be joy
More joyful if it be with sorrow sooth'd.

After Alfoxden the starting point of Wordsworth's poetry is this dynamic and excursive consciousness of self. It is a heart 'Joyous, nor scared at its own liberty' that opens *The Prelude*. The initiative has passed from nature to the poet, but only because anything in nature can quicken him. Sure of the renovating impulse of nature, he is sure of himself, and for the first time he looks at nature steadily. It is a power analogous to the mind and which the mind cannot subdue to itself. Nature is an other; to the natural man *the* other; its divinity is precisely to escape a purely human, selfish use. But how is nature's otherness to be thought of? Here Wordsworth's sanity shines through. He values local superstitions and accepts all kinds of 'animating thought'. There is no harm in generously adding to nature; the danger is in subtracting from it by fixed abstractions; anything which enlarges nature yet does not diminish soul is legitimate. Though Blake would deny the possibility of such coexistence, because for him Nature's life is Imagination's death (and vice versa), Thoreau, without knowing *The Prelude*, almost caught the Wordsworthian relation of poet and nature:

He [the poet] must be something more than natural – even supernatural. Nature will not speak through but along with him. His voice will not proceed from her midst, but, breathing on her, will make her the expression of his thought. He then poetizes when he takes a fact out of nature into spirit. He speaks without reference to time or place. His thought is one world, hers another. He is another Nature, – Nature's brother. Kindly offices do they perform for one another. Each publishes the other's truth.

*   *   *

The otherness of nature is not that of a mysterious solid, 'a solid without fluctuation'. Indeed, Wordsworth cannot be said to discover nature as such but rather the reality of the *relation* between nature and mind. He is now made certain of two things: that there is an indissoluble relation between them, and that this relation is regenerative. In this season of 'second birth' everything turns on the possibility of rebirth, and the view that nature is cosubstantial with mind contributed vitally to his own restoration.

The apogee of Wordsworth's trust in the reciprocity and even 'blending' of consciousness of self and consciousness of nature extended from Alfoxden to the first years of his residence at Grasmere (1800–2). It was at Alfoxden that he composed his manifesto on that wedding of mind and nature for which his proposed epic 'The Recluse' was to be the spousal verse:

> I, long before the blessed hour arrives,
> Would sing in solitude the spousal verse
> Of this great consummation, would proclaim
> Speaking of nothing more than what we are
> How exquisitely the individual Mind,
> And the progressive powers perhaps no less
> Of the whole species to the external world
> Is fitted, and how exquisitely too,
> Theme this but little heard of among men,
> The external world is fitted to the mind
> And the creation, (by no lower name
> Can it be call'd), which they with blended might
> Accomplish: this is my great argument.

It is significant that the manifesto does not announce a poetry dealing with the past. Wordsworth's eye is on present and future; he takes it for granted that the past is recoverable. The past, of course, is not only a body of experience to which that name is collectively given, but also the spirit which informed it. Wordsworth speaks exactly when he says that what redounded on him were 'the first and earliest *motions* of his life'.

Settling at Grasmere in the winter of 1799–1800, Wordsworth begins to implement his manifesto. Here Book I of the 'Recluse', entitled 'Home at Grasmere', is written, as a kind of prologue to the manifesto, and a new launching. By that time, of course, there have already been stirrings of another poem, rough drafts of what is to be *The Prelude*, whose hesitant and reverted eye would displace the forward singing 'Recluse'. 'Home at Grasmere' remains the sole sustained example of Wordsworth making 'A present joy the matter of a song'; only in this poem, swelling to over 700 lines, are the relations between self and nature relatively unproblematic.

JONATHAN WORDSWORTH: FROM *THE BORDERS OF VISION* (1982)

Jonathan Wordsworth's study of the poetry of his great-great-uncle concentrates on Wordsworth's interest in 'border states'.

'One evening, walking in the public way', writes Wordsworth in spring 1804,

> A peasant of the valley where I dwelt
> Being my chance companion, he stopped short
> And pointed to an object full in view
> At a small distance. 'Twas a horse, that stood
> Alone upon a little breast of ground
> With a clear silver moonlight sky behind.
> With one leg from the ground the creature stood,
> Insensible and still; breath, motion gone,
> Hairs, colour, all but shape and substance gone,
> Mane, ears, and tail, as lifeless as the trunk
> That had no stir of breath. We paused awhile
> In pleasure of the sight, and left him there,
> With all his functions silently sealed up,
> Like an amphibious work of Nature's hand,
> A borderer dwelling betwixt life and death,
> A living statue or a statued life.

It is a very characteristic piece of work. No one else could have written it – perhaps no one else could have wished to write it. The faults (lame opening, final over-elaboration) are Wordsworth, and the virtues are Wordsworth. The draft in which it is found never became part of the 1805 *Prelude*, but was an attempt to provide sequels for the Climbing of Snowdon – further evidence that Nature can exert a power that 'moulds . . . endues, abstracts, combines' as does the human imagination. In structure the passage is a 'spot of time', showing the expected progression from detailed and quite ordinary description, through the poet's heightened and heightening response, to a new, odder, and more general vision; the closest parallel in terms of form is probably the account of the blind London beggar in *1805*, Book VII.

Perhaps what one notices first about the poetry is its sense of wonderment:

> breath, motion gone,
> Hairs, colour, all but shape and substance gone,
> Mane, ears, and tail, as lifeless as the trunk
> That had no stir of breath . . .

The reiteration of 'gone' at the end of two consecutive lines, and the insistent return of the poet's mind to the absence of breath, convey a feeling almost of awe at the utter stillness of the animal. All the individually striking features and details – 'hairs' is so much more impressive in this context than 'hair' – have been resolved into the essential facts of stillness, shape, and substance. It is an example if ever there was one of Wordsworth giving us eyes, enabling us to see what we might normally have missed, or passed; but one can overstress the ordinariness of what is happening. What the Grasmere peasant points out to the poet is a horse in the moonlight, sleeping as horses often do sleep, on three feet; what Wordsworth points out to us is something quite different. We are not, in this case at least, laid afresh on the cool flowery lap of earth, shown an object sparkling anew with the dewdrops of childhood. We are offered a strange, personal vision, child-like only in its intensity.

* * *

Wordsworth's borderers, border conditions, states of mind, implications, words, are so numerous and so ramified that they amount to a way of looking at his poetry as a whole.

* * *

Incomprehensibility, or difficulty of perception, is closely related: the songs of the Danish Boy and the Solitary Reaper are in foreign tongues; the 'obscure sense' is valued partly *for* its obscurity,

> Suffering is permanent, *obscure and dark*,
> And has the nature of infinity.

The Wordsworthian double negative, though often tedious, can be very effective in its border implications: 'Not *without the voice*/Of mountain echoes did my boat move on' (1799, i. 91–2),

> the distant hills
> Into the tumult sent an alien sound
> Of melancholy, *not unnoticed* . . .

(1799, i. 165–7)

Such imprecision implies, or allows, the sense of 'something evermore *about to be*', that is essential to Wordsworth's vision, and is so frequently to be found at the centre of his greatest poetry.

No Wordsworth poem more skilfully uses the border language, or more beautifully evokes the yearnings, than *Stepping Westward*. In September 1803, the poet and Dorothy, walking at sunset on the shore of Loch Ketterine, were greeted by the strange half-question, 'What, you are stepping westward?' Almost two years later, in June 1805, when Dorothy was copying her *Recollections* of the Scottish tour, Wordsworth turned the memory into a poem full of tender numinous suggestion [quotes 'Stepping Westward'].

Even though the italics are Wordsworth's, it would be a mistake in *Stepping Westward* to read too much significance into *'heavenly destiny'*, or to see in the glowing beauty of the sky a promise of the Christian afterlife. Associations of the west and sunset with finality – Henry King's 'west of life' (*The Exequy*) – are qualified by Wordsworth's sense of the endlessness of the present participle. Stepping westward has become a guarantee of never-reaching, and therefore of never sinking into stasis and death – never *needing* rebirth. Taking on a life of the mind, the woman's greeting is released not merely from space and time, but from the limitations of language as well:

> 'twas a sound
> Of something without place or bound,
> And seemed to give me spiritual right
> To travel through that region bright.

Dorothy, and the terrestrial journal that she and the poet were making, have disappeared. The greeting has become pure sound, the perfect evocation of boundlessness. It confers the right to travel not in, but *through*, a 'region bright' of childlike wonderment, untrammelled imagination. The poetry, it seems, has floated free of constriction. Fixed on the sunset, the eye has been made quiet, lost its dominance; the senses are laid asleep. And yet the echo of the woman's voice, as it comes back within the mind, brings alongside its intimation of immortality a return of the merely human:

> and while my eye
> Was fixed upon the glowing sky
> The echo of the voice enwrought
> A human sweetness with the thought
> Of travelling through the world that lay
> Before me in my endless way.

The image, if one thinks about it, seems to work in two quite different ways, so that human sweetness may be either cause or effect of the poet's final imaginative response. With such intermingling, perhaps it is safer to say that it is both. Aspiration and the wish for permanence – the world as an 'endless way' – spring from the value that Wordsworth sets on transient human joy; and the joy in its turn is exalted by his feeling that we are greater than we know.

SUGGESTIONS FOR FURTHER READING

Editions

The authoritative edition of Wordsworth's poetry is the Cornell Wordsworth (Ithaca, 1975–). Volumes published so far are: *An Evening Walk*, ed. J. Averill; *Descriptive Sketches*, ed. E. Birdsall; *The Salisbury Plain Poems*, ed. S. Gill; *The Borderers*, ed. R. Osborn; *The Ruined Cottage and The Pedlar*, ed. J. Butler; *Lyrical Ballads and Other Poems, 1797–1800*, eds. J. Butler and K. Green; *Peter Bell*, ed. J. Jordan; *The Prelude, 1798–1799*, ed. S. Parrish; *Home at Grasmere*, ed. B. Darlington; *The Thirteen-Book Prelude*, ed. M. Reed; *Poems in Two Volumes*, ed. J. Curtis; *Benjamin the Waggoner*, ed. P. F. Betz; *The Tuft of Primroses, with other late poems for The Recluse*, ed. J. Kishel; *The White Doe of Rylstone*, ed. K. Dugas; *Shorter Poems, 1807–1820*, ed. K. Ketcham; and *The Fourteen-Book Prelude*, ed. W. J. B. Owen.

See also *The Poetical Works of William Wordsworth*, ed. Ernest de Selincourt and Helen Darbishire (5 vols, Oxford, 1940–9). Other more readily available editions are: *William Wordsworth*, ed. Stephen Gill, in the *Oxford Authors* series; *Lyrical Ballads*, eds R. L. Brett and A. R. Jones (London, 1963); and *The Prelude 1799, 1805, 1850*, eds Jonathan Wordsworth, M. H. Abrams, and Stephen Gill (New York and London, 1979) – known as the 'Norton' Prelude. For Wordsworth's prose, see *The Prose Works of William Wordsworth*, eds W. J. B. Owen and Jane Worthington Smyser (3 vols, Oxford, 1974). *The Letters of William and Dorothy Wordsworth* have been edited by E. de Selincourt, and revised by various hands (Oxford, 1967–88). See also *The Journals of Dorothy Wordsworth*, ed. Mary Moorman (Oxford, 1971).

For a general introduction to the age of William Wordsworth and to the context of the poetry, see *William Wordsworth and the Age of English Romanticism*, eds Jonathan Wordsworth, Michael C. Jaye, and Robert Woof (New Brunswick and London, 1987); and, for more specialized studies, *The Age of William Wordsworth: Critical Essays on the Romantic Tradition*, eds Kenneth R. Johnston and Gene W. Ruoff (New Brunswick and London, 1987).

Biography

See *William Wordsworth, A Life*, by Stephen Gill (Oxford, 1989), and Mary Moorman's *William Wordsworth: A Biography. The Early Years* and *The Later Years* (Oxford, 1957 and 1965).

Criticism

M. H. Abrams, *The Mirror and the Lamp* (New York, 1953) and *Natural Supernaturalism* (New York, 1971): seminal studies of Romantic thought and theory and the intellectual background of the period.

M. H. Abrams, ed., *Wordsworth, A Collection of Critical Essays, Twentieth Century Critical Views* (Englewood Cliffs, N.J., 1972): a useful selection of Wordsworthian criticism.

James Averill, *Wordsworth and the Poetry of Human Suffering* (Ithaca, 1980): an analysis of Wordsworth's response to human tragedy and the use of pathos in the poetry.

F. W. Bateson, *Wordsworth: A Re-Interpretation* (London, 1954): stimulating (and somewhat notorious) biographical criticism.

John Beer, *Wordsworth and the Human Heart* (London, 1978): a revealing study of a compassionate Wordsworth, 'thinking into' the tragedy, and joy, of the human heart.

A. C. Bradley, *Oxford Lectures on Poetry* (London, 1909): could well be regarded as inaugurating modern Wordsworthian criticism.

Marilyn Butler, *Romantics, Rebels, and Reactionaries: English Literature and its Background, 1760–1830* (Oxford, 1981): a clear and accessible introduction to the politics and poetry of the period.

John Danby, *The Simple Wordsworth* (London, 1960): valuable on the complexity of Wordsworth's 'simple' poems.

Thomas McFarland, *Romanticism and the Forms of Ruin* (Princeton, 1981): important on Wordsworth and isolation, the notion of 'the egotistical sublime', and the poet's dealings with society.

Stephen Gill, *Wordsworth: The Prelude* ('Landmarks of World Literature' Series, Cambridge, 1991): an excellent guide through *The Prelude*.

Geoffrey Hartman, *Wordsworth's Poetry, 1787–1814* (New Haven, 1964): valuable analyses of individual poems and the development of Wordsworth's poetry from the early verse to *The Excursion*.

W. J. Harvey and Richard Gravil, eds, *The Prelude* ('Casebook' Series, London, 1972): a *Prelude* companion.

Mary Jacobus, *Tradition and Experiment in Wordsworth's Lyrical Ballads, 1798* (Oxford, 1976): indispensable on the background to Wordsworth's poetry.

John Jones, *The Egotistical Sublime* (London, 1954): a classic study of the poetry.

Alun R. Jones and William Tydeman, eds, *Lyrical Ballads, Casebook Series* (London, 1972): a useful companion to the *Lyrical Ballads*.

Herbert Lindenburger, *On Wordsworth's Prelude* (Princeton, 1963): somewhat outdated, but still valuable.

Lucy Newlyn, *Coleridge, Wordsworth, and the Language of Allusion* (Oxford, 1986): a close study of aspects of the symbiosis of Wordsworth and Coleridge.

Stephen Maxfield Parrish, *The Art of the Lyrical Ballads* (Ithaca, 1973): a study of the revolutionary *Lyrical Ballads* and of the critical theory surrounding them.

H. W. Piper, *The Active Universe: Pantheism and the Concept of the Imagination in the English Romantic Poets* (London, 1962): specialised, but valuable on the influence on Wordsworth and Coleridge of the religious, philosophical and scientific thought of the day.

David B. Pirie, *The Poetry of Grandeur and of Tenderness* (London, 1982): excellent on Wordsworth and human relations.

Robert Rehder, *Wordsworth and the Beginnings of Modern Poetry* (London, 1981).

Nicholas Roe, *Wordsworth and Coleridge: The Radical Years* (Oxford, 1988): a fascinating study of early radical sympathies.

Paul D. Sheats, *The Making of Wordsworth's Poetry, 1785–1798* (Cambridge, Mass., 1973).

Leslie Stephen, 'Wordsworth's Ethics' in *Hours in a Library*: Third Series (London, 1879): a Victorian essay on the importance of the philosophy in a reading of the poetry and on the consoling strengths of Wordsworth.

Jonathan Wordsworth, ed., *Bicentenary Wordsworth Studies* (Ithaca, 1970): an important collection of essays.

Jonathan Wordsworth, *The Music of Humanity* (London, 1969): a close study of *The Ruined Cottage* and *The Pedlar*.

Jonathan Wordsworth, *William Wordsworth: The Borders of Vision* (Oxford, 1982): a study of Wordsworth's interest in 'border states', in things 'evermore about to be'.

ACKNOWLEDGEMENTS

The editor and publishers wish to thank the following for permission to use copyright material.

Carcanet Press Ltd for material from Donald Davie, *Puirty of Diction in English Verse*, 1953.

Faber & Faber Ltd and Harvard University Press for material from T. S. Eliot, 'Wordsworth and Coleridge' in *The Uses of Poetry and the Use of Criticism*, 1933.

John Jones for material from his book *The Egotistical Sublime*, 1954, Chatto & Windus.

Longman Group UK Ltd for material from F. W. Bateson, *Wordsworth: A Re-Interpretation*, 1954.

Modern Language Association of America for material from Robert Mayo: *The Contemporaneity of the Lyrical Ballads*, PMLA, 69, 1954.

Oxford University Press for material from Helen Darbishire, *The Poet Wordsworth*, 1950 and from Jonathan Wordsworth, *William Wordsworth, The Borders of Vision*, 1982.

Random Century Group and the Reece Halsey Agency on behalf of the Huxley Estate and Mrs Laura Huxley for material from Aldous Huxley, 'Wordsworth in the Tropics' in *Do What You Will*, 1931, Chatto & Windus.

Routledge for material from John Danby, *The Simple Wordsworth*, 1960, Routledge and Kegan Paul.

Every effort has been made to trace all the copyright holders, but if any have been inadvertently overlooked the publishers will be pleased to make the necessary arrangement at the first opportunity.